Culture, Citizenship, and Community

A Contextual Exploration of Justice as Evenhandedness

Joseph H. Carens

OXFORD

UNIVERSITY PRESS

OXFORD
UNIVERSITY PRESS

Great Clarendon Street, Oxford OX2 6DP

Oxford University Press is a department of the University of Oxford.
It furthers the University's objective of excellence in research, scholarship,
and education by publishing worldwide in

Oxford New York

Athens Auckland Bangkok Bogotá Buenos Aires Calcutta
Cape Town Chennai Dar es Salaam Delhi Florence Hong Kong Istanbul
Karachi Kuala Lumpur Madrid Melbourne Mexico City Mumbai
Nairobi Paris São Paulo Singapore Taipei Tokyo Toronto Warsaw

with associated companies in Berlin Ibadan

Oxford is a registered trade mark of Oxford University Press
in the UK and in certain other countries

Published in the United States
by Oxford University Press Inc., New York

British Library Cataloguing in Publication Data

Data available

Library of Congress Cataloging in Publication Data

Carens, Joseph H.
Culture, citizenship, and community: a contextual exploration of justice as
evenhandedness/Joseph H. Carens.
Includes bibliographical references and index.
1. Justice. 2. Multiculturalism. 3. Pluralism (Social sciences) 4. Democracy. I. Title.
JC578.C43 2000   323.1'01—dc21   99–048977
ISBN 0–19–829751–3
ISBN 0–19–829768–8 (Pbk.)

1 3 5 7 9 10 8 6 4 2

Typeset in Stone Serif and Stone Sans
by Cambrian Typesetters, Frimley, Surrey

Printed in Great Britain
on acid-free paper by
Biddles Ltd., Guildford and King's Lynn

For
Jenny, Michael, and Daniel

ACKNOWLEDGEMENTS

When I was writing my dissertation which later became my first book, I had the sense that I was writing almost entirely in isolation. For personal reasons, I was living hundreds of miles from the university where I was getting my degree, and so I had little opportunity to interact with my fellow graduate students (or even to have the solace of knowing that others were going through the same misery that I was). My adviser responded promptly whenever I sent him what I had written, but apart from him I had almost no one with whom I could explore the ideas and arguments I was developing.

Writing this book has been an entirely different experience, and vastly more enjoyable. I have had the opportunity to present these ideas both in person and in print in many different contexts, and I have had the sense that I was participating in a community of discourse (or in multiple overlapping communities of discourse) that offered both stimulating challenges to my ideas and a great deal of encouragement and support for my efforts. I am very grateful for both. I want here to acknowledge some of the individuals who have constituted these communities and who have helped me in various ways.

To begin with the most recent, Rainer Bauböck and Jacob Levy provided very detailed comments on an earlier draft of the entire manuscript. Their comments and a nudge from Cliff Orwin encouraged me to undertake much more substantial revisions than I had originally intended. I leave it to others to judge the quality of the final product, but it is certainly a much better book for these changes than it would otherwise have been. Chandran Kukathas's endorsement of the project also played a key role, and he persuaded me to cut the Fiji chapter by a third (though still not as much in places as he would have liked). Dominic Byatt of OUP has been a wonderful editor, first in agreeing to publish the manuscript in the form in which I initially submitted it and then in being patient while I took a long time changing it.

At the University of Toronto I have found an intellectual community that I regard as ideal. Our department treats political theory as central and combines a very wide range of philosophical views with a deep ethos of mutual respect. I am inclined to think that there is no department of political science in the world that is a better place to be a political theorist, certainly none where I would rather be. Five of my colleagues here have read most of this book in one version or another over the years and provided me with very helpful responses: Ed Andrew, Ronnie Beiner, Frank Cunningham,

Cliff Orwin, and Melissa Williams. I owe particular thanks to Melissa Williams for allowing me to use a revised version of an article that we co-authored in Chapter 6. In addition, Steve Dupré, Jenny Nedelsky, Peter Russell, and Don Schwartz gave me valuable feedback on particular parts.

In some ways, I think of this book as the first of two volumes on 'Problems of Political Community' which is the title of a year-long graduate seminar I have taught over the past dozen years. (The second volume, on the ethics of immigration, should appear a year or so after this one.) In this course, the students read works of contemporary theory (including some of mine) in the first half and present normative analyses of actual cases where questions of culture, community, and identity are in play in the second. I have benefited greatly from their reactions to my work, but even more from the case studies they have conducted. I have long thought that political philosophers located in philosophy departments have a comparative advantage in dealing with certain kinds of methodological and foundational questions because of their training in epistemology, metaphysics, and logic, but that political philo-sophers located in political science departments have a (potential) compara-tive advantage in thinking about the relation between theory and practice because we are situated among colleagues whose concern is to study what is actually going on in the world. Too often we don't make use of this compar-ative advantage. The work done by the graduate students in my seminar has confirmed my sense of this potential and strengthened my confidence in the contextual and comparative approach to political theory that I advocate in this book. I want specifically to thank Julia Schtivelman whose paper on Fiji many years ago first sparked my interest in this case.

I have also had the good fortune to receive comments and support from many people outside the University of Toronto. Six of them read earlier versions of most of the work: Howard Adelman, Veit Bader, Rainer Bauböck, Will Kymlicka, Bhikhu Parekh, and Iris Marion Young. Many others commented on one piece or another: Heiner Bielefeldt, Katherine Bullock, Shelley Burtt, Alan Cairns, John Chapman, Dilek Çinar, Marie Deveney, Edie Goldenberg, Amy Gutmann, Danièle Juteau, Peter Lindsay, Jenny Mansbridge, Marie McAndrew, David Miller, Don Moon, Nancy Rosenblum, Jeff Spinner-Halev, Mary Ellen Turpel, Michael Walzer, Myron Weiner, Alan Wertheimer, Ari Zolberg.

Several people provided valuable research assistance: Chloë Atkins, Katherine Bullock, Pak-Cheong Choo, Kathleen Gallivan, Jacob Levy, Jeff Loucks, Ben Moerman, and Richard Verrier. I also want to thank the Social Sciences and Humanities Research Council of Canada and the Department of Political Science at the University of Toronto for financial support. Marian Reed and Mary-Alice Bailey helped with the typing of the manuscript. Judith Neilly and Marcia Weiner provided other kinds of support without which I may never have finished this work. I also want to thank my friends on

Christian Island for providing another kind of community, non-academic in character, but one that provides a congenial context for writing. Special thanks in this regard to Gary Wilde and Tony Vipond whose frequent and generous assistance with cottage repairs greatly reduced the time I spent cursing and correspondingly increased the time available for writing.

Finally, the community that matters most to me. I want to thank Jenny, Michael, and Daniel for the daily joy they bring into my life. It is a great pleasure to dedicate this book to them.

Parts of this book appeared previously in print, sometimes in very different form, in a number of places. I wish to thank the various publishers for permission to use previously published materials here. Part of Chapter 1 draws upon 'Two Conceptions of Fairness: A Response to Veit Bader', *Political Theory*, 25 (6), December 1997: 814–20. A shorter version of Chapter 2 first appeared as 'Complex Justice, Cultural Difference, and Political Community', in *Pluralism, Justice and Equality*, edited by David Miller and Michael Walzer (Oxford: Oxford University Press, 1995: 45–66). Part of Chapter 3 was published as 'Liberalism and Culture', *Constellations*, 4 (1), April 1997: 35–47. Chapter 4 is a much revised version of 'Difference and Domination: Reflections on the Relation Between Pluralism and Equality', in *Majorities and Minorities: NOMOS XXXII*, edited by John W. Chapman and Alan Wertheimer (New York: New York University Press, 1990: 226–50). Chapter 5 was first published in slightly different form as 'Cultural Adaptation and Integration: Is Quebec a Model for Europe?' in *From Aliens to Citizens*, edited by Rainer Bauböck (Aldershot: Avebury, 1994: 149–85). Chapter 6 is a revised version of 'Muslim Minorities in Liberal Democracies: The Politics of Misrecognition', which was co-authored with Melissa Williams and first appeared in *The Challenge of Diversity: Integration and Pluralism in Societies of Immigration*, edited by Rainer Bauböck, Agnes Heller, and Aristide R. Zolberg (Aldershot: Avebury Press, 1996: 157–86). Chapters 7 and 8 draw upon some ideas first developed in a paper for the Royal Commission on Aboriginal Peoples, but presented here very differently. A version of Chapter 7 was published as 'Dimensions of Citizenship and National Identity in Canada' in *The Philosophical Forum*, 28 (1–2), 1997: 111–24. An earlier, longer version of Chapter 9 appears as 'Democracy and Respect for Difference: The Case of Fiji' in *University of Michigan Journal of Law Reform*, 25 (3–4), spring–summer, 1992: 547–631.

I wish to thank the Social Sciences and Humanities Research Council of Canada and the University of Toronto for their generous financial support of my research.

CONTENTS

1

Introduction: Contextual Political Theory, Comparative Perspectives, and Justice as Evenhandedness

This book is concerned with the relevance of culture and identity to justice, citizenship, and political community. As a whole, the book provides a (partial) map of where and how a concern for equality and freedom requires us to respect claims about culture and identity and where and how it requires us to challenge such claims. The central theme is that a commitment to liberal democratic principles is often compatible with and may even require public recognition and support of different cultures and identities. At the same time, the openness to difference that I advocate does not require us to accept every claim put forward in the name of culture and identity. In this broad outline, the view I am advancing is a familiar one today, though still strongly contested. What matters, of course, is the way that view is advanced.

The book has three distinctive features: first, its approach, because of the emphasis I place on the importance of context; secondly, the range of phenomena it considers, because of my concern for cultural differences between political communities as well as cultural differences within them; thirdly, its underlying conception of justice which draws upon two different views of fairness, one requiring that the state be as neutral as possible towards culture and identity and the other that the state be evenhanded. The three features are interrelated, and I will say something briefly about each.

Contextual Political Theory

First, my approach. I have subtitled the book *A Contextual Exploration of Justice as Evenhandedness*. I use the term 'exploration' as a way of indicating that my goal is not to provide a systematic treatise or a comprehensive account. I intend this book to be a contribution to an ongoing conversation among contemporary political theorists. My aim is not to provide a definitive answer to any of the questions addressed in the conversation but to shift the questions a bit and to provoke, prod, and unsettle some of the participants (in a friendly way). I hope that the book will encourage people to become more self-conscious about their own presuppositions, more willing to spell out the implications of their general principles, more open to unfamiliar ways and practices.

If the book achieves its goal it will be because of the emphasis I place on contextual inquiry. I use the term 'contextual' in the subtitle because my project is profoundly shaped by my sense of how much we learn as theorists by confronting the abstract with the concrete and by inquiring into the relationship between the theoretical views we espouse and actual problems, practices, and debates in political life. I seek at every point to consider theoretical claims about equality, freedom, and difference in relation to particular demands or practices in real cases. My basic strategy throughout is to move back and forth between theory and context, articulating intuitive judgements about cases in terms of theoretical principles and critically assessing theoretical formulations in light of their implications for particular cases. The generalization that is essential to theory can be enriched, I believe, through close attention to actual cases. My deepest hope is that the book will illustrate the virtues of taking such a contextual approach to political theory with respect to the issues of culture, citizenship, and community, and indeed with respect to other questions as well.

A contextual approach offers three interrelated advantages. First, it can clarify the meaning of abstract formulations. Secondly, it can provide access to normative insights that may be obscured by theoretical accounts that remain at the level of general principle. Thirdly, it can make us more conscious of the blinkers that constrain our theoretical visions when they are informed only by what is familiar. Let me expand briefly on each of these advantages.

In reading the ongoing and overlapping contemporary debates about liberalism and communitarianism, equality and difference, citizenship and multiculturalism, and public reason and pluralism, I have learned a great deal, but I have also felt that the discussions are usually conducted at such a high level of abstraction that it is often hard to tell whether disagreements are real or rhetorical and difficult to determine what concrete judgements can be inferred from alternative theoretical positions.[1] Of course, there are exceptions, Michael Walzer and Will Kymlicka among others.[2] I discuss Walzer and

---

[1] Will Kymlicka makes a similar point in a recent article defending his own position,: 'Other theorists have sketched some concepts or principles which they think should govern liberal approaches to ethnocultural demands—e.g. Raz, Taylor, Habermas. But these are more outlines than systematic theories. It is impossible (for me at least) to tell what their abstract concepts imply for specific debates about the particular claims of particular groups' (Kymlicka 1997b: 86 n. 1). Ironically, the same objection can be levelled against one of Kymlicka's own key concepts—societal culture—for reasons that I spell out in Chapter 3, although I would agree that he is much more concrete than the authors whom he cites.
[2] Other authors who pay close attention to context along the lines I am advocating here include Veit Bader (1997), Bhikhu Parekh (1990, 1991, 1994a, 1994b, 1997), and Jeff Spinner (1994).

Kymlicka in the next two chapters because their works provide, in different ways, much more concrete, contextually sensitive approaches to these issues than most. But even Walzer and Kymlicka lose their way in theoretical constructs that crumble when confronted with a detailed consideration of the practices they purport to illuminate. In discussing their writings, I hope to illustrate how much a contextual approach can contribute to a critical reading of texts as well as to a clarification of ideas.

To put the main point starkly, we do not really understand what general principles and theoretical formulations *mean* until we see them interpreted and applied in a variety of specific contexts. We may assume we agree on some theoretical point because we have different examples in the back of our minds, different understandings of how the idea would be interpreted and applied. When these come to light, we often find we actually disagree. Or we may be inclined to generalize a claim that really makes sense only in relation to a limited set of cases.

Sometimes what appear to be conventional liberal views are radically at odds with the actual practices and policies of liberal political communities. That is true, as I shall show, of theories that insist that liberal political communities should be culturally neutral. Of course, there is nothing wrong with a theory being radical. That may even be a distinct virtue. But sometimes the persuasiveness of a theory rests in part upon the sense that it fits reasonably well with current arrangements, so it is important to see whether that is really the case. By the same token, theories that are presented as radical critiques of liberalism may gain plausibility from their failure to specify in any detail what alternative practices and institutions would be entailed by the critiques, while leaving the impression that there are viable and preferable alternatives. In the end the concrete arrangements their proponents would defend may not look so different from what passes under the name of liberalism elsewhere.

Pragmatists used to ask about the cash value of philosophical concepts, and while I don't want to endorse the market mentality *tout court*, I think the phrase nicely captures the importance of assessing the merits of competing concepts in the light of their concrete implications for policies, practices, and institutions. In short, to render intelligible and test the persuasiveness of theoretical constructs, we need to consider them in the context of specific cases and examples.

Secondly, a contextual approach encourages us to consider whether existing institutions and practices may embody forms of wisdom that are missed by the prevailing theories. This is a familiar Burkean insight, but there is no reason why it should be embraced only by conservatives. Walzer and Kymlicka recognize it, and their appreciation of this dimension of a contextual approach is another reason why I have made their work the focus of the next two chapters. Walzer argues, for example, that our practices with respect to distributive justice are both more complex and more satisfactory than the accounts provided by our leading theories. Kymlicka contends that liberal democracies have gradually developed institutions and policies for respecting cultural differences in ways that are congruent with liberal principles but that conventional liberal theories have not yet incorporated these insights. It's a familiar (and valid) point that liberal practices often fail to live up to liberal principles. We might also say, however, that liberal theories (and the theories of the critics of liberalism) often do not live up to liberal practices.

Moral judgement is complex, yet theory necessarily simplifies. Our intuitive judgements about particular cases may reflect a variety of relevant but only partially articulated moral considerations. So, we need to juxtapose such intuitive judgements against the conclusions that would seem to follow from the application of our theories to the same cases to see whether the theories might be missing something salient.

I do not mean to suggest that practices and intuitions are always right, theories always wrong. On the contrary, practices may embody ignorance rather than wisdom, domination rather than justice. Intuitions may reflect prejudice not insight. As will become clear, I think there is much to criticize in liberal culture, institutions, and practices. The characteristic danger of a contextual approach is that it will fail to recognize injustices that are pervasive and deeply embedded in practice. 'That is just the way we do things around here' (or in liberal democratic states generally) is never a sufficient justification for our practices. In particular, we should be wary about practices that do not recognize the potential claims of people who are vulnerable or powerless.

It may be the critical perspective of theory that first enables us to see how and why our institutions and practices are unjust and oppressive. In any event, if we think our intuitions and practices are right and the theories wrong, we have to say why, and that starts the dialectic back towards theory. So, a contextual approach requires movement between, and mutual correction of, theory and practice. Rawls's famous phrase 'reflective equilibrium' evokes the spirit of the enterprise, although I'm not so sure that this dialectic ever really finds a settled end-point. Perhaps what I'm advocating is better characterized as reflective disequilibrium, the mutual unsettling of complacent certitudes in theory and practice by their juxtaposition against one another.

This unsettling is all the more likely if at least some of the cases we consider carefully are unfamiliar ones. The third advantage of a contextual approach is its potential capacity to make us conscious of the limiting and often unconscious presuppositions of our theories. To realize this potential we need to turn our attention to examples that don't fit our preconceptions. Every theory casts some things into the shadows with the very light with which it illuminates others. But we have to try to avoid allowing our theories to become rigid frameworks that screen out considerations that ought to matter but don't correspond to the categories we've established. Theories should provide lenses, not blinkers.

Since I insist so much on the importance of context and identity in this book, it may be appropriate for me to elaborate this point with reference to the contexts and identities from which I write. Examples from Canadian politics play a central role in my discussion. Readers may assume that that is because I am a Canadian. That is true but it was not always so. I have lived in Canada only since 1985. For the first forty years of my life I was an American who, like most Americans, knew next to nothing about Canada. When I came to Canada I found that my familiar ways of thinking about theoretical issues were challenged by my experiences in Canada. For example, it soon occurred to me that Rawls could not have been a Canadian. Whatever one's views about Quebec and French language issues, no Canadian would think it appropriate to ignore the problem of language in a comprehensive discussion of justice, just as no American writing about justice would leave out the issues of race and religion. Similarly, questions about cultural minorities pressed themselves upon me much more forcefully in Canada simply because my daily paper would often contain stories about aboriginal people or about Quebec that brought these issues to the fore. This made me more conscious of the ways in which the theoretical debates I was reading often seemed to presuppose a limited set of examples and cases drawn from American experiences. I found it was illuminating to think through the theoretical issues with the less familiar Canadian experiences in mind. Hence the prominence of Canadian examples in this book.[3]

My appreciation for what I was learning by pursuing theoretical questions in the light of Canadian experiences which were only slightly different from American ones made me want to see what challenges would be posed by cases whose context and history were still more unfamiliar. This led me to explore the case of Fiji which I discuss in Chapter 9. I regard the Fiji chapter as a kind of extended preview of what might be gained theoretically by taking up unfamiliar cases, both in terms of a greater awareness of the hidden and limiting presuppositions of our theories and in terms of the range of institutions and policies compatible with justice. To be sure, Fiji is only one more case with its own limitations and idiosyncrasies. No theorist can discuss every case, and if one attempts to be exhaustive one risks losing one's theoretical perspective altogether. But I think there is a lot to be gained by multiplying unfamiliar

---

[3] Of course, I am neither the first nor the only one to draw upon Canadian experiences in these debates. It is no accident, I think, that a disproportionate number of the most thoughtful contributions to contemporary discussions of culture, citizenship, and community have come from Canadian theorists like Taylor (1994), Kymlicka (1989a, 1995, 1997a, 1997b), Beiner (1992), and Tully (1995). What is distinctive about my perspective, however, is that I am that peculiar hybrid, an American–Canadian. (My thanks to Melissa Williams for this category which many would regard as an oxymoron but which nicely captures a key element of my own sense of identity.)

narratives if we can draw out the implications of these narratives for familiar theoretical positions.

One of the differences between my approach and Rawls's reflective equilibrium is that I want to give weight not just to what Rawls calls 'our considered convictions of justice' but also to our intuitive (less considered) judgements about a range of relatively unfamiliar (but real) issues and cases on the assumption that those intuitive judgements may be shaped by relevant moral considerations that are obscured in our theories by the too familiar contours of the issues or cases about which we have 'considered convictions'. Part of the task of the movement between context and theory is to try to bring those relevant but obscured considerations to light and to incorporate them into our moral theory, thus refining our theoretical principles. Of course, the process of reflection may also lead us to revise our initial intuitive judgements. In the long run, I hope to expand my repertoire of cases much further, considering questions about culture, citizenship, and community in the context of a wide variety of comparative cases. For this book, Fiji, Canada, and a few brief examples drawn from other cases will have to do.

Morally Permissible Variations among Liberal Democratic Regimes

The second distinctive feature of this book is closely tied to the comparative perspective I have just extolled. The book links questions about how liberal democratic political communities ought to respond to differences of culture and identity among citizens (or residents) to questions about the differences among liberal democratic cultures. The juxtaposition of Walzer and Kymlicka in the next two chapters highlights this linkage. Kymlicka's *Multicultural Citizenship* (1995) provides a paradigmatic illustration of the way in which debates about cultural difference are usually framed within contemporary theory. The question he asks is whether group differentiated rights are compatible with liberalism. He focuses on the problems raised by the existence of different ethnic and national cultural groups within the same state, and the guiding presupposition of the inquiry seems to be that there is a single set of principles applicable to all liberal democratic states. But Walzer's *Spheres of Justice* (1983) can also be read as a book about cultural differences—not cultural differences within states, which receive little attention in his book, but cultural differences between them. On Walzer's account, each political community has its own distinct set of 'shared understandings'. I take Walzer to mean that each political community has its own distinct culture, reflected partly in its institutions and practices and partly in its articulated ideals. We might call this a political culture (using that term very broadly) to distinguish it from other kinds of culture, such as the culture of ethnic or national groups. Walzer insists that justice is always shaped by and relative to a given community's political culture and that every distinct political culture deserves respect for that reason. Although he does not focus exclusively on liberal democratic states, his principles apply fully as much to the differences between various liberal democratic states as to the differences between liberal democracies taken as a whole and other sorts of regime.

One does not have to accept Walzer's account in its entirety to see that his focus on political culture in this broad sense raises important questions that complement Kymlicka's. When the two perspectives are brought together, they complicate the discussion of culture in fruitful ways. Every liberal democratic political community must recognize certain principles such as freedom of speech, freedom of religion, majority rule, and so on, but there are many different ways of interpreting these principles and many different forms of practice among liberal democratic states. It seems plausible to suppose that there is a range of reasonable disagreement about what the principles of democratic justice require, and that within that range different political communities are morally free to adopt different institutional arrangements and policies. But how wide is that range with respect to the recognition of different identities and the acceptance of cultural differences? That is the question I pursue in various ways throughout this book.

At a number of points, I criticize or defend the policies and practices of particular states in the name of principles that I argue mark off the range of morally permissible institutions and policies for all liberal democratic states. For example, I argue that German citizenship laws are incompatible with the liberal commitment to equal citizenship, that a recent constitution of Fiji violates democratic norms, and that French rules prohibiting *hijab* in schools fail to respect liberal principles of religious freedom. In a positive vein, I contend that Quebec's policies towards immigrants are compatible with liberal democratic standards and that Muslim immigrants do not generally pose a threat to liberal democratic norms and practices. In all these cases and others, I invoke the idea of a common set of liberal democratic principles to consider claims about the respect due cultural difference.

At other points I insist that context is morally decisive, that our moral judgements should turn on our understanding of the history and culture of a particular political community. For example, I defend Canada's override clause, aboriginal demands for self-government and wariness about Canadian citizenship, and Quebec's language legislation. In all these cases, I appeal to particular features of Canada's history and political culture. I defend special land rights for Fijians, a constitutional veto power for Fijian chiefs in some key areas, and the creation of ethnic seats and separate voting lists for Fijians and Indo-Fijians by appealing to particular aspects of Fiji's history. I make no claim that these sorts of policies and institutional arrangements would be justifiable in other liberal democratic regimes.

Thus one of the key features of the book is the attention I pay to the historical and cultural particularity of different political communities (Walzer's concern) and how that affects the claims of groups within a given political community to recognition of their distinct cultures and identities (Kymlicka's concern). Sometimes I defend the distinctive practices of a political community, sometimes I criticize them in the name of the generic requirements of liberal democracy.

Two Conceptions of Justice as Fairness

The third crucial feature of the book is the understanding of justice that informs many of the arguments and moral judgements I make. Since the appearance of *A Theory of Justice*, the phrase 'justice as fairness' has conjured up the idea that to treat people fairly we must regard people abstractly, taking into account only generic human interests (such as primary goods) rather than particular identities and commitments (Rawls 1971). This conception of fairness is closely associated with the view that the liberal state ought to be neutral between competing conceptions of the good. Individuals should be free to make their own choices in the light of what they regard as valuable and important. The task of the political community is to provide a framework within which they can make those choices under equal circumstances, not to support or undermine any particular choice. On this account, justice requires a hands off approach to culture and identity, out of respect for the equality and freedom of individuals. The state has no business supporting or opposing any particular identity or culture.

There is another conception of justice as fairness, however, which is derived from the assumption that to treat people fairly we must regard them concretely, with as much knowledge as we can obtain about who they are and what they care about.[4] This approach to justice requires immersion rather than abstraction. It emphasizes contextually sensitive judgements more than general principles. It requires our institutions and policies to take an even-handed (rather than a hands off) approach in responding to the claims that arise from different conceptions of the good, including matters of culture and identity. And it opens the door to the idea that we may sometimes come closer to equality by adopting practices of differentiated citizenship than by insisting on identical formal rights.

---

[4] This way of thinking about justice owes a great deal to the work of feminist theorists who have emphasized the moral importance of paying attention to the concrete and the particular. See, for example, Gilligan (1982), Young (1990), Benhabib (1987), and Nedelsky (1997).

There are obvious tensions between these two conceptions. An ideal of neutrality will permit us to recognize publicly only thin forms of identity and culture, if any; an ideal of evenhandedness will be open to public support for much thicker versions of identity and culture.[5] Nevertheless, I believe that both the idea of achieving fairness through neutrality and the idea of achieving fairness through evenhandedness have something important to contribute to a fuller understanding of justice. To explain why, I will first show why liberal democratic states cannot be completely neutral with respect to culture and then why a modified version of the neutrality ideal still has considerable power. Then I shall contrast the appeal of this modified neutrality ideal with that of evenhandedness.

Why can't liberal democracies simply take a hands off approach to culture and identity? I want to point to three kinds of answers to this question, the first involving the cultural prerequisites of liberal democracy itself and the other two the inevitable cultural specificity of any particular liberal democratic regime.

A number of contemporary theorists have argued that principles and institutions are not enough to sustain liberal democratic regimes (Macedo 1990; Galston 1991; Bader 1997; Dagger 1997). For liberal democracies to work properly and to endure over time, certain norms, attitudes, and dispositions must be widely shared among the population. Thus liberal democracies require a liberal democratic political culture. This political culture is not neutral because it fits better with some ways of life and conceptions of the good than with others. I emphasize this aspect of the non-neutrality of liberal democracies in Chapters 4 and 5.

The liberal democratic culture required to sustain liberal democratic institutions is a generic culture, not a specific one. In this sense, every liberal democracy has the same cultural prerequisites. For example, in a recent article, Veit Bader provides a list of what he calls the generic virtues of liberal democratic politics (Bader 1997). This would include dispositions to respect the rights of others, to engage in public debate while listening to others, to resolve disputes peacefully, to respect democratic procedures, and so on. The virtues are generic because they distinguish liberal democracies from other sorts of regimes but not one liberal democracy from another.[6] They tell us what it means to be a liberal democrat, but not what it means to be a German or French or American citizen.

How should we regard these more particular national cultures and identities from a liberal democratic perspective? Don't they conflict with the liberal

---

5 Some people have objected to my distinction between neutrality and evenhandedness on the grounds that evenhandedness, too, could be characterized as a form of neutrality. I see the point but if I simply accepted it I would be left without a satisfactory shorthand for the positions I want to describe. Since the idea of liberal neutrality has often been associated with the 'hands off' approach to culture, I have decided to stick with the labels in the text, despite this problem.

6 Bader also provides a list of political virtues that he says apply to all regimes.

democratic commitment to equal citizenship and individual freedom? Sometimes they clearly do, as when a conception of national identity leads to people being inappropriately excluded from formal citizenship. In Germany, for example, because of the links between ethnicity and citizenship in German political culture, most of the grandchildren of Turkish guestworkers are not German citizens even though they, and often their parents, have lived all their lives in Germany. This is a case that I discuss critically in Chapters 2 and 9. Moreover, even when national identities and conceptions of citizenship are publicly proclaimed to be free of ethnicity and open to all who choose to join, they may covertly reflect a particular dominant culture and identity whose prominence subordinates and excludes others. In Chapter 6 I argue that this is the case with the French version of secularism, and Bader contends that the objection applies more generally to the French and American versions of national identity. (Bader 1997).

Given these dangers, why not try to disentangle liberal democratic citizenship altogether from national or ethnic identities and cultures, relying only on a generic liberal democratic identity and culture for the support needed to maintain and reproduce liberal democratic institutions and practices? This initial modification of the neutrality ideal acknowledges that liberal democracy itself supports some values and ways of life and undermines others, but it seeks to draw a line between the unavoidable cultural consequences of liberal democratic commitments and any other kind of support for or opposition to particular cultures and identities. Fairness requires neutrality with respect to the latter.

One objection to this version of the neutrality ideal is that it is impossible. Despite the dangers posed by many actual versions of national culture and identity, we cannot aspire to the complete disentanglement of liberal democracy from specific national cultures and identities for two reasons. The first reason has to do with the indeterminacy of liberal democratic principles. No liberal democratic state may legitimately exclude citizens from the franchise on the basis of race or gender, but there are different acceptable ways of institutionalizing representation, the protection of rights, and so on. Both Canada and the United States are liberal democracies, but the Canadian version of liberal democracy is different in significant ways from the American one. I discuss a particularly controversial example of these differences in Chapter 2 in defending Canada's override clause, but even if one rejects that argument, there are many other ways in which the institutions and practices of the two countries differ. The same is true of other liberal democracies. While I criticize certain aspects of French secularism or German citizenship policy, most of the distinctive features of French and German political institutions and policies seem to me entirely defensible. Such differences reflect (at least in part) differences of national history and culture and they construct (at least in part) differences of national identity. It would be a bold soul who would argue that there is only one right way to instantiate liberal democratic institutions and policies. Yet as Hegel pointed out in the *Philosophy of Right* in his discussion of the transition from abstract morality to ethical life, the instantiation of principles in concrete institutions transforms the principles even as it realizes them (Hegel 1962). To put it another way, every liberal democracy is inevitably culturally specific precisely because of the particular way in which it is a liberal democracy. We should not try to construe this particularism as culturally neutral simply because it is inevitable. Chapter 2 develops this point in the course of my discussion of Walzer.

There is a second reason why every liberal democratic regime is inevitably culturally specific. As Chapter 3 makes clear, Kymlicka's key argument against an unqualified version of liberal neutrality towards culture is that every state will have to choose what languages to use for official business, how to draw internal political boundaries, and what powers to assign to sub-units. Such choices have important implications for specific identities and cultures within the state. The choice of one language rather than another can never be regarded as culturally neutral, even if it is inevitable.

While complete cultural neutrality is impossible, this may be less damaging to the ideal of cultural neutrality than is sometimes suggested by Kymlicka and others. The fact that some development is inevitable does not mean that we should meekly accept it. As Rousseau observes in the *Social Contract*, 'It is just because the force of things tends always to destroy equality, that the force of legislation should tend always to uphold it' (Rousseau 1978). In the same vein we might conclude that the inevitability of cultural particularism means only that we should strive to keep it to a minimum. From this perspective, we could regard cultural particularism as a regrettable necessity, something to be accepted only when unavoidable and to be avoided as much as possible. We have to make some choice about what language(s) we will use in governmental business and in public education, but we can avoid many other particularistic cultural commitments. Even the generic cultural requirements of liberal democracy might be regarded in the same light, so that we should respect non-liberal cultural commitments as much as is possible without threatening the basic stability of the liberal democratic regime.[7] This is essentially a reassertion of the neutrality ideal modified by the recognition that it can never be fully achieved and will always serve only as a regulative ideal.

The attractions of this ideal seem obvious. It is not fair to make people conform to a culture and an identity that they have not accepted for themselves, or to marginalize them if they do not, at least when it is possible to avoid doing so. In Chapters 5 and 6 I implicitly draw upon this conception of

---

[7] That is one view as to why we should respect the concerns of the Amish about compulsory high school education (Spinner 1994). My own view is developed in Chapter 4.

fairness as neutrality in arguing for the limits to what receiving states may demand of immigrants by way of cultural adaptation. From this perspective, it seems possible to require respect for liberal democratic principles and to justify some demands for linguistic adaptation. But to be compatible with the modified neutrality ideal, any identities or cultural commitments that the political community expects or promotes for all must remain very thin.

An alternative answer to the question of what liberal democratic justice requires with respect to culture and identity is what I call the ideal of even-handedness. The guiding idea of evenhandedness is that what fairness entails is a sensitive balancing of competing claims for recognition and support in matters of culture and identity. Instead of trying to abstract from particularity, we should embrace it, but in a way that is fair to all the different particularities. Now being fair does not mean that every cultural claim and identity will be given equal weight but rather that each will be given appropriate weight under the circumstances within the framework of a commitment to equal respect for all. History matters, numbers matter, the relative importance of the claims to the claimants matters, and so do many other considerations. This approach allows for public recognition and support for much thicker versions of culture.

Take a specific example. Having Sunday as a common pause day clearly reflects Christian norms and makes it easier for Christians to go to church (even though most of them do not). Should we abolish the common pause day altogether or choose one (like Wednesday) that has no cultural or religious significance for anyone? From the modified neutrality perspective, this seems like just the sort of policy that is required, given that the selection of a common pause day with some religious or cultural significance is not inevitable. From that perspective, this seems the only way to treat people fairly.

But if we think that fairness requires us to pay attention to and respect people's identities and cultural commitments rather than ignore them, then we may respond differently. Making Wednesday a holiday instead of Sunday makes Christians worse off and doesn't make anyone else better off. So, we shouldn't abolish the Sunday holiday but should think instead about how to respond to the comparable interests of others, say by guaranteeing time off to those who worship on other days or permitting them to keep their businesses open on Sundays if they close them for religious reasons on another day. These sorts of policies aspire to fairness rather than formal equality in the treatment of different religious groups. They seek to be evenhanded, while taking into account relevant differences in the numbers of religious adherents and (perhaps more controversially) the role of a given religion in the history of the country.

What counts as evenhandedness is obviously open to contestation, though that is true also of neutrality. In any event, it is a conception to which minority religious groups often appeal in challenging the status quo. For example, Muslims implicitly employ it when they argue that it is unfair for the British to provide financial support for Christian and Jewish schools but not for Muslim ones or for a city in Ontario to withhold a building permit for a mosque on technical grounds regarding parking requirements that would be waived for other religious denominations. What they are asking for is not neutrality in the form of equal indifference but evenhandedness in the form of comparable support.

What about the non-religious? On the one hand, we might say it doesn't hurt them to have their day off on Sunday. On the other hand, the exemption policy for non-Christians clearly favours religious activities over other sorts. People are guaranteed time off for prayer but not for baseball or bingo, given exemptions from Sunday closing laws for religious reasons but not for other sorts of personal preferences. Is that unfair? That depends in part on whether one considers it acceptable to make political judgements differentiating more fundamental interests from less fundamental ones. The idea of fairness as evenhandedness requires that sort of judgement; fairness as neutrality, even in its modified version, prohibits it (apart from the interests directly derived from liberal democratic citizenship or some notion of universal primary goods).

A conception of fairness as evenhandedness fits better in many respects with the contextual approach I am advocating than a conception of fairness as neutrality. Recall that a contextual approach encourages us to pay attention to forms of wisdom embedded in our institutions and practices that may not be adequately reflected in prevailing theoretical formulations. All liberal democratic states have practices that are hard to reconcile with exclusive reliance on the conception of fairness as neutrality, not only in the area of religion but also in many other areas of public policy as well. For example, consider public expenditures on recreational activities. Should we spend money on a bocce court or on a baseball diamond? The answer is not culturally neutral. Indeed, in existing regimes, there are very few public expenditures that are truly neutral between competing conceptions of the good and very many that support particular cultures or identities in one way or another. Frequently that is the point of the expenditure. It is hard to know what space would be left for ordinary politics if we were to take seriously even the modified version of the neutrality ideal as our sole guide. By contrast, the ideal of evenhandedness provides a critical perspective, but one that is not so much at odds with the way liberal democratic states have come to address not only problems of culture and identity but many other political issues as well.

In the same vein, thinking about fairness as evenhandedness may correspond more closely to our intuitive sense of what justice requires in a variety of situations where questions of culture and identity are at stake. That is another theme that runs throughout this book.

Finally, my contextual approach and the idea of evenhandedness converge on the notion that to determine what justice requires in a particular case one must immerse oneself in the details of the case and make contextually sensitive judgements rather than rely primarily on the application of abstract general principles.

Despite the many virtues of thinking about fairness as evenhandedness, I do not want to abandon entirely the conception of fairness as neutrality (in its modified form). In some contexts, what justice requires is that the state take a hands off approach to culture and identity. As I noted above, Chapters 5 and 6 draw heavily upon the modified version of the neutrality ideal. In my view, both conceptions of fairness play important roles in practice in the institutions and policies of liberal democratic states, and both should play important roles in any satisfactory critical account of what liberal democratic justice requires. Though they stand in considerable tension with one another, each one must supplement and constrain the other.

I have not yet worked out a general theoretical account of how this would work and how the two ideals might be reconciled in principle. I do think, however, that this book shows that such a reconciliation is possible in practice. I make use of both ideals in the book, and yet I think that, taken as a whole, the book offers a consistent and coherent set of views. I give particular emphasis to the idea of justice as evenhandedness, however, both because that conception that fits so well with my contextual approach and because it has received less explicit attention in contemporary discussions of justice.

Thinking about Culture and Identity

I conclude this part of the introduction with a few comments about culture and identity. I will not try to provide a precise definition of culture or identity. Such definitions are rarely helpful, in part because they sometimes exclude things that are morally and theoretically relevant, in part because the limiting implications of the precise definition are often lost sight of in subsequent arguments. I argue in Chapter 3 that Kymlicka's concept of societal culture is subject to both of these objections. I also argue in Chapter 2 that Walzer's conception of shared understandings is a helpful way to think about morality as a cultural phenomenon but that Walzer is wrong to restrict the relevant locus of shared understandings to the political community. In general, I prefer an expansive, open-ended approach to these phenomena, one that does not rule out any arguments or evidence a priori on definitional grounds. Of course, even under this sort of approach one can argue that it is inappropriate to take up a given case or problem under the heading of culture and identity, but I will be surprised if readers want to make that claim about the kinds of cases I discuss in this book. In any event, I am trying to make a contribution to an ongoing, extensive conversation, not to provide a comprehensive and definitive account. The kind of contextual approach I pursue here would not readily lend itself to such larger ambitions.

Despite my aversion to definitions, I do want to say a few things about some of the presuppositions about culture and identity that inform the entire book. I assume that cultures evolve and change over time; that cultures are influenced, directly and indirectly, by other cultures; that cultures contain conflicting elements; that cultures are subject to many different, often conflicting interpretations, by both members and outsiders; that the extent to which a particular culture provides value and meaning to the lives of the people who participate in it may vary among the members of the culture and may itself be a topic of interpretive dispute; and that members of one culture may be exposed to, have access to, and even participate as members in one or more other cultures. Similarly, I assume that identities are partly subjectively determined and partly objectively imposed and that the mix of these two varies from one context to another; that people sometimes experience their identities as given, sometimes as chosen, and sometimes as a combination of the two; that the meaning and salience of a given identity varies from one person to another among those who share the identity, and may shift over time in both of these respects both for the group as a whole and for individual members within it; that people often have multiple identities, each of which may have all of the preceding characteristics; and that group identities may or may not reflect cultural differences between groups (and can be quite powerful even when they do not).

All of the arguments in this book are compatible with the pluralistic, evolving, open-ended view of culture and identity that I have just outlined, including the arguments that defend various forms of public recognition and support for culture and identity. I hope that stating these presuppositions explicitly will reduce misunderstandings of my enterprise and give pause (or at least pose a challenge) to those critics who assume that the kinds of arguments I advance necessarily entail more restrictive and static conceptions of culture and identity.[8]

An Overview of the Book

I turn now to an overview of the individual chapters and of their relationship with one another. Chapter 2 explores the cultural variability of justice

---

[8] For a good discussion of why an anti-essentialist view of culture and identity need not lead to the conclusion that there are no such things as cultural groups or coherent selves, see Modood (1998).

primarily through an engagement with Michael Walzer's *Spheres of Justice*. I argue that Walzer's own understanding of justice is more complex and less particularistic than his rhetoric in *Spheres* suggests. What justice requires or permits is contextually specific in some respects—dependent on the history and culture(s) of a political particular community—but generalizable in other respects, in the form of principles that are morally binding upon all states committed to a liberal democratic political order and, to some extent, even upon states that do not accept such commitments.

The rest of the book should be read in the light of this (neo)Walzerian problematic. For the most part I focus on questions about the morality that applies to all liberal democratic states with respect to differences of culture and identity, but I pursue these general questions through the examination of particular cases. One of my goals is to provide a (partial) map of morally permissible institutions and practices with regard to culture and identity in liberal democratic regimes. At several points, I address questions about how to respond to minorities whose cultural commitments conflict with a liberal democratic state's norms, institutions, or practices. In the final chapter I turn again to the question of how far this liberal democratic morality extends and whether applying it to a state like Fiji shows too little respect for local cultural understandings.

Chapter 3 examines Will Kymlicka's well-known discussion of how liberal political communities should respond to cultural diversity. I celebrate the contributions of *Multicultural Citizenship* but argue that Kymlicka's defence of group-differentiated rights for cultural minorities is weakened by his attempt to construct an abstract theoretical account of the relationship between liberalism and culture on the basis of his concept of 'societal culture'. I argue that this concept is fundamentally flawed in five interrelated and cumulative ways. First, it undermines the case for the kinds of cultural rights for immigrants that Kymlicka himself thinks are needed. Secondly, it fails to provide much guidance for assessing the claims of national minorities. Thirdly, it weakens the claims of smaller, more vulnerable national minorities. Fourthly, and most importantly, it rests implicitly upon a monocultural understanding of the relationship between politics and culture that impedes rather than enhances the quest for a multicultural conception of citizenship. Finally, it homogenizes culture, obscuring the multiplicity of our cultural inheritances and the complex ways in which they shape our contexts of choice. I then argue that much of Kymlicka's analysis can be separated from the concept of societal culture, and I use the example of language policy to show how a conception of justice as evenhandedness offers a more fruitful framework for exploring the questions he has raised. I also use the discussion of Kymlicka to identify many of the issues that I pursue in the rest of the book, such as the relation between culture and opportunity, the kinds of cultural adaptation that may be expected of immigrants, the limits to toleration of illiberal minorities, the political claims and identities of national minorities, and the implications of aboriginal self-government for our understanding of citizenship.

Chapter 4 focuses on the relationship between cultural difference and equal opportunity. Cultural heritages can affect the motivation and the capacity to take advantage of conventionally valued opportunities. This creates a dilemma for those committed to pluralism and equality. Should we respect cultural differences and therefore tolerate the social and economic inequalities that flow from these differences or should we promote equality by trying to override cultural inheritances that affect the chances of conventional success? The key to meeting this challenge, I argue, is to think contextually about the different ways in which culture is connected to inequalities in different cases. In some cases, cultural minorities may achieve disproportionate success in a society in which they enjoy no special power or privilege. I contend that there is nothing morally problematic about that sort of inequality, but that the same sort of argument could not be used to legitimate class inequalities even if there are some cultural differences between classes, because privilege and power are so central to class. Similarly, I claim that from the perspective of justice as evenhandedness we should accept as morally legitimate the lower success rate of a group like the Amish which, for cultural reasons, affirms different goals from the rest of society, but that the same sort of argument will not render legitimate lower success rates for African-Americans and women even if their lower success is partially due to cultural differences. Finally, I point out that respect for cultural differences does not settle the question of whether our institutions and policies should permit wide liberties for social and economic inequalities or try to minimize them, and I suggest that the generally complementary relationship between pluralism and equality is enhanced when social institutions minimize inequalities.

Chapter 5 considers what sorts of cultural adaptations may be expected of immigrants to a liberal democratic state by looking at the case of Quebec. I regard Quebec as an interesting test case for this issue because Quebec's political project of protecting and promoting a culturally distinct society has led elites in Quebec to reflect self-consciously about the cultural integration of immigrants in a liberal democratic regime and the government in Quebec has issued a theoretically sophisticated policy document on the issue. Using this document I show that Quebec's expectations of immigrants are remarkably modest—linguistic adaptation and acceptance of pluralism and democracy as the norms of public life. Even these demands are significantly constrained, once one unpacks them, because of liberal commitments to individual freedom. Here the idea that justice requires the state to take a hands off approach to culture still plays an important role in creating space for immigrants to maintain and pursue their distinctive cultural commitments. Yet in its language policies Quebec promotes an important and particular set of cultural commitments, and it does make specific and significant demands of immigrants. Drawing on my arguments from Chapter 3, I contend that Quebec's language policies and its official expectations of immigrants are morally defensible from the perspective of justice as evenhandedness because these are the sorts of demands that go hand in hand with a commitment to providing immigrants and their children with equal opportunities in Quebec and with the other rights and freedoms that a liberal democratic political community should provide to its members. And I conclude by pointing to ways in which the integration of immigrants is leading to a transformation of the identity and self-understanding of Quebec as a political community.

In developing this line of argument, I claim that the legitimacy of Quebec's expectations is not affected by its status as a province or by the cultural position of French as a minority language in Canada and in North America as a whole, and I contend that more extensive expectations of cultural adaptation would not be justified in any liberal democratic state, including European states. It is a double provocation to suggest that a province of Canada should serve as a model for the states of Europe. This challenges both the presupposition that independent states are the only relevant and meaningful locus of political community (a view also examined in Chapters 2, 7, and 8) and the assumption that the historical and cultural differences between Europe and North America make norms derived from the latter irrelevant to the former (an issue first explored in Chapter 2 in my discussion of Walzer).

Chapter 6 pursues in more detail one aspect of the question of the cultural adaptation of immigrants discussed in Chapter 5: how should liberal democratic states respond to immigrants whose cultural commitments are (or are alleged to be) at odds with liberal democratic norms and practices? The chapter takes as its focus the case of Muslim immigrants because in both Europe and North America this is the group that has most often been portrayed as a cultural threat to liberal democracy. I am deeply critical of this view. I first consider and reject the claim that Islam is constitutive of the identity of Muslims in a way that renders them unfit for democratic citizenship. In the bulk of the chapter, I explore the contention that Islamic beliefs and practices are incompatible with the liberal democratic commitment to gender equality. I take up in turn the assertions that Islam requires or warrants female genital mutilation, wife-beating, polygamy, and a form of dress (*hijab*) that subordinates women. In general, I argue that when one thinks concretely about these issues it becomes clear the critics of Islam misconstrue the normative issues or misrepresent Islamic norms and practices or criticize Islam for practices and beliefs that liberal democracies (rightly) tolerate in other religious traditions. In exploring the debate over *hijab*, I take up again the theme of the cultural variability of justice between different liberal democratic states by considering whether the specifics of the French political tradition should lead to different judgements about this issue from those reached in a North American context

This chapter, like the preceding one, emphasizes the political community's duty to take a hands off approach to culture and religion in many contexts, allowing people to pursue their own traditions as much as possible. At the same time, the chapter draws upon the idea of justice as evenhandedness to explain why some modest departures from normal liberal rules are morally permissible and to show how Muslims can rightly object that they are being judged by different standards than Christians and Jews.

Chapter 7 shows how differences of culture and identity may complicate our understanding of citizenship and political legitimacy. I begin by identifying the conventional unitary understanding of the relationship between citizenship and the state. Against this, I argue that contemporary political practices in Canada and elsewhere differ sharply from the picture painted by the unitary conception of citizenship. Instead of unique, exclusive, compartmentalized versions of membership, we find multiple memberships and overlapping identities along three dimensions of citizenship: the legal, the psychological, and the political. I argue that these ways we have of recognizing collective identity are generally morally permissible and sometimes even morally required under a conception of justice as evenhandedness. Thus I try to clear some space for a conception of citizenship more open to multiplicity and more adequate to our practices, and I try to render problematic the easy equation of state and political community.

Chapter 8 addresses some of the challenges for citizenship and political community that emerge if we accept the legitimacy of distinct political institutions for a cultural minority. Here I assume as background Chapter 7's discussion of citizenship and explore the possibilities of reconciling the demands of aboriginal peoples in Canada for forms of self-government that will reflect and protect their distinct cultural traditions with the idea of a shared Canadian citizenship based on equality and political unity. After a discussion of the multiplicities of membership and identity that aboriginal people themselves experience, I draw attention to another aspect of a contextual approach, namely the way contexts affect the meaning of ideas and ideals. In particular, I outline the long history of the use of Canadian citizenship as a tool of coercive assimilation of First Nations people in Canada and argue that this justifies considerable wariness on their part with regard to any project of civic integration. I then take up the question of whether a common citizenship requires a unitary legal regime, and specifically whether the cultural differences between aboriginal people and other Canadians would warrant some limitations on the application of the Charter of Rights and Freedoms (Canada's Bill of Rights) to aboriginal people. Finally, I consider the objection that differentiated citizenship for aboriginal people would be incompatible with Canada's need for a pattern of civic integration that sustains political unity. I argue that a unitary model of citizenship is bound to fail to provide the desired kind of civic integration and that adopting a version of differentiated citizenship that makes dialogue over justice and cultural difference central is the best hope for achieving civic integration, though it is an approach that carries its own risks.

Finally, in Chapter 9 I discuss the case of Fiji where efforts to protect the cultural traditions of Fijians (the descendants of the original inhabitants) have led to conflicts with Indo-Fijians (the descendants of indentured workers from India and now the largest other group of inhabitants of Fiji). This is the longest chapter by far because it is the richest and most complex, and my personal favourite because it most fully realizes the approach to political theory that inspires this book, the moving back and forth between the concrete particularities of a case and broad theoretical reflections.

I defend the claims of Indo-Fijians to equal citizenship and criticize efforts at political domination and exclusion that some have attempted to justify in the name of culture and history. At the same time, I defend many of the efforts to protect Fijian culture against the pressures of modern liberal institutions and values. In particular, I argue that the creation of a system of collective, inalienable land rights and the institutional reinforcement of deference to Fijian chiefs were methods of preserving Fijian culture that were compatible with a conception of justice as evenhandedness. In the course of this chapter, I take up a number of questions about cultural authenticity and about the moral relevance of history. I also revisit many of the concerns of earlier chapters, exploring the ways in which new light may be shed on these concerns when viewing them through the lens provided by the case of Fiji.

2

Complex Justice, Cultural Difference, and Political Community

> Justice is a human construction . . . The questions posed by the theory of distributive justice admit of a range of answers, and there is room within the range for cultural diversity and political choice.
>
> (Walzer 1983: 5–6)

How much room? How wide is the range? Which constructions of justice should we respect and which should we criticize? These are the questions I will explore in this chapter, using Michael Walzer's *Spheres of Justice* as a focus for the discussion. I have chosen Walzer's book as a vehicle for reflection on these topics for two reasons. First, the way Walzer argues provides a wonderful illustration of the virtues of a contextual, and also a pluralist, approach to political theory. Secondly, Walzer identifies several important concerns about culture and community that shape many of the following chapters.

Let me elaborate briefly on this second point. *Spheres of Justice* is famous for its insistence that we ought to respect cultural differences of a particular kind, namely, the cultural differences between political communities. Justice itself is a cultural construction, on Walzer's account, and inextricably linked to other aspects of the shared culture of a political community. So we should not try to judge a political community's institutions or practices on the basis of criteria that are external to that community's culture.

I think that Walzer has an important insight about the moral significance of differences between political communities, one that is often missed in contemporary discussions of cultural difference. Nevertheless, in my view, he overstates the case for the moral autonomy of political communities. While we should leave room for 'cultural diversity and political choice', there are times when it is appropriate for us to criticize the institutions and policies of political communities to which we do not belong. Indeed, Walzer himself engages in this sort of criticism in his book. I will argue that Walzer's practice as a theorist reflects a more complex and more adequate picture of what justice requires with respect to cultural differences between political communities than the view he formally defends in his theory.

Walzer's Pluralist and Contextual Approach to Theory

I begin with a few remarks about Walzer's philosophical style because I think his style is intimately linked to, and is a manifestation of, his commitment to a deep moral pluralism. Too often we think of intellectual exchange on the model of a fight: you try to knock down my argument and I'll try to knock down yours. Sometimes it is a friendly fight, sometimes not, but it is rarely a shared exploration. Our goal becomes constructing an airtight case, warding off or even submerging doubts, problems, and countervailing considerations (except perhaps as objections to be rebutted). I have certainly written in that style, and I am not alone.

By contrast, Walzer's approach is much more conversational. One has the sense that he is listening as well as speaking. He draws our attention rather than commanding it. He evokes more than he insists. At times he expresses ambivalence and uncertainty. He opens up issues for consideration and invites reflection and response. Walzer takes positions—many of them controversial—and he offers reasons and arguments in support of his views. But his arguments are not, and I think not intended to be, knock-down arguments. On the whole, that is to the good. We are rarely persuaded or enlightened by knock-down arguments even when we cannot refute them.

I do not deny that we can occasionally learn something from pushing an argument as far as it will go or seeing someone else do so. There is something to be gained from a pluralism of styles as well as from a pluralist style. But it seems to me that Walzer's approach is relatively rare among philosophers and political theorists, and that we would learn more if more people followed his lead.

One way to appreciate Walzer's approach to political philosophy is to contrast it with that of Rawls in *A Theory of Justice* (1971), a contrast to which Walzer alludes in the preface to *Spheres*. I mean this not as a criticism of Rawls but as a way of drawing attention to the virtues of both. In my view, every political theory worth taking seriously will have interconnected strengths and weaknesses. In bringing light to bear on some questions, concerns, arguments, and ideas, a theory inevitably casts others into the shadows. It is a mark of a good theory to be both illuminating and comprehensive, but no theory can make everything clear.

Rawls, at least the Rawls of *A Theory of Justice*, offers a model of political theory as an engineer's blueprint. He shows how something can be built from scratch, though, of course, it requires appropriate building materials. Every principle and argument is carefully related to every other one like the beams of a building, with the weight that each will bear carefully specified, and the entire structure resting upon a foundation whose characteristics are essential to the success of the project. By contrast, Walzer offers a model of political theory as an impressionist painting of our moral landscape. He says, in effect, 'See. Isn't it like this?' I am not suggesting that he just points to what people already think is right and wrong. To see a landscape through a painting is not the same as to view it with the naked eye. The artist offers a reconstructive interpretation, drawing attention to colours, shadings, interconnections. Once we've seen the artist's painting, the landscape actually looks different to us, though in important ways what the artist sees was always already there.

I do not offer an unqualified endorsement of Walzer's approach. At times, reading Walzer's work, I would like to see a little more of the Rawlsian structure, some further specifications of what weight particular arguments and principles will bear and of their relation to one another. Perhaps what we need is some combination of the two approaches—say, political theory as architecture. But, on the whole, I think that Walzer's artistic and pluralist style of philosophy is underrepresented.

Now consider the contextual character of Walzer's approach. The most important lesson I have learned from *Spheres of Justice* and related works by Michael Walzer is how much we gain as political theorists if we begin our theoretical reflections with ordinary moral discourse about public affairs—with the concrete judgements we make, the characteristic language we use, the particular principles we invoke, the specific problems we recognize, and the actual arguments we advance when we talk about questions of justice in ordinary life.

In a sense, Walzer is a left-wing Burkean. He would rather rest his moral claims and criticisms on the history, traditions, and practices of a particular community than on abstract general principles, on the rights of Englishmen rather than the rights of man (though Walzer, I suspect, would construe the rights of Englishmen much more expansively than Burke with respect to class and gender).

Walzer is not opposed in principle to general theoretical formulations but he is very sensitive to the blinkers they can impose and to the ways they can embody, in disguised form, moral insights that grow out of, and are only applicable to, particular contexts. *Spheres of Justice* is filled with examples of social practices that are either neglected by, or in apparent conflict with, conventional theories of justice but that, upon reflection, raise issues of justice and seem morally justifiable. Indeed, the book emphasizes the variety and variability of the social goods with which a theory of justice must be concerned. Once we see the richness and complexity of social goods, he says, once we appreciate the different ways in which different communities understand goods, value goods, and think various goods ought to be distributed, we will no longer imagine that it is possible to construct an adequate theory of justice without beginning from and returning to the actual practices of particular societies.

One thing we will discover from such an approach is that we inhabit a rich and complex moral world, a world in which history, culture, and community matter. Theory can clarify and criticize some aspects of this moral world, and no aspect is off limits in principle. But theory cannot replace our moral world or entirely reconstruct it. Indeed, critical reflection should lead us to appreciate not only the morally problematic character of some local practices and understandings, but also the limitations of general principles. The adequacy of a political theory depends in part on its ability to bring into its compass the complex variety of moral considerations that we actually think are morally relevant, even after reflection and self-criticism.

This kind of approach is particularly helpful in thinking about how we should respond to different ways of understanding justice. To say why we should respect some version of local justice in one case and criticize it in another requires a contextual inquiry that begins with actual moral problems and moral judgements and moves back and forth between these particulars and general principles, paying attention in a critical and reflective way to the actual features of our moral world.

I think this approach provides an extremely valuable corrective to the dangers of abstract theorizing. Walzer is surely right to insist upon how much we can learn simply by paying attention to the way people in different societies think about the problems of justice. Unfortunately, Walzer's picture of the moral autonomy of political communities would lead away from the kind of contextual inquiry that he invites.

Moral Community and Political Community

Walzer claims that justice *is* what the people in a particular community *think* it is. More precisely, he argues that when goods are distributed in accordance with the meaning that people in a community attach to those goods, then the goods are distributed justly. The most striking illustration of this argument is his discussion of a caste system in which, by hypothesis, all participants agree to the principles governing the caste system. According to Walzer, criticism of such a cohesive internal society by outsiders would be inappropriate if not incoherent:

Every substantive account of justice is a local account . . . One characteristic above all is central to my argument. We are (all of us) culture-producing creatures; we make and inhabit meaningful worlds. Since there is no way to rank and order these worlds with respect to their understanding of social goods, we do justice to men and women by respecting their particular creations . . . Justice is rooted in the distinct understandings of places, honors, jobs, things of all sorts that constitute a shared way of life. To override those understandings is (always) to act unjustly. (314)[1]

---

[1] For the sake of brevity I will use only page numbers in parentheses, rather than a fuller reference, when citing pages from Walzer's *Spheres of Justice* (1983) in this chapter.

Elsewhere in the book, Walzer says that the locus of these shared cultural understandings is the political community: 'The political community is the appropriate setting for this enterprise . . . [It] is probably the closest we can come to a world of common meanings' (28). He describes the way of doing philosophy that he pursues as 'interpret[ing] to one's fellow citizens the world of meanings that we share' (p. xiv).

Some people have criticized Walzer for characterizing the political community as a world of common meanings and shared understandings (Kymlicka 1989a). They object that his discussion in *Spheres of Justice* paints too homogeneous a picture of culture. Despite the importance of attending to cultural differences within political communities—as I will do in all of the subsequent chapters—I think that Walzer's critics often miss the significance of the point to which he is drawing our attention, namely, that political life both constructs and reflects a shared culture. Members of a political community participate in and are subject to common institutions (courts, parliaments, parties, constitutions) and they transform those institutions over time; they argue about and are subject to the same policies; they contest elections together (whether on the same or opposite sides). Over time, in many and various ways, people who share a common political life develop common practices, norms, and understandings—all subject to contestation and transformation, of course, even while they are shared. The critics are right to insist that political culture, even broadly understood, is not the whole of culture; they are wrong to deny or neglect the fact that long-standing political communities normally have shared political cultures with deep ramifications for how people think about goods and justice.[2]

In what follows I want to focus on the moral significance of political culture, defined in this broad sense. To what extent are different political cultures worthy of respect? When is it morally appropriate for us to criticize the practices or norms of a political community to which we do not belong, and when is that inappropriate? Should moral criticism rely only on standards that are internal to the political community being criticized—their own shared understandings—or is it (sometimes) appropriate for us to invoke our own moral norms?

Walzer's answer to these questions appears radically relativistic: 'Every substantive account of justice is a local account . . . To override those understandings is (always) to act unjustly.' (314). Yet this announced position does not accurately reflect some of the arguments he makes in *Spheres*. Consider,

---

[2] I am deliberately using the term 'political community' rather than 'state' in this paragraph to leave open the possibility of political communities that are not states but that have shared political cultures worthy of respect. I pursue this implication explicitly in Chapters 5, 7 and 8, but I will not make much of it in this chapter because Walzer (like most theorists) usually has the modern state (or the ancient polis) in mind when he speaks of political community, and I do not need to challenge that assumption for the issues I want to take up here.

for example, his criticism of the treatment of guestworkers in Western Europe. Walzer argues that it is unjust if people who live and work in a country are denied (relatively easy) access to citizenship. The German exclusion of Turkish guestworkers and their descendants from citizenship is perhaps the clearest example of the sort of practice Walzer is criticizing, but he says nothing about German or Turkish history, culture, traditions, or conceptions of membership and community. Instead he offers an argument based on general, even abstract, liberal democratic principles (56–60).

Now the German policy that makes naturalization so difficult for guestworkers is rooted in an understanding of citizenship that has very deep roots in German history and culture. Even many of the Turks share that understanding. As Rogers Brubaker puts it:

The ethnocultural inflection of German self-understanding and German citizenship law makes it difficult to reconcile—in the political imagination of Germans and immigrants alike—the preservation of Turkish cultural identity and autonomy, for example, with the preservation of German citizenship. State-membership is too closely tied to nation-membership. To take on German citizenship, in the self-understanding of Germans and Turks alike, requires that one become German in some thicker, richer sense than merely acquiring a new passport (Brubaker 1992: 178).

This view of German citizenship is probably as close as we get empirically to a distinctive and shared understanding of the meaning of a good within a political community. Walzer's position effectively requires the German political community to abandon or at least radically transform this shared understanding. Is this not the very sort of overriding of local understandings that Walzer declared would be unjust?[3]

One possible way to try to preserve the Walzerian emphasis on local understandings is to say that his argument is based on liberal democratic principles that Germans too claim to embrace. In that sense, it remains an immanent critique, though it requires the commitment to liberal democracy to trump conflicting commitments to German history and culture.[4] To construct the

---

[3] Could one argue that the term 'overriding' refers not to judgement and criticism, as I suppose, but to intervention whether military or economic? I do not think that would be a reasonable reading of *Spheres of Justice*. Non-intervention was a central theme of Walzer's earlier work, *Just and Unjust Wars* (1977), but in *Spheres* the central focus is on the appropriateness of different standards of justice and on the relation between those making moral evaluations and the communities they wish to evaluate. Walzer's position seems to be this. Anyone may try to persuade anyone else. You do not have to be a member of a community to engage in conversation about justice. (See, e.g., Walzer 1983: 314.) If you want to persuade others, Walzer assumes, you will have to draw heavily upon some of their existing moral understandings, even if your goal is to transform those understandings in some respects. But, in any event, what counts morally in the end is what the members of the community think. Their judgements are the ones that determine the content of justice. To grant moral weight to the views of an external critic constitutes the kind of overriding to which Walzer objects.

[4] I am assuming here that Walzer's argument is correct, i.e. that the German exclusionary policy on naturalization is incompatible with liberal democratic principles. I have argued for this view in Carens (1989).

argument in this way, however, is to assume that Germans and Americans share an understanding of what democracy means and what it requires. If, as Walzer says, 'in matters of morality, argument simply is the appeal to common meanings' (29), this argument presupposes that our world of common meanings at least partly transcends the boundaries of the particular political community to which we belong. It assumes a shared moral community—to some degree—even among people who are not members of the same political community.

That sort of assumption corresponds much better both to our ordinary moral practices and to Walzer's own theory of justice than do some of his formulations about the moral autonomy of political communities. In fact, *Spheres* does not strike me as exclusively, or even predominantly, an account of the *American* understanding of justice. It is much less explicitly tied to American history and culture than, for example, Judith Shklar's book, *American Citizenship* (1991). Many of Walzer's arguments and examples refer to the experiences of a variety of liberal democratic states, and not with the goal of illustrating how different societies may understand goods differently (which is often the point of his use of historical examples) but with the goal of articulating 'our' understanding of goods like money, political power, and position. That is the way the book has been read and discussed in Europe and elsewhere.[5]

All this suggests that it is a serious mistake simply to equate moral community with political community. The 'we' who share a set of moral understandings should not be identified exclusively with the 'we' who share a political community. It is descriptively inaccurate and conceptually misleading to suggest that every morality is a local morality or that the only morality shared beyond borders is a thin, minimal morality, itself the reiterated by-product of the distinct, thick moralities constructed in particular societies.[6] I am *not* claiming that we should think about the moral community as a universal community. Nor am I saying that there is a minimal morality shared by all contemporary societies. Rather I am claiming that Walzer's own work and the discussion of that work in Europe and elsewhere reflects the existence of a thick, highly developed, richly textured morality

[5] See e.g. several of the essays in Miller and Walzer (1995), especially the introduction where Miller assumes that Walzer is talking about 'the main categories of goods in contemporary liberal societies' (4) and about the 'culture of Western democracies' (15).

[6] In *Thick and Thin* (1994), Walzer extends the argument of *Spheres* by explicitly acknowledging that it is sometimes appropriate to criticize other societies in the name of minimal moral standards, but he insists that these minimal moral standards are themselves embedded in and abstracted from the maximalist moralities of particular societies. There, as in *Spheres*, he writes as though political borders also mark the boundaries of moral and cultural communities, though many of the examples he provides of 'thickly conceived values' such as 'social democracy, moral laissez-faire, republican virtue' clearly generate considerable agreement across borders and considerable disagreement within them (Walzer 1994: 17). I discuss Walzer's position in *Thick and Thin* further in the last section of this chapter.

shared by many people who do not live in the same political community but who share a commitment to liberal democratic norms and ideals. We often engage in debates about what is just and unjust in ways that presuppose this wider moral community.

To repeat, I am not claiming that this wider moral community is co-extensive with humanity. It is obvious that there are many people outside liberal democratic states and some within them who do not share these commitments to liberal democracy. Nor do I mean to suggest that recognition of this wider moral community resolves all of the puzzles about the connections between justice, culture, and political community. On the contrary, it opens the door to more complexity.

Even if we assume a shared commitment to liberal democratic principles, we have to acknowledge (1) some range of morally permissible implementations on any given account of the principles and (2) some range of reasonable disagreement about how to interpret the principles themselves. Within the range of morally permissible implementation and within the range of reasonable disagreements about interpretation, it is morally appropriate to treat the institutions and policies of a particular democratic community as legitimate, even when they differ from the institutions and policies of your own community or from the ones that you think would be best. No one supposes that every liberal democracy is morally obliged to adopt exactly the same institutions and policies. These legitimate differences in institutions and policies will presumably reflect in part historical and cultural differences between democratic states. So, we should not entirely dismiss Walzer's emphasis on the political community as the locus of shared moral understandings that deserve respect.

Democratic Variations: The Canadian Charter and the Override Clause

How wide is this range of legitimate differences? How closely are our interpretations of liberal democratic principles and our understandings of appropriate institutional implementations tied to particular cultures? Consider briefly an example from Canada. One essential component of most contemporary conceptions of democratic justice is the protection of basic human rights such as freedom of religion, freedom of thought and expression, equal treatment under the law, and so on. In 1982, Canada adopted as part of its constitution a bill of rights, called the Charter of Rights and Freedoms, designed to protect such basic rights. The Canadian Charter is like the American Bill of Rights in many ways, but it has some interesting differences. For example, it says at the very beginning that the rights and freedoms it guarantees are 'subject . . . to such reasonable limits prescribed by law as can be demonstrably justified in a free and democratic society', thus rejecting any absolutist conception of rights and drawing attention to the need for public deliberation about the relationship between individuals as rights-bearers and the political community to which they belong. (Constitution Act 1982: 385).[7] The Charter also has clauses explicitly endorsing affirmative action in various contexts, acknowledging distinct aboriginal rights, prohibiting gender discrimination, affirming multiculturalism, and so on. So, it reflects a particular (and, of course, contested) view of the proper place of individual rights in Canadian democracy.

The particular feature of the Charter that I want to highlight concerns the limits on judicial review. As in the United States, Canada's Supreme Court can declare laws that violate the Charter to be invalid, but there is this important difference. A simple majority, either of Parliament *or of a provincial legislature* can pass a law that is immune to such judicial scrutiny, with respect to certain sections of the Charter, simply by announcing that as its intent. This is called the notwithstanding or override clause.[8] The law has to be renewed every five years or it automatically lapses.

Americans may be tempted to think that this provision just shows that the Canadian Constitution is built on a misunderstanding of the nature of fundamental rights, which are supposed to be trumps (to use Dworkin's famous phrase), not something that can be overridden by a democratic majority. Many Canadians would agree with this (Whyte 1990). But the override clause has many defenders as well, and I am now inclined to be one of them.

The short version of my defence goes like this.[9] We should assess political institutions, including institutions for protecting human rights, not only by their announced aspirations but also, and more fundamentally, by how well they work in practice. The US Supreme Court, for example, whose task (one might say) is to interpret and apply the Constitution in an uncompromising fashion, without regard for democratic majorities, immune from easy democratic override, is the very Court that has brought us such decisions as *Dred Scott* (which upheld slavery) and *Plessy vs. Ferguson* (which upheld segregation).[10] To put it very cautiously, the Court has not been an

---

[7] Of course, many interpreters of the US Constitution would argue that it does not provide for absolute rights either, but the language of the Bill of Rights creates scope for absolutist readings that would be much harder to defend in the Canadian context.

[8] 'Parliament or the legislature of a province may expressly declare in an Act of Parliament or of the legislature, as the case may be, that the Act or a provision thereof shall operate notwithstanding a provision included in section 2 or sections 7 to 15 of this Charter.' The sections referred to deal with such rights as freedom of religion, freedom of expression, freedom of assembly, freedom of association, the right to habeas corpus, and other basic legal rights (Constitution Act 1982; section 33).

[9] The account which follows is heavily influenced by Peter Russell (1991).

[10] In *Dred Scott* (1857) the Court struck down as unconstitutional a federal law prohibiting slavery in certain territories of the United States and held that 'negroes' were not citizens of the United States and could not become so, even if free, saying that the Constitution reflected the

unqualified success in protecting basic human rights, especially of minorities.

The way an institution works depends in part on the history and culture of the society in which it is embedded. Any institution has to be evaluated in context. The case for the override clause is that, given the Canadian context, this arrangement is a reasonable experiment whose goal is to promote public deliberation about individual rights and to assign political responsibility for transgressions. In a society like Canada, where people are deeply attached to fundamental rights, invocation of the override clause will be likely to generate public criticism and debate. Canadian parliamentarian traditions ensure that, in most cases, a debate will occur and political responsibility for the action will be clear. If an override can be publicly defended as a correction of judicial injustice or perhaps judicial imperialism, then it will provide a better outcome than the judicial decision. If it cannot be reasonably defended in this way, the government will back down or the issue may well be a significant factor in the next election. This might ultimately secure rights more effectively, because more democratically, than an American-style system of judicial review would have done in the Canadian context.[11]

A recent case illustrates the way this can work. The provincial government in Alberta passed a law providing compensation for disabled people who had been forcibly sterilized under a eugenics law passed by a much earlier Alberta government. One part of this legislation specified that the victims of the sterilization policy could not sue the government for additional compensation (regardless of whether they accepted what was offered). The Supreme Court of Canada struck down this provision as a violation of the Charter's guarantee of equal rights under the law. At first, the Alberta government reacted to the Court's decision by announcing that it would invoke the override clause and re-establish the ban on litigation. (From the government's perspective, the compensation it was providing was reasonable, and it wished to avoid protracted and expensive litigation as well as potentially higher costs from a court judgement.) But the suggestion that it would invoke the override clause was met with widespread public condemnation, and the government backed down, accepting the Court's decision. It is important to note that the initial legislative restriction on litigation had not

---

long-standing view that negroes were 'beings of an inferior order . . . and so far inferior that they had no rights which the white man was bound to respect'. In *Plessy v. Ferguson* (1896) the Court held that compulsory segregation of the races did not violate the Fourteenth Amendment, an amendment explicitly passed to overturn *Dred Scott* and to guarantee equal protection of the laws to all. According to the Court, it was fallacious to assume that 'The enforced separation of the two races stamps the colored man with a badge of inferiority. If this is so, it is not by reason of anything found in the act, but solely because the colored race chooses to put that construction upon it' (quoted from Kutler 1984: 153 and 216.)

[11] I am not arguing that an override clause would be a desirable innovation in the American context. On the contrary, given the different history, traditions, and culture of American politics, I would suppose that such an innovation would be extremely unwise.

evoked comparable public opposition. It was the Court's decision that changed the political climate, shaping public opinion about what justice required in this case.

Of course, one case like this is not enough to prove that an institution works as intended or at least well enough to justify its continuance. There are other cases (e.g. the use of the override to restrict the rights of organized labour) that might lead to a less optimistic assessment, and, in any event, it is too recent an innovation to reach any firm conclusions (except that, thus far, with the exception of one brief period in Quebec, the override has rarely been used). But at least one can see why such a device, if it did function as intended, might be preferable to an unrestricted form of judicial review.

So goes one argument for the notwithstanding clause, and, if you accept it, you can already see that cultural differences *between* democratic societies can have an impact on what democratic justice requires and permits. Of course, some people will not be persuaded by my defence of the override clause. As I said, many people in Canada think the override clause is a bad idea. But even if one thinks the American approach to protecting rights would be superior, would it be appropriate for non-Canadians to call the override clause unjust, or is this the sort of judgement that ought to be left to Canadians? If you consider the override clause unjust, what would you say about the system in place before the Charter (with its override clause) was adopted, the system of parliamentary sovereignty that continues in Britain today? Is that sort of system unjust?

The point of this example is to unsettle a bit the sense that we know what liberal democratic justice entails with respect to institutions and policies and to draw attention to the ways in which even countries that are very similar in many respects can have understandings that are very different. I am not suggesting that there are no limits to these differences. On the contrary, in discussing German citizenship policies, I have already drawn attention to one sort of limit. That is exactly the point of these two contrasting examples.

In thinking about justice, we should try to map out the range of the morally permissible (and also the range of reasonable disagreements), and in constructing this map, we should begin by identifying some of the actual differences of institutions and policies in existing states and by considering their connections to cultural differences. When we speak of 'contemporary liberal societies' or 'contemporary democracies', do we include Japan and India in the mental list conjured up by these phrases? Do the cultural differences between countries like Japan and India on the one hand and Western countries on the other have any bearing on how we think about democratic justice? I would be surprised if they do not. The challenge is to say how.

Consider again the issue of German citizenship policy. When defenders of that policy argue that a critique like Walzer's is a form of North American cultural and moral imperialism, an attempt to project an understanding of membership appropriate to the immigrant societies of North America onto European societies with very different histories and traditions, this is an argument that deserves to be considered seriously.[12] In this case I would ultimately reject that argument, but I do find it somewhat troubling that the model that Walzer and I hold up as a standard fits so comfortably with the practices of the societies of which we are members.

We make moral arguments against a background of cultural assumptions that are never fully explicit and often not even conscious. I may have enough of a feel for the way that German culture is similar to and different from the North American cultures that I know best that I can make reasonable critical judgements about German citizenship policy, despite the fact that I do not know German culture well. Would I be willing to make the same critical judgements with respect to Japan's citizenship policy? Japan, like Germany, has a restrictive naturalization policy and an understanding of citizenship closely tied to an ethnocultural conception of the nation. In the end, I would criticize Japan's policies too, but I would do so with somewhat more trepidation. The cultural differences between Japan and North America are much greater than the cultural differences between Germany and North America, and so, the risk of missing something that would make a difference to the moral argument seems greater.

I draw attention to my doubts and trepidations not as a way of providing information about my psychic life but because I regard these feelings as morally relevant. In moral deliberation, what matters is not only the ultimate conclusion we reach but also the considerations we regard as relevant (even when they are outweighed) and the degree of confidence we feel in our judgements. These things matter because they affect our view of the range of reasonable disagreement which in turn affects our view of the kinds of differences that deserve respect.[13]

Justice as Concentric Circles

So far, I have been exploring some of the implications of cultural differences for the ways in which we think about justice in liberal democracies. Would it be appropriate for us to extend the critique of exclusionary citizenship policies to states like Kuwait and Saudi Arabia that have large guestworker populations but that do not claim to be liberal democracies? I am not sure how Walzer would answer this. On the one hand, this sort of critique can no

---

[12] See, e.g. Hailbronner (1989). Hailbronner's essay is, in part, a response to an article by me, but since I defend Walzer's position, Hailbronner's objections to me would presumably apply to Walzer as well.

[13] See Gutmann and Thompson (1996). See also Rawls (1993) and Gutmann (1993).

longer easily be construed as an appeal to shared moral understandings. To do so would presumably require one to argue that most people in Saudi Arabia or Kuwait accept democratic principles that their governments reject. Of course, one immediately has the further problem, characteristic of all inquiries into shared understandings within a political boundary, of whose understandings count. For example, do the views of those living there but currently excluded from citizenship matter? How do we judge whose interpretation of the shared moral understandings of Saudi Arabia or Kuwait is the best? However these questions are answered, it would be difficult, I think, to make a convincing case that a critique of Saudi Arabian or Kuwaiti policy from a liberal democratic perspective is a critique driven by an appeal to shared understandings. For that reason, one might expect Walzer to oppose it.

On the other hand, Walzer is quite prepared to make this sort of critical judgement in what seem like comparable cases affecting citizenship. In *Spheres* (42–3), Walzer says that it is wrong for new states formed after the demise of colonialism to expel current inhabitants who do not share the race or ethnicity of the newly established dominant majority. The sort of case he has in mind presumably is the expulsion of Asians from Kenya and Uganda in the 1970s. But he makes no appeal to African or even Asian understandings of community and of responsibilities towards those seen in some way as outsiders. Instead he cites Hobbes. In the same context, he says that he will later consider and reject the possibility that such inhabitants should be permitted to stay but excluded from citizenship, thus implicitly extending his critique of exclusionary citizenship policies beyond the confines of affluent liberal democratic states.

For the moment, I don't want to try to settle the question of how Walzer would answer this particular question or how it ought to be answered. It is enough to note that Walzer's critique of the expulsion of residents from postcolonial regimes shows that he is sometimes willing to criticize the practices of others without making any explicit reference to their own understandings. If we combine this point with my previous discussion of his critique of German citizenship policies on the basis of liberal democratic principles, we can see that Walzer's own practice as a theorist depends upon a richer, more complex, and, in my view, more satisfactory theory of justice than his rhetoric in *Spheres* sometimes suggests.

One way to read (or reconstruct) *Spheres of Justice* would be to say that it reveals a theory of justice with three distinct parts. To employ an alternative spherical model, we might think of these three parts as concentric circles, the later contained within the earlier. I do not mean to suggest that the inner circles are derived from the outer or even that the boundaries between them are hard and fast. Rather the point is that as one moves outwards, the understanding of justice is thinner in the sense that it settles fewer questions, but more extensive in the sense that it applies to more contexts. As one moves inwards, the understanding of justice is thicker and less extensive. It is more culturally specific, settles more questions or more details, but for fewer places.

The first part, the outermost circle, contains minimal standards of justice applicable to all contemporary states, regardless of their own particular histories, cultures, or political arrangements. The theory is universal in the sense that it applies to all, at least all in the present. It is particular in the sense that this understanding of justice is acknowledged to be the product of a particular time and place, a particular culture and history. It is *our* understanding of justice. The 'we' here is indeterminate and open, however. It includes more than the members of any particular political community but perhaps less than all humanity. Thus there are some policies, practices, and institutions that we will criticize in the name of justice, even though we recognize that the people whose policies, practices, and institutions are being criticized may not share our understanding of justice. Critiques advanced in the name of human rights offer one paradigmatic illustration of this sort of approach. Walzer's criticism of the expulsion of long-term residents is another.

The second part of the theory, the middle circle, contains standards of justice applicable not universally, but only to contemporary liberal democratic states. Within this circle we can distinguish two different kinds of norms. The first involves standards more or less directly derived from liberal democratic principles. Even these are historically and culturally specific, in the sense that the very ideal of liberal democracy is itself obviously the product of a particular historical and cultural development. But this development is not societally specific. Its cultural and historical characteristics are shared by many contemporary societies whose cultures differ in other ways. The liberal democratic conception of justice may not be a universally shared understanding, but it is certainly one that is shared across the borders of many different political communities. Many arguments of this kind can be found in *Spheres*, not only in the critique of the treatment of guestworkers cited above, but in many parts of the discussion of money, power, office, and so on.

The other kind of norm found in the middle circle involves standards of justice that are more contingently linked to commonalities of culture and history among liberal democratic states. Walzer's discussion of medical care provides a good example. While he focuses on the American case, he never suggests that he is presenting a distinctive American understanding. (It is the opponents of communal provision who insist that there is a distinctive American understanding of medical care.) The understanding of medical care that Walzer presents—that it is a basic need that ought to be provided by the community to all—is a cultural understanding shared (at the least) by all affluent liberal democratic societies. So, justice requires communal provision of medical care to all citizens, at least where that is economically feasible. Yet Walzer is surely right to insist that this view of what justice requires is an

historical and cultural development, closely linked to a particular understanding of medical care. It is not intrinsically linked to the principles of
liberal democracy or to any universal conception of justice.

The third part—the innermost concentric circle—contains standards of
justice that are intimately linked to the history and culture of a particular
political community. Walzer's discussion of integration and school busing
offers one prime example. It is impossible to separate our sense of what justice
requires with respect to this issue from the history of American racism, and
the particular forms it has taken. Indeed, Will Kymlicka argues, persuasively
in my view, that liberal theorists like Rawls and Dworkin have failed to appreciate the ways in which the famous claim 'separate is inherently unequal' was
tied to the particular case of African–Americans and thus have not seen that
justice may not only permit but require separate arrangements for cultural
minorities in other circumstances (Kymlicka 1989a).[14] My own discussion of
the Canadian Charter and the override clause is designed to illustrate the
same phenomenon. What justice permits or requires with respect to institutional arrangements and policies may be intimately linked at times to the
particular culture and history of a given political community.

Walzer's rhetoric suggests that this third part, the innermost concentric
circle, constitutes the core of his theory of justice, but his actual discussion in
Spheres ranges over all three parts, and I would venture to say that considerably more of it is situated in the middle circle than in the innermost one.
Most of his claims about the meaning of various social goods (work, leisure,
education, marriage, and so on) and the distinct principles of justice that flow
from these meanings clearly apply to all advanced industrial liberal democratic states and emerged from the same historical and cultural processes.
Many fewer apply only to the United States or are distinctively American in
their evolution.

The picture I have sketched of what Walzer actually does in *Spheres* (as
opposed to what he says he does) provides an important model for thinking
about justice. What justice requires and permits is intimately linked to culture
in myriad ways (some of which I explore in the subsequent chapters). It is
entirely appropriate therefore that we become more tentative in our judgements and more cautious in our criticism, the more we move onto culturally
unfamiliar ground. The broad outlines of justice may still be clear but the
nuances and subtle shadings may be different.

As Walzer's own discussion shows (and in contrast to what he says), the
degree to which cultural understandings relevant to justice are shared is not

---

[14] Kymlicka does not connect his project to Walzer's and indeed devotes a whole chapter of his
1989 book to a critique of *Spheres of Justice*, but I think Kymlicka's argument fits very well with
Walzer's emphasis on what we can learn about justice from looking at the problems and practices
of different societies. See the next chapter of this volume for an elaboration of this point in my
discussion of Kymlicka's more recent work, *Multicultural Citizenship*.

determined by the allocation of political authority or by political boundaries. A political community may sometimes be the locus of distinctive cultural understandings that instantiate justice and deserve respect. But our cultural and moral understandings are not uniquely and often not primarily the product of processes internal to the political community. In a number of the following chapters, I will try to clarify the relationship between these two *loci* of justice, by exploring the extent to which the policies and practices of various liberal democratic communities with respect to cultural issues are compatible with the requirements of liberal democratic justice.

In the remainder of this chapter, I want to focus not on the border between the innermost and middle circles but on the border between the middle and outer circles. Is that a defensible border? How extensive are the minimal moral standards that we use to criticize others? Should we regard liberal democratic principles as particularistic, applicable only to those political communities in which they are culturally embedded, or should we regard them as universal in the sense of providing critical moral standards that are appropriately applied even to communities which do not present themselves as committed to liberal democracy and which may even find such ideas to be culturally alien?

Should we make Moral Judgements about the Past?

In *Spheres,* Walzer makes frequent use of historical examples. These kinds of references raise the question of how we should think normatively about the past. The 'other' that emerges from history reproduces in many ways the puzzle of the 'other' that emerges from comparative studies of contemporary societies. When should we seek to understand without judging, when should we criticize (or praise) on the basis of standards internal to a community, and when should we invoke our own moral understandings as critical standards even if these moral understandings are not shared by those we criticize?

Walzer often uses historical examples to point to similarities and differences between the ways we think about goods and the ways in which various societies in the past have done so. One of his goals seems to be to make us aware of differences in social understandings of goods without arousing the urge to judge these differences because moral criticism would be pointless and anachronistic. In *Thick and Thin* (1994), Walzer revisits the example first discussed in *Spheres* of the differences between the medieval and modern understanding of the relative importance of physical and spiritual health and concludes: '. . . it makes no moral sense to wag our finger at medieval Christians, insisting that they *should have had* our understanding of life and death' (Walzer 1994: 29–30, italics in original). Walzer's point is not simply that you cannot change the past and so it makes no sense to criticize it, though I think he draws implicitly upon that view at times. It would be different, he says, if these understandings were 'imposed by force, the mere ideology of the ruling class'. Then criticism would be appropriate in the name of social meaning. But these understandings emerged, he says, from 'a maximalist morality, a thick understanding of life and death, a human culture' and '[t]o this we ought certainly to defer'. (Walzer 1994: 29).

One might wonder whether it would really ever make sense on Walzer's view to 'wag our finger' at people from the past. The phrase suggests that deference, at least in the form of a reluctance to pass critical judgement, is always the appropriate stance towards deeply rooted social practices and moral views from the past. Yet another, more critical perspective on history also plays a role in his discussions. In exploring the good of membership in *Spheres*, Walzer takes up the case of exclusions from citizenship in ancient Athens. He focuses on metics rather than slaves because, he says, 'the injustice of slavery is not disputed these days, at least not openly' (53). That comment is a striking and puzzling form of deference to contemporary standards of justice. From a Walzerian perspective, it is not clear why present views about the injustice of slavery, however widely shared, would be relevant to the question of whether slavery was unjust in ancient Athens. If one asked instead (as Walzer's approach would presumably require) whether Athenians regarded slavery as unjust or whether they ought to have done so given their shared social understandings of various social goods, the answer would, I suspect, be openly and vigorously disputed. That sort of contextual question seems to be the one Walzer has in mind in his extensive discussion of the metics. He spends some time exploring, without finally resolving, the question of whether the Athenian treatment of metics was unjust, given the conception of citizenship that prevailed in Athens. In any event, this perspective seems to provide some basis for criticizing past societies and cultures, namely, that social practices are not faithful to the shared understandings of the time. In other words, it is appropriate to criticize people for failing to live up to their own principles, but not for failing to live up to ours. That seems to me the approach that Walzer wants to urge upon us with regard to contemporary societies as well.

Here as elsewhere, I share Walzer's concern about the inappropriateness of certain forms of criticism. There is always the danger of anachronism in making critical judgements about past societies. It would seem to violate the maxim that 'ought implies can' to criticize people for failing to meet moral standards that were entirely unknown and unarticulated in their own time. Yet that need not entail an uncritical acceptance of the conventional view of an era. For example, in the *Philosophy of Right*, Hegel was sharply critical of the Roman legal system for treating children as the property of their father, because the Roman legal system was built upon a conception of the distinction between persons and things that should have enabled them to understand why treating children as property was wrong (Hegel 1962). By contrast, Hegel has nothing comparably judgemental to say about Babylonian practices even more at odds with modern moral norms, presumably because Babylonian civilization did not have the conceptual resources for a critical perspective on these practices.

The approach to the past that I am advocating here does not limit itself to criticism of the gap between principles and practices but opens up space for criticism of the principles or understandings that people actually had in the name of principles or understandings they should have had, given their overall cultural context. This may appear to go beyond Walzer, but I think that this sort of critical stance towards the past is compatible with Walzer's insistence that his interpretive approach to morality does not entail a passive acceptance of prevailing ideas and practices and is fully compatible with radical social criticism (although he himself does not deploy this critical perspective much in his discussions of examples from the past).

Finally, I want to open the door to a less connected form of criticism of the past, one that makes assessments of the goodness or badness of different kinds of social arrangements independent of their cultural context. Consider again the example of Athenian slavery during the Periclean period that Walzer chose not to discuss because 'the injustice of slavery is not disputed these days, at least not openly'. Suppose we concluded upon investigation that the shared understandings of Athenians (perhaps of Greeks) during this period provided no good grounds for regarding slavery as unjust. After all, it was a common practice among the Greeks to enslave other Greeks on the losing side of a war. Perhaps they regarded the institution of slavery as inevitable, and the condition of being a slave as unfortunate but not unjust. (There are, of course, countervailing readings of Plato and Aristotle, among others, but this is not an implausible reading of the time. Remember that Hegel dates the conceptual resources for the critique of slavery to the Romans not the Greeks.) Would it follow that we should not say that the institution of slavery during this period was unjust? I don't see why. It seems to me both possible and sensible to conclude that a particular set of social practices was unjust, even if the people engaged in those practices could not be held responsible for the injustice. At the very least, we can make assessments about better and worse ways to organize human affairs even apart from a consideration of what cultural possibilities are open in a given context. So, too, today. In the next section I will argue that it is justifiable today to criticize forms of social organization in which women's life chances are severely restricted or in which the rulers make no effort to secure the consent of the people, even if we do not know the extent to which these arrangements fit with the prevailing culture.

Gender Equality and Cultural Difference

One way to specify how much room a theory of justice provides for particularity and cultural difference between societies is to look at crucial topics where our understanding of justice is not shared by others to see whether we regard these different understandings as ones we should respect or not. I propose to take up two topics in this context: gender equality and democracy.

How should we think about the way women are treated in other countries? Of course, we need to *understand* how they are treated before passing judgement. We can't simply assume that what would be a form of oppression in our society is necessarily one in theirs as well. But should we limit *our* judgements to *their* understanding of what justice requires in relations between men and women with respect to economic opportunity, education, health care, access to office, and so on? If we recognize that both justice and gender are cultural constructions, what should we think about the ways in which cultures that are not our own have constructed them?

Walzer's discussion of the caste system suggests that the only meaningful criticism is internal criticism, but, as I have tried to show, other parts of his discussion are less particularistic. He is surely right to draw our attention to the fact that cultures vary and to insist that justice, like all morality, is a cultural creation, at least in many important respects. It is all too easy to project our own particularistic understanding as a universal norm and to misunderstand institutions and practices different from our own. As liberals, we have good historical and theoretical reasons to be wary of such projections and misunderstandings. Would anyone today want to endorse (or reproduce) the smug superiority displayed by so many nineteenth-century liberals towards indigenous cultures in Asia, Africa, and America?[15] On the other hand, appeal to difference is every tyranny's first line of defence against external criticism. 'You don't understand our circumstances, our way of life, or our people', they say.

Take the issue of female circumcision (as it is usually called by its defenders) or genital mutilation (as it is usually called by its opponents), a practice with deep cultural roots in some countries, mainly in Africa but also in the Middle East and Southeast Asia, in which the genitalia of young girls are removed in whole or in part. Those who object to Western criticism of this practice usually argue that the criticism is a contemporary manifestation of Western cultural imperialism and hence is illegitimate. It seems essential, however, to distinguish between two kinds of objections that can be posed to this or any other sort of external criticism. One kind, which I'll call a moral

---

[15] For a telling critique of this smug superiority, including its contemporary manifestations, see Parekh (1994*c*).

or principled objection, challenges the intrinsic merits of external criticism, insisting that outsiders are not morally entitled to judge insiders. (I'll return to this in a moment.) The second kind, which I'll call a political objection, challenges the effectiveness of external criticism or seeks to interrogate its meaning and purpose in a particular context.

Political objections to external criticism sometimes—though not always—have considerable merit. One sort of political objection is the argument that external criticism is counter-productive, causing people to be defensive and to continue an objectionable practice longer than they would if left to their own internal debates and deliberations. Thus some people argue that it is a mistake to oppose genital mutilation in the name of human rights or of women's right to control their own sexuality or perhaps even to call it genital mutilation as opposed to female circumcision, because these sorts of arguments and categories will be experienced as an alien discourse in the cultural contexts in which the practice takes place. Instead, one should find resources from within the local culture, as, for example in local commitments to the physical health of women and children, and use them as the basis for opposition to the practice. Note that this position presupposes the illegitimacy of the practice and merely claims that one set of tactics is better than another in arriving at the agreed-upon goal of eliminating it. In my view, this kind of argument will have merit in some cases but not in others, and I don't know how well it works here. Perhaps the relevance of the argument varies from one cultural and political context to another. In any event, on this approach, the question of how to respond to a deeply objectionable cultural practice in another society becomes an empirical matter calling for political judgement. It is implausible to suppose that it will always require us to argue from within. Constructive engagement is not always more effective than confrontation as a means of bringing about a desired change in attitudes or policy.

A second kind of political objection draws attention to the fact that moral discussions of particular issues may have symbolic and political functions that deserve critical scrutiny. When I was educated in primary and secondary school, the only thing I ever learned about India concerned *sati*, the Hindu practice in which widows were burnt alive on their husbands' funeral pyres and which was outlawed by British colonial authorities. It is no defence of *sati* to suggest that there are other, perhaps more important things one could learn about Indian civilisation and that the focus on this practice was not an accident. It served to identify the British with civilization and Indians with barbarism and thus to legitimate British colonialism.[16]

The debate over genital mutilation often plays a similar role, especially in contemporary discussions of immigration.[17] Such discussions often focus on

---

[16] For an illuminating discussion of *sati* and other issues of cross-cultural criticism from a feminist perspective, see Narayan (1997).
[17] I owe the argument in this paragraph to Dilek Çinar.

the 'problems' raised by the 'alien' values of immigrants, especially with respect to the issue of gender equality. In this context, the issue of genital mutilation is frequently used to illustrate and define the nature of the presumed conflict of values. The effect is implicitly to create an identification of the West with civilization and of other cultures with barbarism, and to define immigrants as threats because they are bearers of a barbaric culture. These identifications are possible because nothing is said about any internal opposition to these practices within the countries of origin, about the ways in which immigrants may not fully embrace the dominant cultural traditions of the countries they have chosen to leave, or, for that matter, about the failures and inadequacies of Western liberal democratic states with respect to gender equality.[18]

One can grant the force of both of these political objections without accepting the view that the only legitimate moral critique of a cultural practice is one based on the local understandings of the community in which it is practised. That is what the moral or principled objection to external criticism seems to require, and what Walzer's rhetoric seems sometimes to endorse. How might he respond to the issue of female circumcision/genital mutilation? Walzer takes it up in *On Toleration* (1997), where he argues that it is right for European and North American states to prohibit the practice among immigrants (though not necessarily by means of criminalization) because of the commitment of these states to certain conceptions of equal citizenship and individual rights. He is more circumspect about what stance he would take towards the practice in the countries of origin, noting only that no one has proposed humanitarian intervention to eliminate it and in that sense international society tolerates it at the state level while a number of organizations in international civil society work to oppose it (Walzer 1997: 62–3). But this is only a descriptive comment. The key question (for my purposes) is not whether one advocates armed intervention but whether one is willing to criticize the practice at all when carried on elsewhere and, if so, on what basis. Leaving aside the political considerations discussed above which would affect how one might act with regard to this issue, how should we think about the practice? Should our judgement depend upon our understanding of the underlying norms and values of the local culture in which the practice is embedded, or should we make an independent judgement about it based on our own norms and values?

For my own part, I find this a relatively easy case. Female circumcision is clearly a practice loaded with cultural significance, intimately connected to the meaning of sexuality and gender in particular communities. Nevertheless,

---

[18] Chapter 6 takes up this issue again in the context of a detailed exploration of the supposed clash between liberal democratic norms and the cultural commitments of Muslim immigrants. For a related critique of the role played by discussion of genital mutilation in contemporary politics, see Tamir (1996).

it causes permanent and significant physical harm to young girls. In the face of this fact, its local meaning and the degree to which that meaning is accepted by people subject to the practice (e.g. the women who perform it on their daughters) seem to me irrelevant. I regard it as an unjust practice, rightly characterized as genital mutilation.[19] In making this judgement, I am not rejecting the political objections discussed above to some of the ways in which critiques of genital mutilation have been advanced, and I am certainly not advocating armed intervention to end it. Moreover, it may well be that there are important points of contact between the fundamental grounds for my rejection of the practice (physical harm to children) and the values available in local cultures for opposing it. Nevertheless, my own reasons for rejecting it do not depend on those points of contact. If we take seriously, as I think we should, Walzer's insistence that people can construct very different social and moral worlds, then we cannot simply assume that such points of contact exist, or, if they do, that they are sufficiently powerful to outweigh the other elements in the culture. Walzer's account of the profound differences between medieval and modern Europe in the relative importance attached to physical and spiritual well-being illustrates the point. My critical reaction to genital mutilation is undoubtedly shaped by certain views of physical health, including unimpaired sexuality, as a human good, and people who practice female circumcision (as they see it) may have quite different views of the relative importance of this good compared with other culturally constructed concerns. We should try to understand, we should listen respectfully, but we should not abandon our own commitments for the sake of respecting those of others.

Because it involves serious physical harm to children, genital mutilation is a hard case to defend on grounds of local understanding. What about gender-related practices in which such harm is not involved? Here the answer is less obvious. One way to test how much of your theory of justice falls within the outermost circle and how much within the middle one would be to ask the following question. Are there any gender-related norms or practices that you would regard as just (at least in the sense of being morally permissible) on the grounds that they are accepted by the people of a particular society as integral to their culture and way of life, even though you would regard such practices as unjust in your own society on the grounds that they are incompatible with a commitment to equal citizenship?

In formulating the question in this way, I do not mean to imply that contemporary liberal democratic states have achieved gender equality. On the contrary, I take it to be obvious that the opposite is the case with respect to physical security, economic opportunity, political power, and virtually every

---

[19] This judgement presupposes that the practice is carried on in its current form. See Chapter 6 for a more detailed discussion, including a consideration of possible alternative, acceptable forms of female circumcision.

other important life chance. But I do assume that gender equality (the meaning of which is, of course, contested) provides a critical standard of justice for evaluating public institutions and practices in Canada, the United States, and every other liberal democratic state. The question is whether it provides the same kind of critical standard for evaluating public institutions and policies in other societies.

I hope that readers will think about this question for themselves. I confess myself to be uncertain about how to respond. On the one hand, I feel the power of Walzer's argument about the importance of cultural particularity. On the other hand, I cannot think of any actual example of a gender-differentiated practice that I would be willing to defend as just in another society but not in my own. I could probably construct an imaginary example, but it seems to me to be crucial to appeal only to actual, not hypothetical cases, and to ones drawn from contemporary societies so as to avoid the problems of anachronism that emerge with historical cases. I am not ruling out the use of hypotheticals in moral inquiry. Rather the point is that if you cannot think of (m)any actual examples of gender-differentiated practices that are just in other societies but would be unjust in your own, then your understanding of justice has a powerful universalistic cast in practice, whatever its formal room for particularity.

These questions emerge not only as theoretical puzzles about how to think about justice but also as concrete problems requiring action. For example, several Third World countries led by China have pressed for revision of various international human rights codes, especially with respect to gender, on the grounds that they reflect a specifically Western liberal view of the proper role of women in society. How should we respond to these demands?

Related questions emerge within liberal democratic states because of the presence of people who reject or challenge the idea of gender equality in ways that raise questions about public policy. Some of these people are recent immigrants, others members of long-standing ethnic or religious minorities. In what ways should liberal democratic states respect and in what ways should they challenge these cultural commitments? If we think of an inquiry into justice as a matter of evaluating conflicting interpretations of shared understandings, what do we say when disagreements about what justice requires come from deep differences in cultural traditions? I pursue these questions, including their implications for gender equality, in Chapters 4, 5, and 6.

Democracy as a Universal (Contemporary) Norm

The kinds of questions I have asked about gender can be extended to the idea of democracy. How should we think about democracy as a normative ideal or standard? Can democratic principles properly be used to criticize any state that fails to live up to them or only states whose political culture is democratic? Recall Walzer's central claim in *Spheres* which I cited earlier:

One characteristic above all is central to my argument. We are (all of us) culture-producing creatures; we make and inhabit meaningful worlds. Since there is no way to rank and order these worlds with respect to their understanding of social goods, we do justice to men and women by respecting their particular creations (314).

Where does this idea of justice come from? Isn't the idea that we should respect the shared understandings or cultural creations of other communities itself a democratic argument, a kind of modified consent theory with the fact that the culture is *shared* substituting for other forms of consent as the basis of legitimacy? But *that* argument comes from *our own* traditions and understandings, not from the particularistic cultures of other societies. Some of them may share this commitment to democracy and some may not. So then the fundamental question that Walzer is addressing is not really what do *they* think is right, but rather what do *we* think is right or what *should* we think is right? (Indeed, given Walzer's view of theory as interpretation, what other question could he ask?) In other words, the question is to what extent our (culturally constructed) understanding of justice requires us to respect the cultural constructions of others (including their constructions of justice)? Now, our conception of justice does include respect for cultural creations different from our own as one of its components. Walzer is surely right about that. But respect for such cultural creations is only one aspect of our understanding of justice, and one that must be balanced against concern for human rights, gender equality, and democracy among other things.

So, to assess the force of democracy as a normative ideal, we must ask a more concrete question. Is there any actual state today where the absence of democratic institutions—to put it more starkly let me say liberal democratic institutions—should not be regarded as deeply problematic from a moral perspective? In less convoluted form, is there any actual state that is undemocratic but not unjust because of the absence of democracy? Again, I pose this question both as a challenge to Walzer's theory and as a vehicle for the reader to use in clarifying the character of his or her own understanding of justice. If the answer to the question is 'no', for whatever reason, that would suggest either that one rejects Walzer's account of justice or that the idea that justice is determined by the shared understandings of particular communities is far less radically relativistic and justice far less culturally specific than many readers of *Spheres* would have supposed. Indeed, the distinction between the outermost and middle concentric circles collapses. If the answer is 'yes', then the challenge is 'name it' and say why it is not unjust.

As in the discussion of gender, I want to make a plea here for actual examples. The undemocratic but just state has to be a real state, not an imaginary one, and a contemporary state, not an historical one. It is one of the great virtues of Walzer's approach to theory that he starts with real moral arguments and real political cases. He rightly criticizes some philosophers for relying too heavily upon implausible hypotheticals to support their intuitions. So, it is striking that, while the general principles of *Spheres*—particularly the arguments about shared understandings—*seem* to open the prospect of a just state with social arrangements radically at odds with contemporary liberalism, the only actual example of such a radical yet just departure that he gives is an idealized picture of an Indian village based on the caste system. It is not a state. India is a state, but such a description could not plausibly apply to the entire state of India. It is not even an actual village, with all the complexities and messiness that actual village cultures contain. If there are no real cases to support these principles, perhaps the principles themselves are less sturdy than they appear.

For my own part, despite my considerable sympathy for Walzer's approach and for his openness to cultural difference, I cannot think of a single actual case where the absence of democracy is not unjust. I do not mean to suggest that democracy must always and everywhere take the same forms or that history and culture are irrelevant to the question of what justice requires and permits in political arrangements. On the contrary, In Chapter 8 dealing with aboriginal self-government and Chapter 9 discussing the case of Fiji, I defend arrangements that deviate from conventional liberal practices. Nevertheless, I cannot think of any existing state in which the absence of such liberal democratic arrangements as freedom of political opinion and expression and open elections is morally defensible.

Moral Minimalism and Democracy: Relativism Revisited

How might Walzer respond to this sort of challenge? I have a good sense of the answer to this because an earlier version of this chapter appeared in a book in which Walzer wrote the concluding chapter responding to the criticisms that the other contributors (including me) had advanced. In replying to my essay, Walzer introduces the example of contemporary Iran which he describes as a 'religious republic . . . where there is no separation of mosque and state and no effective citizenship for non-Muslim minorities' (Walzer 1995: 288). Walzer does not argue that Iran as it actually exists is just, but he does say that 'the requirement of justice in an Islamic republic might be the full autonomy of all the other religious communities' (Walzer 1995: 288). This seems to me a fair response to my challenge even though it does not name an actual state that is just though undemocratic. After all, one might argue that no liberal democratic state really lives up to the principles of liberal democracy or deserves to be called just. To say that an Islamic republic that was undemocratic but respected the autonomy of other religious communities would be a just regime is clearly to reject the notion that liberal democracy provides a normative standard that is appropriately applied to all contemporary states, and Walzer says that it is not a 'requirement of justice' that Iranian Muslims adopt the democratic ideal (Walzer 1995: 289).

Walzer insists further that his requirement of religious autonomy for other communities is not properly characterized as a minimalist and universalist standard that emerges only from the outermost circle of our own moral views and is external to Muslim culture. Instead, he says, this is simply a requirement of reciprocity, a principle with deep roots in past Muslim practices. He insists that it is inappropriate to criticize other societies on the basis of our own minimal standards unless these standards are also shared by the society that we are criticizing.

I think this position is too restrictive in some respects and too expansive in others. Let me begin by distinguishing two kinds of questions one can ask about minimal morality. The first is whether there are any moral norms that are universally shared among all people despite the obvious differences among societies and cultures on a wide range of moral issues. The second is whether *our* morality includes any norms that we think apply universally (regardless of whether these norms can also be derived from some other community's culture). Walzer is interested in both questions, and, in my view, he sometimes confounds the two. I am interested only in the second.

With regard to the first question, Walzer argues in *Thick and Thin* that there is a universal minimal morality, but that it is a mistake to imagine that this is independent from particular cultures and directly shared by all human beings. As a corollary, he rejects any philosophical project that would seek to establish the foundations of such a minimal morality (e.g. in human nature or reason) and use it as a base for a more expansive universal conception of justice. Instead he insists, '[T]he moral minimum is not a free-standing morality. It simply designates some reiterated features of particular thick or maximal moralities' (Walzer 1994: 10). I have no quarrel with this aspect of Walzer's argument, with the important caveat that these thick or maximal moralities should not be imagined always to be the product or property of a particular political community but may instead be shared across borders or even continents as deep elements of culture often are. Walzer's own example of the changing attitudes towards care of the body and the soul illustrates the relevance of this caveat. The contrast is not between the shared understandings of different political communities but between the shared understandings of Europeans in one age and in another.

As my discussion in Chapter 1 of my contextual approach to political theory makes clear, I am not trying to find (or construct) a minimal universal morality that can serve as the foundation for all moral judgements or prescribe all social practices. So, I am perfectly prepared to acknowledge that the outermost circle of our morality, the one in which we apply our critical standards universally, is a feature of *our* morality. Indeed, what is so striking about this part of our morality, in my view, is that we *are* prepared to apply it even to people who may not share it, whereas we have many moral norms that we think should apply only to people who share our commitments. In my view, Walzer obscures this aspect of our moral views in *Thick and Thin* (1994) by taking up the question of the moral minimum in a context in which he imagines critical questions already being raised elsewhere and in which the issue is how we should respond and the extent to which our critiques have the same basis as theirs. Walzer insists it is more a matter of the overlap of principles and ideas, abstracted from independent, thickly contextual moralities than of an agreement on general principles. This implicitly sets to one side the question of whether we would have any basis for criticism, if this overlap were absent, if they were not raising critical questions about their own practices.

I am inclined to leave open the question of whether there are any moral standards universally shared by all human societies, past and present, or even only by contemporary ones. It sounds like an empirical question, but even if we can get enough information, much will depend on how we classify different norms. For example, all societies prohibit some forms of human killing, and many tolerate or approve others. Should this be regarded as a point of agreement or disagreement? I'm not sure this is a fruitful question. In any event, it is one I do not want to pursue. Walzer's view that such universal standards as exist (if any) are rooted in and abstracted from thick, particularistic moralities seems to me plausible, but again I want to set that issue to one side. Instead I want to focus on the question of when we feel we ought to judge others and when we feel we ought not to do so (recognizing that we disagree among ourselves about this). In that sense, my question is an internal, interpretive one, which seems to me more in the spirit of Walzer's own basic project than the question he himself addresses.

Walzer says that we should not think of ourselves as applying minimal moral standards when we criticize other societies, but should look instead for the overlap between the criticisms that emerge from the minimal standards derived from our own thick moralities and the minimal standards that can be derived from the thick morality of the society we are criticizing (1994: 10, 1995: 289). I worry that this sort of approach will bias our inquiry into other cultures and lead us to distort their moral views. Note that on my account— a descriptive and interpretive account of our moral practices—we do not normally feel entitled to criticize other societies as much as our own and the more cultural distance there is the more we are (and ought to be) hesitant to criticize, but nevertheless we still feel we ought to make critical judgements on some matters even when there is great cultural distance. Suppose that we have passed that threshold, that we find an issue (like genital mutilation or the expulsion of long-established residents) where we feel we ought to pass critical judgement on the practices of another society. If, as appears to be the case on Walzer's account, we are entitled to pass judgement only if there are points of overlap between our moral views and theirs on this issue, then we have a powerful incentive to find such points of overlap. This is not conducive to an open-minded inquiry into their culture and morality.

Consider again the case of contemporary Iran. Walzer argues that we can hold Iran to a norm of reciprocity but not democracy because reciprocity is internal to Muslim culture and democracy is not. But what sort of internality is required for such a claim? At one point, Walzer suggests that reciprocity is 'not wholly external to any . . . culture' (1995: 289). Perhaps not, but I'm inclined to think the same could be said about gender equality and democracy, broadly understood. If there is anything the postmodernist turn has taught us, it is that a suitably motivated interpreter can find almost anything he or she wants somewhere in a text. If we are to treat other cultures with the kind of deference Walzer wants, then surely we have to say more than that the norms and standards we are using to evaluate their practices are not 'wholly external' to their culture. Walzer observes that 'some version of [reciprocity] has been accepted by Muslim states in the past' (1995: 289), but this is open to the obvious objection that those versions of reciprocity (not to mention Walzer's) do not reflect the most satisfactory understanding of (a) Islam and (b) Iran. (Note again the ambiguities about the relationship between the political and the moral communities.) To argue that reciprocity (in the form of the full autonomy of all religious communities) is the appropriate norm for the Iranian Islamic community, given its own cultural commitments, would require a detailed knowledge of a thick moral world, a knowledge that I do not possess and that I suspect Walzer does not either in this case.

One illustration of the dangers of the course that Walzer is advocating is provided by a controversial Supreme Court case in India, the Shah Bano case.[20] India provides a measure of autonomy for the Muslim community with regard to matters of personal law, including family law. In a recent case, a woman argued that the financial support provided by her husband after a divorce, which had been judged acceptable by the Muslim courts in India, was incompatible with India's constitutional commitment to gender equality. In upholding her claim, the Indian Supreme Court, composed primarily of Hindu and secular Indians, did not limit itself to an interpretation of the correct balance within the Indian Constitution of the (at least potentially)

---

[20] For information on this case I rely on Engineer (1987). My thanks to Ashok Acharya for bringing this case to my attention. Acharya has a very illuminating discussion of this case in his unpublished dissertation.

competing commitments to gender equality and religious communal autonomy but went on to argue that the Qur'an itself required a higher level of
payment to the divorced wife. The Muslim community in India was outraged
at the decision, but especially at the fact that the Court had taken it upon
itself to decide what was the best understanding of Islam. It seems to me that,
whatever the merits of the outcome, it would have been better for the Court
to limit itself to an interpretation of the Constitution for which it was clearly
responsible and to leave aside its understanding of the Qur'an.

To insist that we can criticize only on the basis of norms internal to a
cultural tradition is to create powerful incentives to interpret that tradition in
ways that satisfy our desire to criticize, a desire often generated in the first
instance not by the cultural tradition in question but by our own. In such a
context, interpretations by outsiders will rarely seem persuasive, and often
offensive, to insiders.

It is only fair to acknowledge that so long as we stay within our own
cultural commitments we are not providing others who do not share those
commitments with reasons to change their views or practices. But my focus
in this essay is on the interpretation of our own shared understandings (to use
a Walzerian phrase), and, in particular, of our understanding of when it is
appropriate and when inappropriate to make critical judgements about the
practices of others. I am not suggesting that every time we reach a critical
conclusion about views or practices in another culture, we should launch a
missionary crusade. On the contrary, I think that we should state our criticisms and the reasons for them respectfully and listen with an open mind to
the response. Perhaps we will learn something that persuades us either that
we've misunderstood their practices or that there are other grounds for modi-
fying our views. I will try to show in Chapters 8 and 9 how listening sym-
pathetically to other cultural perspectives can enable us to appreciate the
moral virtues of practices that depart from conventional liberal arrangements.
If we are not persuaded by others' justifications of their practices, it may then
be appropriate to try to persuade them by looking for points of contact
between their cultural commitments and the views we are advocating, without disguising the fact that our arguments are motivated, in the first instance,
by our own commitments (just as they may try to persuade us that our
commitments to freedom and respect for other cultures should lead us to
abandon our critique of their practices). Whatever the outcome of such a
conversation, our views of the minimal moral standards that can appropriately be applied to other cultures does not and should not depend upon
whether we can show that those standards can be derived from those cultures.

I return finally to the question of whether it is appropriate to criticize
contemporary Iran for being undemocratic. Note first that, as in other examples discussed above, Walzer's own discussion of Iran contains elements of the
kind of external criticism that he says he wants to exclude. At the end of his

response he says: 'Is the absence or ineffectiveness of democratic citizenship in Iran morally problematic? Yes, because it blocks the full development of complex equality and because it puts justice at risk—at greater risk than it is in more differentiated societies' (Walzer 1995: 289).[21] Why should blocking the full development of complex equality be morally problematic for Iran from Walzer's perspective? Isn't complex equality precisely the kind of moral notion that derives its critical power from its location within a particular, thick moral tradition, a tradition that is Walzer's and mine, but not that of the Iranian Muslims? More fundamentally, in acknowledging that the absence of democratic citizenship is morally problematic, Walzer has retreated a long way from his initial suggestion that reciprocity would be morally sufficient. Why does Walzer find it so hard to avoid this kind of external criticism? Because, as his own theory suggests, he thinks and argues from within a particular tradition, and within that tradition democracy is a norm with a powerful universalistic cast. But I would go a bit further than he does.

Iran is a modern state, not a medieval empire. That sort of political community is morally constrained. It could not rightly exclude people who live there from citizenship, even if it did grant full autonomy to their religious communities. It cannot rightly deny their basic human rights, and their political authorities will lack moral legitimacy if they are not chosen through elections that are, broadly speaking, fair and open.[22]

As I emphasized in the first half of this chapter, I am not suggesting that we can specify in precise detail what institutions and practices Iran ought to adopt as a matter of justice, but I do think we can establish some constraints, rule some things out of (moral) bounds. In *Thick and Thin,* Walzer says that he supported the Chinese students in Tienanmen Square in 1989 in their demands for democracy but that he could not say what sort of democracy the Chinese ought to have, except that it would have to be *Chinese,* to reflect Chinese history and culture (Walzer 1994: 59–60). I entirely agree that we cannot determine what Chinese democracy should look like, but that does not mean that as non-Chinese we can make no critical comments. It is easy to claim the name 'democracy' and many states do so that are entirely undemocratic. I would want to insist that Chinese democracy must not only be

---

[21] Walzer also insists that we should not regard non-democratic societies as unjust 'by virtue of that fact alone' (i.e. the absence of democracy) because understandings of justice that resonate with our own in important ways can be found in many such societies. In elaboration, Walzer cites a passage from Deuteronomy calling for the pursuit of justice, a passage that Walzer says is not about democracy but about the denunciation of 'corrupt judges who bent the law in the interests of wealthy and powerful men', an important matter of justice today as well as then (Walzer 1995: 289–90). I don't doubt that there are links between the biblical conception of justice and our own (which is, of course, in part derived from it), but this seems to me irrelevant to the point at hand. The question is whether the absence of democracy in a contemporary state is *an* injustice, not whether it is the whole of justice. Justice is multifaceted and complex. Even in regimes with profoundly unjust forms of social domination (e.g. the American South under slavery and segregation, South Africa under apartheid), it was possible for people to criticize corrupt judges.

[22] Iran has elections, though I'm in no position to assess their character.

Chinese, it must also be *democratic*. If we cannot specify what the regime should look like in advance, we also cannot avoid judging the concrete institutions and practices that emerge and determining whether we think they deserve the name 'democracy'. And if they do not, then they deserve criticism.

Let me conclude with a caution. I don't want to overstate the universalism of the last few pages. As subsequent chapters will show, I think there are indeed many important areas of local justice, many situations in which we should simply respect the shared understandings of other communities even when they differ from our own. But there are many other situations where we don't and shouldn't respect these shared understandings. How we sort these cases out, and on what basis, and whether our sorting makes sense, are all important questions. Answering them requires just the sort of contextual inquiry that Walzer invites. But that is not what Walzer himself says. In granting such strong priority to the shared understandings of particular communities, he stops a bit short of the more fully satisfying sort of political theory that his own work has enabled us to see.

3

Liberalism and Culture

Most countries today are culturally diverse. According to recent estimates, the world's 184 independent states contain over 600 living language groups, and 5,000 ethnic groups. In very few countries can the citizens be said to share the same language, or belong to the same ethnonational group.

(Kymlicka 1995: 1)

How should we respond to differences of culture and identity within political communities and to the many conflicting demands that emerge from them? In this chapter, I will use Will Kymlicka's work to open up a set of questions about cultural diversity that I will pursue throughout the book. As in my discussion of Walzer, I will show both how much we learn from Kymlicka's contextual approach, and how some of his abstract theoretical formulations lead us astray, obscuring more than they reveal about the normative justifications for our practices. Once again, I will argue that an even closer attention to context will lead to a richer, more complex, and ultimately more satisfactory theoretical account.

Kymlicka's Contextual Defence of Multiculturalism

Kymlicka's attention to the theoretical significance of liberal practices is what identifies him as a practitioner of the kind of contextual theory that I am advocating in this book. This approach to political theory initially emerges in the second half of Kymlicka's first book *Liberalism, Community, and Culture.* (1989*a*). The first half of that work defends contemporary liberal theory, especially Rawls and Dworkin, against communitarian critics and others. In that part, the argument is advanced almost entirely at a theoretical level. References to actual practice are rare and are used only as examples. The second half is quite different. There, after noting that theorists like Rawls and Dworkin treat cultural differences as morally irrelevant in a just society, Kymlicka appeals to the actual practices of liberal democratic states, especially, but not only, Canada, to challenge these theories. In effect, he says something like this: 'Look, many of the people in Canada who care most strongly about liberal democratic principles like freedom and equality are passionately committed to the protection of minority cultures, even to the point that they are willing, in some circumstances, to limit some of the basic rights of citizenship like freedom of movement or the right to vote. Let's not assume that they are wrong just because the prevailing theories say so. Instead, let's consider whether it is the theory that needs to be changed rather than the practice.' Kymlicka himself did not use this folksy style in the book, but that seems to me the gist of his approach.

In *Multicultural Citizenship*, Kymlicka extends this strategy of inquiry (1995). He draws our attention to some of the ways in which various liberal democratic states deal with cultural issues. Overall, he makes three main points about these practices. First, he observes that all liberal states have policies that reflect and promote some aspects of the majority's culture. Secondly, he points out that virtually all liberal states also recognize and promote minority cultures, often through the use of various types of group-differentiated rights. Thirdly, he notes that most of these states distinguish between two kinds of cultural minorities, granting much more extensive linguistic and self-government rights to national minorities (groups with a shared language, culture, and identity that have lived on the territory of the state over several generations or more) than to ethnic groups (groups constituted by immigrants and their descendants). Canada continues to figure prominently in the discussion, but the book refers to a wide variety of practices in different countries.

As Kymlicka shows, these practices pose a deep challenge to the conventional liberal view that the state should take a hands off approach to culture, because this conventional view presents itself as defending existing liberal arrangements against demands for group recognition that would represent a radical departure from the status quo. By showing how much current practices in liberal states already recognize the claims of cultural groups, Kymlicka shifts the burden of proof. Conventional liberals must say whether they are prepared to revise all of the current practices that favour particular cultural groups, including the majority, and if they are unwilling (or unable) to endorse that course, they must explain why the new group claims are morally different from the ones already recognized.

Kymlicka argues persuasively that it would be impossible to abandon all of the practices favouring specific cultures. The ideal of cultural neutrality is an illusion. There are certain issues on which the state cannot avoid making decisions that have a significant impact on culture, and, if the polity contains people from different cultures, that advantage some and disadvantage others. The most obvious and important example is that of language. Whether or not a government adopts an official language, it cannot avoid deciding what languages will be used in legal settings, in the provision of public services, and in schools. Of course, such decisions may be made at local or regional levels rather than at the level of the polity as a whole, but that merely shows that decisions about internal boundaries, jurisdictions, and powers have implications for cultural groups as well, enhancing the ability of those who constitute a majority within a jurisdiction with relevant authority to use government power to promote and protect their cultural interests, especially in policies with regard to language. Public holidays and state symbols are other examples of topics that are always culturally laden. Moreover, public policies often impinge differently on different cultural groups, even if that is not the explicit intention.

Liberal Theory and Societal Cultures

Since neutrality is impossible, what should be done? Kymlicka's answer is that some policies favouring cultural minorities, the ones that are justifiable, provide a way of fulfilling rather than undermining liberal commitments to freedom and equality. He takes his principal challenge to be showing how culture matters from a liberal perspective. Kymlicka addresses this challenge most directly in chapters 5 and 6 where he uses the concept of 'societal culture' to provide a theoretical explanation of why the practices of liberal states with regard to culture are generally compatible with liberal principles. He notes that the term 'culture' can be used in a variety of ways but says that he will focus on what he calls:

a societal culture—i.e., a culture which provides its members with meaningful ways of life across the full range of human activities, including social, educational, religious, and economic life, encompassing both public and private spheres. These cultures tend to be territorially concentrated, and based on a shared language (76).[1]

He emphasizes that societal cultures 'involve not just shared memories or values, but also common institutions and practices' and that a societal culture 'must be institutionally embodied—in schools, media, economy, government, etc.' (76). Citing Gellner, Kymlicka says that societal cultures in the sense in which he uses the term 'did not always exist, and their creation is intimately linked with the process of modernization' (76). The term 'societal culture' is also closely linked to the term 'nation', so that at one point he says that he uses the terms culture and nation synonymously (18) and at another says, 'just as societal cultures are almost invariably national cultures, so nations are almost invariably societal cultures' (80).

Kymlicka then argues that the liberal freedom to choose one's own path in

---

[1] In this chapter, numbers in parentheses refer to pages in Kymlicka (1995).

life depends, in significant ways, upon having access to a societal culture, because it is only in the context of a societal culture that we can understand the options available to us and make intelligent judgements about which ones to pursue. In other words, a societal culture provides the context within which meaningful choice is possible. In this light, access to a societal culture can be seen to be a fundamental interest of human beings, the sort of thing that Rawls calls a primary good.

Why does the societal culture within which one makes choices have to be the one within which one was born and raised? Kymlicka says that it does not have to be that one, noting that immigrants often function well in the context of the societal culture of the place to which they have moved. But he argues that the transformation required to adapt to a new societal culture is normally very difficult and demanding, so that it is reasonable for people to regard access to their native culture as a fundamental interest or a primary good, something they should not normally be expected to give up.

Having established the moral importance of societal cultures, Kymlicka then argues that fairness requires that 'we should aim at ensuring that all national groups have the opportunity to maintain themselves as a distinct culture, if they so choose' (113). In other words, protecting societal cultures promotes freedom because it protects the contexts that make choice meaningful and protecting all of the distinct societal cultures within a given state promotes equality because it gives people access to their own societal cultures instead of placing them at a disadvantage by requiring them to adapt to another culture. In a democratic state, the mechanisms of majority rule will ensure that the language of the majority national group is an official language and that its culture is supported and protected in other ways as well. To ensure that members of minority nations also have secure access to their own societal cultures it is necessary to recognize the languages of minority nations as official languages and to draw boundaries and distribute powers so as to enable minority nations to support and protect their own cultures. Thus group-differentiated rights designed to protect minority societal cultures can be seen as a way of promoting equality by compensating for unequal circumstances.

If people's native societal cultures are so important to them, why should not immigrants be able to bring their societal cultures with them and establish them in their new home? Kymlicka says that they are not entitled to do that because they have come voluntarily. In choosing to come, they have agreed to waive their normal entitlement to access to their original societal cultures.[2]

---

[2] Kymlicka's position is considerably more ambivalent, and, I think, ambiguous than some of his statements suggest. He concedes that refugees do not come voluntarily and that the assumption that other immigrants come voluntarily may be inappropriate given the vast economic inequalities in the world. Moreover, he seems to slide from the empirical observation that states are not likely to give immigrants and refugees the resources needed to enable them to preserve their original societal cultures to the normative conclusion that they are not obliged to do so. I discuss these issues more fully later in this chapter.

In Kymlicka's view, immigrants' claims to equal access to a societal culture can be met satisfactorily by enabling them to integrate effectively into the 'mainstream culture(s)', which is to be achieved mainly 'by providing language training and fighting patterns of discrimination and prejudice' (114). For them, unlike national minorities, 'equality with respect to cultural membership' ought primarily to be pursued through 'rigorously enforcing the common rights of citizenship [rather] than providing group-differentiated rights' (114). However, he does qualify this, saying that 'equality does justify some group-specific rights' for ethnic groups (114). He calls these 'polyethnic rights' (30) and cites exemptions from Sunday closing laws or dress codes for government officials as examples of the sorts of rights that are warranted (though he is not clear whether they are morally required).

Kymlicka intends the concept of societal culture to provide a theoretical foundation for his analysis. In my view, however, this concept is an abstraction that distorts his argument and appears persuasive only because he fails to think concretely about its implications for particular cases, including many that he himself mentions. The concept of societal culture is fundamentally flawed in five interrelated and cumulative ways. First, it undermines the case for the kinds of cultural rights for immigrants that Kymlicka himself thinks are needed. Secondly, it fails to provide much guidance for assessing the claims of national minorities. Thirdly, it weakens the claims of smaller, more vulnerable national minorities. Fourthly, and most importantly, it rests implicitly upon a monocultural understanding of the relationship between politics and culture that impedes rather than enhances the quest for a multi-cultural conception of citizenship. Finally, it homogenizes culture, obscuring the multiplicity of our cultural inheritances and the complex ways in which they shape our contexts of choice. I will use a critical analysis of the concept and its limitations to explore what is required by a more satisfactory approach to the problem of multicultural citizenship.

Immigrants and Liberal Neutrality

Consider the question of immigrants first. I do not deny altogether the moral relevance of a distinction between immigrants and national minorities, as I will show below. Nevertheless, by drawing the distinction between these two types of cultural minorities so sharply and by grounding his moral argument for the rights of cultural minorities on the concept of a societal culture as a context of choice, Kymlicka has fatally undermined the principled case for policies designed to take the cultural concerns of immigrants (and their descendants) into account, despite his efforts to defend them. When Kymlicka addresses the question of why liberals might be justified in using public policies to protect or promote culture, he frames his response entirely in terms of the concept of societal culture. In his theory, specific cultural commitments are a (potentially) legitimate object of public solicitude only in so far as they are part of a particular societal culture that is entitled to support. But on his account, immigrants have access to the societal culture of the state they have entered and have waived the right to maintain their original societal culture. So, it is not clear why immigrants are entitled to any special rights to maintain their distinctive cultural commitments.

Kymlicka's defence of the cultural rights of immigrants ends up sounding very much ad hoc. He tries to draw upon the general point that the state is not culturally neutral to argue that it is unfair not to grant special rights to ethnic groups who do not share the dominant culture reflected in public practices and institutions, but he has undercut that argument himself with his insistence that immigrants have consented to join the societal culture(s) of their new state. Given the emphasis he places on the centrality of language to culture, I suspect that he is particularly concerned to preclude claims for official language status for the native languages of immigrants, and I'll pursue that concern below. But the logic of his argument precludes any distinctive cultural claims for immigrants altogether.

Why would Kymlicka construct his argument in this way? The answer, I think, is that despite his criticism of the idea that the state can be neutral with respect to culture, Kymlicka remains implicitly wedded to a version of liberalism that requires the state to be neutral between competing conceptions of the good.[3] Given this commitment, culture can be morally relevant to politics only as a precondition of choice, not as an object of choice.[4] By insisting that a societal culture only provides a context of choice, that it makes choices possible, Kymlicka hopes to defend the claims of cultural minorities without abandoning the ideal of neutrality.

I think this sort of enterprise is ultimately doomed to failure, but I don't mean to dismiss the dilemma with which Kymlicka is struggling. I noted in the previous chapter that it is a deep part of our (liberal) tradition to recognize that people are entitled to make their own choices about how to live their lives, and that we often regard it as inappropriate to judge, much less interfere with, the choices of others. This applies not only to people in other societies but also to people in our own. Thus, not using the power of the state

---

[3] Kymlicka explicitly defends a version of liberal neutrality in an earlier article (1989b) and so far as I know has not subsequently repudiated that position, although the commitment to liberal neutrality is much more evident in his first book than in *Multicultural Citizenship*.

[4] I do not mean to deny that societal cultures are also objects of choice on Kymlicka's account in the sense that the members of a culture decide how it is to evolve. But in this respect, the transformations that a culture undergoes are construed as the by-products of individual choices not as the outcome of collective political action. At the same time, this whole approach stands in some tension with the Gellnerian account that Kymlicka endorses that sees societal cultures as the product of state actions.

to celebrate this particular identity or to promote that specific cultural good is a way of respecting the rights of people to choose different, possibly conflicting goods and identities for themselves. Yet, as I also observed in the previous chapter, sometimes we do make judgements about the choices others make or the way they live their lives. Again, this is true within societies as well as across them. So, the challenge in thinking about cultural differences within a state as well as between them is to say when we should judge and when we should not and why. Kymlicka's concept of societal culture does not help in this task. Rather it obscures the need for it. Although Kymlicka defends an autonomy interpretation of liberalism against more relativistic toleration and political accounts, he remains like Walzer locked into a theoretical position that should prevent him from making the kinds of judgements that he is clearly inclined to make.[5]

We cannot provide an education for citizenship that says nothing about the history or identity of the citizenry. So, one question is what place should be given to the histories and identities of various immigrant groups in such accounts. We cannot have culturally neutral work schedules or public holidays. Almost everything about public education—not only the formal classes but the rules regulating social interactions, the school lunch programmes, the recreational activities, and so on—involves the transmission of cultural norms and values. So, again we have to think about what justice as evenhandedness requires for people (whether immigrants or others) whose cultural commitments differ from those of the majority (assuming there is some clear majority). We have to decide whether to transform existing rules and practices altogether or to keep them in place but make exceptions or to require all to conform to them as they are or to pursue some other alternative. And we may well make different decisions in different cases.

In thinking about such issues, as I do throughout this book, respect for the choices of individuals will play an important role because autonomy is an important good but so will our own judgements about people's interests, about what is good for them. As Chapters 4 and 6 make clear, the need for such judgements is especially clear when one is dealing with policies towards children and when the political majority is also a cultural majority with different views of what is good for children from the families and minority cultural communities to which they belong. Even when it is a question of adults, however, such judgements cannot be entirely avoided. Ultimately, we will not be able to say what is fair without also saying something about what we think is good. If we attempt to do so, we simply smuggle in substantive judgements about what is good under other guises. Thinking about justice as evenhandedness brings this challenge directly into sight. In my view, an

---

[5] For Kymlicka's defence of his autonomy version of liberalism against other liberal alternatives, see chapter 8 of *Multicultural Citizenship* (1995).

open-minded liberalism should not restrict itself to a single narrow conception of the good and should perhaps even find ways of appreciating the goodness of non-liberal ways of life, for reasons I explore most fully in Chapters 8 and 9. More generally, I think these sorts of questions can be most fruitfully addressed in specific contexts, and that is what I try to do in several of the chapters of this book. For now, the main point is that the concept of societal culture simply does not aid us in the kind of thinking that is required.

Indeterminacy and National Minorities

This problem becomes even more apparent if we consider the implications of the concept of societal culture for national minorities, the groups whom the concept would seem to be designed to protect. The first issue is that the concept is radically indeterminate with respect to its normative implications for national minorities. At best it clears a bit of space to show that certain kinds of cultural protections are not necessarily wrong. But what is right or required by justice is much less clear. Elsewhere Kymlicka criticizes other theorists like Raz, Taylor, and Habermas on the grounds that 'it is impossible . . . to tell what their abstract concepts imply for specific debates about the particular claims of particular groups.' (Kymlicka 1997*b*: 86 n. 1). Exactly the same objection applies to the abstract concept 'societal culture'.

I do not mean to argue that indeterminacy is always a bad thing. On the contrary, the kind of contextual approach I am advocating in this book necessarily entails a great deal of indeterminacy in generalizing about what ought to be done. But there the indeterminacy is acknowledged from the outset and is a necessary component of a contextual approach. Kymlicka's concept of societal culture is much more problematic because it creates the illusion of offering a highly determinate principle for assessing particular claims in particular cases while failing to do so.

Let me elaborate. One deep problem with Kymlicka's line of argument is that it is unclear how secure access to one's societal culture is to be measured in relation to the benchmark of equality, both by itself and in relation to other primary goods. Is everyone (except for immigrants) entitled, as a matter of justice, to equally secure access to her societal culture (or, what is not the same thing, to an equally secure societal culture)? Kymlicka calls secure access to one's societal culture a primary good, thus evoking Rawls. Rawls addressed the benchmark problem by creating a short list of primary goods, then establishing his priority principles, then assuming that the goods subject to the difference principle were highly correlated so that the indexing problem (i.e. the problem of evaluating trade-offs among primary goods) could safely be ignored. Kymlicka's use of the term primary good is less clear. Would secure access to one's societal culture count as a basic right that must be equally distributed or would it be subject to the difference principle? If the latter, how would we assess trade-offs between it and other primary goods?

This is not just an abstract philosophical concern. Consider the case of aboriginal peoples in Canada, an example often cited by Kymlicka of the kind of cultural minority whose moral claims his theory is designed to defend. I agree entirely with Kymlicka that forced assimilation is wrong, but I do not think his framework provides much guidance about what is right. Take the issue of language, which Kymlicka makes central to his concept of societal culture. Some aboriginal languages are spoken only by several thousand people, others by several hundred thousand, but none by millions. Now it is one thing to say that aboriginal people should be able to be educated in their own languages, at least if they (or their parents choosing for young children) wish it. That seems to me a minimum requirement of justice (though, as I'll argue below, it is possible to explain why without resorting to the concept of societal culture). And, conversely, the previous policy of prohibiting such education was clearly unjust. But how extensive is this obligation? For example, does it require Canadian society to pay for the translation of textbooks into aboriginal languages? If so, what sorts of choices should aboriginal peoples have among textbooks, including the possibility of choosing new ones as they appear? To reproduce the extensive choices available in English or French would be extremely expensive, while to limit the choices is to disadvantage aboriginal students in relation to those educated in the dominant languages. What limits do equality and justice set here?

Or consider the implications of making aboriginal languages official languages. As a form of symbolic recognition, that seems to me desirable. Is it required as a matter of justice? That seems less clear. In any event, it is clearly not practical to make aboriginal languages official languages in the way that French and English are, for example, with requirements that all packaging information be published in both languages. But how is this impracticality (i.e. the costs of such a project) related to the principles of justice and to the benchmark of equality in the distribution of primary goods?

Furthermore, no aboriginal person can routinely expect to communicate with doctors, lawyers, dentists, bureaucrats, television technicians, and so on in her native language, much less to find employment in that language in the economy outside the reserve. There is a deep tension, which aboriginal people experience daily, between secure access to their cultures (which are themselves threatened in various ways by the forces of modernization) and access to other primary goods like income, wealth, opportunities, and power.

What are we to think about this tension? To what extent and in what ways does our commitment to liberal equality require us, as a matter of justice, to reduce the tension? To what extent and in what ways are we permitted to say to aboriginal people, 'The trade-offs you face are hard but not unjust. We are not obliged to try to change your circumstances.' Kymlicka's concept of societal culture provides little help in thinking about this question.

In some ways, Kymlicka's project in *Multicultural Citizenship* continues to be guided by an ideal of equality that was more fully discussed in his first book, namely, that outcomes for individuals should be a product of choices rather than circumstances. (This is a version of the liberal neutrality ideal.) His concern is that the relative security of a person's access to her own societal culture is a function of circumstances rather than choice (except for voluntary immigrants). Although this ideal is intuitively attractive in some respects, I think that it is ultimately incoherent.[6] The more immediate problem is that his account provides no way to assess the extent and the limits of our obligations to equalize this particular circumstance, namely, secure access to one's societal culture. In my view, there is no general answer to that question. What is needed instead is a contextual analysis that takes into account the competing moral considerations in particular cases and that aspires to treat people evenhandedly. I will show later in the chapter that this provides a feasible and preferable alternative approach to questions like the extent of our obligations to minority languages.

Protecting Small Minorities: The Limits of the Quebec Model

More troubling than the indeterminacy issue is the way the concept of societal culture implicitly undermines the moral claims of small and vulnerable (non-immigrant) cultural minorities. I've been assuming above that the concept of societal culture could be applied to aboriginal groups and used to justify their claims to self-government, and it's clear from many passages in his book that this is what Kymlicka intends. But consider more carefully the disjuncture between what Kymlicka says about societal cultures and the cultural circumstances of aboriginal peoples. In the first place, Kymlicka says that societal cultures did not always exist and that their emergence is intimately linked with the process of modernization. Aboriginal cultures emerged long before modernization and have often been seen (both from within and from without) as in deep tension with modernity. Even if one accepts (as I certainly think one should) that aboriginal cultures may successfully adapt to modern conditions, they cannot be understood as the product of modernization.

Moreover, the link to the process of modernization is not just a matter of historical origins. What does it mean to say that a societal culture 'provides

---

[6] For an argument as to why this ideal is incoherent see Carens (1985).

its members with meaningful ways of life across the full range of human activities, including social, educational, religious, recreational, and economic life, encompassing both public and private spheres' (76)? How are we to interpret 'meaningful ways of life' and 'full range of human activities' in this sentence? The words 'meaningful' and 'full' remind us of the impossibility of avoiding judgments about the human good in these debates. Perhaps Kymlicka means to make these terms entirely relative. Ways of life and ranges of activities are meaningful and full if the members of a culture regard them as such. But that would be a difficult position to defend because it calls into question the responsibility of the majority non-aboriginal society to promote equal opportunity for aboriginal people in non-aboriginal social institutions. This issue raises complex questions about the interrelationship between culture and opportunity that I will pursue later in this chapter and again in Chapter 5. In any event, I think that in this passage Kymlicka is implicitly evoking a picture of a modern industrial society with its characteristic liberal rights and market opportunities.[7] Would traditional aboriginal communities fit within this picture? Do contemporary ones?

Even leaving aside the relationship between modernization and culture, we have good reason to doubt whether most national minorities have (or could have) a societal culture in Kymlicka's sense of the term. He insists that immigrant groups do not. The institutions and cultural practices that immigrant communities routinely create and sustain in their new countries have social, educational, religious, recreational, and economic dimensions and exist in the public as well as the private sphere, but, in Kymlicka's view, these are not of sufficient scope or depth to count as a 'societal culture'. Thus, in a recent work, Kylicka insists that 'to maintain a separate societal culture in a modern state is an immensely ambitious and arduous project' (Kymlicka 1997a: 52). He describes at length what the Québécois had to do to maintain their societal culture as a way of showing why it is virtually impossible for immigrants to do so. He observes that the Québécois had to establish the right to use their language not only when interacting with government institutions ('courts, legislatures, welfare agencies, health services, etc.') but also in employment in the public and private spheres (Kymlicka 1997a: 53–4). This implies the need, he says, 'that the minority be able to create and run its own higher education system—not simply at the elementary and secondary school levels, but up to university and professional schools' (Kymlicka 1997a: 54). Moreover, he says, 'a minority which seeks to sustain a distinct societal culture must . . . have some control over immigration policies' and 'there must be some political body or political unit which they substantially control'

---

[7] One might object that this is a much too narrow view of what constitutes 'meaningful ways of life' or the 'full range of human activities', and I would agree as will become clear in my discussion of the traditional Fijian way of life in Chapter 9. Nevertheless, I think it is the only reading that makes sense of Kymlicka's account.

which has the power to adopt and implement all these policies (Kymlicka 1997a: 54).[8] He concludes:

To put it another way, it is not enough for a minority to simply resist the majority's efforts at diffusing a single common language. The minority must also engage in its own competing form of modern, state-sponsored nation-building. Nationalists in Quebec realize that to sustain their national culture, they too must seek to diffuse a common culture and language throughout their society so as to promote equality of opportunity and political solidarity. And they must use the same tools that the majority nation uses in its program of nation-building—i.e., standardized public education, official languages, including language requirements for citizenship and government employment, etc (Kymlicka 1997a: 55–6).

Kymlicka's point is that immigrant groups have neither the motivation nor the capacity to undertake this sort of nation-building. Yet the same incapacity characterizes most non-immigrant cultural minorities. Kymlicka's insistence on dividing all cultural minorities into ethnic (immigrant) groups and national minorities simply obscures this important fact. If the sole justification for group-differentiated cultural rights is that they can contribute to the maintenance of a societal culture, then how can a group be entitled to such rights if it does not have the capacity to sustain a societal culture?

As I have pointed out above, for reasons of numbers and resources that cannot possibly be overcome, aboriginal people in Canada cannot hope to have their languages become languages of public life in the way that French has nor can they hope to establish an elaborate system of higher education or the full range of economic and professional opportunities and services within the boundaries of the political units that they (aspire to) control. Of course, this raises questions about what aboriginal self-government means and I pursue some of these questions in Chapters 7 and 8.

Kymlicka says he recognizes that some indigenous peoples may not be able to sustain their societal cultures, but that these are the hard cases, as though the

---

   [8] Kymlicka frequently refers in his writings to Quebec's powers over immigration as a key to the capacity of the Québécois to maintain their societal culture and suggests that the rights of aboriginal people to determine who may live on aboriginal reserves is comparable. I agree that Quebec's powers over immigration are significant and I discuss their implications at length in Chapter 5, but it is important to note some crucial differences between Quebec's situation in this regard and the situation of most independent states on the one hand and of aboriginal people on the other. Quebec does not have the power to control immigration into Quebec from the rest of Canada, and those living in Quebec (whether citizens or permanent residents) are free to move elsewhere in Canada if they choose. Even Quebec sovereigntists do not generally perceive this open border with Canada as a threat to Quebec's culture and hope to maintain it if Quebec becomes independent. The situation of aboriginal peoples seems to me quite different because their land is collectively held and inalienable (with the result, for example, that aboriginal individuals cannot use their land as collateral in market dealings with non-aboriginals). This arrangement stands in deep tension with Kymlicka's picture of societal cultures in liberal states. I think that it is an arrangement that may be justifiable under some circumstances, as I argue in Chapter 9 on Fiji, but also that the justification cannot entirely abstract from an assessment of the goodness of the way of life that it helps to preserve. As my discussion there will show, this is not just another form of immigration control.

Québécois were somehow a norm which many indigenous groups could replicate. In fact, indigenous people who are in a position to sustain a societal culture are the rare exception, and the case of Fiji which I discuss in Chapter 9 provides an interesting opportunity to explore what such an exception entails. But, in this respect, it is not most aboriginal people but the Québécois (and the Fijians) who are the exception. Within Canada, for example, the millions of francophones outside Quebec cannot aspire to maintain a societal culture in the way that the Québécois do, even though many of them are not simply emigrants from Quebec (or their descendants) but people with quite distinct group identities and long collective histories (in the Canadian context). Outside Canada, the number of cultural minorities who have the size and resources to pursue a project like Quebec probably number no more than a dozen or two.

Recall the quotation with which I opened this essay (which is the opening passage of *Multicultural Citizenship*). There are 5,000 ethnic groups and over 600 language groups within the world's 184 states. Most of these 5,000 are not groups of recent immigrants with ties to some other homeland (which is how Kymlicka subsequently uses the term 'ethnic group') but long-settled cultural minorities. Are they 'national minorities' in Kymlicka's sense of the term? Not if being a national minority means that a group has to have the capacity to create a modern liberal industrial society (a societal culture) as the Québécois have, though many of them would count as national minorities under conventional uses of the term. Few of these groups have numbers or resources comparable to those possessed by the Québécois (not to mention the cultural advantages of using as their national language a language which is also employed by a much larger industrial state with a much older cultural history as well as by many other former colonies). And, like aboriginal groups, most of these group identities and cultures are not simply the product of modernization, even if they have been significantly shaped by interactions with modernizing forces including colonizing powers. Yet if they are not national minorities with societal cultures, what sorts of moral claims do they have, on Kymlicka's account, to any rights and resources for the maintenance of their cultures and identities? Treating the Québécois as the norm for national minorities and (non-immigrant) cultural minorities incapable of sustaining their societal cultures as exceptional hard cases both misrepresents the empirical situation and weakens the normative claims of the vast majority of (non-immigrant) ethnic and linguistic minorities.

Societal Culture as Monoculturalism: Reproducing the Logic of the Nation-State

This point about the way the concept of societal culture undermines the claims of smaller, more vulnerable cultural minorities leads directly to the fourth criticism, namely, that the concept of societal culture rests upon an understanding of the relationship between politics and culture that impedes rather than contributes to a multicultural conception of citizenship. The deepest problem—and the greatest irony—of Kymlicka's concept of societal culture is that it is much better suited to a *monocultural* conception of citizenship than to a multicultural one. This is not surprising if one considers how heavily Kymlicka's concept of societal culture rests upon Gellner's discussion of nationalism. Gellner is concerned with accounting for the rise of the modern nation-state, understood as a political unit in which almost all of the citizens share the same national culture and identity. Gellner's distinctive contribution was to emphasize the extent to which the nation was the product of the state rather than vice versa, but in the course of making this argument, he insists that considerable cultural homogeneity is a prerequisite for the modern state to function effectively (Gellner 1983: 140–1). Both Gellner and Kymlicka have intelligent things to say about the process of nation-building, the ways in which a modern state (or its equivalent as in the case of Quebec) constructs and diffuses a common language and common social institutions, and, through them, shared identities. But this focus on the way a *common* culture is constructed and transmitted inevitably draws our attention away from the problem of *multi*culturalism understood as the persistence (or emergence) of cultural differences *within* a given state and the moral and political relevance of such differences.

In a multicultural state, people with different cultural identities and commitments belong to and are members of the same political community. Sometimes people make demands upon the state in the name of their cultural identities and commitments, asking for recognition or support or changes in institutions and policies or exemptions from normal rules.[9] These sorts of demands are familiar aspects of the landscape of contemporary multiculturalism, and they pose a challenge both to the conventional liberal understanding of the proper relationship between the individual and the state and to the view that the modern state must be a nation-state (even on a Gellnerian account of how nations arise). Nevertheless, these sorts of demands do not challenge the conception of the state itself as the locus of legitimate political authority.

Sometimes, however, the cultural identities and commitments of some people within a state include the sense of belonging to a distinct community that is or ought to be self-governing in certain respects. To the extent that this sense gives rise to demands for a separate state, it simply reproduces rather than challenges the logic of the nation-state. But when these cultural identities and

[9] Different sorts of demands raise different sorts of normative issues and pose different sorts of challenges to liberal views of the proper relationship between the individual and the state. For a very illuminating taxonomy of cultural rights and of the kinds of normative questions they raise, see Levy (1997).

commitments do not lead to such demands (or not only to such demands), people may have the sense of belonging simultaneously to a state and to another political community, that is distinct from the state and not necessarily subordinate to it even though contained within it. This is the distinctive feature of the general landscape of multiculturalism to which Kylicka seeks to draw our attention with his emphasis on national minorities. This is indeed a very important problem, neglected by many other discussions of multiculturalism, and Kymlicka is right to underline it. I offer my own reflections on what the Canadian case tells us about this problem in Chapters 7 and 8. But the concept of societal culture obscures rather than illuminates the distinctive questions that national minorities raise.

When Kymlicka says a societal culture is 'more or less institutionally complete' (18), it is the old logic of the nation-state that he is evoking, the view that every nation (societal culture) should have its own state, civil society, and so on. What is characteristic of states with national minorities is precisely the institutional incompleteness of all of the nations that compose it, because no nation, not even the majority, can claim all of the economic, social, and political institutions as its own. Different national identities share and contest the public space, even the right to exercise political authority.

At the same time, institutional incompleteness varies by degrees, and national minorities are apt to be more incomplete than majorities because numbers and concentration play a major role in determining the kinds of institutions a cultural group can construct and maintain. So, the normative problem is to think about what justice prohibits, permits, and requires in the face of this sort of multiplicity. Kymlicka emphasizes the legitimacy of self-government rights for national minorities, though he is not always clear about whether he regards such rights as morally required or merely as permissible. In any event, as we have seen above, the implications of his argument are much more indeterminate than his analysis seems to suggest. In my view, the range of plausible answers will vary from one context to another and will involve judgements about how to balance a number of competing considerations. In some cases, extensive self-government for a national minority will be best, but in others a more limited, partial form of autonomy may be preferable, and in some situations self-government may be morally undesirable even for a group that clearly qualifies as a national minority.[10] In many cases asking what a group would need to maintain a societal culture will not provide a helpful guide but will lead us away from the kind of contextual reflection that is required.

[10] In an important unpublished paper, Elizabeth Kiss argues that there is no absolute right to self-determination for national minorities, even though such groups are entitled to insist on institutional arrangements that will enable them to maintain their distinct cultural identities. She uses a detailed discussion of the situation of ethnic Hungarians in Slovakia, Romania, and Serbia to explore the moral complexities of alternative arrangements for meeting the cultural claims of groups. Her approach in this paper is closely related to the kind of contextual theory I am advocating here (Kiss 1996).

Kymlicka's conception of societal culture links politics and culture too tightly, at the expense of politics. The state appears as an agent only in its diffusion of national culture. Otherwise it seems only to reflect and embody societal culture. What is missing here is precisely what Walzer's analysis reveals, the importance of the shared political culture and identity constructed by people living together in a political community even when they speak different languages and possess different cultural identities. The ways in which a political community determines how collective cultural differences will be recognized and addressed cannot itself be construed as the product of a single societal culture (unless that culture is hegemonic). In any event, in a multicultural state, politics cannot be only about what goes on within a societal culture. It must also be about what goes on between societal cultures (assuming that concept to be useful in some form). Moreover, it would be a mistake to assume that an individual's relation to the state is (or should) always be mediated through the institutions of her societal culture. There are some rights and duties that individuals possess (and should possess) as citizens of the state, not as members of a societal culture.

At one point, Kymlicka suggests that the liberal ideal of a society of free and equal individuals should be interpreted as referring to arrangements within a nation, that it is freedom and equality within a societal culture that matters (93). This is a startling claim in the context of a book about multicultural citizenship.[11] It is as though the freedom and equality of *citizens* does not matter, as though the liberal state need not concern itself with questions about freedom and equality across cultural boundaries but only with freedom and equality within the bounds of each of the societal cultures that compose it. In fact, this is very much at odds both with liberal theory and with the practices of liberal states which characteristically seek to ensure the freedom and equality of all citizens (indeed, in many respects, of all persons) living within the state's territory.

In Canada, for example, there are a great many laws and institutional arrangements that extend throughout the state and apply to all Canadians.[12] The Charter of Rights and Freedoms is one obvious example, but there are many others. Market arrangements matter, too. A Quebec francophone who speaks English can apply for jobs anywhere in Canada, but not in the United States or the United Kingdom. An anglophone Canadian who speaks French can apply for jobs in Quebec but not in France. The arrangements that ensure this (and that seek to prevent discriminatory treatment of qualified applicants)

---

[11] So far as I know the claim has drawn little comment, and I assume that is because it rests implicitly on the familiar assumption of a correspondence between state and nation, and the disjuncture between this assumption and Kymlicka's inquiry into multiculturalism has been overlooked.

[12] One might call these 'national' institutions, but to do so would immediately give rise to controversy about the use of the term 'national' and what collective units are entitled to claim it.

flow from the characteristic liberal concern for freedom and equality *within the state,* not across states but also not only within societal cultures.[13] The federal government communicates in both French and English, but it is supposed to ensure not only that francophones receive equal treatment with other francophones, and anglophones with anglophones, but that all Canadians receive equal treatment in the areas of its responsibility. Of course, what those areas of responsibility are is constantly debated and contested (as is the meaning of equal treatment).[14] Still, it would be a radical departure to suppose that what matters morally from a liberal perspective is only what goes on within each societal culture in Canada (assuming, for these purposes, that that category makes sense). Comparisons across societal cultures and the possibilities of moving between them also count.

I do not wish to overstate this critique. Language is a very important factor in marking off the boundaries of social interaction, and even more powerful when it is linked (as it is in Quebec) with significant jurisdictional powers. Civil society in Quebec has much less interconnection and overlap with civil society in Canada's other provinces than each of those does with one another (despite their own differences of culture and identity). To cite only one illustration, most professional associations in Canada have separate anglophone and francophone organizations, with the francophone branch identified as Québécois. I certainly think that Quebec is a distinct society in a way that the other provinces are not. Nevertheless, there is an anglophone minority in Quebec and there are francophone minorities outside Quebec, and aboriginal minorities in both. Moreover, all Canadians share common political institutions that have social, economic, and cultural consequences. So, the question is how to fit all these differences together, both morally and politically. The concept of societal culture draws attention only to what distinguishes one group from another. It entirely neglects what connects people, institutionally and culturally, across those differences. But in thinking about multicultural

---

[13] One might think that the characteristic liberal willingness to accept state boundaries as appropriate limits to our concerns for freedom and equality is itself a betrayal of deeper liberal commitments. I have argued for this view in Carens (1987). Kymlicka is far more sympathetic to this view than his surface rhetoric suggests. At one point in his text, he tries to shift the burden of proof from those who defend group rights to those who oppose them by arguing that the state system itself, and particularly the assumption that states have the right to control immigration as they wish, is itself a version of group rights. In this context, he uses the idea of open borders as a *reductio ad absurdum* argument, trying to show that those who oppose all group rights should logically be committed to open borders (124–6). Yet in a footnote to this section he says that rich states that do not meet their redistributive obligations under international justice have forfeited their moral right to exclude (224 n. 18). Since no rich states come close to meeting what Kymlicka clearly regards as their obligations, this seems to commit him in practice to something close to an open borders argument himself, at least with respect to affluent states.

[14] In Canada, the debate over the extent of the federal government's responsibilities is not only a debate between Quebec and the federal government. Many of the other provinces are jealous of their prerogatives, and there is an ideological dispute about the appropriate division of responsibilities that is reflected in the differences between political parties. This complicates political and normative analysis in ways that do not fit well with the concept of societal culture.

citizenship, we must address both aspects (difference and connection) simultaneously. That is what I try to do in Chapters 7 and 8.

Multicultural Contexts of Choice

Consider finally how Kymlicka's discussion of societal culture as a context of choice homogenizes culture, excluding many of the other cultural differences *within* states that ought to fall within the range of his concerns.[15] He begins by saying that he is adopting a stipulative definition of culture in order to mark off his concern with 'the sort of "multiculturalism" which arises from national and ethnic differences' from other kinds such as those that arise in debates over the rights of gays and lesbians or the disabled (18). I have no objection with an attempt to narrow one's focus to manageable proportions, and indeed in this book I adopt the same kind of (narrow) focus on national and ethnic identities and the cultural differences associated with them. (Like Kymlicka, I intend this as a way of making my topic more manageable, not of denying the moral and political relevance of other sorts of differences.) But Kymlicka's stipulative definition soon begins doing explanatory and prescriptive work and claiming rather more space than is its due.

The key problem is the way he links freedom and societal culture. Instead of claiming (as is plausible) that the language and national culture of the place where one lives will normally play *an* important role in shaping the sorts of choices one faces, Kymlicka presents societal culture as if it were the sole and comprehensive determinant of one's context of choice. Societal culture is what makes freedom possible. In one passage he says, 'Put simply, freedom involves making choices among various options, and our societal culture not only provides these options, but also makes them meaningful to us' (83). Later he talks about 'the shared vocabulary of tradition and convention' or the 'shared vocabulary of social life' and the institutions in which that shared vocabulary is embedded as the things that make choices available to us (103). And in a summary of his view he says:

freedom of choice is dependent on social practices, cultural meanings, and a shared language. Our capacity to form and revise a conception of the good is intimately tied to our membership in a societal culture, since the context of individual choice is the range of options passed down to us by our culture. Deciding how to lead our lives is, in the first instance, a matter of exploring the possibilities made available by our culture (126).

---

[15] For a complementary critique of the restrictiveness of the way Kymlicka thinks about cultural contexts of choice and an appeal to an ideal of fairness that seems similar to the one I am defending here, see Walker (1997).

Notice how comprehensive a societal culture is according to this picture. All of the cultural differences *within* a society are rendered invisible and irrelevant to 'the context of individual choice' which is defined exclusively in terms of the 'options passed down to us by our culture' and 'the possibilities made available by our culture'. It is as though all those who belong to a societal culture have the same cultural options and possibilities. Moreover, the societal culture is what gives meaning to these options.

Now try to think concretely about what this sort of claim might mean with regard to some major cultural variable like religion.[16] Would it make sense to say that Quebec's societal culture passes down Judaism as an option to its members or that Islam is a possibility made available by Canada's anglophone culture? Of course, both Quebec and Canada as a whole are liberal polities that guarantee freedom of religious practice (within broad limits) and the right of individuals to leave a religion or join one (if the religious community will accept them). But are such liberal legal rights what come to mind when one speaks of a culture as providing options? Are these religions part of the 'shared vocabulary of tradition and convention' or the 'shared vocabulary of social life' in these societies in the same way that various forms of Christianity are? And could anyone say that it is the societal culture of Quebec or Canada that makes Judaism or Islam (or even Christianity) 'meaningful to us?' To be sure, Jews and Muslims use French or English for some (though not all) communications about religious matters, but to describe this as what makes the religious practices meaningful to believers would be missing something important.

To speak of freedom as taking place within a context of choice and to investigate what determines that context of choice can be very illuminating. But language is not the only, and often not the most important, factor in determining the context of choice for individuals, if one uses the phrase 'context of choice' in any substantive sense. For example, being raised in a religious tradition is (often) a major determinant of one's context of choice

---

[16] One might object that religion should not be regarded as a cultural variable. It is certainly not only a cultural variable. From the perspective of believers it is inappropriate to treat religion (only or primarily) as a cultural variable, and even from a secular sociological perspective, it is clear that the great world religions cannot be adequately studied through the lens of particular national cultures. Both these points are implicit in my insistence in the text that it is inappropriate to regard religious traditions as being generated or rendered meaningful by societal cultures. Nevertheless, I do not think that any discussion of the multiculturalism associated with national and ethnic differences can leave questions about religion entirely aside. Religion and ethnicity are intertwined in many complex ways, and I won't try to sort them all out here. It is an obvious point, however, that the liberal states of North America and Europe have been overwhelmingly Christian, and that many of the most hotly contested issues in contemporary debates over multiculturalism are connected to values and practices that are associated with the religious traditions of immigrant groups and national minorities. The examples that Kymlicka himself discusses illustrate the point many times over. Indeed, in Europe, the debate over multiculturalism is intimately linked to the arrival of Muslim immigrants. That is why I have devoted Chapter 6 to this topic. So, the question of how to respond to religious differences cannot be simply set aside.

(whether one remains a member of the religion or leaves it). This is the sort of thing that often shapes one's identity and values, sometimes reactively. Even if everyone has the freedom to join or reject any religion, the context of choice is not the same. To choose to become a convert is different from being raised in a religion. To choose to abandon a religion is different from never having belonged to it.

There are many aspects to culture besides religion, and Kymlicka's account of the way a societal culture creates a context of choice for its members is no more satisfactory in dealing with them. Again, when one thinks concretely about what Kymlicka's theoretical claims seem to entail, it becomes apparent that they are either misleading or false. It is one thing to say that immigrants (and especially their children) can reasonably be expected to learn the language of the country they enter and that their life choices will be affected by their formal legal rights and freedoms. It is quite another to claim that their entire context of choice is or ought to be determined by the social practices and cultural meanings made available by the culture of their new land. The latter is clearly implausible both empirically and normatively, yet Kymlicka says that immigrants can be expected to join the societal culture of the place where they settle, and that this societal culture is what provides them with their context of choice.

A sense of identity and of a shared history connected to their society of origin often constitutes a very important dimension of life for many immigrants and their descendants. Immigrants bring with them from their cultures of origin various values, conceptions, and commitments that shape the meaningfulness of the options open to them, sometimes in ways quite different from those of other members of society. Of course, Kymlicka does not really want to deny this, but if he brought it clearly into view he could not maintain the fiction that the societal culture creates *the* context of choice for individuals (as opposed to a more modest claim that it helps to shape their context of choice).

Consider, for example, the similarities and differences between the range and the meanings of the options available to native-born Québécois on the one hand and those available to native-born anglophones in Canada on the other. These two groups belong to different societal cultures according to Kymlicka. Now contrast both of these sets of options with the range and the meanings of the options available to immigrants to Toronto from, say, Korea or Nigeria or Pakistan. All of them, on Kymlicka's account, share the same societal culture as anglophone Canadians. It should be immediately clear (even to those who do not know much about any of these groups) that the options passed down by their different cultures to native-born anglophones and francophones are much more similar to one another than either of them is to the options passed down to the immigrants and their children by their (combined) culture of origin and culture of adoption.

To cite only one example, think of how much more alike anglophone and francophone Canadian conceptions of family responsibilities are than Korean or Nigerian or Pakistani conceptions (granted that there is variation within all of the cultures and between them). Conceptions of family responsibilities shape our options in life and are often intimately connected to the way we form and revise our conceptions of the good. Over time immigrants, and especially their descendants, may adapt their conceptions to conform more closely to the dominant ones. But the transformation will not be immediate and it may never be entire.

So, in any reasonable sense of the term 'context of choice', the context of choice for immigrants and their descendants is shaped by both their old culture and their new one, in varying and shifting degrees. These sorts of differences between the contexts of choice of immigrants and long-settled residents are obscured when Kymlicka asserts that immigrants join the societal culture of the place to which they immigrate and thereby enjoy a secure context of choice. This suggests somehow that everyone belongs to one (and only one) societal culture which then shapes the context of choice in the same way for all who belong to it. It may be plausible to say that everyone (including immigrants) can belong to a societal culture in a thin sense (shared language and liberal rights) but it is not plausible to characterize such a thin societal culture as providing people with the context that makes choices meaningful or that makes it possible for them to form and revise conceptions of the good.

In sum, it can be helpful to think of culture (broadly construed) as providing the context within which we choose, but culture, in this sense, has multiple sources and will not be the same even for people who live within the same state, speak the same language, and participate in the same public institutions. Kymlicka's concept of societal culture includes only one of the sources of culture as a context of choice, and so cannot help us to think about the multiplicity and variability that characterize the contexts of choice of people who live in a multicultural society.

Why does someone like Kymlicka who is so clearly concerned with multiculturalism adopt this implausibly monolithic account of culture as a context of choice? The answer again stems I think from his implicit (and perhaps unconscious) commitment to the norm of liberal neutrality. If culture creates people's contexts of choice, and if culture is interpreted to mean only societal culture, then it appears plausible to argue that in providing support for a particular societal culture, we are not favouring one conception of the good over another but helping to maintain the conditions within which free choice among different conceptions of the good is possible. But if one acknowledges that the cultural contexts of choice for people within the same society are multiple, variable, and overlapping, then it becomes less obvious that it is appropriate to provide public support for all these different contexts of choice and impossible to argue that such support is neutral between different conceptions of the good. One response is to return again to the idea that there should be no public support for culture (Waldron 1992). I think this is unsatisfactory for reasons spelled out in this chapter and elsewhere in this book. The preferable alternative in my view is to see a concern for preserving or protecting or promoting culture as one sort of human interest that may legitimately be taken into account in public decision making within the constraints imposed by familiar individual freedoms and by a general concern for justice as evenhandedness. I will try to give an illustration of what this might entail later in this chapter in a discussion of the justifiability of public support for particular languages.

One implication of thinking about culture as creating the context of choice in the way I have suggested is that it draws our attention to questions about what kinds of choices people should have, not just formally but also substantively. Kymlicka notes that the diffusion by the state of a common culture is instrumentally necessary to the fulfilment of liberal commitments to equal opportunity (77). This raises a number of important questions that Kymlicka himself does not pursue about the ways in which cultural inheritances may depart from the norm, how such deviations affect people's life chances, and whether the state should intervene in the name of equality to challenge or restrict cultural inheritances that disadvantage (or privilege) people with regard to the sorts of opportunities that the common culture values. Kymlicka is clearly concerned about the problem of marginalization both for immigrants and for national minorities, but he constructs this almost entirely as a problem of fighting discrimination against immigrants and ensuring that national minorities have what they need for cultural survival. This simply leaves to one side the question of whether it may be justifiable (or even morally required) to promote certain kinds of cultural transformations in the name of equality. Chapter 4 is entirely devoted to these questions, and I pursue them at a number of other points as well.

The Contextual Alternative to Societal Culture

If we abandon the concept of societal culture for the reasons I have advanced, how can we address the question of how culture matters from a liberal perspective? Fortunately, Kymlicka offers us a guide out of the morass as well as into it. The best alternative is to begin by thinking concretely about how liberal states actually deal with cultural issues and to reflect upon which practices we think are justified and which are not and why. Kymlicka's work is filled with these sorts of reflections. One important starting-point is to recognize that not all cultural claims take the same form or raise the same sorts of normative issues. Kymlicka makes a number of useful distinctions that help us to see this.

First, as I have already noted, he draws our attention to the fact that most states adopt different policies towards national minorities and ethnic groups. I think Kymlicka exaggerates the differences to some extent, but there are important differences, and I will try to explain below how these can be defended without the concept of societal culture.

Secondly, Kymlicka notes that the term 'collective rights' is often used in a way that suggests a false dichotomy with individual rights. He observes that many forms of group-differentiated rights are exercised or even held by individual members of the group. For example, individuals in Canada have a right to use French as well as English in federal courts, a right that is clearly constructed with the minority francophone population in view. One might object that this is not a group-differentiated right, since it is possessed by everyone, but that simply begs the question as to why it is justifiable to favour these two languages, one of which is not the language of the majority, when many Canadians have other languages as their native tongues. And if these language rights can be presented as, in some sense, universal individual rights, others cannot. For example, under the Canadian Constitution, individuals are guaranteed a right to an education in French or English only if one of their parents was educated in that language in Canada and if they live in an area 'where numbers warrant' collective provision of education in that language (Reaume and Green 1989). This is clearly a group-differentiated right, though again one that provides individual entitlements that the group in question cannot control. (I will discuss the moral legitimacy of these linguistic arrangements later in this chapter and again in Chapter 5).

Still other group-differentiated rights are controlled by the group but may be delegated by the group to individual members and exercised by them as individuals. Kymlicka mentions aboriginal fishing rights as an example, since the rights are often not possessed directly by individual aboriginals but by a community that assigns them to particular members. Other collective rights may be exercised by the group as a whole (e.g. some land rights). In other cases a governmental unit may be granted certain powers precisely because it is a jurisdiction in which a cultural group forms a majority and this will enable the group to protect or promote its culture more effectively. Quebec is the obvious example here. It has demanded and received a number of powers in order to promote Quebec's distinct culture. (I discuss how Quebec exercises some of these powers in promoting the cultural integration of immigrants in Chapter 5).

Any of these arrangements may be criticized as unjust or unwise, but the issue is unlikely to be settled by deciding whether it is correct to call it an individual or a collective right. The real question is whether a given arrangement that takes account of cultural differences is morally required or at least morally permissible, and, if so, why and under what circumstances. To address that question requires a careful contextual analysis that takes account of how such an arrangement affects people's interests, how it enhances or restricts freedoms, how it reduces or increases inequalities, and so on.

Thirdly, Kymlicka makes a number of distinctions among different kinds of cultural rights and the different purposes they serve that help us to see more clearly why different ways of protecting culture raise different sorts of issues. For example, he draws a distinction between external protections (ways of reducing the vulnerability of members of a minority cultural group to the decisions of the larger society) and internal restrictions (ways of limiting the freedom of members of the group to promote some collective goal of the group). He argues that the two functions are distinguishable in principle, and often separable in practice as well. From a liberal perspective, he argues, external protections are easier to justify, although particular forms of external protections have to assessed for their impact on individual freedoms and overall inequalities. Not every external protection is justifiable. Internal restrictions are far more problematic, in so far as their goal is the restriction of freedom. Kymlicka concedes that the distinction between the two is not always easy to draw and that internal restrictions are sometimes an unavoidable by-product of arrangements (like collective, inalienable land rights) whose basic goal is a justifiable form of external protection. Nevertheless, this sort of distinction can be very helpful in explaining why some ways of protecting culture are morally defensible and others are not, as I'll show in my discussion of Fiji in Chapter 9.

Kymlicka also distinguishes between three kinds of group-differentiated rights: self-government rights, polyethnic rights, and special representation rights. Self-government rights involve the allocation of political powers so that members of a cultural group are able to act authoritatively to protect the group's cultural interests. Kymlicka mentions the powers exercised by Quebec and by aboriginal governments as examples. He uses the term 'polyethnic rights' to characterize such things as entitlements to financial support for a group's cultural practices (e.g, funding for arts or for heritage language programmes) and exemptions from laws and regulations that disadvantage people because of their religious or cultural traditions (e.g. exemptions from Sunday closing laws for people like Jews and Muslims with other traditions regarding a weekly day of rest, exemptions from dress codes that conflict with religious requirements). Special representation rights involve guarantees of group representation in political institutions. Kymlicka mentions Canada's constitutional guarantee that three Supreme Court justices will come from Quebec as an illustration. Again, these distinctions are very helpful in enabling us to see the variety of mechanisms actually employed to take cultural concerns into account and the ways in which different mechanisms raise different issues and require different sorts of justifications.

One can object that these distinctions obscure certain issues as well. For example, the way in which he constructs his three categories of group-differentiated rights is unduly shaped by his focus on the distinction between national minorities and immigrant groups. Kymlicka wants to establish both empirical and normative links between self-government rights and national minorities on the one hand and between another kind of group-differentiated rights and ethnic groups on the other hand. But calling the second type of rights 'polyethnic rights', as he does, is an exercise in persuasive definition, suggesting that only members of ethnic groups do (and perhaps should) possess such rights. This is not helpful conceptually because it does not draw attention to what it is about the rights (as opposed to who exercises them) that distinguishes them from self-government rights. As I see it, the key difference between the second kind of rights and self-government rights is that the former do not necessarily require any control by the cultural group itself over the legislative or administrative process establishing and carrying out its rights. A better term than polyethnic rights might be something like 'recognition rights' or 'accommodation rights'.[17] This would give some indication of what function the rights perform, which is, broadly speaking, to provide public recognition of and support for certain minority cultural practices or forms of identity.

While there is nothing comparably problematic about the term 'self-government rights', Kymlicka tends to restrict his use of the term to relatively extensive versions of self-government, as in the cases of Quebec and aboriginal peoples, perhaps because he has the concept of societal culture implicitly in mind. In principle, the category of self-government rights might be usefully extended to include any exercise of state power by and on behalf of a minority cultural group, even if it involved a smaller jurisdiction (e.g. a municipality) or a limited set of powers (e.g. a school board, parts of the criminal justice system). This would provide a clearer conceptual framework, leaving open both the question of whether it might sometimes be justifiable or even morally required for ethnic groups as well as national minorities to have self-government rights and the question of how extensive those self-government rights should be in any given case.

Other authors have gone beyond Kymlicka's categories to construct a more refined set of classifications for cultural rights. Levy (1997) provides a particularly illuminating account that shows why some forms of cultural rights pose much more serious problems for liberals than others. The main point here, however, is not to assess the relative merits of the particular distinctions that Kymlicka and others draw, but rather to see that a careful analysis of our prac-

---

[17] In an earlier discussion of Kymlicka, I suggested the term 'recognition rights.' (Carens 1997a). Kymlicka acknowledged the potential bias in the term 'polyethnic rights' but suggested 'accommodation rights' was preferable to make clear that the issues are not purely symbolic (Kymlicka 1997b).

tices enables us to think critically about how liberal states do and should respond to the claims of cultural groups without employing the distorting lens of the concept of societal culture.

Evenhanded Justice and Culture: Language Policy, National Minorities, and Immigrants

Let me show concretely how it is possible to pursue this sort of contextual inquiry by taking up one of the issues that is central to Kymlicka's discussion of culture: language. How should political authorities decide what languages to employ and how to employ them? In particular, how does justice constrain the range of acceptable language policies?

In Chapter 1, I identified two conceptions of justice as fairness, one advocating that the state take a neutral or hands off approach to culture, the other that it take an evenhanded approach. Each of those conceptions has a role to play here, though the role of the former is more limited.

Consider the ideal of neutrality first. There are some important respects in which the state should take a hands off approach to language. Some language policies are unjust because they violate the basic rights of individuals to freedom of expression, which must normally include the right to communicate in the language of one's choice. People may disagree about how freedom of expression is to be interpreted and what sorts of constraints on expression are legitimate, but political authorities ought not to try to suppress a language or a linguistic community. It was wrong when Canadian educational authorities placed aboriginal children in residential schools and prohibited them from speaking their own languages in an effort to force them to assimilate to the dominant culture. It is wrong for Turkish authorities to prohibit the use of Kurdish in public broadcasts and in educational and political communications in an effort to suppress Kurdish culture and identity. As a general rule, it is wrong to prohibit people from speaking a language, or teaching it, or publishing books or newspapers in it, or using it generally as a vehicle of personal, cultural, or political communication. These moral restrictions on state action normally apply regardless of the size, location, circumstances, or history of a linguistic community. The kind of contextual approach I am advocating in this book is not incompatible with general principles of this sort. In Chapter 5 I will consider (and largely reject) the claim that Quebec's language policies are guilty of violating these restrictions, and I will try to show there how a contextual approach can deepen our understanding of such principles.

A neutral, hands off approach to language sets some important limits to language policies but it is clearly insufficient as a general guide. A political community cannot be entirely neutral with regard to language, taking a hands-off approach and letting people use whatever language they choose in whatever contexts they choose. Here Kymlicka's arguments are compelling. We cannot avoid deciding what language or languages will be used by the government in courts, legislatures, the distribution of public services, and, above all, in public schools. And there is no culturally neutral language.[18] Beyond what is strictly unavoidable, we may want to provide positive support for some languages. Are we permitted to do so? Is there a range of morally permissible, discretionary choices with regard to language? In short, what does justice require or permit or prohibit with respect to language policies, apart from non-interference with certain kinds of linguistic freedom?

I don't think there is a single principle or a simple answer to this question. It strikes me as just the sort of issue where many different considerations are relevant, and what justice requires is an evenhanded approach that takes account of history, numbers, patterns of concentration, and other factors. A language policy that might be unjust in one set of circumstances might be morally permissible in another and even morally required in a third. Let's consider some concrete cases. I want to focus first on language policies affecting a national majority and immigrant minorities, leaving consideration of national minorities for later.

In many countries (e.g. the United States, the United Kingdom, France, and Germany) there is a single dominant language. Whether it is designated the official language or not, everyone knows what it is. It is the language that the vast majority of people speak as their native tongue. It is the language that will be spoken by legislators and judges, by police officers and fire-fighters, by bureaucrats and civil servants, by teachers and telephone operators, by postal workers and physicians, in short, by most people in most walks of life. It is the language in which children are educated in schools.

If you are an immigrant in such a society and do not speak this language, you are simply at a disadvantage which people will normally feel no obligation to rectify in day to day interactions, except perhaps in a few, highly specialized situations like a legal trial. If you are lucky in other situations, you may find someone who can interpret for you. If there are enough others like you, you may find an enclave where it is possible to conduct most of your affairs in your native tongue rather than the dominant language of the larger society. No one will forbid you to use your language either in the enclave or outside it, but outside the enclave, few people will understand it. If you hope to act effectively outside the enclave, you have to learn the dominant

---

[18] Although there is no culturally neutral language, there is sometimes a politically neutral one. Thus several former colonies in Africa and Asia (India and Nigeria, to name only two) retained the colonial language as an (or the) official language, precisely because its use did not favour the culture and identity of one indigenous group over another.

language. If you send your children to public schools, they will be taught in the dominant language—if not immediately, then eventually.

Is there anything morally objectionable in this typical pattern? The policies I have described clearly favour the language of the national majority. Is that justifiable? Do they pay adequate attention to the linguistic claims of immigrant minorities?

To answer these questions we must start by considering the interests involved in this issue. It is of considerable importance to most people whether their native language is used in the delivery of public services. This will be instantly appreciated by anyone who has ever struggled to communicate in a crisis with doctors or bureaucrats in a foreign country using a language that one has not thoroughly mastered. Having one's language as a language of public education is especially important to many parents because it makes it much easier for them to pass on their cultural heritage to their children. People's interests in language policies may flow from concerns about identity as well as from more practical cares. For many people having their language established as one that is used in public services and in public education provides an important form of recognition of their cultural identity as one that matters in the society. Sometimes a language may be explicitly designated as an official language. This is an additional means of recognition.

There is also a public interest at stake here. As Kymlicka argued following Gellner, under modern social conditions a shared, standardized medium of communication is an essential public good, so that political authorities have a positive obligation to promote a common language. Furthermore, because the ability to navigate in civil society and to take advantage of educational, economic, and social opportunities is so dependent on linguistic competence, a commitment to equal opportunity entails an obligation to ensure that all members of society are able to function effectively in the common language.

None of this means that language policy must be absolutist. The need for a common language does not mean that a political community cannot designate two (or more) languages as official languages and use them in public services and public education. Canada, Belgium, and Switzerland provide just three obvious examples from Europe and North America, while India and Nigeria provide two examples among many from other continents. Moreover, the place of a language in public life is not an all or nothing matter. A language may be designated as an official language without being widely used in public life or it may be widely used without being designated as an official language. A language may be employed as the primary language of instruction in schools but not in the delivery of public services. Or it may be used in the delivery of some services and not others. One can imagine an almost infinite array of possibilities and see many actual variations.

What are the implications of all this for the picture I painted above of a country with a single dominant language? Consider the support given to the majority's language first. As I observed above, people normally have an interest in having their native language used in public life. The vast majority has the same interest, and, for normal democratic reasons, this majority is entitled to have its interest satisfied. So, it is perfectly justifiable for the language of the majority to be established as a language in which public education normally takes place and in which public services are normally delivered and as an official language (if there is one) of public life. Moreover, given the long historical entrenchment of the majority's language in social institutions and the sheer weight of numbers, the majority's language will normally dominate social, economic, and political life. There are certainly unjust ways of augmenting the hegemony of the majority's language, but there is nothing inherently unjust in the hegemony itself. It's neither good nor bad, just a fact of social life.

Given this fact of social life, even if another language were to be used in the delivery of services and in public education, people who could not speak the majority's language reasonably well would be at an immense disadvantage in terms of conventionally valued social opportunities. I recognize that non-native speakers often face highly objectionable forms of discrimination and disadvantage. But even if the objectionable practices were eliminated, people who could not use the dominant language effectively would face significant disadvantages. There is no way to change this social reality. So, immigrants and especially their children have an enormous interest in mastering the language of the majority. Furthermore, as I noted above, the normal liberal commitment to equal opportunity means that the government has a moral obligation to make mastery of the dominant language possible and likely.

Even if we accept the argument to this point, that the hegemony of the language of the majority is justifiable and that immigrants and their children ought to learn this language, we can still ask whether immigrants have some claim to have their languages used and recognized in public life in addition to the dominant language. One common justification for not using immigrants' languages is that they have consented to the use of the majority's language in deciding to immigrate. Kymlicka, for example, explicitly uses this argument to distinguish between the claims of immigrants and national minorities. '[P]eople should be able to live and work in their own culture', he says, and this is what justifies the language rights and self-government rights of national minorities:

But like any other right, this right can be waived, and immigration is one way of waiving that right. In deciding to uproot themselves, immigrants voluntarily relinquish some of the rights that go along with their original national membership. For example, if a group of Americans decide to emigrate to Sweden, they have no right that the Swedish government provide them with institutions of self-government or public services in their mother tongue (96).

This argument is clearly insufficient. Contrary to what Kymlicka says, we do not think that every right can be waived. Some rights, like the right to freedom of religion or the right to a fair trial or the sorts of language rights that go with freedom of expression are inalienable. And even if a right to public services in one's native language is not inalienable, we should hesitate to assume from the fact of immigration alone that immigrants have agreed to alienate it or, if such an alienation was a condition of admission, that this condition was a reasonable demand. Many immigrants are so desperate that they would agree to anything. Kymlicka himself recognizes this point a few pages later when he says that refugees cannot be viewed as voluntary immigrants and then acknowledges:

The line between involuntary refugees and voluntary immigrants is difficult to draw, especially in a world with massive injustice in the international distribution of resources, and with different levels of resources for human rights. If a middle-class American chooses to emigrate to Sweden, that is clearly voluntary, and very few of us would think that she had a claim of justice that the Swedish government provide her with free English-language services. . . . But if a peasant from Ethiopia emigrates to the United States, her decision is voluntary in a very limited sense, even if she was not subject to persecution in her homeland, since it may have been the only way to ensure a minimally decent life for herself or her children (99).[19]

I do not claim that the argument from consent has no relevance at all, but rather that it must be used with great caution.

A second, related argument against language rights for immigrants is the lack of demand for such rights. Kymlicka insists that most immigrants do not aspire to set up separate institutions based on their language and want their children to be educated in the dominant language of the receiving society (61–3, 176–81). This is clearly true as an empirical matter, but as with consent we have to be wary of taking this lack of demand at face value. It may be the product of what Elster has called adaptive preference formation (Elster 1983). People don't ask for and even say they don't want what they know they cannot have. Immigrants may know that they cannot get the receiving societies to provide extensive services or public education in their native tongue, and that is why they don't demand these things. But that leaves open the question of whether they ought to get them if they do demand them. As I noted in Chapter 1, in adopting a contextual approach, we must be careful not to use appeals to practice to legitimate deeply embedded injustices.

What if immigrants did make demands for education and public services in their languages? Or what if they made somewhat lesser demands, but ones

---

[19] Ironically, even the example of purely voluntary immigration that Kymlicka cites, a middle-class American moving to Sweden, is less self-evident than he supposes. The largest group of American expatriates in Sweden is composed of people who went there in the 1960s as draft dodgers and deserters to avoid being sent to fight in Vietnam. It is not clear that they should be classified as purely voluntary immigrants.

that went beyond existing practices? For example, suppose they asked that public education be provided in their native tongue along with the cultivation of capacities in the dominant language. Or suppose they asked that public officials (police, bureaucrats, and so on) communicate with them in their native tongues without demanding formally separate, self-governing institutions. As I noted above, language rights are not an all or nothing matter. Immigrants clearly have the same interest as anyone else in having their services delivered in a language they understand fully, and some of them at least might feel they have an interest in having their children receive a formal education in their native tongue (as well as the dominant one) as a way of maintaining and transmitting their cultural heritage and identity. Kymlicka himself draws attention to the latter possibility. He insists that a public policy of trying 'to make immigrants and their children as close as possible to unilingual native-speakers . . . rather than aiming to produce people who are fluently bilingual' (in both the dominant language and their native tongue) is 'a deeply misguided policy' (97). The question is whether this policy is not just misguided but unjust. How far do the language claims of immigrants extend?

It may be easier to address this question if we first consider linguistic minorities that possess much more extensive language rights than immigrants and ask why these minorities have such extensive rights and what (if anything) would be wrong with removing them. As usual the idea here is to start from practice, to try to identify the moral norms embedded in practice, and to reflect critically upon those norms. So, take cases like Canada, Belgium, and Switzerland, each of which has at least one relatively large, long-settled, territorially concentrated linguistic community that constitutes a significant minority of the state's overall population, and an overwhelming majority within a given area. These minorities are prototypical examples of what Kymlicka calls national minorities, and he is right to draw our attention to the fact that these groups normally possess much stronger linguistic rights than do immigrant groups. In each of these cases, the state recognizes more than one official language, and there is at least one sub-state political unit within which a minority linguistic community constitutes the vast majority and within which its language is the primary language of education, public services, and public life. In such cases, it seems intuitively obvious that state policies establishing the majority's language as the only official language and the only language of public life throughout the country would be unjust (assuming, as is clearly true in these cases, that such a policy would conflict with the desires of a majority of the minority linguistic community).

But what lies behind this sense that the current arrangements are in some sense required by justice? What makes the situation of these national minorities so different from that of immigrants? Why would it be unjust to require them to learn the language of the majority? I think we have to look at the

ways in which various factors—history, numbers, and concentration—
strengthen the interests people have in maintaining their language of origin
to such an extent that neglecting those interests is incompatible with any
notion of fair or evenhanded treatment.

The most powerful argument as to why immigrants and their children
should learn the majority's language is that this is necessary to have access to
a reasonable range of opportunities to participate in economic, social,
cultural, and political life. But if a linguistic minority is sufficiently large,
territorially concentrated, and numerically dominant in a given area and if it
is not economically and politically subordinated within that area, then that
argument will not apply. The normal range of activities characteristic of a
modern civil society will usually be conducted in the minority language, and
it will be feasible to provide not only primary and secondary but also higher
and professional education and a full range of public services in that
language. So, members of the minority linguistic group will find that a formal
education in their own language will open up a reasonable range of opportunities for most purposes and will offer distinct advantages over an education in
the majority language with regard to the appropriation of their own cultural
heritage and identity. This capacity of a large, territorially concentrated
minority to maintain an extensive civil society and corresponding political
and educational institutions is what gives a surface plausibility to Kymlicka's
concept of societal culture.

Of course, acquisition of the majority language may open up a wider range
of opportunities, but the importance of this will vary widely according to
individual aspirations, the relative size of the majority and the minority, and
other factors. In any event, acquisition of the majority language as a second
language is not precluded by having one's own language as the primary
language of instruction. As we have already seen, people have a strong interest in having their services delivered in their own language, at least whenever
that does not reduce the quality of those services as is certainly the case in the
examples I have mentioned.

Under these circumstances, to require the minority group to have its public
services delivered and its children educated in the language of the majority
would rightly be perceived as a form of majority tyranny, a blatant disregard
for the interests of the minority in a context where those interests could be
taken into account with comparatively little cost to the majority. Similarly,
relatively large linguistic minorities such as the ones we are considering are
justified in expecting that their languages will be recognized as official
languages of the country, that they will be used in the legislature and in official communications from the federal government that affect them. As I
argued above, people also have an interest in the extent to which their
language receives symbolic recognition because there are often close links
between language and personal identity.

Someone may object that all this understates the importance of a common language for building a sense of shared identity and making possible a shared public conversation, both of which contribute greatly to the successful functioning of a democratic political community. There is something to this concern. Other things being equal, it is plausible to suppose that it is easier to build a solidaristic political community when people share a common language than when they do not. But when one starts from a situation of linguistic differences, other things are not equal. If the majority imposes its language on the minority against the will of the minority, that is unlikely to foster a sense of solidarity or community.

In sum, justice sets some limits to what may be regarded as reasonable language policies. Compromise and mutual accommodation are essential to a well-functioning democracy. The majority is not entitled to pursue its interests to the exclusion of those of the minority. The norm of evenhandedness constrains the range of acceptable policies and entails the right of large, territorially concentrated, and long-settled linguistic minorities to expect that their languages will be used in public education and in the delivery of public services and will be recognized as official languages in laws and other formal state settings.

The claims of these linguistic minorities mark one end of a continuum. At the other end, one could imagine, as Kymlicka does, the isolated middle-class American moving to Sweden (or middle-class Swede moving to the United States). In such a case, history, numbers, and concentration all come together to minimize the strength of the language claims that could be put forward. Such an individual is entitled to the normal rights anyone should enjoy to use her language freely but cannot expect to receive public services in her language of origin or to have her children receive a public education in that language or to have that language receive public recognition. But this is a hypothetical extreme. As one moves away from it towards more realistic cases, the linguistic claims of immigrant minorities become stronger. Similarly, as one moves away from the model of the large, territorially concentrated national minority to ones that are smaller or more scattered, the linguistic claims become weaker. Let me elaborate.

Consider again contemporary practices in liberal democratic states. In most societies with any substantial amount of immigration, it would not be accurate to say that no education or public services are delivered in the language of the immigrants. Where there is any significant concentration of immigrants speaking the same language, a sector of civil society conducted in that language usually emerges. People find stores and shops and restaurants where they can use their native language, and they can usually find professional services as well—doctors, lawyers, dentists, accountants, estate agents, bankers—who provide services in their own language and thereby mediate the public services provided by the state in the dominant language.

What I have described so far requires no effort or commitment by the public authorities, but often there is some commitment as well to provide public services in the language of the immigrants. Some societies have heritage language programmes either during regular school hours or after school designed to provide formal instruction in the children's native language. Official communications about important public issues or public policies are sometimes printed in one or more immigrant languages. (For example, in the school that our boys attend, some of the communications sent home are printed in Chinese, Portuguese, and one or two other languages and interpreters are available at public meetings with parents). In places where there is some significant concentration of immigrants who do not speak the dominant language, authorities often try to ensure that some public employees in health care, social services, law enforcement, emergency response functions, and other areas can communicate in the language of the immigrants.

All of these measures cost money. They are not culturally neutral expenditures. On the contrary, they provide public support for the language and culture of the immigrants. It seems obvious that such expenditures are morally legitimate in the sense that they are morally permissible and that it is not necessarily unjust to spend public funds in this way. Are they morally required as a matter of justice? That is certainly not the conventional view. What is characteristic of all the arrangements I have described is that they are regarded as discretionary expenditures rather than fundamental entitlements. The various ways of providing public services in the language of the immigrants differ from one state to another and often from one local jurisdiction to another and are normally regarded as expenditures that can be expanded or contracted (like many other public services) in accordance with changing social, economic, and political circumstances. No liberal democratic state recognizes any fundamental obligation to use the language of immigrants in public life.[20] No state recognizes the language of immigrants as an official language. In sum, providing services in the immigrants' languages is generally regarded as morally permissible but not morally required.

Is this basic stance justifiable? In my view, it is for the most part. It is normally appropriate to think of demands for public services, including education, in one's native language as interests that should be considered in the context of competing interests. The norm of justice as evenhandedness constrains the range of acceptable policies but inevitably leaves considerable

---

[20] Even the apparent exception to this rule—the obligation to provide a person accused of a serious crime with an opportunity to understand the accusation and to respond to it—illustrates the point. This obligation does not require communication in the language of the accused if the person understands the dominant language, and even if he or she does not understand that language, the obligation only requires communication in a language that he or she does understand, not communication in one's language of origin. Thus, this is not in any sense a fundamental cultural right.

scope for differing views as to how the competing interests should be accommodated. This indeterminacy should not be interpreted as *carte blanche*,
however, particularly with regard to the delivery of essential services. As the
number of immigrants speaking a given language increases in a given area,
the justification for not having public service providers who speak the
language decreases, and it would undoubtedly be possible to find cases where
the discrepancy is large enough to count as an injustice. But there are almost
no cases where the numbers and concentration of an immigrant group are
comparable to those of the national minorities I discussed above. The few
exceptions like Spanish speakers in certain areas of the United States or
Russian speakers in the Baltic states usually have some distinctive feature of
their history that makes them a more ambiguous case morally and empirically.

   If the language claims of immigrant groups increase as their numbers and
concentration increase, so the language claims of national minorities decrease
as their numbers and concentration decrease. For example, Canada provides
a constitutional guarantee of a public education in French or English (if one
parent was educated in that language in Canada), but only 'where numbers
warrant' (Reaume and Green 1989). So, members of a national minority who
reside in an area where there are few other native speakers of their language
will not be able to get a public education for their children in their native
language. Moreover, the right to receive governmental services in French or
English applies only to services provided by the federal government. Several
of the provinces provide services only (or primarily) in English or French.
Again, the language rights tend to reflect numbers and concentration. In
other states like Belgium and Switzerland, the linguistic regime is even more
strongly territorial. The language of public education and public services
(whether the majority or the minority language) depends on the majority
within a given jurisdiction. These different arrangements seem to me to fall
within the range of the morally permissible.

   Similarly, if there are long-settled and concentrated minorities whose
numbers are small, their language rights are likely to be fewer than those of
large minorities. In Switzerland, for example, Rhaeto-Romansh is recognized
as a national language of Switzerland as a way of providing symbolic acknow-
ledgment of the historical position of the Rhaeto-Romansh community, but
Rhaeto-Romansh is not an official language of state business in the way that
French, German, and Italian are, precisely because there are relatively few
native speakers of Rhaeto-Romansh (Levy 1997).

   Aboriginal peoples also are numerically small national minorities. As I
have already pointed out above, it is difficult to say what justice requires with
regard to aboriginal languages. In one important respect, the linguistic situation of aboriginal people is comparable to that of immigrants, namely, that
their opportunities will be severely constrained if they do not acquire

command of the dominant language. Many aboriginal people will want to take advantage of the educational and economic opportunities that the wider society provides and that cannot be reproduced within any aboriginal society. They will be able to do this only if they can use the language(s) of the wider society. Moreover, many will spend some or most of their lives in the wider society, and even those who do not will normally have to interact with actors from the wider society. Again, they will need to use the dominant languages for this. Finally, many younger aboriginal people, like the descendants of immigrants, no longer have a fluent command of their aboriginal language and would be severely disadvantaged if public services were delivered and public life conducted only in their aboriginal language. So, aboriginal people, like immigrants, normally have a deep interest in acquiring a command of the dominant language of the wider society in which they live. On the other hand, I think that aboriginal peoples do have a stronger claim than immigrant groups to public recognition and support for their languages in areas where they are concentrated because of the historical role of aboriginal peoples in the settling of North America and because of the deep distinctiveness of their cultures and identities, topics I will discuss more fully in Chapter 8.

Conclusion

I have not attempted to be comprehensive in this brief discussion of language claims. I will explore other aspects of this issue in Chapter 5. My goal here has been simply to say enough to show that it is possible to think intelligently about the normative claims of cultural minorities from a liberal perspective without employing the distorting lens of societal culture. A contextual approach, guided by the norm of justice as evenhandedness, offers a more promising avenue of inquiry.

I conclude again with a caveat. I would not want this extended critique of the concept of societal culture to create a false impression of my evaluation of Kymlicka's work. It is precisely because it is so important that it deserves such sustained scrutiny. Kymlicka has performed an extremely valuable service in *Multicultural Citizenship* by enabling us to see that liberals do and should find institutional means of respecting cultural differences. Kymlicka's work as a whole remains extremely valuable. His book is filled with distinctions, arguments, and insights that will advance the thinking of anyone concerned with questions about multiculturalism. My goal here has been to show why the most fruitful direction for further exploration lies along the paths he has opened up in his contextual discussions rather than in his theoretical account of societal culture.

4

Distinguishing between Difference and Domination: Reflections on the Relation between Pluralism and Equality

In the previous chapter, I suggested that Will Kymlicka had opened up a fruitful line of inquiry by urging us to think of culture as providing the context within which people choose, but that he had narrowed and distorted that inquiry with his problematic concept of societal culture. If we take seriously the idea that culture provides the context of choice, we cannot avoid asking what sort of context that should be. What sorts of choices should people have? To what degree does the liberal commitment to equal opportunity require that people have the same cultural framework and the same cultural resources for their choices? Liberals are committed to both pluralism and equality, but some people see a deep tension between these values. Some egalitarians worry that emphasis on group identities and cultural differences will legitimate social and economic inequalities or at least distract from them as a focal point of concern (Fraser 1997, 1998; Gitlin 1995; Walker 1997). Some pluralists worry that a commitment to equality will bring with it an assimilationist overriding of the respect due to group differences. On their view, it is only to be expected that cultural differences will have social and economic consequences, and a genuine commitment to pluralism requires us to accept the inequalities that result from the cultural differences between groups (Simon 1990).

In my view, both concerns have some merit but are greatly exaggerated. The right sort of egalitarianism does not require us to make everyone like everyone else or to make minority groups conform to the dominant majority. The right sort of pluralism rarely entails inequality. Pluralism and equality are usually compatible and often mutually reinforcing. To see why, we have to take up specific cases in which there is some connection between group differences and social inequalities. To make substantive judgements about whether such inequalities are legitimate or illegitimate, we have to investigate the contexts in which the group differences have emerged. In particular, we have to consider the ways in which power may have shaped cultural differences before we rely on those cultural differences to legitimate inequalities.

In this chapter, I will take up several examples of groups in the United States, whose members are either more successful or less successful than average with respect to certain conventional socio-economic indicators or measures of achievement. I will show how attention to context and an understanding of fairness as evenhandedness enable us to regard some of these inequalities as morally defensible and others as morally problematic.

I begin with a caveat. The most important sorts of social inequalities, both historically and today, are not a product of internally embraced identities and cultural commitments but of externally imposed markers and ascribed cultural characteristics. In other words, the link between inequality and group difference is often not cultural difference but enforced subordination. As one small but telling illustration of this phenomenon, recall Malcolm X's story about his experience in the eighth grade. He was at the top of his class, a class with both white and black students. His teacher, whom Malcolm describes as a well-meaning person full of advice on how to succeed in life, asked him if he had given any thought to a career. Malcolm said that he wanted to be a lawyer. His teacher replied:

Malcolm, one of life's first needs is for us to be realistic. Don't misunderstand me, now. We all like you here, you know that. But you've got to be realistic about being a nigger. A lawyer—that's no realistic goal for a nigger. You need to think about something you *can* be. You're good with your hands—making things—Why don't you plan on carpentry? (Haley 1966: 36).

Whatever one thinks of the teacher's behaviour—note his attempt to get Malcolm to internalize the externally imposed limitations—his assessment of the social situation facing Malcolm was entirely accurate. Becoming a lawyer was a relatively unrealistic goal for an African-American in the first half of the twentieth century no matter how talented and hard-working he or she was. No one would openly defend that sort of social arrangement today (however much the same message is covertly communicated to young African-Americans in schools and elsewhere). But in considering whether a commitment to cultural pluralism requires us to accept inequalities between groups, we should not ignore the possibility that actual group inequalities are simply the result of differences of power rather than differences of culture.

But suppose group differences and inequalities are not linked in this way. What if it is not a question of restrictions and exclusions imposed on people against their will, but of the way in which being raised in a group shapes one's talents, character, motivation, and values?

We might draw on a useful distinction that James Fishkin makes between two components of the idea of equal opportunity: the principle of merit ('There should be widespread procedural fairness in the evaluation of qualifications for positions') and the principle of equality of life chances ('The prospects of children for eventual positions in society should not vary . . .

with their arbitrary native characteristics') (Fishkin 1983: 22, 32). Defenders of the view that pluralism entails inequality might reasonably say that it is only the latter construction of equality of opportunity that they want to challenge.[1] They accept the merit principle. Positions must be open to all in a fair competition. However, they say, we should not be surprised if cultural differences result in people having different aspirations and different capacities to achieve any given aspiration, even if all other factors are the same (natural talents, information, opportunity, and so on). The very concept of equal life chances presupposes a consensus on what counts as a 'life chance', that is, a consensus on what is important in life. But that sort of consensus is incompatible with pluralism. Moreover, equal life chances would require 'equal developmental conditions' (Fishkin 1983: 32). But different cultures place different emphasis on hard work, discipline, ambition, education, money, and so on, and these different emphases inevitably affect 'developmental conditions' and hence the relative likelihood of success for members of different groups. Truly equal developmental conditions could be created only by eliminating all cultural differences between groups, that is, by homogenization and assimilation, and that is clearly undesirable. So goes the general argument that cultural differences between groups will inevitably generate morally legitimate inequalities. I will call this the inegalitarian pluralist view.

Advantaged Groups: Asian–Americans and the Upper Class

What sort of example might support this line of argument? In an article defending the inegalitarian pluralist view I have just described, Robert Simon suggests that Asian-Americans fit the bill (Simon 1990). He observes that Asian-Americans made up only 2 per cent of the US population in 1987 but 11 per cent of the Ivy League's first-year class, an inequality between groups that he clearly regards as morally legitimate. The implicit argument seems to be that Asian-American culture (assuming that to be an appropriate category) places great emphasis on higher education and perhaps on related values like work, discipline, and achievement, and that this cultural pattern accounts for the higher than average success rate of Asian-Americans in applications to prestigious universities. What should we make of this argument?

One might object, of course, that the category *Asian-American* is itself insufficiently sensitive to pluralism because it lumps together many different

---

[1] I take this to be the view of Robert Simon, for example (1990). The account of the link between cultural difference and inequality that I present in this paragraph is a loose reconstruction of Simon's argument.

ethnic groups and cultural traditions (e.g. Chinese, Japanese, Korean, Indian, Pakistani, and so on, to mention only national cultures). Indeed, one might object that this category entails a racialization of culture, implicitly linking historically contingent and variable cultural characteristics to an imaginary common genetic pool. For the purposes of this chapter, however, I want to leave that sort of criticism aside. Instead, I will assume, for the sake of this argument, that it is possible to generalize about Asian-American culture (say, in contrast to European-American culture) and that Simon is right about the effects of that culture. We might conclude that it is an advantage to be born an Asian-American. It is an accident of birth, but it improves your chances of success in life. Is there anything wrong with that, any reason to regard the cultural advantage that Asian-Americans enjoy as morally problematic? Not at all. The success of Asian-Americans is something we can rightly celebrate as a triumph of pluralism. But let us pause for a moment to consider why this is the case.

Note first that the example supports one part of the inegalitarian pluralist argument—the moral legitimacy of different cultural starting-points—by undermining another—the significance of the diversity of group goals. What makes the Asian-American example effective as an illustration of a legitimate inequality resulting from cultural differences is the implicit assumption that *most* people (and not just Asian-Americans) would find an Ivy League education and the opportunities it brings highly desirable. We only care about the effect of different starting-points on the distribution of things that are widely desired. Even the fiercest egalitarian would not be troubled if it turned out that Japanese-American children had advantages in composing *haiku*. A Harvard degree is not like that (at least in the eyes of most people). The idea of merit itself presupposes a shared understanding of what life chances matter (at least to most people), and that shared understanding is itself an important element of cultural commonality, not cultural difference, as Michael Walzer's work reminds us.

One important reason why it seems morally unobjectionable for an Asian-American cultural heritage to increase one's chances of conventional success is that, as a group, they have not enjoyed power and privilege in American society. On the contrary, they have been the targets of racial hostility and oppression, both overt and covert. No one can suppose that they have rigged the rules of the game in their own favour or that they have tailored the definition of merit to fit their own particular characteristics. So, there is nothing unfair about their success, no violation of the idea of justice as evenhandedness. Indeed, it sounds ironic to say as I did above that it is an advantage to be born an Asian-American. Their success has come in spite of the disadvantages the larger society has imposed upon them. That is why it does not seem problematic. But all this is a contextual judgement. If Asian-Americans had had a long history of disproportionate success and had not been subjected to racial oppression, we might view their advantaged position more sceptically.

Consider another example of disproportionate success that evokes more doubt about its legitimacy: the upper class. Recall that Asian-Americans constitute only 2 per cent of the population but 11 per cent of the first-year Ivy League class. I have no precise statistics on the financial background of Ivy League students, but I think it safe to say that at least 11 per cent of the Ivy League student population (and probably a much higher proportion) comes from the richest 2 per cent of the population. Should we celebrate this as a triumph of pluralism, too? Presumably not, but why not?

Part of the answer is that we may suspect the success of the rich applicants has more to do with the size of the parents' bank-books than the size of the children's brains. This is the type of advantage that wealth and power often provide. Nevertheless, let us assume away any suspicion of abuse of power or special treatment. After all, lots of rich kids don't get into Ivy League schools. Those who do are usually talented and hard-working. Working-class applicants are rarely denied admission just because they are poor. It's a question of grades, test scores, writing ability, and so on. In short, of merit. Would the knowledge that only qualifications count eliminate the sense that there is something unfair about the disproportionate success of this group? Not entirely, for we also know that the qualifications are, in large part, a product of the environment that money buys. Lots of working-class kids are bright and hard-working but never get the chance to develop their talents or the encouragement to do so. They may not be as qualified now, at the time of application to college, but if they had had the same sort of schooling when they were younger, they would be. It is not so easy to place great weight on the distinction between merit and life chances.

I have been suggesting that the advantages in life chances enjoyed by the rich are more problematic from a moral perspective than the advantages in life chances enjoyed by Asian-Americans. I suspect that is a view that will fit with the moral intuitions of most (though not all) of my readers. But why? If poor children can complain because they have not had the opportunities provided by inherited money, why can't Italian or Irish American children complain because they have not had the opportunities provided by an inherited Asian-American culture? Is the inherited cultural tradition of Asian-Americans a form of unfair advantage after all?

Intuitively, inheriting a culture seems different from inheriting wealth. We do not think of the advantages enjoyed by Asian-Americans and the upper class in the same way, and that is not just because Asian-Americans have been subjected to racism. We would not think of success due to the Protestant Ethic in the same way as success due to schooling at a fancy private academy, even though the lessons of both have to be internalized if one is to be successful. Perhaps it is because a genuine culture seems more central to the self, less detachable and transferable than the things that money can buy (including a prep school education). But I don't want to press this too far. In what follows, I want to assume for the time being the moral legitimacy of social inequalities that arise from a cultural inheritance like that of the Asian-Americans and to explore other cases where inequalities are linked to cultural differences between groups to see whether we should draw the general lesson that cultural differences between groups make inequalities between them legitimate. At the end, I will return to this deeper egalitarian challenge.

Group Culture and Legitimate Inequality: The Amish

Consider first another example that I think illustrates the possibility of a morally legitimate connection between culture and inequality, even though in this case the group is less rather than more successful in conventional terms: the Amish in the United States.[2] The Amish are people whose religious and cultural traditions lead them to live simple lives, largely independent of the technologies that most people in the United States rely upon so heavily and free from the consumerism that is so central to the dominant culture. For the most part, they engage in farming and handicraft production. They place great emphasis on work, family, and community. They do not generally seek higher education; indeed they have resisted the compulsory education required of all young children in the United States. So, the Amish have less of many things that most Americans want. We could reasonably predict that Amish children are less likely than most American children to acquire advanced degrees or enter prestigious, high-paying occupations.

Is this sort of inequality morally objectionable? One reason for thinking that it is not unjust is that the inequality results largely from the values and practices of the Amish themselves, not from their treatment by others. It is significant that the Amish themselves do not complain about this inequality. They see it as an outcome of their way of life, and, for the most part, they do not want the things they have less of. (The absence of complaint is not proof of the absence of injustice, but it is a relevant indicator.) Moreover, individual members of Amish society are free to leave the local community and to seek other goals, including the conventional American dream. So, those who stay choose to do so.

The account I have just offered depends implicitly upon a conception of justice as neutrality, a hands off approach to culture. It treats the cultural

[2] For information about the Amish I rely upon Hostetler (1980) and Kraybill (1989). For an account of the Amish that supports the distinctive arrangements for them but on somewhat different grounds, see Spinner (1994). For an opposing view, see Arneson and Shapiro (1996).

commitments of the Amish as freely chosen. The inequality that results from these commitments is therefore a product of choice not circumstances (to use the language of Kymlicka and Dworkin).

One objection to this line of argument is that Amish children do not choose to be brought up in the Amish tradition. By the time they are adults their options outside the Amish community may be severely constrained by the limited training and education they have received while growing up. So, they are deprived of equal life chances with other Americans, even if it is their own parents and community who are depriving them.

This objection should not be dismissed lightly. Indeed, the state requires that Amish children be educated in certain ways and up to a certain age, in part to enable them to participate as citizens in public life (if they choose to do so) and in part to ensure that they will have some basic capacities relevant to the social and economic life of the larger society (if they choose to join it). But this can hardly be said to create equal life chances for these children to succeed in the ways most Americans think of as success. Why not go further?

The answer to that question depends both on how one thinks about liberalism and on how one thinks about the Amish way of life. One cannot make sense of the concept of equal opportunity without addressing the question, 'opportunity for what?'. The answer to that question depends upon our ideas about the good life (or the range of good lives). While the idea of justice as neutrality does play an important role in the liberal tradition, liberalism is not neutral among competing ways of life.[3] It values individual development and especially forms of development that involve rationality, purposiveness, and choice (Galston 1982). In contemporary liberal democratic societies, these ideals of development are conventionally linked to certain kinds of achievement, especially in the economic sphere. Not all ways of life encourage this sort of development.

At the same time, liberalism also values diversity; it believes in the desirability of different experiments in living, some of which are possible only in the context of a group life with shared traditions. Now it is obviously impossible for people to have an equal opportunity to participate in every experiment in living. If you are raised in one tradition (e.g. Catholicism), you cannot simultaneously be raised in another (e.g. Judaism) or, if you are, as in a 'mixed' marriage, that is a different experience and experiment from being raised in either alone. And no one can choose the tradition into which he or she is born. But these facts alone do not create a problem for the liberal ideal of equal opportunity, for there may be many different paths to development. For example, both Catholicism and Judaism may develop (in different ways) the characters, talents, and motivations (e.g. guilt)

---

[3] As Kymlicka (1995: 158–63) and Spinner (1994: 92–4) argue, even political liberalism cannot manage to avoid this.

needed to achieve those things that are widely valued in contemporary liberal democratic society. In this situation there is no conflict between equal opportunity and pluralism.

The conflict emerges only when a tradition or way of life does not offer a comparable path to conventional success (as in the Amish case). Then whatever course is taken requires the sacrifice of something valued in liberal democratic societies. The approach adopted in the Amish case is a compromise, partially infringing upon the Amish way of life and yet not really providing the Amish children with equal opportunity in the full sense. What this compromise reflects, I believe, is an implicit attempt to apply a norm of justice as evenhandedness.

What is at issue here is the extent to which the political community has a responsibility to shape the contexts of choice of Amish children in the name of equality.[4] It is impossible to make a judgement about this issue that is neutral between competing conceptions of the good. In the case in which the Supreme Court upheld the right of the Amish to keep their children out of the local high schools, the majority opinion spent a good deal of time discussing the Amish way of life and expressing admiration for it, (*Wisconsin v. Yoder* 1972). It seems clear that this admiration played an important role in the Court's willingness to exempt the Amish from the state's normal educational requirements. In my view, that was entirely appropriate. The desire of the Amish for this exemption has weight at least in part because we can recognize that the Amish way of life does make possible certain kinds of human goods that would be jeopardized by adherence to the conventional rules regarding education. So, permitting an exemption is a form of just (i.e. evenhanded) treatment of the Amish children, only because the interests they have in living their lives as members of an Amish community count in the balance over against the interests they have in being well equipped for conventional forms of success in the United States.

The Court's decision seems to me to be a reasonable compromise. It does not alter the core of the Amish tradition and yet it ensures that the Amish children have some of the basic capacities that liberal democratic societies value so highly. This course is far preferable to one that would emphasize only one of the competing values. It is an evenhanded approach even though it means that Amish children are disadvantaged in conventional terms.

Of course, some people think that the Court (and those who agree with its decision) are unduly romanticizing the Amish way of life with its emphasis on obedience and conformity, patriarchy and hierarchy.[5] There is

---

[4] A different concern about the Amish focuses not on the inequality between them and other Americans but on the conflict between the Amish way of life on the one hand and the cultural requirements of a liberal democratic political community and the responsibilities of citizenship on the other. This is the issue that Spinner focuses on in his discussion.

[5] Even some who agree with the Court's decision share this worry. See Spinner (1994).

doubtless something to this concern, but one might ask in turn whether the liberal critics of the Amish are unduly romanticizing the liberal way of life. How good is the fit between the deepest ideals of liberalism with regard to the development of human talents and capacities and the sorts of development most valued and encouraged by the institutions and social practices of contemporary liberal democratic societies? (Beiner 1992). Liberal theorists tend to say that liberal political communities develop our capacities to evaluate and revise our conceptions of the good, that they promote autonomy and critical reflection. These are liberal ideals, of course, but is this really what goes on in the high schools of Wisconsin? If so, they are rather different from most American high schools. Kymlicka says that the Amish 'wanted to withdraw their children from school before the age of 16, so as to limit severely the extent to which the children learn about the outside world' (Kymlicka 1995: 162). Even someone relatively sympathetic to the Amish like Spinner says, 'the possibility that liberal institutions might succeed in encouraging citizens to think critically leads the Amish to shy away from these institutions' (Spinner 1994: 95). It seems to me that we should consider the possibility that what the Amish are shying away from is as much consumer culture as it is critical thinking. When Amish parents say that they are worried about the 'worldly' influences of the public high schools and the ways in which peer pressures might draw their children away from their communities, I suspect it is fast food and fast cars that they fear (not to mention drugs, sex, and rock and roll) more than philosophy.

Indeed, one could take an even stronger position and argue that the Amish way of life comes closer to realizing worthy human purposes in terms of a broad understanding of the human good and perhaps even in terms of fundamental liberal ideals itself than the conventional way of life in contemporary liberal societies. One might say, for example, that the Amish way of life has a purposiveness and rationality to it while liberal societies inculcate a blind dedication to acquisition and consumption, to meaningless and frivolous choice. Furthermore, the Amish practice adult baptism, insisting that the decision to join the community must be a voluntary one. Given the inevitable exposure of Amish youth to the wider society (even with their removal from the public high schools), it is arguable that the Amish have more scope for genuine choice among alternative ways of life than most people in American society (Spinner 1994).

Still, I don't want to push this line of argument too far. The liberal commitment to equal opportunity means that a liberal democratic society has some obligation to ensure that all its members have access to the kinds of developmental opportunities that the society as a whole considers valuable, even if the society is wrong about what is valuable. To act differently would be hypocritical.

Group Culture and Illegitimate Inequality:
African-Americans

Consider now another minority group that has less of what most Americans want: African-Americans. Are the inequalities between African Americans and other Americans morally objectionable? Again, part of the answer depends upon what one thinks are the sources of these inequalities. No one denies that African–Americans were oppressed and kept down both during slavery and after, and almost no one now defends that history. But what about today?

In my view, racism remains a powerful and pervasive force in American life, often exercising its influence openly, but even more often covertly and in ways that the actors themselves do not understand. It is not just a question of discrimination that violates the merit principle, although that is common enough.[6] The problem goes much deeper than the word 'discrimination' suggests. In a multitude of ways, American society creates a hostile environment for African-Americans, one in which it is harder for them than for whites to develop their potential and to flourish.

These considerations have important implications for our understanding of pluralism. It is not just a group's own culture that may affect its members' life chances, but also the cultures of groups with which it interacts. When considering the legitimacy of inequalities between groups, we cannot simply assume that interactions among groups are benign and that all group cultures are equally legitimate regardless of their implications for those in other groups. In the Amish case, it seems reasonable to claim that Amish children have lower expectations (in conventional terms) primarily because of Amish culture and the values and motivations it inculcates rather than because of the way they are regarded and treated by the non-Amish majority. But that is not a plausible account of why the life chances of African–Americans are lower than those of whites. This is precisely what we must consider in making a moral judgement about inequality between groups in the real world.

This general point about what is relevant to the evaluation of pluralist inequality is valid even if one rejects my claims about racism in American society. Some clearly disagree with me. They claim that racial domination is

---

[6] One of the reasons why I think that affirmative action programmes, even ones that use quotas, are morally justifiable in principle is that I do not think it possible in most spheres to create procedures for evaluating merit that are free of racism, at least of the unconscious variety. It is a separate question whether the political and other costs of such programmes outweigh the benefits they provide. The fact that a course of action is morally justifiable does not necessarily mean that it is wise to pursue it. I am uncertain about the wisdom of affirmative action programmes. On the one hand, political forces opposed to the interests of African-Americans have used the widespread hostility to affirmative action programmes as a mobilizing tool to organize opposition to other policies and programmes that might help African-Americans. So, affirmative action programmes have a high political cost. On the other hand, if such programmes are abandoned, it is not clear what will prevent a return to a complacent acceptance of covert, perhaps unconscious discrimination.

a thing of the past and they point out that laws mandating segregation have been replaced by laws prohibiting discrimination in education, housing, and employment. They do not claim that racial prejudice has disappeared but rather that it no longer has any significant impact on the distribution of education, income, and employment. They point to the success of other groups like Jews and Asian-Americans who have also been the victims of discrimination and exclusion and who now do better in many ways than other Americans. They conclude that the lower than average success rate of African-Americans must therefore be due to cultural characteristics of African-American life. For example, some authors suggest that African-American culture does not promote educational achievement, an important key to employment and income. In their view, it is not domination but difference that is the source of inequality between African-Americans and whites today.[7]

I have made clear my disagreement with the position I have just described, but I do not want to pursue that debate here. On the contrary, I want to assume, for the sake of argument, that my opponents are correct and African-American culture is the major cause of the continuing inequality between African-Americans and whites. After all, even if my claims about the ongoing force of racism are correct, African-American culture could still be a contributing factor and it is important to see how this would affect the moral argument. Moreover, by framing the question in this way, we can focus on the implicit suggestion that inequalities that can be traced to cultural differences are morally legitimate.

If African-American culture were the cause of their lower rate of success in areas like education and income, would the inequality be as morally unobjectionable as the inequality between the Amish and other Americans? No, it would not. The connection between inequality and culture is different in the two cases, different in ways that are morally relevant.

Let us suppose that African-American culture does not promote educational achievement. Why might that be? One plausible answer is that African-American culture is in important respects a culture of subordination. Socialization is a source of power, and cultural differences between groups may reflect and embody relations of domination and subordination. Children from dominant and subordinate groups receive different sorts of socialization. As Malcolm X's story illustrates, children from subordinate groups are taught by schools (but also by their families and peers) not to aspire to positions possessed by members of the dominant group, not to expect equal treatment from authorities, not to challenge the status quo or to show initiative, and so on. In some respects this reflects a prudent recognition of the dangers of 'excessive' ambition, but it also reflects (at least in part) the internalization of

---

[7] These views can be found in Glazer (1975) and Glazer (1983), though Glazer (1997) reflects a changed assessment of American social reality with regard to race.

subordination. A group that has consistently been denied access to things the dominant groups in society value may come to say that it does not want these things anyway. Jon Elster calls this adaptive preference formation, like the fox saying that the grapes that were out of reach were probably sour and not worth eating (Elster 1983). A group culture that has been significantly affected by this sort of adaptation cannot be used to legitimate the inequality of which it is a product.

All this applies to African-American culture much more than to the Amish tradition. African-American culture has been shaped profoundly by the long and recent history of racial domination. Even if we assume that the domination has now finally ended, we cannot assume away its cultural legacy. If African-American culture contributes to lower rates of African-American success in education, we should not simply accept this as a morally legitimate by-product of pluralism, as part of the African-American way of life. By contrast, the Amish opposition to technology, consumption, and higher education is not the result of an adaptation to a recent history of deprivation and discrimination. This is not to say that the Amish have not been subject to discrimination at all in the United States, but rather that this has not been central to the formation of their culture and values.

Someone might object that the Amish suffered from persecution in Europe and this shaped their culture. Should it matter from a moral perspective that this happened long ago and far away? Yes, it should. The fact that the Amish have affirmed the distinctive features of their culture over time under circumstances in which they were not primarily reacting to domination gives legitimacy to the elements that differentiate them from the majority. It makes their culture more a product of their own inner life, of their own collective choice as a group.

Does this mean that there is nothing of distinctive value in African-American culture, that assimilation is, after all, the ideal at least for African-Americans and groups like them whose culture is in important ways a response to recent domination? No. We have to avoid two different dangers. The first would reproduce domination in the name of pluralism by uncritically accepting the social consequences of a culture of subordination. The second would reproduce domination in the name of equality by uncritically accepting the culture of the dominant group as a valid norm for all. It is characteristic of oppressed groups struggling for liberation that they want to affirm the value of their collective experience without endorsing the history of their oppression and to celebrate their distinctiveness without legitimating ongoing domination.

Unlike the Amish, African-Americans want to improve their educational achievements and to take advantage of the opportunities educational success offers. We do not find the same deep conflict between the goal of equal opportunity and the goal of respecting African-American culture. If African-American culture is an obstacle to educational success, African-Americans themselves want to transform it, but they want to do so without abandoning it altogether. This has clearly been a central element of the African-American struggle for equality from Frederick Douglass through W. E. B. DuBois and the black power movement. It remains a challenge for African Americans today.

Again, there is a general lesson about pluralism that is valid even if one does not accept my specific claims about African-American culture. Showing that inequality results from a group's own distinctive culture is not sufficient to establish the moral legitimacy of the inequality. We have to consider both the wider social context in which the group currently exists and the context in which the group's culture has developed before we can use the distinctiveness of culture as a justification for inequality.

Culture and Gender: Are Differences Legitimate?

Now consider the issue of gender differences. Women are not a cultural group in the way that Asian-Americans and African-Americans and the Amish are, but women do less well on conventional socio-economic indicators of success than men, and it is plausible to suppose that this has something to do with cultural constructions that distinguish their roles and responsibilities from those of men. What are we to think of such cultural constructions?

As usual what is needed to address these issues is more attention to context. If we are asked how to respond to culturally constructed differences between men and women, we should begin by distinguishing between two cultural contexts: the culture of a religious or ethnic group and the public culture of a liberal democratic society such as Canada or the United States. A commitment to pluralism will require us to respect or at least tolerate many of the norms about gender differences that emerge from the internal culture of a group. It does not require us to endorse gender differences in the public culture. Pluralism is not relativism, and respect for diversity does not entail indifference to the way the public culture treats gender.

Let us begin with the issue of gender construction within groups. Different traditions have different views of the proper roles of men and women and the proper relations between them. For example, some religious and moral traditions sharply differentiate the roles of men and women, assigning women to the domestic sphere and limiting their public activities, and emphasizing the authority of the husband within the family. Other traditions, particularly as they have evolved in recent years, seek to minimize gender differences, encouraging both females and males to develop their talents and capacities whatever these might be and teaching that men and women have similar responsibilities in the public and domestic spheres. Within broad limits, a liberal democratic society ought to tolerate these sorts of cultural differences among groups and thus cultural differences between the sexes when these emerge from a group's inner life. This follows from a general commitment to pluralism.

These differences may affect the life chances of group members. For example, other things being equal, women raised in the former sort of tradition seem less likely to pursue professional careers than women raised in the latter. But these sorts of consequences of group differences are an inevitable by-product of respect for people's religious and cultural commitments.

There are limits to toleration, of course.[8] Some traditions might oppose formal education for women on principle, but, as in the case of the Amish, a liberal democratic state will override that position and insist on certain kinds of education for all children, girls as well as boys, up to a certain age. A liberal democratic state may also try to limit the ability of people to act on the basis of their group culture in their relations with those who do not share their views, at least in certain contexts. For example, laws that prohibit discrimination on the basis of gender are supposed to prevent men whose group culture teaches that women belong in the home from acting on those beliefs in the public sphere.

Even where it does not impose formal limits on group cultures, the public culture is not neutral. For example, a liberal democratic regime will tolerate a patriarchal religion as part of its commitment to pluralism. But if it grants equal legal rights to women, it communicates a message about the status of women that is subversive of traditional patriarchal values and creates a resource that makes it easier for a woman to leave a group life based on that patriarchal religion than it would be in a regime that endorsed and reinforced those patriarchal norms.[9] A young girl raised according to traditional norms in Canada or the United States receives one image of what it is to be a woman from her family and another quite different one from the larger society. Her socialization and her objective situation are very different from those of a girl raised in a society where the public institutions explicitly support patriarchal values.[10] A liberal democratic regime ought to respect diversity, but it cannot be equally congruent with all values and ways of life and should not try to be. It will quite properly support some and undermine others simply by being true to itself.

---

[8] In Chapter 6, I take up the question of whether Islamic practices transgress these limits.

[9] I do not mean to suggest that legal equality is enough to overcome patriarchy or that patriarchal domination is not a powerful force in contemporary liberal democratic societies. But I do think that legal equality is a necessary step in overcoming patriarchy and that it makes a difference.

[10] Again, I do not mean to suggest that societies like Canada and the United States have actually achieved gender equality. On the contrary, I take it as obvious that they have not, that women are disadvantaged with respect to virtually every important life chance, including the most basic one of personal safety. Nevertheless, it matters that gender equality is a public norm.

What should the public culture of a liberal democratic regime communicate with regard to gender? I cannot answer that question fully, but I can
make a few general points. As the preceding discussion makes clear, a central
part of the message must be equality. Gender is not a relevant difference when
it comes to legal rights and social opportunities. No one seriously questions
that now. As in the case of race, liberal democratic societies have become
committed to gender equality in many areas where they previously tolerated
or even enforced inequality. This sort of equality is not in conflict with pluralism. Pluralism does not require one always to favour difference over sameness, regardless of context.

Does our commitment to equality require that socialization be the same
for both males and females? Is every social difference between girls and boys
or men and women a form of domination? To answer these questions we
must first ask what a particular difference means in a concrete social context.
We cannot answer that on the basis of a priori principles. ('All differences of
X type mean Y.') Nor is it something that can be determined by the subjective will of an individual. ('I do (or do not) experience this difference as a form
of domination.') Instead it is a matter of interpreting a culture, of understanding a social reality.

Let me offer an illustration. In *Plessy v. Ferguson*, the Supreme Court majority who upheld the 'separate but equal' doctrine contended that, if blacks
found their separate treatment stigmatizing or degrading, that was their problem. Racial segregation alone carried no implication of inferiority, so long as
the treatment was equal (e.g., comparable facilities). Given the *actual* dispar-
ity between the treatment of blacks and whites at the time, it would be kind
to call this argument disingenuous. But later, in an attempt to maintain segregation, some communities did upgrade the facilities available to blacks (e.g.
physical plants, money spent on educational resources, and so on), so that
the claim that the treatment was separate but equal was not absurd on its face,
as it had been in the past. Still, everyone knew what segregation was all about.
Whites regarded blacks as inferior. That is why the whites wanted them kept
separate. Given the history of American race relations, for whites to keep
blacks apart was inevitably stigmatizing and degrading. That is why the later
Supreme Court was correct to rule in *Brown v. Board of Education* that separate
treatment of blacks was inherently unequal.

What is, or is not, stigmatizing is not merely a matter of the subjective
perceptions of individuals. It is a social construction and a cultural reality.
Particular claims about what is stigmatizing may be contestable, but some
claims are clear beyond a reasonable doubt. That the segregation of blacks was
stigmatizing is clear in that way.

The claim that separate but equal is inherently unequal is not an analytic
truth, however. When an amendment to the US Constitution guaranteeing

equal rights for women was proposed, opponents argued that it would require the elimination of separate toilet facilities for men and women, on the 'separate is inherently unequal' hypothesis. Now there is nothing stigmatizing in our culture in having separate public toilet facilities for men and women. The practice reflects cultural norms about gender, bodily functions, and privacy. These are perhaps funny norms—as anyone who has seen *The Discreet Charm of the Bourgeoisie* can recognize. (Bunuel has a scene in which people retreat quietly to locked rooms to eat and sit on toilets around a common table to talk). It may also be an incoherent norm, as many people suggested in noting that men and women normally use the same bathrooms in private homes. But no one, as far as I know, supposes that the separation of public facilities is in itself stigmatizing, or degrading, or disadvantaging to one sex over another.

The fact that the separation of toilets is not stigmatizing does not necessarily settle the question of what counts as equal treatment. If one aimed to be evenhanded in the treatment of men and women, one might focus not on footage of lavatory space but on time spent waiting in queues to use the facilities. With such a measure I suspect we would indeed conclude that women are usually disadvantaged by the 'separate but equal' treatment. But they are not stigmatized. So, in this case, separate but equal is not inherently unequal. The inequality is something that could be solved with additional plumbing. That is simply not the case with racial segregation, which included, not incidentally, public toilets. No improvement of facilities could have made separate toilets for blacks equal in the United States. The social meaning of that difference was clear.

This long excursus on toilets reveals both that it is possible to think of cases in contemporary liberal democratic states where social differences between the men and women do not entail domination or objectionable forms of inequality, and that it is very difficult to do so. In my view, most differences in the ways males and females are treated in these societies, including gender-related patterns of socialization, embody and maintain patriarchal domination. But I will not try to support that claim here. If the claim is correct, it has important implications for the question of what the public culture ought to be with regard to gender. In general, distinctions based on gender should be suspect. In this context, justice as evenhandedness does usually require the elimination of difference.

Let me immediately add two important caveats to that general conclusion. First, in a context of piecemeal social change, the elimination of difference in one area (while others remain intact) may actually aggravate patterns of domination. For example, the move to have men assume more responsibilities for child-rearing has been accompanied, in some legal jurisdictions, by a change in assumptions about who would get custody of the children in case of divorce. The traditional assumption was that the mother would normally get primary custody. Now some jurisdictions have eliminated that assumption, making it easier than before for fathers to get joint custody or even primary custody. But the social reality continues to be that, in most cases, women care much more than men about rearing their children. Often the man uses his potential legal claims to custody as a bargaining chip in negotiations over finances, agreeing to give primary custody to the woman if she will settle for a lower level of child support. So, the effect of the change has been to transfer power from women to men, leaving women in a worse position than they would have been under legal rules that assumed a traditional sexual division of labor. A number of 'egalitarian' reforms in the area of family law seem to have generated this sort of inegalitarian effect. This shows that we have to pay attention not only to the symbolism of a social arrangement but also to how it actually works if we want our policies to be evenhanded in their treatment of different groups. It also indicates why one cannot use the moral judgements offered here, even though they are themselves contextual judgements, as a simple blueprint for social change.

The second caveat concerns the androgynous ideal that is implicit in the arguments I have presented in this section. Some feminists have suggested that the ideal of androgyny is not sufficiently sensitive to women's differences from men (Gilligan 1982). It is not merely that we have to avoid constructing the ideal primarily from a male model. Any plausible androgynous ideal will require that men become more like women as well as women more like men. It will require men to integrate traditionally female roles, values, motivations, tasks, and dispositions into their lives. For example, if traditional female socialization is criticized for having discouraged women from fully develop-ing their mental and physical capacities, traditional male socialization is crit-icized for having discouraged men from developing their emotional and affective capacities (Dinnerstein 1976). Women are to pursue careers and to act in the public sphere, but men are to assume equal responsibility for child-care and domestic activities. I take that much as implicit in what I said above.

The new feminist challenge goes deeper still, suggesting that women have a distinctive voice that men cannot hear easily and perhaps not at all, that women have a distinctive and valuable way of being that risks being lost if men and women become too much alike. Some trace the difference to bio-logy, while others emphasize the long history of enforced difference under patriarchal domination.

To speak of men and women as fundamentally different will remind many people of the traditional defenses of gender distinctions. The feminist writ-ers are well aware of this and see it as a danger. They want to find ways to identify and respect women's differences from men without providing a justification for past and present subordination. They want to pay tribute to women's historical experience without simply endorsing women's traditional roles. I do not think that any of those struggling with this approach has yet succeeded entirely, but I do think they are asking the right questions. If an effective challenge to the androgynous ideal is mounted, one that emphasizes difference rather than sameness, it will come from this sort of inquiry not a retreat to traditionalism or an abstract general commitment to group pluralism.

Conclusion: The Egalitarian Challenge Reconsidered

Throughout this chapter I have implicitly taken the basic institutional framework of contemporary liberal democratic societies, including their capitalist economic arrangements, as a given. Within that framework, the claim that cultural differences between groups give rise to morally legitimate inequalities between groups needs to be modified by stipulating that the claim applies only to *morally legitimate* cultural differences. The Asian-American and Amish cases can be used to support this modified claim But even within that framework, we can often criticize inequalities linked to cultural differences and argue that pluralism and equality are complementary and mutually reinforcing. The cases of African-Americans and women illustrate this theme. Now I want to conclude by suggesting that pluralism and equality are compatible at a much deeper level.

Some people seem to assume that if cultural differences are morally legitimate, whatever inequalities they might give rise to in a capitalist market society are also morally legitimate (Simon 1990). We should be wary of making such an assumption. We ought to accept cultural differences among groups as a good thing (within the limits discussed above) and to recognize that some group cultures will emphasize certain forms of aspiration and accomplishment more than others. Group cultures will affect people's motives and values and goals, and achievements will vary from one cultural group to another. But this does not settle the question of what sort of social institutions and policies we should have, that is, of the framework within which these group differences are to operate. There is no such thing as a neutral social structure. We have to decide whether and to what extent and in what ways certain forms of achievement will receive external rewards (in addition to the intrinsic rewards that come from the achievement itself). This obviously includes deciding what role the market will play in society and how it is to be constrained if at all.

In my view we are most likely to encourage genuine diversity (both among individuals and among groups) if we minimize the role of the market as an arbiter of human worth. We should try to reduce invidious distinctions and differential material rewards in relation to education and occupation. People should be encouraged to develop those talents and capacities that offer an opportunity for personal growth and self-realization (often achieved through social contributions) and to respect achievements in diverse fields. In the end, a society in which there are relatively few inequalities among individuals (and hence among groups) will be the one in which the kinds of differences we want to affirm (among individuals and groups) will be most likely to flourish.

5

Cultural Adaptation and the Integration of Immigrants: The Case of Quebec

Questions about liberalism and culture have come to the fore in the past decade in part because of the growth in international migration. Many European states that had not thought of themselves as countries of immigration found themselves with substantial populations of immigrants, and states like Canada and the United States that were self-consciously countries of immigration found that the sources of immigration had changed.[1] In both Europe and North America, many people saw immigrants as the bearers of alien cultures, radically different from and perhaps incompatible with the existing cultures in these liberal states. These developments have raised urgent questions about the cultural adaptation of immigrants in liberal states. In this chapter and the next, I will explore some of those questions.

In broad terms, the key questions for this chapter are these: to what extent and in what ways may liberal states legitimately expect immigrants and their children to conform to the dominant culture of the society they have entered? To what extent and in what ways may immigrants expect the states they have entered to respect their pre-existing cultural identities and commitments and respect whatever concern they have to pass on these identities and commitments to their children?

I use the term 'expect' in a normative not an empirical sense. There is an extensive empirical literature on the cultural adaptation of immigrants that seeks to describe and explain how and why immigrants change (or do not change) culturally in response to their new environment. From such a perspective, one might say, for example, that one can expect a high degree of linguistic adaptation among the children of immigrants. That sort of expectation is sociological or predictive. By contrast, I am interested in the question of whether states are *entitled* to expect this sort of linguistic adaptation (and

---

[1] In both cases this was partly the result of forgetting one's own history. Several European states had experienced substantial immigration flows earlier in their history, and people in the North American states had forgotten how alien Irish, Eastern European, and Mediterranean cultures had seemed to the long-settled inhabitants of Canada and the United States in the nineteenth and early twentieth centuries.

other forms of cultural transformation) as a condition of full membership for immigrants and their descendants. My questions are not about how immigrants *will* adapt in the course of living in a new society, but about how they *ought* to adapt.

I do not assume that all liberal democratic states ought to follow exactly the same policies with respect to the integration of immigrants. Different states have different histories, cultures, institutions, and goals. These differences may legitimately lead to different policies with respect to, say, education or health care, and presumably may legitimately lead to different policies with respect to the integration of immigrants as well. I do assume, however, that a commitment to liberal democratic principles sets limits to the range of morally permissible policies. There are some things that no liberal democratic state may legitimately do and other things that every liberal democratic state is obliged to do. Identifying those limits with respect to the cultural integration of immigrants is the principal task of this chapter.

In talking about integration, I have used the word 'membership' rather than 'citizenship'. This is deliberate. States may require certain kinds of cultural adaptation as a prerequisite for admission to citizenship, but they may also expect resident aliens who do not become citizens to adapt culturally in various ways and they may expect further cultural adaptation even of those already admitted to citizenship. Elsewhere, I have argued that access to legal citizenship should not be conditioned upon cultural adaptation but should be tied almost exclusively to length of residence (Carens 1989). I will not repeat those arguments here. Instead, I will focus on the question of how liberal democratic communities may legitimately expect new arrivals to change, regardless of their formal citizenship status, and how they may not. To put it another way, what moral principles ought to undergird and guide public policies with respect to the integration of immigrants?

Why the Case of Quebec?

Traditional countries of immigration like Canada, the United States, and Australia have all undergone broadly similar patterns of development with respect to the selection and integration of immigrants. For much of the twentieth century, each of these countries had in place a system for selecting immigrants that was racially and culturally biased and mechanisms of integration that were built upon the assumption that immigrants should assimilate to the prevailing, hegemonic culture. (Even the melting-pot myth was built upon the assumption that certain flavours would be dominant.) Over the past few decades, each of these societies has abolished its overtly discriminatory criteria of selection and each has adopted, in one form or another, an

ideal of multiculturalism rather than assimilation. Should these developments be viewed merely as a response to the particular historical situations of
the countries in question or should they be viewed as required by—I do not
say caused by—a new understanding of the requirements of liberal democratic principles? I believe the latter, but instead of trying to demonstrate that
abstractly, I propose to explore it concretely by looking at a case in which a
political community has an explicit collective cultural project and seeks to
integrate immigrants into that project. Seeing what such a community thinks
it can demand of immigrants may reveal a lot about liberalism and culture,
both in terms of the kinds of cultural projects that a liberal political community can pursue and in terms of the way liberal principles limit the demands
that can be placed on immigrants to adapt.

The case I will take up is Quebec. I propose to focus on what Quebec says
about the principles guiding its policies with respect to the integration of
immigrants and to critically evaluate Quebec's principles in the light of liberal
democratic theory.

This may seem an odd way to proceed in two respects. First, Quebec is
not—at least, not yet—an independent state. (There is a strong independence
movement in Quebec, and Quebec's separation from Canada seems a realistic
possibility in the near future). Secondly, what political communities say
about the moral principles underlying their policies is a notoriously unreliable guide to their practices. Let me say why I think this is an appropriate way
to proceed nevertheless.[2]

Although Quebec is not an independent state but a province of Canada,
the Quebec government has negotiated with the federal government and
acquired virtually complete authority over policies affecting the integration
of immigrants to Canada who arrive in Quebec. None of the other Canadian
provinces has shown any interest in exercising authority in this area. The
Quebec government sought these powers precisely because it thinks of
Quebec as a 'distinct society' from the rest of Canada and sees control over
the selection and integration of immigrants as essential to the project of
maintaining and developing this distinct society.

What makes Quebec a distinct society is the fact that the vast majority of
the population (over 80 per cent) are francophones descended from the original French and other settlers of New France during the seventeenth and
eighteenth centuries, whereas in the rest of Canada the overwhelming majority of the population are anglophones descended either from English settlers
or subsequent immigrants who learned English. Moreover, many Quebec officials and intellectuals are hostile towards the term 'multiculturalism' because
they regard the term as a way of placing francophone culture on a par with

---

[2] A third possible objection is that Quebec is not a liberal political community because of its
collective project. I try to address this issue later in the text.

the cultures of ethnic minorities who became established in Canada through immigration in the late nineteenth or twentieth centuries or who are now still arriving. In the eyes of many Québécois, multiculturalism does not do justice to the conception of Canada as a country built upon two 'founding nations'—the French and the English.[3] The Quebec government insists that Quebec has a distinct history and culture and it aims to integrate new immigrants to Quebec in a way that contributes to its distinct society.

I should add that immigration policy is not the subject of serious dispute between the federalist party (the Liberal Party) and the main elements of the separatist party (the *Parti-Québécois*) which is currently in power. Even if Quebec becomes independent, it seems unlikely that Quebec's immigration policy will change much.

In thinking about the issues posed by contemporary immigration in Europe, one objection to drawing lessons from classical countries of immigration like Canada and the United States is that the self-understandings of European countries are very different. Even a country like France that has traditionally accepted immigrants does not conceive of itself as a country built by immigration, and most European countries have much less ethnic and cultural diversity and populations with much deeper historical roots than the countries of immigration. These objections have a good deal less force when applied to Quebec, for the reasons outlined above. At the same time, Quebec officials have given a great deal of careful and explicit attention to the question of how to integrate immigrants in a way that preserves and contributes to Quebec's distinct society, so their reflections may illuminate some of the possibilities and limits of the demands a liberal democratic society can make of immigrants with respect to cultural adaptation.

Why focus on what Quebec *says* about its principles with respect to the integration of immigrants? Formal policy pronouncements are notoriously unreliable as a guide to actual practice. What is said in one document may be contradicted in another, or officials may speak in codes, using language that formally respects certain conventions while expressing the opposite in a way that is understood by all who care to listen. Moreover, actual policies often differ greatly from formal policies, and outcomes often do not correspond to intentions.

In studying social policy, social scientists tend to follow the advice of H. R. Haldeman (an aide to President Nixon subsequently sent to jail for his role in the Watergate scandal) who said, 'Don't watch what we say; watch what we do'. (To his chagrin, some reporters heeded his recommendation). So, social scientists want to learn about what is actually done, and, if they do study

---

[3] The conception of Canada as having two founding nations is one that aboriginal people in Canada find particularly objectionable because of the way it ignores their prior settlement on the land. I discuss questions about aboriginal people in Canada further in Chapters 7 and 8, especially the latter.

what is said, they pay particular attention to the contradictions and codes rather than the formal pronouncements. This approach is justified on the grounds that the real commitments, values, and principles of the government are manifested in practice. Indeed, this sort of approach is entirely appropriate, in my view, when the task at hand is to explain what the government is doing and why.

But if the question is what people think is morally right (and what they should think), then a formal statement of principles becomes much more important. For purposes of critical reflection on legitimation, public discourse matters. Even the use of codes reveals something important about public criteria of legitimation. Hypocrisy is the tribute vice pays to virtue, as the old saying goes, and what public officials say they are doing can be an important indicator of what they think is generally regarded as the boundaries of the morally permissible, especially when they actually intend to do something else. Moreover, there are often genuine disagreements about what is and is not morally permissible. To criticize actual practices or even codes—except perhaps on grounds of ineffectiveness or inconsistency—one has to speak from a normative perspective. My task is to elucidate that normative perspective and to subject it to critical reflection.

Questions about Belonging in Quebec

In what ways (according to Quebec) ought immigrants to change their behaviours, their beliefs, their cultural practices, or their identities? What does Quebec think they ought to do in order to become Québécois, not just legally but in some deeper, social sense? When, in Quebec's view, are they morally entitled to feel that they belong, that they are full members of Quebec society? And how does Quebec think it ought to adapt to the immigrants? In what ways does Quebec feel obliged to respect the immigrants' existing behaviours, beliefs, cultural practices, and identities? What sorts of acceptance and welcome does Quebec think it ought to extend? In short, in Quebec's view, what do the immigrants owe Quebec and what does Quebec owe the immigrants?

Let me repeat that I am not primarily concerned here with legal status and legal rights. Immigrants to Quebec normally become permanent residents of Canada when they arrive, with most of the rights of citizens apart from the right to vote. They are eligible to apply for citizenship after three years, and the requirements for admission are limited: modest linguistic competence, rudimentary knowledge of Canada's political institutions and history, no serious criminal record. These requirements would not be likely to change much in an independent Quebec.

My focus is on the normative conceptions of membership and community that Quebec says should govern the process of integrating immigrants into Quebec and that should inform particular policies, regardless of whether those immigrants have become citizens. My primary task is to identify and evaluate these normative conceptions.

There is one last preliminary complication. When I hypostatize Quebec, as in speaking of Quebec's demands or goals, I am referring implicitly or explicitly to the government of Quebec. When one considers the issues of social expectations, membership, belonging, and identity, however, the attitudes and behaviour of the whole population matter. An immigrant is not likely to feel as though she belongs, regardless of what government officials say, if most of the population see her as an outsider. To say that Quebec expects this or that of immigrants or that Quebec feels it owes this or that to immigrants thus risks a certain ambiguity. It is reasonable to ask whether the population as a whole shares the government's attitudes and assumptions. Despite this complication, I will focus primarily on the government's view of these issues, because I am trying, in this chapter, to identify and evaluate the normative presuppositions of public policies with regard to immigration. Moreover, while the government cannot entirely control the process of social integration, its policies and pronouncements play an important role in constructing norms of discourse about immigrants, membership, and community.

Quebec's Moral Contract with Immigrants

Quebec has issued a policy document that is particularly revealing about the government's normative presuppositions.[4] It proposes a moral contract between immigrants and Quebec as a society, and it outlines the rights and

---

[4] The document is entitled *Vision: A policy statement on immigration and integration*. It was issued by the Ministry of the Cultural Communities and of Immigration of the Government of Quebec (in French and English) in 1990 after a great deal of highly developed and highly moralized public debate about the place of immigrants in Quebec's distinct society. For a government document it is truly remarkable. Instead of the bureaucratic banalities that such documents usually contain, this one offers a sophisticated, self-conscious articulation of the goals of Quebec's policies and of some of the normative presuppositions underlying those policies—presuppositions about rights, duties, membership, community, democracy, pluralism, history, culture, and individual identity. Of course, any government document has its limits. As policy, it could be changed by this government or a new one. As an account of Quebec's understanding of immigration and political community, it cannot claim to be a reflection of the views of the population as a whole or even of all current government practices. As the title itself indicates, the policy statement is about a vision, a goal, rather than an accomplished fact. Nevertheless, the statement puts forward a set of standards, principles, and ideals that it says should guide the development of policy. As such, it invites comparison with alternative policies and rationales and that from a moral and theoretical perspective as well as a political and practical one.
Page numbers in parentheses in the text of this chapter refer to this document.

responsibilities of each party in the integration process. By explicitly invoking the language of morality to describe the principles undergirding Quebec's policies, it sets out a clear claim to moral legitimacy that invites scrutiny—and, in my view, can largely sustain that scrutiny.

According to the document, three principles guide the integration process in Quebec, principles based on the 'social choices that characterize modern Quebec' (15). On this account, Quebec is:

- A society in which French is the common language of public life;
- A democratic society where everyone is expected and encouraged both to participate and contribute;
- A pluralist society that is open to multiple influences within the limits imposed by the respect for fundamental values and the need for intergroup exchanges (15).

Immigrants are expected to accept these characteristics of Quebec society. That is their primary moral responsibility with regard to integration. These characteristics also entail certain rights for the immigrants, not only legal rights but also moral rights in the sense of legitimate expectations about the way they will be treated and accepted in Quebec. For its part, Quebec as a society has a moral right to expect immigrants to accept these three characteristics but also a moral duty to meet the legitimate expectations of the immigrants and to make possible the integration that it expects.

What should we say about this moral framework that the government says is to guide Quebec's integration process? Obviously, we need to unpack it a good deal before we can evaluate it adequately. Still, one feature of the general picture is striking. Given the emphasis that Quebec has placed on building a *distinct* society and the importance it has attached to gaining control over all aspects of immigration and social integration, one might expect Quebec's policies on the integration of immigrants to be strongly assimilationist. What is surprising from this perspective is how little adaptation Quebec expects of immigrants and how little of that seems 'distinct'.

French as the Language of Public Life

Let us consider each of the three characteristics of Quebec society in more detail and what each entails for the integration of immigrants. First, consider the context of the assertion that French must be accepted as the common language of public life. The fact that a substantial majority of the Québécois (over 80 per cent) are francophones is at the heart of Quebec's self-understanding as a political community, as is the potential vulnerability of that fact given the overwhelming dominance of the English language in the rest of North America and given Quebec's history.

The Québécois are acutely aware of the rapid and substantial diminution of the use of French among francophone emigrants from Quebec to parts of Canada where anglophones constitute a majority. In many cases in the past, the French language was deliberately and forcefully suppressed. But even if one sets aside such overt suppression and indeed takes the cases today where the francophone population outside Quebec receives the strongest public support, with bilingual institutions ostensibly in place and systems of public education in French, assimilation to English is rapid and widespread except in those cases where a particular francophone population is relatively isolated and self-contained geographically. In the North American context, the English language has an overwhelming presence. That is why the Québécois have concluded that bilingualism in Quebec would lead to the erosion and eventual demise of French.

Compared with the position of French in the rest of Canada, not to mention the United States, English has enjoyed a privileged position in Quebec until quite recently and, in some important respects, it still does. There was never any suppression of English in Quebec. On the contrary, Quebec established a system of anglophone public institutions—not only schools but also hospitals, a major university, legal and social service institutions—that has no parallel in terms of francophone public institutions outside Quebec. The creation of these anglophone institutions may have been the result of anglophone political and economic hegemony, but they remain largely in place even now after anglophone hegemony in Quebec has disappeared. Despite the fact that anglophones have always been a minority in Quebec, they dominated commercial life, including most managerial posts down to the shop floor. Until quite recently—the last twenty-five years or so—it was more advantageous in terms of economic opportunity to be a unilingual anglophone than to be a bilingual francophone, and many francophones could not use French in the ordinary course of their work. These are the sorts of facts that the Québécois remember and resent when Quebec is criticized for its efforts to ensure that the French language will be the central language of Quebec's public life.

Prior to the 1970s, immigrants to Quebec tended overwhelmingly to learn English rather than French (if they were not themselves already francophones) and, most importantly, to send their children to public schools in which English rather than French was the language of instruction, an option that was normally completely open to them. They chose this course because knowledge of English offered social and economic advantages even within Quebec and was overwhelmingly advantageous in the rest of North America and because the francophone community had a largely closed and insular character. Some francophone parents sent their children to anglophone schools for the same reasons.

Beginning with the Quiet Revolution of the 1960s, successive governments in Quebec have taken various actions to establish and secure the position of French.[5] The French language is to be 'the language of Government and the Law, as well as the normal and everyday language of work, instruction, communications, commerce and business' (15). But the centrality of the French language is politically important for more than instrumental reasons. 'It is also a symbol of Quebec identity' (16). The Quebec government thus takes the preservation of the French Fact and the promotion of the French language as a central political goal. Any foreseeable future government, whether Quebec remains part of Canada or not, seems certain to share this commitment:

What does this mean for immigrants to Quebec? In general terms, the following:

[T]he Government and the vast majority of Quebeckers view the learning of French and its adoption as the common language of public life as the necessary conditions for integration. . . . The host-community therefore naturally expects immigrants and their descendants to be open to the French Fact, to make the necessary effort to learn the official language of Quebec and to gradually acquire a sense of commitment to its development. (16)[6]

The central message seems clear. If you want to belong in Quebec, both to feel that you belong and to have the rest of the population feel that you belong, you have to learn French and accept the central place of the French language in Quebec society. At one point, the government's document speaks 'about 'the need to send immigrants and Quebeckers from the cultural communities a message about the importance of French. This should be correctly perceived as a message about belonging to Quebec society' (47). It is hard to be more explicit than that. There is nothing wrong, the government seems to be saying, in making full social membership contingent upon this sort of adaptation. It is a reasonable expectation that immigrants are morally obliged to meet.

Linguistic adaptation is the strongest demand that the moral contract proposed in the policy document makes upon immigrants. Moreover, this is one moral demand that the government is prepared to enforce with legal

---

[5] The 'Quiet Revolution' refers to the dramatic transformation of Quebec society during the early 1960s. Prior to this time, the anglophone minority in Quebec dominated the economy. The francophone community (including the elite) was predominantly conservative and Catholic, wedded to a rural way of life and traditional values, hostile to liberalism and capitalism. In the space of a relatively few years, the francophone community (especially the elite) became predominantly secular, liberal, modern, and entrepreneurial, active rather than passive, aggressive rather than defensive. Modernizing francophones gained control of Quebec's government and of its economy and used the two together to transform Quebec society.

[6] The document uses the term 'Quebeckers' to refer to the inhabitants of Quebec, whereas I use the term 'Québécois' in this book, except when quoting directly from the document. Usage in the literature on Quebec varies a good deal, and I am treating this entirely as a matter of stylistic preference. I do not intend the choice of words to imply anything substantive about my views on Quebec.

requirements in certain respects. For immigrants, the most important of these requirements is the law that says the language of instruction in the public schools to which immigrants send their children will be French, thus removing the option which had previously been available to them and is still available to anglophones in Quebec, of sending their children to schools in which the language of instruction is English.[7] This requirement ensures that most children of immigrants will learn French, whether their parents do or not.

What are the limits on the demand for linguistic adaptation? First, the government asserts that the expectation that immigrants learn French and accept its place as the language of public life is not a demand for 'linguistic assimilation' (16). Individuals have the right to use the language of their choice in 'private communication' (16). Moreover, 'heritage languages' are viewed as 'an economic, social and cultural asset for the whole population of Quebec' (16). Thus Quebec actually promotes the retention of heritage languages among the children of immigrants through various publicly funded school programmes. Finally, the government recognizes that linguistic adaptation is something that occurs over time, and that the length of time required depends in important ways on people's circumstances.

What may immigrants expect of Quebec with regard to linguistic adaptation? First, the government acknowledges that expecting immigrants to adapt linguistically entails an obligation for the government to provide services that make it possible and attractive for them to learn French. Secondly, the government says that the existing francophone community has an obligation to be open to immigrants, as it was not prior to the Quiet Revolution, and that the desired linguistic adaptation will not occur without that openness. The goal, according to the government, is make it possible for 'the French language [to] become part of the shared heritage of all Quebeckers, whatever their origin' (16).

Learning the official language of the society to which they are moving might seem like the prototypical example of the sort of adaptation a society can reasonably expect of its immigrants. And so it is, or so I shall argue below. But this paragraph shows that even in the case of linguistic adaptation, the expectations for change are not all on one side. Before examining the merits of Quebec's claims to be making legitimate demands of immigrants in asking

---

[7] This way of describing the requirement oversimplifies things a bit. The actual rule stipulates that only children who have at least one parent who received a primary education in English in Canada are entitled to have access to the English language public school system in Quebec. Thus, for example, the children of British or American immigrants to Quebec would not be entitled to an education in English. Some have proposed softening this rule to permit immigrants whose native tongue is English—a relatively small proportion of the immigrants to Quebec—to send their children to the English language schools, but this proposal has not yet been adopted. My analysis later in the chapter implies that children of immigrants whose native tongue is English would have stronger moral claims to an English language education than the children of other immigrants. Whether the failure to provide them with such an education exceeds the bounds of justice as even-handedness is another question.

them to learn French, however, I want to consider more briefly the two other elements of Quebec's moral contract with immigrants: democracy and pluralism. Commitment to these principles may entail some kinds of adaptations by immigrants, but it also sets strong limits to the kinds of changes that can be demanded and imposes obligations on the receiving society as well.

Democracy and Pluralism

The principle that Quebec is 'a democratic society in which everyone is expected and encouraged to participate and contribute' seems to demand more of Quebec as a society than of immigrants. On the one hand, this does entail a duty for immigrants to exert themselves. Quebec 'is entitled to expect newcomers to make the necessary effort to engage gradually in the economic, social, cultural and political life of Quebec' (17). On the other hand, it requires Quebec to make this participation possible and to encourage it.

Quebec's commitment to the democratic ideal means that it 'assigns the highest importance to the values of equal opportunity and social justice' (16). Thus, Quebec has promulgated various human rights documents committing Quebec to principles of non-discrimination on various familiar liberal grounds, including language and ethnic or national origin, categories of special significance for immigrants. But the government goes further than a promise of formal equality:

[I]mmigrants can expect the host-society to provide them socio-economic support during the initial period and to back them up whenever they or their descendants confront institutional or social barriers that deny them equal access to employment, housing or various public and private services. Furthermore, immigrants can also expect the host-community to allow them, like all Quebeckers, to help define the major orientations of our society (17).

Thus Quebec acknowledges a duty to promote the full participation of immigrants in economic and political life.

With respect to pluralism, the government draws a sharp contrast between traditional Quebec society which it says 'advocated a uniform cultural and ideological model to be shared by all Quebeckers' and modern Quebec which it says 'has for more than 30 years resolutely styled itself as a pluralist society' (17). People in Quebec are free to 'choose their own lifestyles, opinions, values and allegiances to interest groups within the limits defined by the legal framework' (17). Ethnic minorities, including recent immigrants, have 'a right to maintain and develop their own cultural interests with the other members of their group' (17). All this clearly is incompatible with the notion that immigrants have an obligation to repudiate their cultures of origin and to adopt the culture of Quebec or that this sort of cultural transformation is a prerequisite for becoming full Québécois. The principle of pluralism seems to rule out any strong version of cultural assimilation.

What does Quebec demand of immigrants with respect to the principle of pluralism? Does Quebec expect any cultural adaptation beyond the learning of French? It does expect immigrants, like all Québécois, to respect the democratic values in which the commitment to pluralism is embedded. The government emphasizes three concerns in this context: 'equality of the sexes, the status of children and the censure of all discrimination based on race or ethnic origin' (18). Beyond this, the language is much more tentative. The main emphasis is on openness between groups. The government certainly suggests that immigrants will integrate more effectively if they learn about the history and culture of Quebec, but it is also at pains to acknowledge that immigrants and 'the cultural communities' have contributed to Quebec's history and culture in the past and continue to do so in the present, and that Quebec has an obligation to be open to these contributions. It talks about the history of Quebec as a 'common heritage', while insisting that 'Quebeckers from the cultural communities must be recognized as full-fledged Quebeckers with their similarities and differences' (75). Moreover, these differences may sometimes oblige Quebec to adapt, to modify its practices out of respect for these differences. Thus, for example, it acknowledges that in matters of 'dress, dietary prescriptions, work schedules and the observance of religious holidays' the practices of religious minorities may differ from those of the Christian majority and these differences should be respected wherever feasible (72).

In all this, the contrast with the much stronger demand for linguistic adaptation is striking. There the message was 'Learn French and adopt it as the language of public communication if you want to be accepted'. Here the message is not at all 'Learn about Quebec culture and adopt it as your own public culture if you want to be accepted'. There the message was 'The immigrants' responsibility is to learn French and the government's responsibility is to make that possible and attractive'. Here the message is not (as it could conceivably be) 'The immigrants' responsibility is to internalize Quebec's culture, at least with respect to public interactions, and the government's job is to facilitate that adaptation for them'. On the contrary, the message is that all Québécois, whatever their cultural origins and commitments, have an obligation to be open to one another.

Evaluating the Moral Contract

How should we evaluate this moral contract that Quebec proposes to establish with immigrants? Is it morally permissible for a liberal democratic society to impose these sorts of expectations on newcomers?

Let me make one preliminary point. Talk of a 'moral contract' may seem to suggest that the expectations are legitimate because immigrants were informed about them in advance and came anyway, thus accepting the terms of the contract. The government's document evokes this normative view by saying that 'Applicants will be able to make an informed choice between Quebec and other host-societies' (18). This moral appeal to contractual agreement is seductive but specious. Most immigrants are not able to pick and choose among alternative host societies. They must choose between moving to the one that has admitted them and staying at home. That is still a choice, of course, but it is misleading to construct it as an entirely free choice. It is no doubt true, given the conditions in the world today, that most immigrants would readily agree to Quebec's requirements. But many would undoubtedly agree to much harsher terms, even perhaps indentured servitude. No one today would defend that sort of contract. Consent alone cannot make any agreement whatsoever legitimate, regardless of the circumstances. There are standards of fairness and justice beyond actual consent for assessing the ways in which states treat their own citizens and others. So, the mere fact that Quebec informed immigrants in advance about its expectations would not make the expectations legitimate, not even if the immigrants explicitly said that they understood and accepted them. Quebec does indeed have an obligation to let the immigrants know what it expects, even if the expectations are morally permissible. To that extent, the idea that informed choice matters is correct. But we have to employ independent moral standards for evaluating the legitimacy of the expectations themselves. At a minimum, they must be compatible with liberal democratic principles and respect for human rights to be morally defensible.

Do Quebec's expectations meet these standards? I think so. Let me reverse the order of exposition by starting with an assessment of the way Quebec invokes the principles of democracy and pluralism before I turn to its demands with respect to French.

The Demands of Democracy and Pluralism

Some immigrants may come from cultural traditions in which democracy and pluralism are not valued.[8] That is clearly the presupposition of the

[8] This is not to say that one can presuppose anything about the values of particular immigrants on the basis of the dominant cultural traditions in the countries from which they come. After all, they may have left in part because they rejected elements of their inherited culture and wanted to live under a liberal democratic regime. More generally, one should not assume that immigrants are hostile to liberal democratic values while native-born members support them. Many people who have been born and raised in liberal democratic states have deep commitments to illiberal and undemocratic values, whereas, as just noted, many immigrants have such deep commitments to liberal democratic values that they have left home to live in a state that is committed to respect them. Nevertheless, in thinking about what sorts of cultural adaptation one may expect of immigrants, it is not unreasonable to assume that at least some of the immigrants come without a commitment to liberal democratic values and to inquire what that entails for the issue of cultural adaptation.

government's document at many points. But Quebec says that immigrants ought to recognize and respect Quebec's fundamental commitment to the values of democracy and pluralism. In other words, democracy and pluralism are aspects of Quebec's political culture, and Quebec aims to protect and maintain that culture and to demand that immigrants accept it. How can that demand be justified?

One answer is that immigrants to Quebec ought to recognize and respect the values of democracy and pluralism, not (as the government's document seems at times to suggest) because these are Quebec's 'social choices', but rather because respect for these values is the precondition for the maintenance of a morally legitimate political order. To repudiate these values, at least with respect to the public culture, is to advocate injustice. This answer obviously presupposes that liberal democracy is the only just political order, at least under modern political conditions. I suggested in Chapter 2 that this is the view of most contemporary liberals, even one like Michael Walzer who appears to deny it but then implicitly relies upon it for his own arguments. In any event, it is my view. That view requires a defence, of course, but the elaboration of such a defence goes beyond the scope of this book.

A second answer might be connected more specifically to the immigrants' position *vis-à-vis* the receiving society. Immigrants should accept the values of pluralism and democracy because these are the very values that provide immigrants with a moral basis for challenging certain kinds of demands for cultural adaptation or cultural conformity. Why are the Québécois morally obliged to respect the pre-existing social identities of immigrants at all? What would be morally objectionable about coercive forms of assimilation or about the social and political subordination of those who refuse to assimilate or are incapable of doing so? If the answers to these questions depend on appeals to liberal democratic conceptions of people as free and equal moral agents, as I think they do, then they presuppose a commitment to the values of pluralism and democracy as outlined in the government's document. Hence it would not be possible for immigrants to reject pluralism and democracy without rejecting the very principles they need to employ in order to claim moral standing in the first place.[9]

These general arguments conceal some deep perplexities, however. In what sense are immigrants morally obliged to accept the values of pluralism and

---

[9] This argument presupposes that immigrants are seeking to engage in a moral dialogue with Québécois who themselves accept democracy and pluralism and that the immigrants are seeking to appeal to principles that such Québécois would respect. To develop this argument at a deeper level, one would have to show that there is no alternative (illiberal and anti-democratic) set of principles that is morally superior to democracy and pluralism, or at least one would have to make a positive case for democracy and pluralism. But as I say in the text, that goes beyond the scope of this book. In this project, I am simply assuming the moral validity of liberal democratic principles and trying to explore what they entail.

democracy? Is 'acceptance' a question of behaviour or belief, of external conformity or internal integration?

All that is required, in my view, is that people accept these values as political values, as the principles that regulate the public life of the society. Liberal democratic principles establish norms about actions and even discourse that people are morally obliged to respect in the public sphere. But this does not mean that every person must be a liberal democrat in her heart of hearts. It is not morally forbidden in liberal democracies to believe, say, that Plato's views on justice and the relative ranking of regimes are correct.[10]

Liberal democracies have a very deep commitment to freedom of religion, of conscience, of thought, and of opinion. One might expect sociologically that most people's beliefs will eventually tend to conform to their actions and that they will find ways to reinterpret their values so as to make them compatible with the ways in which they are expected to behave, so that people living in liberal democratic regimes will tend to adopt liberal democratic values, at least over the long run. But that is very different from saying that people have a moral obligation to abandon their philosophical judgements, moral convictions, or religious beliefs to the extent that these conflict with democracy and pluralism. On the contrary, it is characteristic of liberal democratic societies that they are (or ought to be) open even to views that challenge the basic presuppositions of the regime.[11]

Take the norm of 'equality of the sexes' which Quebec cites as a fundamental democratic value. The government's document seems to suggest at various points that immigrants who come from cultures that do not accept this value must learn to do so. But as I argued in the previous chapter, we must distinguish between the public political culture of a liberal democratic state and the cultures of religious and ethnic groups. It is right to insist that the public political culture must be committed to gender equality, but, at the same time, the commitment to pluralism requires liberal democratic states to tolerate group cultures that conflict with this norm.

Let me place this issue in a more concrete context with regard to Quebec. The traditional Catholicism that was such a deep part of Quebec's culture prior to the Quiet Revolution was deeply patriarchal. Indeed, it seems fair to

---

[10] Of course, Plato himself thought that democracies permitted all sorts of opinions, including opinions about the merits of different regimes. This uncontrolled freedom—of opinion and everything else—was what made democracies such an inferior form of regime in his view. See *Republic* Book VIII (Plato 1991).

[11] I am not suggesting that this openness is unlimited. For one thing, there is the familiar problem of the toleration of the intolerant in liberal democratic societies, and it can be argued that there is no obligation to tolerate those who actually threaten the existence of the regime. But the mere fact that some people may hold illiberal or undemocratic views does not in itself constitute such a threat (Rawls 1971: 216–21). For another thing, particular cultural practices may be so incompatible with liberal democratic norms (e.g. regarding gender) that they should be prohibited, even though they pose no political threat to the regime. I explore the claim that Muslim immigrants have such practices in the next chapter.

say that it was hostile to the principles of democracy and pluralism, at least as they are generally interpreted in Quebec today.[12] But like every revolution, the Quiet Revolution met some resistance. It did not elicit unanimous support. Presumably there are people in Quebec today who still hold to this traditional Catholicism, perhaps even young people who have acquired traditional Catholic beliefs and values from their parents.[13] What does Quebec expect of them? Presumably it does not expect them to abandon their religious convictions. Certainly it does expect them to obey the laws which include various laws against discrimination on the basis of sex and also laws requiring them to send their children to schools where they may be exposed in various ways to the values of gender equality, and more broadly of pluralism and democracy.[14] Quebec can reasonably demand the same of immigrants. But no more.

Democracy, Pluralism, and the Distinct Society

Thus far I have been exploring whether Quebec is morally entitled to expect immigrants to accept the principles of pluralism and democracy, two of the three elements in Quebec's proposed moral contract with immigrants. My answer to that has been 'yes', with the qualifications and clarifications that I have just discussed. But Quebec is entitled to expect this of immigrants, at

---

[12] This is evident even in the government's document (17). It is this earlier illiberal Quebec that opponents of Quebec often evoke in criticizing the delegation of the central government's powers to Quebec and in insisting that final authority on matters relating to individual rights and liberties should rest with the central government.They imply and sometimes even explicitly say that the transformation is only skin deep. The Québécois respond with understandable irritation to all this, noting that the record of the rest of Canada, both the central government and the other provinces, is far from unblemished when it comes to protecting rights and liberties (not least of francophones) and that the Québécois almost always do as well as or better than non-Québécois in surveys on toleration and liberal values generally.

[13] The Catholic Church went through its own revolution with Vatican II, but not everyone joined that revolution either and it has arguably been reversed much more than Quebec's Quiet Revolution. There are many traditional Catholic beliefs and values (e.g. on issues of gender equality) which continue to play an important role in the lives of some Catholics and which are not easily reconciled with Quebec's current understanding of democracy and pluralism.

[14] This is undoubtedly an optimistic reading of what goes on in Quebec's schools (if they are anything like other schools in North America), but it would not be unrealistic to think that the messages the students get from Quebec's schools today are generally more sympathetic to gender equality, pluralism, and democracy than the messages they would have received in a traditional Catholic education forty years ago.

Quebec does permit private schools, but even private religious schools are subject to public regulation to some extent. In fact in Quebec, as in other parts of Canada, much of the public school system has an explicit religious affiliation as either Catholic or Protestant, so that the incentive for the Christian segment of the population to create separate private schools is substantially less than in the United States where the constitutional requirement of the separation of church and state greatly restricts the connections between religion and public education. Of course, these denominational public schools are subject to closer and greater restraints than private religious schools.

least according to my analysis, only because these principles are not unique to Quebec but are characteristic requirements of all liberal democratic societies.

Not only are Quebec's demands regarding democracy and pluralism not unique to Quebec, but the very liberal democratic commitments that Quebec wants immigrants to respect severely limit the kinds of cultural adaptation or personal transformation that Quebec can demand of immigrants. We see here why the idea that justice requires a hands off approach to culture has such power. Justice does require a hands off approach to many of the choices people make about how to live their lives. The fact of becoming an immigrant cannot mean that one has given oneself up to the receiving society to be made over according to its will, at least not in a society that respects liberal democratic principles. The government's document is obviously well aware of this and develops the point in talking about free choice of 'lifestyles, opinions, [and] values' as well as in its affirmation of the rights of minorities to pursue their own cultural interests. Given such principles, on what basis could Quebec claim that immigrants have an obligation to accept some specific aspect of Quebec's culture? It will never be a sufficient reason to expect conformity to say that the values and norms in question are shared by most of the non-immigrant population. In their dress and diet, in their reading and recreations, in their interests and inclinations, in their relationships and, generally, in how they live, immigrants should be left free to choose their own course, including retaining as much of their culture of origin as they wish, without suffering any moral disapprobation or social pressures to the contrary from the government or the people of Quebec.

I do not mean to overstate the likelihood that immigrants will not adapt to the dominant culture of Quebec. On the contrary, as a matter of sociological fact, most immigrants do undergo profound cultural transformations if they move to a country in which most people share a very different culture. Even trying to retain one's original culture in that sort of environment requires adaptation and change. Moreover, market forces and the mass media have powerful socializing and homogenizing effects in modern mass consumption, capitalist societies. Furthermore, one should not assume that adaptation always goes against the grain for immigrants. Many immigrants have a strong desire to integrate culturally, at least to some extent. In addition, the children of immigrants face even more powerful and fundamental socializing experiences in the public schools, even if the schools are committed to pluralism and are open to influences from sources outside the dominant culture. For all these reasons and more, immigrants to Quebec are likely to become much more like the rest of the population of Quebec after they have lived there for a while than they were before they arrived.

But would Quebec be satisfied with such empirical expectations, coupled with and constrained by the public recognition that Quebec as a society is not entitled to expect or demand any specific cultural adaptation from immigrants? I think not. What would this leave of the vision that immigration can help Quebec to build a distinct society? The phrase 'distinct society' certainly evokes the image of a society with a distinctive culture. Immigrants can contribute to building a distinct society then, only to the extent that they contribute to and share in that distinctive culture. Is that to be left as a purely contingent, empirical development? Is there no sense in which Quebec can say that it *expects* immigrants to join in building the distinct society? Clearly the whole thrust of the document we have been considering is exactly the opposite. The whole point of the 'moral contract' between Quebec and its immigrants is to provide a normative foundation for the claim that immigrants will contribute to building Quebec's distinct society, to say that Quebec can legitimately expect them to contribute to the project of building the distinct society (as well as to identify Quebec's obligations to them in return). But what we have just seen is that the principles of democracy and pluralism are in no way distinctive to Quebec and that commitment to these principles limits severely any normative demand for adaptation to a distinctive, local culture. So, what kind of obligation might the immigrants have that would be specific to Quebec's distinct society, not common to any liberal democracy?

The Moral Status of Quebec's Commitment to French[15]

The answer, of course, is the third element of the moral contract, the principle that immigrants should accept French as the language of public life in Quebec. As we have seen, there are specific and strong normative expectations of immigrants put forward in connection with this principle, such as that immigrants should try to learn French and should accept the fact that their children will be educated in French in the public schools and that French is the language of public life. Are these expectations justifiable? I will argue that they are, but also that the corresponding obligations they impose on Quebec require a public, official understanding of the distinct society that is at odds with, and may eventually lead to a transformation of, the popular understanding of the distinct society.

In considering Quebec's language policies, we must keep in mind the distinction between claims about what is morally permissible and claims about what course a society ought to take among the morally permissible alternatives. Many of the objections to Quebec's policies are inspired by a particular vision of the kind of country Canada ought to be, not by a claim

---

[15] My position in this section is, I think, generally compatible with the one taken by Charles Taylor in his well-known discussion of these issues, though I construct my arguments rather differently (Taylor 1994). See also Tully (1995).

about what justice requires, though the two are sometimes confounded. Some people think that English should have an even more hegemonic position than it already enjoys in Canada, because it is the language of the majority. On this view, French should not have equal official status with English because francophones comprise only about 25 per cent of the population of Canada. Others remain committed to the idea that Canada should be a bilingual state but favour what has been called personal bilingualism. They want a Canada that has two official languages throughout its territory, so that (ideally) citizens could use French or English as they wished wherever they were in Canada. At the very least, they would be able to receive public services in French or English, including public education, anywhere in the country.[16] Quebec's government also has a vision of Canada as a bilingual country, with two official languages for its federal institutions. But most social institutions are under provincial jurisdiction, and Quebec's view is that each province should be free to establish itself as bilingual or to adopt one of the two official languages. This approach has been called territorial bilingualism. Quebec, of course, has followed this policy, establishing French as its official language.

I do not intend to try to assess the merits of these competing visions of Canada.[17] Rather I wish only to argue that Quebec's vision is a morally permissible one, that it does not violate the minimal moral standards that a liberal democratic society ought to meet. As we saw in Chapter 3, Belgium and Switzerland have versions of territorial bilingualism that resemble Quebec's vision in many respects, although Quebec provides more extensive public services to its anglophone minority than the sub-units of these states usually do to their linguistic minorities. With respect to public schooling, this largely reflects the requirements of the Canadian Constitution, but in other important ways the services go well beyond what is required by federal law. As I argued in Chapter 3, this basic pattern of linguistic policy falls within the parameters of what is required by a conception of justice as evenhandedness.

While territorial bilingualism may be broadly justifiable as one way of accommodating linguistic differences within a state, there may be objections to particular features of the way such a policy is implemented. I can imagine three moral objections that might be launched from the perspective of immigrants to Quebec against Quebec's language policies. (1) Some parts of Quebec's language legislation not only promote the use of French but restrict the use of other languages, thus interfering with the linguistic freedom of individuals in a way that is morally impermissible. (2) It is not justifiable to treat the

---

[16] Various aspects of this policy have been implemented, at least in theory. This includes a requirement that commercial packaging contain product information in both French and English. However, in some parts of Canada, one is much more likely to find a cereal box with French on it than a public servant who understands French.

[17] Some versions of English hegemony would be unjust for reasons spelled out in Chapter 3, but that is not my focus here.

acquisition of French as a precondition for full acceptance into Quebec society and to impose a moral duty to learn French and to accept French as the language of public life. (3) The policy of requiring immigrants to send their children to French language public schools (if they send them to public schools) is unfair when native-born anglophone Canadians have the right to send their children to English language public schools.

Of the three objections, I regard the third as the most important for the purposes of this chapter because it entails a specific demand relating to linguistic integration aimed primarily at immigrants. I will argue that Quebec's policy is entirely defensible. With respect to the other two, I see some merit in the objections, but I do not regard either one as especially important. All of the policies to which the objections refer must be understood in the context of the potential vulnerability of the French language for the historical and demographic reasons that I discussed above. All of the policies are defensive. In other words, they are not aimed at establishing the hegemony of French over the disparate languages of origin of the immigrants. If the contest were between French and the immigrants' languages of origin, Quebec could simply rely on the normal social advantages of the majority language in a society to create sufficient incentives for immigrants and their children to learn French. Indeed, as I noted above, Quebec actually spends money to support heritage language programmes for immigrants. Quebec's primary concern, obviously, is that immigrants will choose to learn English rather than French, because of the dominance of English on the North American continent and that such a pattern of linguistic adaptation in Quebec would render French vulnerable over the long run, especially if Quebec took in substantial numbers of immigrants.

I start with the first objection. Most of Quebec's language legislation is aimed at promoting French, rather than at restricting any other language, and to the extent that it is restrictive, the target is clearly English not the various other languages that immigrants bring with them to Quebec. Moreover, it is aimed primarily at the regulation of commercial activities. It seeks to ensure both that the francophone majority will not be disadvantaged in the workplace because of their language, as they had been historically, and that the public face of Quebec, as presented in commercial advertisements, will be a French face. Quebec explicitly affirms, as I noted above, that individuals may use the language of their choice in private interactions and in cultural and political expressions. It is only commercial speech that is regulated. Nevertheless, one law did prohibit people from posting commercial signs outside their place of business in any language other than French. The main object of the legislation was undoubtedly to prevent highly visible commercial advertising in English, especially by large Anglo-run enterprises. Nevertheless, the law was comprehensive and thus also formally prohibited immigrant shopkeepers from posting signs in their language of origin outside their shops, even though their primary clientele might be fellow immigrants.

This is a small issue in many respects, but I do regard it as an unreasonable restriction of linguistic freedom. As I argued in Chapter 3, the conception of justice as neutrality rightly condemns prohibitions on a person's use of her own language. If someone wants to communicate in her native tongue, the political community should keep its hands off. Moreover, as anyone who has walked through the ethnic neighbourhoods of Toronto or New York can testify, the signs on the shops are an integral part of the cultural life of the local communities, so that prohibiting such signs has a restrictive impact beyond its effect on the individual shopkeeper. The fact that the law was normally not aggressively enforced in immigrant neighbourhoods lessened the damage somewhat but did not make it legitimate in principle. A number of commentators (including the Supreme Court of Canada) suggested it would not be objectionable to have legislation requiring that signs using languages other than French also communicate their messages in French and could even require that the French lettering be more visible. A positive requirement for French along with other languages can be seen as a way of addressing in an evenhanded fashion both the interests of individuals in communication in their own language (even in commercial contexts) and the interests of the francophone majority in the political community in creating a French linguistic landscape as part of its effort to secure the place of French in a North American context dominated by English. Avigail Eisenberg has conducted a careful and illuminating study of the judicial reasoning of the Canadian Supreme Court in cases affecting this language legislation and related issues (Eisenberg 1994). She shows that the judges do not think of these issues primarily as ones involving a conflict between individual and group rights but rather as ones raising the question of the appropriate recognition due to different cultures and identities. The problem with the Quebec sign law was not that it required French (an appropriate insistence on cultural recognition) but that it prohibited other languages, denying their speakers the recognition that was due to them. In response to these criticisms, perhaps especially to a critical judgement by a United Nations human rights tribunal, Quebec revised its legislation to require only that French be predominant on signs.[18]

The second objection is partly informed by the sense that expecting people to learn French, or at least treating the acquisition of French as a moral duty, asks too much of people. The overall approach of the policy document is to present a version of liberal democracy that links rights with duties both for the immigrants and for Quebec. In that respect, it differs from some versions of liberalism that focus almost exclusively on the rights of individuals against society, and I think it is generally on the right track. The duty to learn French

---

[18]   For further discussion of these cases see Tully (1995).

is intimately connected to the duty to contribute to and participate in society, which is connected, on this account, to fundamental democratic principles. Learning French is, among other things, a necessary means to participation in society so that if one can defend the duty to participate, and I think one can, one can defend the duty to learn French. Moreover, the goal of this discourse about duty is not the legitimation of moral condemnations of, say, isolated immigrant women for failing to learn French. On the contrary, the document makes clear that Quebec must reach out to immigrants, especially to those who are socially isolated, to make it possible and attractive for them to learn French. Furthermore, the document recognizes that language acquisition is something that occurs over a long period of time. Undoubtedly, there might be particular circumstances in which it would be unreasonable to expect an immigrant to learn French, but on the whole it seems to me that the document is balancing the relevant considerations in an evenhanded way and establishing a reasonable expectation that immigrants to Quebec ought to meet.

Despite this general defence, it may be useful to consider more closely what is being demanded, to see whether it asks too much of immigrants. What does it mean from the immigrants' perspective to have to learn French as a condition of integration into Quebec? What sort of personal transformation does this entail? How significant a demand is it in terms of the immigrants' pre-existing or future cultural commitments?

In addressing these questions, let me distinguish between two conflicting ideal types of what language acquisition entails with respect to one's own cultural commitments. The first sees language in purely instrumental terms, as a means of communication and no more. On this account, learning a language has no necessary or even likely impact on one's other cultural commitments. Call this the thin theory of language. The second view sees a shared language as centrally connected to and expressive of the culture of a community. On this view, learning a language shapes our cultural options and commitments in profound ways. Call this the thick theory of language.

My own view is that what language acquisition entails for other dimensions of one's cultural world ranges between these two ideal types, varying according to the circumstances in which the language is acquired and other circumstances as well. An immigrant who learns French as an adult may have already adopted deep cultural commitments. Learning French does not require her to abandon any of them, although it is likely to open her to new influences and to make her less tied to, because less dependent upon, her culture of origin. For adults then, learning French is, at least potentially, a liberating experience that opens new possibilities without foreclosing old ones (though I have to acknowledge immediately that not everyone experiences liberation as a positive thing).

An immigrant to Quebec who learns French as a child is likely to be much more profoundly affected by the experience than one who learns it as an adult. To learn a language as a child is normally to acquire a culture, at least to some extent, in part because one learns the language primarily in the course of learning other things. In school, children hear stories and acquire models for behaviour, both formally through the things they read and experience in the curriculum and informally through their interactions with other people, especially with their peers. Thus, it seems plausible to argue that a language acquired as a child is normally much more likely to have the intimate connection to one's most fundamental cultural commitments that the thick theory ascribes to it than a language acquired as an adult. Still, one ought not to overstate the cultural significance of language or to posit a necessary connection between language and cultural orientation. In a society committed to pluralism, as Quebec is, the same language may be a vehicle for widely different and conflicting cultural values and perspectives. And the cultural messages a child receives from her family and local community may or may not be congruent with the ones she gets at school from authorities and peers.

On the account I have just given, the norms about learning French are much more significant for the cultural commitments of children than of adults. That makes the third objection, which focuses on the exclusion of immigrants' children from the English language public school system in Quebec particularly important. Some people see this as the kind of policy that Kymlicka calls an internal restriction, a means of maintaining a cultural community by limiting the rights of members and forcing them to belong (Moon 1993). Primary education is compulsory in Quebec (as in every Western society), and in restricting immigrants to French language schools, Quebec has indeed deprived recent immigrants of a legal right that previous immigrants had enjoyed. Nevertheless, I think that Quebec's policy is entirely justifiable. The previous legal right was never a fundamental moral entitlement. As I argued in Chapter 3, no one is entitled to an education at public expense in the language of his or her choice. And the previous system did not provide that option. It offered education in only two languages. In removing the English language option for immigrants (and for francophone Québécois, too), the Quebec government was making the sort of choice among alternative educational policies that democratic governments are fully entitled to make, judging what allocation of educational resources and options will best meet the needs of the community as a whole over the long run as well as the needs of particular students in the near term. No action has done more to integrate immigrants with the francophone community and none is more likely to have lasting, long-term effects with respect to linguistic integration. These are important and legitimate social goals. The change reduced the options for immigrants, but it did not deprive them of anything to which they had a fundamental right and it does not violate the norm of justice as evenhandedness.

If Quebec were an independent state without any system of public education in English, no one would suppose that immigrants had a moral right to
expect that their children should be educated in a language other than that
used by the vast majority of the population. For reasons explored in Chapter
3, it is normally justifiable to require immigrants to be educated in the dominant language of the territory they have entered. In other linguistically
divided societies like Belgium and Switzerland, the children of immigrants
(like the children of citizens) do not normally enjoy the right to demand an
education in any of the state's official languages. It is only because Quebec is
part of Canada (which does have extensive provisions for education in both
official languages) and because Quebec has a system of public education in
English in place that the view that immigrants should have the option of an
English language education seems at all plausible.

One argument against Quebec's policy focuses on the principle of equal
treatment. It goes something like this. Perhaps Quebec has no moral obligation to provide a system of public education in English, but if it does provide
such a system it must provide it as an option to all, not just to some. The
suggestion is that restricting the English language system to the children of
people educated in English in Canada, Quebec is discriminating against the
children of immigrants.

If the option of attending English language public schools were open to
the children of francophone Québécois, but not to the children of immigrants, this argument would be more persuasive. Then one could claim that
immigrants were selected for disadvantageous treatment, that the government was not being evenhanded. As it is, the argument depends on the claim
that the children of anglophone Canadians are unduly privileged in Quebec
in relation to everyone else. It is a claim that seems implausible on its face.
An independent Quebec could respond to such a criticism by abolishing the
English language system of education altogether, thus treating everyone the
same. The harshness of that approach reveals the flaws of a formalistic
approach to equality. To treat everyone the same is not always to treat them
evenhandedly. As I argued in Chapter 3 long-settled linguistic minorities have
much stronger interests in having public education provided in their own
language than do recent immigrants. In Quebec's unusual circumstances (i.e.
its position as a French island in an English sea and the extensive English
language institutions already established in Quebec), immigrants might have
some interest in being able to have their children educated in a language
which is not that of the majority in the territory, but this interest should not
be regarded as so weighty that it would be unjust not to satisfy it. The immigrants' interest in choosing the language of education of their children may
properly be weighed against the interests of the francophone majority in
securing French as the language of public life.

As a province of Canada, Quebec is bound by constitutional requirements to provide an English language public education to the children of any Canadian who received an English language education in Canada, but not to other children. The critics of Quebec's policy rarely mention that the other provinces of Canada are under no obligation to offer a French language education to their inhabitants (whether recent immigrants or citizens of long descent) unless the children have a parent who received a French language public education in Canada. Even when there is a system of French language public education established, anglophone parents can be and often are denied the right to send their children to these schools.[19] Thus the question becomes whether the Canadian Constitution is morally justified in providing special guarantees regarding education in the language of one's parents to the two major language groups in Canada. I think that is a morally permissible policy, for the reasons I have offered here and in Chapter 3 regarding the differences between the interests of immigrants and long-standing linguistic minorities.

Integration and Identity in Quebec

Having argued for the moral permissibility of Quebec's policies on integration, at least for the most part, I want to turn in the final part of the chapter to the question of how Quebec's policies on integration affect its self-understanding as a political community, or, to hypostatize less, how Québécois who support these policies are likely to think of Quebec as a distinct society.

So far we have seen that Quebec's commitment to pluralism means that the only distinctive cultural commitment (i.e. the only commitment that is not common to every liberal democratic society) that Quebec requires of immigrants for full social membership is knowledge of French. There is no requirement that immigrants prove their loyalty to Quebec by proclaiming an attachment to its symbols or an identification with its history, though Quebec seeks to promote both of these attitudes as we shall see. Immigrants can be full members of Quebec's distinct society even if they look and act differently from the substantial segment of the population whose ancestors inhabited Quebec and even if they do not in any way alter their own customs and cultural patterns with respect to work and play, diet and dress, sleep and sex, celebration and mourning, so long as they act within the confines of the law.

On this account, given the commitment to pluralism, Quebec's distinct

---

[19] It is often the francophone schools that choose to exclude anglophone children whose parents want them to receive a French language education. They do this out of fear that the anglophone children's lesser competence in the language will have a deleterious effect on the overall quality of the education provided to those whose native tongue is French. But this still illustrates the point that there is no individualized right to instruction in the official language of one's choice.

society becomes identified, almost exclusively, with the French Fact. That is, Quebec's distinctiveness consists essentially in the fact that it is a society situated in North America in which the vast majority of the population speak French (whether as a first or second language is irrelevant) and in which French is the language of public life. There may be other facts about Quebec that would mark it off to an outside observer as different from other societies or other cultural commitments that are widely shared by Québécois and not by members of other societies, but such facts and commitments are not and cannot be normatively central to Quebec's project of building a distinct society.

Some see Quebec's claim to cultural distinctiveness as superficial, if not false. They argue that Quebec's embrace of liberal capitalism since the 1960s has essentially destroyed the distinctive culture it once enjoyed and rendered it virtually indistinguishable from other North American societies, despite the linguistic differences. Can one build a distinct society on the basis of language alone? Is a shared language sufficient for a claim of cultural distinctiveness? I do not have any particular views on this question. It seems to me to be just the sort of issue that ought to be left to the people of Quebec to decide. How much do they value this form of distinctiveness? Do they regard it as significant, as something relevant to their identities as individuals and as citizens?

These questions point to an ambiguity in the principle that French is to be accepted as the language of public life, because immigrants must be included in the group to whom these questions are addressed. Unlike the commitment to democracy and pluralism, which can be defended on independent moral grounds, the commitment to French as the language of public life clearly is something that derives its normative status entirely from the fact that it is Quebec's 'social choice', that is, from the fact that the majority of Québécois are deeply committed to this principle. But that commitment could change. In saying that immigrants are morally obliged to accept French as the language of public life, then, the government must appeal to respect for the democratic process. But once immigrants are members of Quebec's society, and certainly once they have become citizens, they have a right to participate in that process, or, as the document itself says, 'to help define the major orientations of our society' (17). But language policy cannot be excluded from the democratic process in which the immigrants participate. If immigrants or their adult children choose to try to reshape Quebec's linguistic orientation, say, by supporting a more bilingual public policy, they cannot be criticized for violating the moral contract.

The importance of this issue will increase as the proportion of immigrants in Quebec's population increases, which it will if the policies outlined in the document are followed. Moreover, immigrants would not have to constitute a majority of the population in order to have significant, perhaps even decisive weight, if the Quebec-born francophone population were divided. In

the long run then, the viability of Quebec's distinct society and the maintenance of the French Fact may depend in important respects on the extent to
which immigrants and their children identify with, and are committed to,
that project. To be sure, if the children have been educated in French, if they
have become francophones, they may feel that their interests would be served
most by preserving the position of French in Quebec. But the project of maintaining the distinct society may well depend on their having a deeper, less
instrumental commitment than that.

How can that commitment be created? By making sure that the project of
the distinct society is genuinely open to them, that it is not too closely identified with a particular group, namely, those descended from the francophone
settlers of the seventeenth and eighteenth centuries. What appeared above as
a moral imperative arising out of a commitment to pluralism—a conception
of Quebec society with no specific cultural commitments beyond democracy,
pluralism, and the French language—reappears here as a political imperative
arising out of the need to enlist the support of immigrants and their children
in the project of maintaining the French language in Quebec. In integrating
immigrants, Quebec is transforming not only their identity but its own as
well.

In Quebec, the word 'multiculturalism' has pejorative connotations, in
part because a federal commission which was charged several years ago with
the task of developing policies for Canada based on its *bicultural* and bilingual
character emerged, after consultation with immigrant groups among others,
with a recommendation that Canada think of itself as a *multicultural* and
bilingual country. Francophone Québécois were outraged by this decision,
seeing it as a policy that placed francophone culture on a par with that of
minority ethnic groups and that betrayed the conception of Canada as a
country built upon two 'founding nations'.[20] But now they face the same
dilemma in Quebec, whatever term they choose to use. If the collective identity of Quebec is too closely tied with the 'founding nation' and with its
particular history and culture, then immigrants and their children will find it
hard to feel as though they belong to that collectivity and will be disinclined
to support its projects. But if the collectivity is defined in the open way that
I have been suggesting, with an almost exclusive emphasis on the French
language as the shared cultural commitment and without any claim of privilege or priority for the more particular features of the history and culture of
the descendants of the settlers, then Quebec is committed to its own internal
version of multiculturalism, even if it rejects that term.

One might object here that the policy document upon which I have been
relying so heavily in my analysis is not representative of the views of the
government as a whole, not to mention the population at large. After all, it

---

[20] See note 3 above.

was issued by a ministry which is responsible not only for immigration but also for 'the cultural communities' of Quebec. It would not be surprising if this institutional location led to an official line from this ministry which was more open and more pluralistic than the position of other parts of the government.

There is certainly something to this concern. Indeed, the document itself is titled *Vision* which certainly suggests that there is some gap between the principles it professes and the social and political realities of immigration in Quebec.[21] Surveys of the population on attitudes towards immigrants and membership in Quebec indicate that the positions proposed by the document are not universally accepted. Moreover, the document itself expresses a degree of frustration that other parts of the government do not seem to feel it necessary to think about the implications of their policies for immigrants and the cultural communities, treating that as the preserve of a single ministry.

While there are reasons for caution therefore in viewing Quebec through the lens provided by this document, I think that the document nevertheless captures something fundamental about the normative logic of immigration in Quebec, and perhaps in any modern liberal democratic society. I will try to illustrate the working of this normative logic by discussing briefly a couple of examples of the ways in which the presence of immigrants has affected discourse about Quebec's identity and policies in apparently unrelated areas.[22]

The first illustration concerns a report drawn up for Montreal's School Council, called 'Les Francophones québécois' (Bouchard *et al.* 1991) The Council had already commissioned a series of reports on Montreal's ethnic communities and their cultures and thought it would be useful to commission a report on that huge part of the population that had French as a mother tongue and that was not composed of or descended from recent immigrants. I use this awkward phrase because, as the report indicated, there was no convenient label. It rejected the terms 'Canadiens' and 'Canadiens français' which were formerly used about this population but which fell into disfavour with the rise of a nationalist sentiment closely tied to the territory and government of Quebec. What about 'Québécois français?' Too narrow, it said,

---

[21] One famous incident illustrates some of the ambiguities of contemporary Quebec nationalism. In 1995, Quebec held a referendum on sovereignty. The pro-sovereignty forces were defeated very narrowly (i.e. by about 1 per cent of the vote) and received a clear majority of francophone votes according to all subsequent surveys and analyses. On the evening of the vote, after the outcome was clear, Jacques Parizeau, the then Premier of Quebec, gave a speech announcing his resignation and asserting that the defeat was due only to 'money and the ethnic vote' and that a majority of the Quebec people had clearly expressed their desire for sovereignty. But most other major sovereigntist figures, including Lucien Bouchard, the leader of the movement and the current Premier of Quebec, repudiated Parizeau's exclusion of ethnic groups (i.e. immigrants) from the Quebec people and his implicit denial of the legitimacy of their participation.

[22] Normative logics do not always triumph in politics, but it is instructive to understand them none the less.

because settlers from Ireland, Scotland, and elsewhere integrated with this group culturally and linguistically centuries ago. And, I suspect, that phrase might have sounded a bit too much like the description of an ethnic group, and the authors did not want this population to be thought of as just another ethnic group, no matter how large. Finally, it settled on 'Francophones québé- cois' while acknowledging that this label, too, was unsatisfactory because it placed primary emphasis on language and the point was to identify and describe a shared historical culture. Besides, did the term include recent fran- cophone immigrants from places like Haiti and Belgium? To exclude them would seem insulting. What are they if not *francophones québécois*? But to include them would distract the project from its central focus.

This long discussion of labels reveals an ambiguity about identity and legit- imacy that runs throughout the report. The authors are clearly committed to linking Quebec's distinct society and its nationalist project to a specific history and culture, but they want to do that without repudiating pluralism and democracy. They want to affirm a Quebec in which everyone is a full member, regardless of origin, and simultaneously one in which a particular culture holds a privileged place. This leads to a tortuous discussion at many points.

In general, the report faces the following dilemma. The more closely it identifies Quebec with the francophone community and francophone culture, the more open that community and culture have to be to people who speak French but are not descended from French settlers and thus open to diverse cultural influences. The more it ties the identity of the francophone community to a specific history, to specific cultural practices, and especially to specific lines of descent (i.e. the more particularistic it is), the stronger the claim for the distinctiveness of this francophone community but the weaker the claim for identifying this particular community, even though numerically very large, with Quebec as a state. Others can then say, 'We are citizens too, and we clearly do not belong to your group and can't join it because it's an ascriptive group, so it is not fair to identify the state with a group that comprehends only part of the population, even if it is the largest part. In particular, it is not fair to use the state to impose the norms and values of your group on people whom the group is not willing to accept.'

The report dances around these issues in various ways, at times emphasiz- ing the historical particularity of the *francophonie québécoise* and at times emphasizing its openness to others on pluralist, not assimilationalist, terms. One striking feature of the report is that despite the authors' commitment to making the historical francophone community central, when it turned to the question of the integration of immigrants it came up with a list of expectations remarkably similar to the one provided in the document that I have discussed at length here: learning French; sharing fundamental values of democracy, liberty, toleration, citizenship, and equality of the sexes; participation in

economic, cultural, and political life. To this it added learning about the territory, institutions, and history of the *francophonie québécoise* and respecting and
appropriating the symbols at the heart of public life in Quebec, such as the flag
and the national holiday. (The last addition brought a sharp retort from a
representative of ethnic groups in Quebec about preferring the Canadian flag,
a retort that illustrates again the ways in which Quebec's status as a province
creates dilemmas for its nationalist project, since Canada provides alternative
symbols of political legitimacy to which those who are disaffected with
Quebec's course or who feel excluded from its project can appeal.)

In the minds of most people, both inside and outside Quebec, the phrase
'distinct society' is intimately connected to the preservation and development of the (evolving) historical culture shared by people who are largely
descended from the original French settlers in Quebec. But in a society which
takes in substantial numbers of immigrants and tries to integrate them with
francophone institutions and public life without requiring cultural assimilation, that connection is harder to maintain. It does not entirely disappear, of
course, but it loses much of its normative force. Such historical links can no
longer serve as a criterion of authenticity for what is or is not part of the
culture of Quebec's distinct society. With the opening of francophone institutions and public life to immigrants, it becomes necessary to think of the
culture of Quebec's distinct society as including whatever is part of the culture
of the inhabitants of Quebec.[23] Indeed, the very concept of francophone
culture in Quebec takes on a systematic ambiguity.

Let me conclude with another story that illustrates the dynamics at work
here and the ways in which immigration transforms the identity of Quebec
as a community even while immigrants are being transformed into
Québécois. The Quebec government set up a programme in Ontario (and a
few other provinces) to support francophone culture outside Quebec. This
was motivated largely by a desire to respond in some way to the complaints
of francophones outside Quebec that they had been thrown to the anglophone wolves by Quebec's focus on provincial autonomy rather than linguistic solidarity, and those complaints aroused some sympathy in Quebec
because of the sense that these francophones elsewhere shared the same
cultural and ethnic roots as francophones in Quebec. But then representatives
of a group of francophone African–Canadians applied for a grant under this
programme to support a cultural newspaper for francophone
African–Canadians in Ontario. How were Quebec officials to respond? This

---

[23] Perhaps I should say the culture of those inhabitants who use French (and not simply those
for whom it is the mother tongue). The latter more qualified phrase leaves open, in particular, the
possibility of thinking about anglophone culture in Quebec as a minority culture rather than as an
integral part of the culture of the distinct society. Many people would object to that, arguing that
Quebec anglophones must also be counted as full Québécois and that their anglophone culture also
contributes to Quebec's distinct society. I do not want to enter that debate here.

was clearly not the sort of thing they had in mind in setting up the programme. If they gave the grant, people in Quebec might ask why the Quebec government was spending its money on multicultural activities for recent immigrants to Ontario. Wasn't that the job of Ontario or of the federal government? What did these people have to do with Quebec? But if they denied the grant, what grounds could they use? The applicants were francophones after all. Could they say that they had intended the programme for those with ethnic ties to Québécois? Not really. Besides some of these people probably did have ethnic ties to Québécois, that is, to the new Québécois from francophone Africa. And if francophone culture within Quebec is now genuinely open to Asian and African francophones, as the public rhetoric declares, how could the francophone culture outside Quebec worthy of support be narrowly defined in terms of ethnic or historical links to Québécois of European descent? In the end, the Quebec officials could not say no (though they did not just say yes either).[24]

The case shows, I think, how the integration of immigrants within the francophone community of Quebec has begun to and will continue to change the identity of that community. Where once francophone Québécoi implied a specific culture, ethos, history and way of life, all of which played a role in defining Quebec as a political community, now a logic of multiculturalism (both sociological and moral) has been introduced which will lead Quebec to look more and more like a French-speaking version of English-speaking multicultural Canada or at least will make it hard to defend an alternative vision of Quebec in public.

The Lessons of the Quebec Case

What does the Quebec case reveal about the general principles that apply to all liberal democratic states with regard to the integration of immigrants? For example, does it have implications for the way European states ought to deal with the immigrants in their midst?

I think it does. In brief, I want to suggest that no European state can legitimately demand much more of immigrants by way of cultural adaptation than Quebec does. On the one hand, this means that states can make some significant demands because, as I argued above, being educated in a language normally has significant cultural consequences. Thinking about the education of children and the thick theory of language acquisition deepens the point that there is no culturally neutral language.

---

[24] The final decision was to grant less than the group had requested and to try to tie the grant in various ways to the francophone, rather than African, dimensions of the newspaper though this merely continued the contradiction.

On the other hand, the whole point of my analysis of Quebec's demands with respect to pluralism and democracy was to show both that Quebec's public commitment to these principles was common to all liberal democratic states and that these principles drastically limit the ability of a liberal democratic state to require cultural conformity. If that argument was correct, it should apply to European (and other) states as well. The same moral principles that constrain demands for adaptation to Quebec's distinct society also constrain whatever demands for cultural adaptation European states might put forward.

I recognize, of course, that many of the cultural traditions within the various European states are more ancient and more deeply rooted than are those in Quebec and that the populations of some European states are more culturally homogeneous than the population of Quebec (though it may be useful to recall here that one of my reasons for choosing Quebec as a subject of study was that its population is more like those of many European states in terms of the degree of cultural homogeneity than are the populations of other parts of North America). But I do not see how the relative thickness, depth, or uniformity of the cultural commitments of the population in a receiving country affects the *moral* argument about what may be demanded of immigrants. European states, too, are committed to respecting individual freedom, and so, they cannot avoid the pluralism that is legitimated by that freedom. On what moral grounds could any European state demand, as a condition of full acceptance, that immigrants dress, eat, read, think, play, pray, or live differently from the way the immigrants themselves choose?

I recognize that European states have traditions of citizenship and membership at odds with the overall line of argument I am taking here. France, for example, while traditionally open to immigration, has also insisted on the homogeneity of French culture and on cultural assimilation as a condition of full membership. Germany has had an ethnocultural conception of the nation that has effectively excluded the possibility of any substantial number of outsiders from joining (Brubaker 1992). But how can one defend either of these traditions today, at least if they are interpreted as requiring more by way of personal transformation than Quebec requires? It is not enough to say that these are 'our' traditions. The challenge is to show that these traditions are compatible with liberal democratic commitments.

From a liberal democratic perspective, the German understanding of membership is particularly hard to defend, as I have argued above in Chapter 3. The French tradition draws upon a secular, rational, universal ideal of citizenship which may be easier to reconcile with liberal democratic principles, but only if it does not place too much weight on French content, as it were. I will pursue this issue a bit further in the next chapter in a discussion of the famous debate in France over *les foulards*.

Let me conclude with a reminder and a caveat. As I emphasized at the beginning, I am writing primarily from a normative perspective. From a sociological perspective, and even from a political perspective, the historical and cultural differences between Europe and North America (even Quebec) may play a crucial role in shaping both public debate about immigration and the process of integration. After all, there are many factors at play here besides liberal democratic principles. Indeed those principles could be compromised or defeated in the political struggles and social practices affecting immigration.

I know, furthermore, that no European state currently recruits new immigrants as Quebec does and that none of them faces quite the same political need to win the attachment, loyalty, and identification of its immigrants. Nevertheless, all of the European states have significant immigrant populations. If the immigrants and their descendants are not successfully incorporated, this is bound to create serious social problems over the long run. More fundamentally, from a normative perspective, these settled populations have a moral claim to belong to the societies in which they live. They deserve to be accepted. To repeat, I do not see how any European state can justly demand more, as the price of that acceptance, than Quebec demands of its immigrants. While multiculturalism is the *bête noire* of many Europeans as it is of many Québécois, any defensible version of liberal democracy today entails a commitment to pluralism that inevitably opens the door to multiculturalism in some form.

6

Muslim Minorities in Contemporary Democracies: The Limitations of Liberal Toleration

In the previous chapter, I used Quebec's policies on the integration of immigrants to explore some questions about how liberal democracies should respond to cultural differences. In this chapter, I want to pursue further one of the issues raised in that discussion, namely, the question of how liberal democratic commitments constrain cultural differences, and more specifically, what sorts of cultural differences should not be tolerated.

The 'Clash of Civilizations'

In exploring this topic, I will focus on immigrants of Islamic faith. Muslims have featured prominently in a number of recent political conflicts in Western states. In Britain, there was the Salman Rushdie affair; in France, *l'affaire des foulards*; in Germany, the debate over the status of the descendants of the Turkish guestworkers. In all these cases and others, questions about the relation of Muslim immigrants to the states where they have settled have provoked public debates about the meaning of citizenship and the requirements of liberal democratic principles. Some people speak almost apocalyptically about a 'clash of civilisations' between Islam and the West (Huntington 1993).[1] Much of this alleged clash involves relations between states, but immigrants of Islamic faith are often constructed as a kind of fifth column in this struggle, because they live in the West yet (supposedly) carry with them these threatening values and alien ways of life. Thus, some people argue, it is particularly important to identify the conflicts between Islamic beliefs and practices and those that undergird the liberal democratic institutions of the West and to limit the capacity of

---

[1] For a review and critique of this view of Islam, see Esposito (1992).

Muslim immigrants to pass on their norms and values to others, including their children.

I think that this stance is wrong, both in the way it portrays Muslim migrants as a threat and in the way it fails to respect their legitimate concerns. While it is reasonable to ask questions about the kinds of cultural adaptation receiving states can expect of immigrants, any serious commitment to liberal democratic principles requires a much greater openness to Islam and to Muslim migrants than those allegedly concerned with defending Western civilization seem prepared to acknowledge. In particular, a commitment to the idea of justice as evenhandedness requires us to consider whether there are relevant similarities between Western cultural and religious practices that are generally regarded as morally permissible and Islamic practices that are widely seen as morally problematic. I will argue that these similarities are greater than is commonly thought.

I begin by considering the claim that the centrality of Islam in the lives of Muslims conflicts with the requirements of democratic citizenship. In the bulk of the chapter, I take up common critiques of Islamic practice and doctrine among would-be defenders of liberal democracy and gender equality and show how these critiques tend to mischaracterize the normative issues that particular practices raise, wrongly attribute objectionable practices to Islam as such, or employ a double standard by ignoring parallel issues within other religious traditions.

Islam as a Communal Identity in Liberal Society

One question that one encounters frequently, either implicitly or explicitly, is whether Muslims can be full members of liberal democratic societies given the strength of their communal identity. In the view of some democratic theorists, participation in the democratic process requires a capacity to distance oneself from one's identity, in order to put oneself in the position of another. On this view, this capacity for reflective distance from one's commitments is a prerequisite for genuine dialogue. But both Muslims and non-Muslims have argued that Islam constitutes, for many of its members, a communal identity which is, to borrow Sandel's term, thoroughly constitutive of their identity as individuals, something from which they cannot and do not wish to distance themselves (Sandel 1982). As Anne Phillips has articulated this concern in general terms:

Democracy surely does imply tolerance of difference . . . [yet] it is nonetheless hard to conceptualize without some means of distancing ourselves from those qualities we used to think of as most intrinsic. Somehow or other, we have to be able to stand back from the things that are peculiar to us . . . and try to think ourselves into another person's place. Part of the anxiety generated by fundamentalism—whether it is of a religious or political variety—is that it makes it impossible for its adherents to engage in this process, for even in principle they cannot treat their beliefs as detached (1991: 57).

Does this pose a problem for the position of Muslims in liberal democracies?

In a related vein, Charles Taylor suggests that there is a fundamental conflict between Islamic conceptions of the relation between religion and politics and liberal conceptions:

For mainstream Islam, there is no question of separating politics and religion the way we have come to expect in Western liberal society. Liberalism is not a possible meeting ground for all cultures, but is the political expression of one range of cultures, and quite incompatible with other ranges. (Taylor 1994: 62)

In considering this challenge, we should first pay attention to the variability among Muslims. Muslims do not all fit a single mould. We should not suppose that they all have exactly the same understanding of Islamic doctrine and its implications for social life, the same unqualified and unambivalent commitment to Islam, and so on. In fact, there is enormous variability among Muslims as there is among Christians, Jews, and other religious groups, with respect to doctrine, practice, and ways of life. For some immigrants, Islam may be primarily a cultural marker, a symbolic locus of identity that has little bearing on the norms that guide their actions in public and private life. For others, the commitment to Islam is at the centre, guiding every activity and choice. For many, it is something in between.

Secondly, if we focus only on those Muslims who do have a powerful sense of communal identity as described, we have to consider whether the same questions would be raised about Christians or Jews with comparably strong senses of religious identification. Anyone who reads the anti-immigrant literature from the nineteenth and early twentieth centuries is bound to be struck by the similarity between the doubts and fears expressed with respect to Catholics and Jews then and the doubts and fears expressed with respect to Muslims now. One finds the same rhetoric about alien invasions, with Catholics and Jews portrayed as threatening and unassimilable because of their illiberal and undemocratic values.[2] Nobody today would defend those earlier views (or at least nobody should). Nobody today would question whether Christians or Jews could be full members of a liberal democratic society, whatever their religious beliefs, although many committed Jews and Christians would reject the idea that they are obliged to distance themselves from their own religious identities to engage in the democratic process. One of the recurring and largely justifiable complaints of Muslims is that the standards used to evaluate their behaviour and beliefs are different from those used to judge others. In other words, they complain of a lack of evenhandedness.

---

[2] For original sources see (Wilkins 1892) and the thirty entries in Buenker and Burckel (1977): 208–210. For scholarly discussion see Divine (1957); Garrard (1967); Gainer (1972); Higham (1963) and 1975.)

Finally, we might ask whether the problem here lies not with the Muslims but with an understanding of democracy that would exclude or require fundamental changes from many other people as well as Muslims, at least if applied consistently. This model of deliberative democracy requires that people abstract themselves from their identities. But there is an alternative model of democracy that simply requires that people listen and engage with each other. To treat other people with respect—which is a requirement of deliberative democracy—does not necessarily require that one suspend one's own commitments or distance oneself from one's own identity. Indeed, conversations are often most fruitful when people speak from their deepest selves.

Someone might object that religious beliefs can have no standing in a pluralist society that must be committed to respect for all religions. But consider the case of Martin Luther King, Jr., whose effective leadership of the civil rights struggle in the United States, a struggle for democratic justice, was inextricably linked to his religious rhetoric. King's understanding of justice was rooted in his Christian convictions, and he could not have articulated it adequately without reference to them. Of course, other Christians were staunch defenders of segregation, while many of those who supported the civil rights struggle were not Christian. But that does not make King's method of communication inappropriate. To be sure, religious rhetoric can often be abused and manipulated. But so can a purely secular rhetoric. So, Muslims, too, should be free to bring their religious views to the democratic dialogue, recognizing, of course, that to be effective in persuading others they will have to find a way (as King did) to communicate their convictions in ways that resonate with people who do not share their religion.

Doubtless there comes a time when the claims of religious community become incommensurable with the claims of democratic citizenship. This seems especially likely to occur at the point at which religious communities seek to reshape the public sphere in their own image and at the expense of other religious or moral conceptions. An inquiry into the deeper question of what liberal democracies may in general claim of religious communities would take us far beyond the scope of this chapter.[3] The point here is simply that it is wrong to make allowances for Christian and Jewish communities and to refuse to make them for Muslim communities.

Islam and Gender Equality

To acknowledge the right of Muslims to participate in the democratic dialogue without abandoning their fundamental convictions is not to say

---

[3] Other theorists, however, have taken this question up directly For illuminating recent discussion, see Burtt (1994); Levinson (1990, 1992); and Macedo (1995).

how non-Muslims should respond to them. In the rest of this chapter, I will focus on one particular area where the beliefs and practices of Muslims are often alleged to be in fundamental conflict with the values and practices of liberal democratic societies: the issue of gender equality.

I begin by articulating views critical of Islam that I wish to challenge. According to the critics, Islamic practices and conceptions of women's role in society are incompatible with the liberal democratic commitment to equal citizenship. The critics say that Islam authorizes the genital mutilation of young girls, that it legitimates patriarchal authority and even wife-beating, that it permits polygamy, and that it requires women to dress in restrictive ways that limit their capacity to act in the public sphere. From the critics' perspective, rather than accommodating these practices as a way of respecting the cultural commitments of Muslim immigrants, liberal democratic states should challenge and constrain these practices as much as possible, prohibiting some of them and insisting on a legal regime and an educational system based on principles of gender equality.

In my view, the critics' account is mistaken both about Islam and about liberal democracy. Some of the practices mentioned above are deeply objectionable and should be prohibited, but it is wrong or at least deeply misleading to describe them as Islamic practices. Some of the practices are Islamic but are less in conflict with gender equality than the critics suppose. Finally, as the previous chapters have argued, liberal democracies do and must tolerate some departures from gender equality in the name of respect for religious freedom.

Let me begin with the last point. It is unreasonable to make demands of Muslims that are not made of adherents of other religions with comparable views and practices. The overall claim that women are subordinated within Islam is a claim that can also be made about Christianity and Judaism. Both Christianity and Judaism have deeply patriarchal elements in their religious traditions. Some versions of both religions, as they are understood and practised today, have very negative views of female sexuality, teach that women's primary responsibilities are in the home, assert the authority of the husband within the household, and so on. Yet no reasonable person suggests that traditional Catholics or fundamentalist Protestants or orthodox Jews should be required to modify these religious beliefs and practices as a condition of full membership in liberal democratic societies.

Some might object that there is a tremendous range of theological views within Christianity and Judaism and that this deep patriarchalism is characteristic of only a small part of each. But there is great variability within Islam as well, both in practice and in theological interpretation. Muslim feminists argue that there is nothing in Islam properly understood that requires the subordination of women (Ahmed 1992; Mernissi 1987, 1991; Sa'dawi 1980; Wadud-Muhsin 1992). The question here, however, is how to respond to those elements in a religious tradition—whether Islam or Christianity or Judaism—that see patriarchalism (in some form) as religiously mandated.

Why are patriarchal versions of Christianity and Judaism tolerated? Perhaps because the commitment to gender equality in liberal democratic states is not as deep in practice as is alleged when ideological contrasts are drawn between Islam and the West, but also because, even at the level of principle, the commitment to gender equality stands in some tension with other liberal democratic commitments. Liberal democratic principles entail a deep commitment to freedom of religion, of conscience, of thought, and of opinion. For that reason, a liberal democratic state cannot require intellectual or moral conformity, not even to its own ideals, although the state may legitimately try to inculcate key elements of the public democratic culture through the educational system and may establish a legal order that reflects its basic principles. Furthermore, a commitment to individual autonomy entails the recognition of some sort of private or personal sphere that the state may not regulate, including much of the activity within the family sphere. At a minimum then, any liberal democratic state will have to leave untouched some beliefs and practices that conflict with gender equality. From the perspective of justice as evenhandedness, it is unreasonable to demand more of Muslims in this respect than of the adherents of other faiths.

Genital Mutilation

How should we respond to the specific practices that critics claim are characteristic of Islam and in conflict with gender equality? Consider first the charge that Islam authorizes the genital mutilation of young girls. I have already argued in Chapter 2 for a general moral condemnation of genital mutilation regardless of its cultural or religious significance because it causes permanent, serious physical harm to children. Here I want to refine that argument by considering how our assessment of the practice would be affected if it were performed only upon consenting adults or were significantly modified in the way it was performed. I will also argue that it is misleading and harmful to claim that Islam authorizes the practice.

Let me begin with a brief restatement of the nature of the practice and the reasons for opposing it. In a number of countries in Africa, Asia, and South America—mainly in twenty countries in the middle belt of Africa—girls commonly undergo some form of ritual cutting of the genitalia. The procedure ranges from what is sometimes called 'circumcision proper' (incision or removal of the prepuce of the clitoris), to clitoridectomy or excision (removing part or all of the clitoris and often part or all of the labia minora as well), to infibulation (removing the clitoris, the labia minora, and part of the labia majora and sewing together the two sides of the vulva, leaving only a small opening for menstrual blood and urine).[4] Some people object to the use of the term female circumcision precisely because it suggests a procedure analogous to male circumcision and thus conceals the much more drastic character of infibulation or even of clitoridectomy. They insist on the term genital mutilation. (See, for example, Winter 1994: 941.) I use the term female circumcision at some points in the text because it is a broader term and includes both practices that might not be morally objectionable (as I argue later in the text) and ones that are. It is precisely because it enables one to make this distinction that I find the term useful.

The most common version of this practice appears to be some form of excision. In the mid-1980s, it was estimated that 75–80 million females in Africa were affected. This is an ancient practice whose origins are unclear. The (overlapping) reasons offered for continuing the practice are that it is traditional, that it is connected to cultural norms regarding sexuality and reproduction, that it is religiously required or at least encouraged, and that girls will not be accepted as eligible marriage partners and full members of the community unless they have been circumcised. These reasons continue to have weight for some immigrants who have their daughters circumcised either in the West (usually covertly) or in their countries of origin while visiting on vacation, although most immigrants from countries where female circumcision is common do not continue the practice after they have arrived in the West and some people leave their countries of origin (even seeking refugee status) precisely to avoid having their daughters subjected to circumcision.

It has been argued that female circumcision should be permitted in liberal democratic states because it is clearly an important social practice for some people and immigrants cannot reasonably be expected simply to abandon their pre-existing cultural and religious commitments.[5] How should we respond to this argument?

---

[4] For information on this topic I have drawn upon Dorkenoo and Elworthy (1992); Hosken (1983); UNCHR (1986); Koso-Thomas (1987); Toubia (1995); Aldeeb Abu-Salieh (1994); and Boddy (1998). There is some variation in terminology in the literature, with some people restricting the use of the term circumcision to the less radical procedures, though the broader usage (which I follow here) seems more common. The use of the term 'circumcision proper' for the mildest form of the procedure clearly takes male circumcision as the standard of reference. Some people refer to (removal of the prepuce) as 'sunna circumcision', an Islamic term whose significance in this context I discuss later in the text. Toubia says that, in her medical practice in Sudan, she has 'not found a single case of female circumcision in which only the skin surrounding the clitoris is removed, without damage to the clitoris itself' (1994: 712, cited in Boddy 1998).

[5] This sort of argument has actually been advanced in public debates and in legal trials in France. See Winter (1994) for a review and discussion. The question of what it is appropriate to permit within the legal framework of a Western liberal democratic state is different from the question of whether it is appropriate for Westerners to intervene in some way against female circumcision in the states where it is traditionally practised. The latter question raises a host of complications that I do not attempt to address here. For a sensitive discussion of some aspects of the issue, see Boddy (1998). For a discussion of whether Westerners have any moral standing to comment on this practice in other societies, see the discussion of Walzer in Chapter 2 above.

My basic answer is this. The respect due to particular cultural and religious commitments must be assessed in the context of their implications for other fundamental human interests. Female circumcision as normally practised has horrific physical and psychological consequences that have been well documented. Even the mildest form of clitoridectomy is painful, permanent, debilitating, and devoid of health benefits. One crucial responsibility of any liberal democratic state is to protect the physical safety and bodily integrity of its inhabitants, including children. This responsibility obliges the state to set strict limits to the authority of parents over their children, regardless of the parents' motives (i.e. even if they believe themselves to be acting in the best interests of the child). Thus, it is proper for the state to restrict or prohibit cultural and religious practices that cause serious harm to children. Given the consequences of female circumcision, any liberal democratic state not only may but should regard the practice as genital mutilation and prohibit it from being performed upon young girls.[6]

This general line of argument is subject to two important qualifications, the first focusing on the involuntary nature of the procedure, the second on the degree of harm it causes. So far, I have described female circumcision as it is most widely practised, that is, upon girls who are usually not consulted and who are too young to consent even if they were. But suppose it were a question of an adult woman voluntarily undergoing circumcision? This is not a purely hypothetical or unimaginable example. Bhikhu Parekh told me in conversation that after giving a lecture in which he criticized the practice of female circumcision, he was challenged by a Nigerian woman who said that she had voluntarily undergone excision as an adult just before the birth of her first child as a way of reducing her sexual desires. She described this adult, pre-child-bearing circumcision as the normal practice of her community.[7]

Would it still be obligatory or even permissible for a liberal democratic state to ban the practice for adults? Every liberal regime must grant considerable latitude to individuals to lead their lives and even to treat their bodies however they choose. Liberal states permit women to undergo a wide variety of cosmetic surgeries (breast enlargement and reduction, liposuction, facelifts, and so on) and bodily alterations (tatooing, body piercing) in order to meet cultural norms regarding beauty and sexuality. On the one hand, feminists rightly criticize many of these practices for the ways in which they reflect, serve, and reinforce problematic ideals of the female body (Morgan 1991). These practices, too, could be described as forms of bodily mutilation. But feminists also insist on the rights of women to control their own bodies and

---

[6] To say that genital mutilation should be legally prohibited is not necessarily to say that an aggressive criminal prosecution of those who continue the practice is the best strategy for eliminating it In France, for example, the opponents of genital mutilation are divided among themselves about the best approach to the problem (Winter 1994).

[7] For a general account of the practice in Nigeria, see Myers *et al.* (1985).

are wary of granting state authorities the power to restrict women's choices. Criticism is one thing, prohibition and control another. Why should female circumcision be treated differently from these other forms of bodily mutilation?

One possible answer to this question would be that female circumcision has much more harmful consequences than the other forms of mutilation both in terms of health risks and in terms of normal bodily functioning even if it is performed under sound medical conditions.[8] This answer carries some weight although it may underestimate the health risks of the other procedures which have become apparent with the public controversy over the consequences of breast implants. In any event, it points to what I think is the right principle here. There are some limits even to control over one's own body. People are not permitted to sell their organs, for example. Some forms of bodily alteration are so harmful that they should not be permitted even if the person consents.

Does female circumcision fall into this category? In my view, infibulation probably does, but as one moves in the direction of less radical forms of circumcision, the answer is much less clear. I find the practice of clitoridectomy abhorrent and would want to challenge anyone who would defend it. But should an adult woman like the one who confronted Parekh be legally prohibited from undergoing such a procedure in a licensed medical facility? I think not. My tentative view is that such a ban interferes too much with the right people ought to have to conduct their lives in accordance with their own convictions and cultural commitments.

What should we think of what has been called 'circumcision proper' (i.e. removal only of the prepuce of the clitoris)? Some discussions of female circumcision seem to dismiss altogether the cultural and religious dimensions of the practice, as though these should carry no weight at all, at least in deciding whether infants and children may be subjected to circumcision. But on such a view it seems hard to understand why the practice of male circumcision should be tolerated either, at least in the absence of evidence about its health benefits. Medical views of male circumcision have varied over the years, and I am not in a position to assess them. At a minimum, it seems safe to say that there have been times when the prevailing view was that there was

---

[8] Many of the worst consequences of female circumcision stem from the fact that it is normally performed without anaesthesia and in unhygienic conditions. In recent years, people committed to having their daughters circumcised for cultural and religious reasons but concerned about the health consequences have sought to have the procedures performed in modern medical facilities when they could afford to do so. While this would doubtless reduce some of the negative health consequences of circumcision, the World Health Organization and other agencies concerned with the practice have consistently opposed this sort of effort and have urged professional medical personnel not to be involved in performing female circumcisions (WHO 1986). I think this is the right course. On the other hand, see the subsequent discussion in the text of why a much modified form of the practice should be permitted.

no medical justification for circumcising most male children.[9] Nevertheless, so far as I know, no liberal democratic state in recent times has tried to prevent people from having their male children circumcised for cultural and religious reasons. (Male circumcision is traditionally practised by Muslims, Jews, and some Africans who are neither Muslim nor Jewish.) Some people have argued for the prohibition of male circumcision on the grounds that male circumcision involves cutting healthy tissue without medical reason, causes some pain, occasionally leads to serious complications, and so should be regarded as a form of child abuse (Aldeeb Abu-Salieh 1994; Zwang 1978; and sources cited in Coleman 1998). These arguments have never prevailed politically even though in most jurisdictions male circumcision has religious or cultural significance only for a minority of the population. The conventional view seems to be that the minor pain and small risk associated with the practice are outweighed by the meaning attached to it by the child's parents and the cultural and religious community to which they belong and which the child will therefore join. I think that is a reasonable view. Physical well-being is essential but it is not the only human interest. It is entirely appropriate to give weight to the concerns people may have to maintain rituals and practices that have deep importance in a community.

If female circumcision were culturally important and caused no more harm than male circumcision, I think that it would be appropriate to permit it, too, even for children. Would 'circumcision proper' fall into this category? That requires information about its health consequences that I do not have. At the least though, I can say that it is possible to imagine a form of female circumcision in which the health risks would be small enough that it should be permitted for cultural or religious reasons. Suppose Muslim women who want their daughters to maintain the cultural ties and communal standing that come with passage through this rite of initiation into womanhood but do not want them to suffer the physical consequences of mutilation persuade the relevant actors in their community (themselves female) to accept a pinprick of blood from the clitoris as a satisfactory performance of the ritual. It may be objected that this is not the traditional practice, but traditions can evolve without disintegrating. If a particular community were to find that this sort of ritual played an important cultural role, it is hard to see why it should be prohibited.

Again, this is not merely a hypothetical possibility. Doriane Lambelet Coleman has written a richly detailed and nuanced account of an attempt by Somali immigrant women in the United States to have their daughters circumcised by having 'the doctors perform a symbolic *sunna* that would have involved only a small incision or "nick" on the foreskin or prepuce (also

---

[9] For a discussion of current medical views on male circumcision see Coleman (1998: 757 n. 185).

called the hood) of the clitoris, just enough to draw blood' (Coleman 1998: 739). This procedure would have involved less physical harm than that caused by male circumcision. After considerable discussion and reflection, the doctors and the hospital agreed to perform this type of female circumcision, but they were forced to abandon that policy as a result of political pressure brought to bear by people who saw even this modified version of the practice as genital mutilation or at least as an implicit legitimation of genital mutilation.

In this case as in many others, critics of multiculturalism worry that any public accommodation of cultural practices of immigrants that seem at all problematic will put us on a slippery slope, implicitly legitimating radical departures from liberal norms and standards in the name of cultural difference. In some criminal cases, for example, defendants have appealed to their cultural heritages as a justification of (or at least excuse for) crimes of violence against women. Coleman argues, however, and I agree, that the proposed policy on female circumcision was an appropriate way of accommodating the cultural concerns of the Somali immigrants without compromising fundamental liberal principles. The cultural significance was great, the harm was small, and we already make accommodations for procedures that are very similar but culturally more familiar (i.e. male circumcision). Thus the proposed policy was a nice illustration of the application of the idea of even-handed justice. Coleman's position on this issue is particularly significant because she is the author of a well-known critique of use of the 'cultural defence' in criminal law (Coleman 1996). Thus her work illustrates the ways in which a contextually sensitive approach can distinguish between the merits of different sorts of claims for cultural recognition.

I have one disagreement with Coleman. In my view, she places too much weight on what is essentially a prudential argument and too little on the normative importance of cultural practices. The doctors who agreed to perform the modified form of female circumcision apparently were persuaded largely by the argument that if they did not perform this mild procedure in the hospital the parents would probably have much more radical forms of circumcision performed clandestinely either within the United States or abroad. The doctors also expressed the hope that this procedure could serve as a transitional mechanism of accommodation that would be unnecessary in subsequent generations. Coleman appears to agree with these views. In my opinion, both are inappropriate if not mistaken. As I observed above, the World Health Organization has rightly urged medical practitioners not to carry out the conventional forms of female circumcision, even though many of the health complications associated with female circumcision are the result of the procedure being performed under insanitary conditions or by insufficiently trained personnel, and the refusal to perform circumcisions in medical facilities leads many parents to have them performed in traditional ways. If the World Health Organization's position is correct, as I think it is, claims about what the parents in the Seattle case would have done if the hospital did not cooperate should not have been given decisive weight. And it is clear that the Seattle doctors would not have agreed to perform any kind of genital mutilation. Medical personnel should not cause serious harm to people in order to prevent others from causing them even more serious harm. To do so is to yield to, and invite further forms of, blackmail. What made the proposed policy morally permissible was the fact that the physical harm was relatively minor and the cultural significance great, the same considerations that justify medical personnel in performing male circumcisions. For that reason, it seems as inappropriate to expect or hope that a modified form of female circumcision will fade away as it would be to expect or hope that male circumcision will fade away among those who attach religious significance to it.

Let us turn now to the question of the relation between Islam and female circumcision.[10] Female circumcision is practised by Muslims in some countries, but it is not practised by Muslims in other countries including Saudi Arabia, Algeria, Iran, Iraq, Libya, Morocco, Tunisia, and Indonesia, and is little known in Pakistan or Bangladesh. All of these countries have predominantly Islamic populations. I have not been able to find any estimates of the overall percentage of Muslims who practise female circumcision, but judging from the relative populations of countries in which it is and is not practised, it would appear to be a minority practice within Islam. Furthermore, in those countries in Africa where female circumcision is most common, it is practised by Christians, animists, and others besides Muslims and it clearly predates Islam. Interviews with women who have been circumcised or have had their daughters circumcised cite a variety of reasons for continuing the practice, as noted above, with religious motivations playing some role but generally a less important one than tradition and social acceptance.

From a doctrinal perspective, the status of female circumcision within Islam appears to be contested, in contrast with the status of male circumcision which all Muslims agree is mandatory. The debate focuses mainly around the interpretation of the Prophet Muhammad's injunction to a traditional practitioner of circumcision not to go to extremes. Most Muslims take this as a criticism of the most severe forms of female circumcision such as infibulation, and in countries where Islamic revitalization movements have had success (as in Sudan) there have been religious pressures to modify traditional practices. What seems more in dispute is whether the statement by the Prophet implies some endorsement of the practice in a less severe form. Some argue that it does not and further claim that other Qu'ranic injunctions

---

[10] My discussion of circumcision and Islam draws upon Dorkenoo and Elworthy (1992: 13–14); UNCHR (1986: 13, 23); Boddy (1989: 53); and Aldeeb Abu-Sahlieh (1994).

against bodily harm provide an Islamic basis for opposing the practice of female circumcision altogether. Others claim that the statement implies that female circumcision is '*sunna*' which is sometimes presented as meaning permissible and other times as recommended for those aspiring to be good Muslims. And among those who take the view that female circumcision is '*sunna*', there seems to be disagreement about whether this only applies to 'circumcision proper' or, on the one hand, to the more severe practices such as some forms of clitoridectomy or excision or, on the other hand to a milder, symbolic practice such as the one discussed above.

In sum, many Muslims do not practice female circumcision or see it as part of Islam, but some do. This makes it descriptively misleading, though not entirely inaccurate, to describe female circumcision as an Islamic practice. But how is this relevant to the question of how liberal democratic states should respond to Muslim immigrants? After all, it is not the business of political authorities in a liberal democratic state to pass judgement on what is authentically Islamic.[11]

In one sense this objection is certainly correct. As I argued in Chapter 2, for the most part, it is appropriate for political authorities to take religious claims at face value. If some Muslim immigrants say that they feel they have a religious obligation to practise female circumcision, it is not the responsibility of state officials to challenge their interpretation of Islam, in the absence of evidence of deliberate deception. Some immigrants will undoubtedly defend the practice in this way, emphasizing their religious motivations (and downplaying other factors like tradition) because of the privileged status normally granted to religious practice in liberal states.[12]

The problem with characterizing female circumcision as an Islamic practice is not located primarily in the sphere of interactions between officials enforcing laws and immigrants advancing religious claims but rather in the sphere of public discourse in which this characterization contributes to the construction of a negative image of Islam and of Muslim immigrants. As Chapter 2 pointed out, discussions of female circumcision frequently have a political subtext, identifying its practitioners with barbarism and its opponents in the West with civilization. So, identifying female circumcision as an Islamic practice serves to discredit Islam. The headline of one recent article on the topic illustrates the point: 'Women are Being Abused, Even Mutilated . . . All in the Name of Islam' (Bardach 1994). The message is typical.

Imagine a comparable attempt to discredit Christianity. The people who engage in violent opposition to abortion (bombing abortion clinics, murdering doctors who perform abortions, and so on) frequently describe

---

[11] See my critique of Walzer on this point in Chapter 2.
[12] As I argued above, I think such an attempt to defend female circumcision on grounds of religious freedom should fail and that liberal states can and should prohibit the practice of most forms of female circumcision, even if sincerely motivated by religious beliefs.

themselves as acting out of a sense of Christian religious duty. In most cases, there is no reason to doubt the sincerity of these claims, and, in any event, state officials (such as judges in a criminal trial) should not try to assess the doctrinal merits of their beliefs, at least under normal circumstances. They need only conclude that such actions are not legally permissible, regardless of their religious foundations. But most Christians (even among those opposed to abortion) would object strenuously if such activities were described as Christian practices, because they do not engage in these activities themselves and do not wish to be associated with them. Similarly, most Muslim immigrants do not practise female circumcision and do not wish to be identified with the practice. Of course, the construction of public discourse is multi-sided, and Muslims can contribute to a dissociation between Islam and female circumcision by criticizing the practice publicly as unIslamic, just as, for example, some Catholic bishops in the United States recently criticized violence against abortion clinics as unChristian.

Wife-Beating

Consider now, much more briefly, the claim that Islam legitimates patriarchal authority within the household, including the right of the husband to beat his wife under certain circumstances. Interpretations of religious traditions are always subject to contestation. Muslims disagree among themselves, to some extent, about the correct understanding of Islamic teaching on the family and relations between spouses. For example, one author develops a highly egalitarian reading of Islamic teaching and insists, among other things, that 'The Qur'an never orders a woman to obey her husband' (Wadud-Muhsin 1992: 77). Another, perhaps more common view asserts at least some duty on the part of a wife to obey her husband:

Because of his natural ability and his responsibility for providing for his family, the man is the head of the house and of the family. He is entitled to the obedience and cooperation of his wife, and accordingly it is not permissible for her to rebel against his authority, causing disruption (al-Qaradawi 1993: 205).

Of course, the same range of views can be found within other religious traditions such as Christianity and Judaism. Apart from physical violence, in addressing the issue of Islamic legitimation of patriarchal authority, we encounter the problem, discussed in previous chapters, that liberal democratic commitments to religious freedom and personal autonomy preclude any attempt to regulate directly the character of relationships between spouses or between parents and children, even where some cultural tradition prescribes patterns of authority and deference within the household that are quite at odds with equality of the sexes.

Physical violence is, however, another matter. As I noted above, protection of physical security is a core task of any liberal democratic government. Cultural and religious commitments cannot provide a ground for exemptions from the general prohibitions on violence, including domestic violence. But is there any reason to believe that it is appropriate to identify Muslim immigrants as a special focus of concern in this regard? The actual record of Western states with respect to domestic violence provides no grounds for self-congratulation or complacent comparisons with non-Western cultures. The use of violence by men against their partners and children has deep cultural roots in the West, and until quite recently has been largely supported by the legal system. Even now when public norms have apparently begun to change, the amount of domestic violence is staggering. It might be instructive to compare the actual use of force by Muslim men within their own households (in Western societies) with the use of force by non-Muslims. What if the Muslim rate turned out to be lower than that of other groups? Would that have any bearing on the question of what sorts of cultural adaptation were required to meet the requirements of the Western commitment to gender equality?

I have not been able to find any empirical studies on the relation between culture or religion and domestic violence that would help us to address the questions I just posed. In the absence of such data, is there any reason to suppose that Islam legitimates wife-beating? Critics of Islam point to a passage in the Qur'an which allows a husband to strike his wife under certain circumstances. But Muslims insist, with good reason, that it is unfair to take the passage out of context. Some argue that the passage should be read as severely restricting the practices prevalent at the time rather than as granting ongoing permission for this sort of behaviour (Wadud-Muhsin 1992: 74–8). Even conservative Islamic scholars emphasize the steps that must be taken before the husband may use physical force and the drastic limits on the kind of physical force that may be employed (al-Qaradawi 1993: 205). I would want to challenge even this highly circumscribed legitimation of physical force in relations between spouses, but clearly this cannot be taken as a general legitimation of domestic violence. Spousal abuse is undoubtedly a problem among Muslim immigrants as it is among every group in Western societies, and it may be that some Muslim men seek to justify their actions by appealing to the Qur'an, but both their behaviour and their appeals are contrary to Islam as understood by most Muslims (Memon 1993).

In sum, my response to the issue of spousal abuse parallels the one given to female circumcision. The state can and should prohibit domestic violence, but it is deeply misleading and harmful to say that Islam legitimates wife-beating.

Polygamy

What about Islam's endorsement of polygamy? First, it should be noted that many authors have argued that there are resources within Islam for prohibiting polygamy, based on the Qur'anic injunction that a husband must treat each of his wives justly, and, if unable to treat more than one justly, should marry only one (Esposito 1991: 96). Furthermore, a legal prohibition of polygamy does not prevent a Muslim man from doing anything required by his religion (provided that he has not yet taken more than one wife) but only limits something that is permitted by Islam.

Polygamy is significantly different from female circumcision and wife-beating in one important respect, however. It is not obvious why it should be legally prohibited. Every Western liberal democratic state does forbid it, of course, but it is not clear how that fits with the general principle that adults should normally be able to enter into whatever contracts or personal relationships they choose. If the defence of the prohibition rests on a concern for the well-being of women and children in such relationships, it would seem appropriate to consider the effects of easy divorce as well. Muslim commentators rightly point out that the relative ease of divorce and remarriage in Western states creates a kind of *de facto* serial polygamy, and studies show that the economic position of women and children after the breakup of a marriage is usually greatly reduced for a significant period while that of men often improves (Weitzman 1985). If the issue is asymmetry between men and women, that would appear to be remedied by a legal regime that permitted women as well as men to have multiple spouses, even if, among Muslims, only men availed themselves of this opportunity (Gutmann 1993).

Hijab and *L'Affaire des Foulards* in France

Consider finally the issue of Islamic dress. This is a particularly puzzling issue. The right to dress as one chooses—subject only to standards of public decency (themselves highly contestable and often gender biased)—would seem the quintessential liberal right. Indeed, one of the objections against some Islamic regimes is that they require all women to conform to a narrow, publicly determined dress code, thus unduly restricting their personal liberty. So, why would anyone object if Muslim women choose to wear the *hijab* as a way of expressing their cultural identity or religious convictions?[13]

[13] It is striking what passions this form of dress can arouse A graduate student in my department whose strong feminist views were well known converted to Islam after years of study and reflection, and, after her conversion, began to wear the *hijab* out of conviction that this was the

In some contexts, there are norms of dress so that wearing the *hijab* would require an exemption from the norms that others are expected to follow. For example, in Montreal recently a judge expelled a Muslim woman for refusing to remove her head covering on the grounds that there was a prohibition against wearing anything on one's head in court. The judge's action was widely condemned in the press on the grounds that it was insensitive to the cultural and religious significance of the *hijab*. One Muslim critic wondered rhetorically whether the judge would have required a Catholic nun in a traditional habit to remove her head covering. In the Canadian context, with its institutionalized commitment to multiculturalism, it seems obvious that the judge was wrong. A Muslim woman shows no disrespect to the legal system by wearing her *hijab* in court. If the right to do so is considered a special right, it is precisely the sort of special right required by the deeper commitment to evenhanded justice. It does not privilege Muslim women over other people but merely ensures that their cultural and religious differences from the majority do not become unfair sources of disadvantage.

In France, the expulsion of three girls for wearing the *hijab* to a public school became the focal point for a national debate on special rights, the integration of immigrants, women's equality, and the principle of secularity in French public life (Feldblum 1993; Silverman 1992; Galeotti 1993; Moruzzi 1994; Gaspard and Khosrokhavar 1995). I cannot recapitulate all of the elements of that debate here, but I can perhaps use it to draw attention to one of the important complicating considerations in thinking about gender equality and Islam in liberal democratic states, namely, the range of legitimate variability among liberal democratic regimes.

As previous chapters have pointed out, every liberal democratic state must recognize certain principles such as freedom of speech, freedom of religion, majority rule, and so on, but there are many different ways of interpreting these principles and many different forms of practice among liberal democratic states. Now the mere fact that a practice exists in a state that we call liberal democratic does not make it morally legitimate. One need only mention the example of legally supported segregation in the United States prior to 1954 to make that clear. Yet it would be astonishing if someone argued that there was only one correct way to institutionalize liberal democratic principles. It seems far more plausible to suppose that there is a range of reasonable disagreement about what the principles of democratic justice require, and that within that range different states are free to adopt different institutional arrangements. But how wide is that range with respect to gender equality and the toleration of difference?

proper thing for her to do as a good Muslim. It is hard to imagine a more apt case for the Millian injunction about respecting the right of a mature adult to live her life in the way she sees fit and avoiding the tyrannical intrusions of public opinion. Yet she was subject to disapproval and even hostility from many of her peers.

One central element of the argument for prohibiting the wearing of the *hijab* in the French public schools emphasized the distinctiveness of the French political tradition, especially as compared with Anglo-Saxon traditions. France has a tradition of a strong state and an expansive public sphere. One French author writing about the challenge posed to the French by Muslim immigrants wrote that in the 1980s 'the state got the impression that it no longer had complete control over the norms of society' (Leveau 1992: 173). No American author could have written such a line about the United States, for it would never occur to an American that the state could or should have complete control over the norms of society. But does that mean that the French model is undemocratic and illegitimate?

The French political system has a history of strictly limiting the role of intermediate groups in public life, of confining religious matters to the private sphere, and of insisting on the strict secularity of the state. Again, all of these fundamental principles of the modern French state differ in various ways from the practices of Anglo-Saxon states. (For example, marriages in France must be performed before a civil authority to be legally binding, whereas other states delegate to religious officials the authorization to perform legally binding marriages). The French tradition of dealing with immigrants has strongly resisted the sort of ethnic group formation that developed in North America and has pursued a strategy of assimilating immigrants as individuals, relying heavily upon the public schools (and the army and the unions) to bring about the necessary cultural transformations.

One may object that these generalizations say more about the myths of French political traditions than about the realities of French political life. The objection has merit, but it would be exaggerated to claim that there are no significant differences along these lines between, say, France and the United States. In any event, many prominent intellectuals and public figures in France feared that what they regarded as deep and distinctive principles of the French state would be threatened by the wearing of the *hijab* in the public schools. This is, at the least, a more plausible claim in the French context than it would be in a North American context. Whether it is sufficient to warrant the requirement that girls not wear the *hijab* to school seems more doubtful, however.

The claim that the *hijab* as a religious symbol was incompatible with the secularism of the public sphere was weakened in the actual case by the fact that no such restrictions had been placed on the wearing of Christian religious symbols like crosses. Even if that inconsistency were tidied up, however, the question remains whether the French state could legitimately ban all religious symbols from a compulsory institution like public schools, as some of the defenders of secularism advocated. In my view, the answer is no. Here it is important to reassert the idea that the state should sometimes take a hands off approach to culture, and especially religion, as a way of respecting individual

choice. It should certainly count as a powerful argument against such a prohibition that, in some religious traditions (including some forms of Islam), the
wearing of certain items is seen not merely as an admirable expression of faith
but as obligatory. In such a context, the prohibition interferes with religious
practice in a way that calls for a stronger justification than appeal to a political tradition of secularism.

The French *Conseil d'État* took a somewhat similar view, ruling that the
mere wearing of religious signs could not be prohibited. The *Conseil* went on
to assert that it was permissible to prohibit students from wearing religious
signs in such an ostentatious way that it would pressure other students or
amount to a form of proselytization or provocation and left it up to local
administrators to decide when that was the case. Drawing upon this opening,
some people have argued that, in the current context in France, wearing the
hijab is not so much an expression of faith as a political challenge to French
liberal democracy. They note that most of France's Muslim population is of
North African origin or ancestry. They draw attention to the rise of Islamic
fundamentalism in North Africa and the use of terror in some states there
against females who do not wear the *hijab*. They note the experience in
France itself of terrorist attacks in the name of these fundamentalist movements. They say that the fundamentalists see female separation from and
subordination to males as an essential element in their project and thus view
Muslim girls as a particularly important target for their efforts and public indicator of their success or failure. In all these circumstances, they argue it is
appropriate to construe wearing the *hijab* in school as both a political provocation and as a threat or at least a form of undue pressure against Muslim girls
who do not wear it. For all these reasons, they claim, it is legitimate to ban
the *hijab* from French public schools (Badinter *et al.* 1989; Lacoste-Dujardin
1990; William 1991; Aulagnon 1994).

The view I have just described offers a contextual defence of the ban on
hijab. In my view, the kinds of considerations it adduces on behalf of a restrictive policy in France are relevant, and, in that respect, it seems clear that a
stronger case can be made for banning the *hijab* in French schools than could
be made in most other liberal democratic states. Still, the mere fact that a
contextual account is offered does not mean that we have to accept it. Here I
do not think the case is strong enough. I would agree that what people wear
often carries symbolic meaning and that the meaning depends in part on the
social context. I would even stipulate, though some civil libertarians would
disagree, that it might be permissible to restrict certain forms of dress in
school because of their symbolic associations. For example, the wearing of
Nazi insignia is banned in schools in a number of states. Some schools in Los
Angeles have banned the wearing of colours associated with gangs. But the
hijab cannot reasonably be equated with Nazi insignia or gang colours, even
allowing for the differences in circumstances.

The *hijab* has long played a central role in the Western imagination, standing particularly as a symbol of the subordination of women within Islam and hence as a proof of the moral superiority of the West. Precisely for that reason, many women in the anti-colonial movement who had never worn the *hijab* began to put it on, using it as a symbol of their rejection of Western values. Doubtless the contemporary wearers of the *hijab* in France mean sometimes to evoke this rejection of French colonialism and to assert an alternative set of norms. Yet part of what they deny in doing so is that the *hijab* does stand for the subordination of women. Indeed, one could make a plausible case that French *haute couture*, by constructing female identity in terms of a woman's ability to dress in ways that are attractive to men, has contributed more to the subordination of women— think of short skirts and high heels—than the *hijab* ever did. But even if the *hijab* does stand for the subordination of women within Islam, why shouldn't Muslim girls be permitted to wear it if they choose to do so?

Some allege that the girls who first wore the *hijab* were pressured into doing so by their parents and were not acting out of religious conviction but were being used as tools by others for purposes of political mobilization (Monnet 1990). It is remarkable how this sort of construction treats all of the pressures within French society *not* to wear the *hijab* (including perhaps pressures from Muslim parents who want their daughters to conform more to the dominant French norms) as background conditions of free choice and only pressures from parents or others to wear the *hijab* as coercive. Of course, there are some sorts of pressures the state must intervene to prevent, notably the threat of bodily harm. And there are states such as Algeria and Iran where girls and women face physical threats for failing to conform to what some people regard as the norms of Islamic dress. But that is not the case in France today. If anything, the pressures for most Muslim girls are overwhelmingly in the other direction. Once again we are reminded that one's context of choice is shaped by many different factors, none of them neutral.

There may well be a good deal of truth to the claim that non-religious motives play a role for some of the girls who wear the *hijab*, but it can hardly be denied that the *hijab* has a deep and long-standing religious significance within Islam or that devout Muslims living in the West frequently wear the *hijab* without any political goals in view. In the end, I do not see why the potential of the *hijab* to serve multiple purposes, including political ones, should have any bearing on the right of the girls to wear this religiously important form of dress.

Conclusion

Over the past several years, I have been struck by the vehemence of anti-Muslim sentiment not only in Western societies generally, but particularly within the academy. This was one of my principal motivations for using Islam as a focus in this chapter. I have argued here that liberal states are not obliged to tolerate every practice that some people claim is justified by Islam but that it is wrong to suggest that Muslims cannot be good citizens. The various examples of alleged conflicts between liberal commitments and the place of women in Islam that I have considered suggest that, in fact, liberal critiques of Islam often demand more of Muslims than of members of other religious communities. An understanding of justice as evenhandedness would seem to require more modifications of Western attitudes towards Muslim immigrants than of Muslim practices. I am well aware that I have only scratched the surface of this rich and challenging subject and that any complete account of the appropriate relationship between Muslim immigrants and their liberal democratic host countries must consult the voices of Muslims themselves. My goal here was simply to use a contextual analysis to unsettle some of the assumptions that critics of Islam often make.

7

Multiple Political Memberships, Overlapping National Identities, and the Dimensions of Citizenship

In the previous two chapters I have been considering some of the ways in which cultural commitments may stand in tension with liberal principles, thus raising questions about the meaning of equal citizenship. In this chapter, and the next two, I will continue to explore the meaning of equal citizenship, while examining cultural identities that raise questions about the meaning of citizenship itself.

In the modern world, talk about citizenship sometimes presupposes, as a background assumption, an idealized (and misleading) conception of the nation-state as an administratively centralized, culturally homogeneous form of political community in which citizenship is treated primarily as a legal status that is universal, equal, and democratic. In this idealized conception, the nation-state is the only locus of political community that really matters and citizenship just means membership in a nation-state. Everyone in the world is supposed to belong to one such state and only one. Although the state may delegate its authority to sub-units, it retains ultimate authority because it exercises a legitimate monopoly of violence over the territorially based society that it governs.[1]

This picture of citizenship is inadequate in many respects. It is conceptually inadequate in the sense that it does not appreciate the multiple dimensions of citizenship and the complex relationships among these dimensions. It is empirically inadequate in the sense that it does not correspond to actual practices in Canada and in other states that embody a recognition of multiple forms of belonging and of overlapping citizenships. And it is theoretically inadequate in the sense that it fails to see the ways in which recognition of difference may be essential to fulfil the commitment to equality that is often expressed in the language of citizenship.

---

[1] For an instructive account of the conventional view and some of its limitations, see Brubaker (1989: 1–27). I argued in Chapter 3 that Kymlicka's conception of societal culture presupposes this conventional view despite his focus on multiculturalism.

In short, our existing institutions, practices, and values provide many ways of recognizing claims of identity and community that are at least morally permissible and in some cases morally required, even though they are incompatible with the unitary model of citizenship. Once we see the legitimacy and desirability of these non-unitary arrangements, it may become easier to contemplate others as well. We may become less imprisoned by conventional conceptions and more willing to consider how we want to live together and why. In my view, our conceptions of citizenship and political community should grow out of, rather than determine, the political and social arrangements that we choose.

If the conventional understanding is inadequate, how should we think about membership in political communities? What does it entail? How *do* people belong to a political community? How *should* they belong? In this chapter, I will address these questions by identifying and exploring three different dimensions of citizenship—the legal, the psychological, and the political. The legal dimension of citizenship refers to the formal rights and duties that one possesses as a member of a political community; the psychological dimension to one's sense of identification with the political community or communities to which one belongs; the political dimension to one's sense of the representational legitimacy of those who act authoritatively on behalf of and in the name of the political community. I will argue that people often have multiple memberships within each of these dimensions, and that the three dimensions interact with each other in complex ways. An adequate conception of citizenship will have to leave room for these various forms of multiplicity, and whatever form that conception finally takes, it will have to differ markedly from the conventional unitary understanding if it is to provide a satisfactory empirical and normative account of citizenship in the modern world.

The Legal Dimension

One way to belong to a political community is to possess the legal status of a citizen. The unitary model of the nation-state both expects and prescribes that every individual possess the legal status of citizenship only in relation to one political community. Yet this model fails to capture contemporary realities or to provide good reasons for changing current practices to conform to the unitary ideal.

Even if one accepts the underlying presupposition that state citizenship is the only kind that matters, the conventional view is built upon shaky empirical and normative foundations. Consider the social and legal reality of state citizenship first. I do not know of any empirical studies estimating the number of dual citizens in contemporary liberal democratic states, but there is no doubt that the incidence of dual citizenship has grown considerably in recent years and is likely to continue doing so (Spiro 1997; Schuck 1998). One reason for this phenomenon has been the gradual elimination of gender bias in laws regulating the transmission of citizenship (Bauböck 1994). Most such laws made the citizenship of children dependent exclusively upon the citizenship of the father. Now citizenship normally passes through either parent, so that if the parents have different citizenships, the child will possess both. In addition, in states where citizenship is determined by place of birth (as in the United States, Canada, and a number of other countries), children born to foreign parents acquire dual (or triple) citizenship at birth. Some states (like Canada and Australia) do not require renunciation of one's previous citizenship as a condition of naturalization so that immigrants normally retain their old citizenship even after acquiring a new one. And legal rulings in some states (like the United States) have made it more difficult to take away people's birthright citizenship as a consequence of naturalization elsewhere. The general growth of international migration makes the impact of these legal rules more significant.

One could imagine various legal attempts to restrict dual citizenship in ways that were not gender biased. Some states require immigrants to renounce previous citizenships. Such rules could be made more rigorous and could be applied to existing citizens who naturalized elsewhere. One could require children who acquired dual citizenship at the time of birth to renounce one of them at the time of majority. But these sorts of rules would seek to reverse current trends. The reasons for the expansion of dual citizenship seem good ones, rooted in our aspirations for equal treatment and the protection of vital human interests. Is there any good reason to resist this development? Why might some people see dual citizenship as a bad thing?

Objections to dual citizenship are closely tied to the picture of the nation-state sketched at the beginning of this chapter. In a world organized entirely on the basis of independent sovereign states, each state is supposed to bear certain responsibilities for its own citizens. If people hold more than one citizenship, who bears the responsibilities? Are not dual citizens potentially subject to two, possibly conflicting, sets of laws (e.g. with respect to such matters as marriage and divorce) and to two, possibly overlapping, sets of obligations (e.g. with respect to such matters as taxation and military service)?

In practice, these sorts of problems have proved highly tractable (Hammar 1989; Spiro 1997; Schuck 1998). Potential conflicts in legal rules and obligations are usually resolved through bilateral or multilateral negotiations that normally give priority to the place of domicile. In other words, dual citizens pay taxes and fulfil military or other obligations in the state in which they reside and that state's laws take precedence in cases of conflict.

A second set of objections to dual citizenship links legal status to issues of democratic legitimacy. If people have dual citizenship, does that mean that they can have a say in governing two different states by voting in the elections of each? If people live in one country but vote in another, doesn't that mean that they will not be subject to the government and policies they are helping to select? Doesn't that violate democratic norms? Double voting is indeed anomalous from a democratic perspective, but it need not be a major policy concern so long as the percentage of the electorate living outside the polity is small. In any event, there are some obvious mechanisms for addressing the problem (such as limiting the possibilities of absentee voting or prohibiting dual voting). Again, the norm would be to restrict participation to the country of residence.

People also object sometimes that dual citizenship gives rise to dual and potentially conflicting loyalties. Here I will anticipate a few points I will discuss in more detail below in the section on the psychological dimension of citizenship. Multiple, overlapping, and even conflicting identifications and loyalties are a widespread phenomenon in the modern world, and one that has little to do with dual citizenship as a legal status. It is an open question how much these psychological attachments are affected by legal status. My guess is that permitting dual citizenship does little to exacerbate whatever problems such multiple identities create and eliminating it will do little to solve it.

In sum, dual citizenship creates few serious problems in practice, despite its obvious incompatibility with the conventional unitary model of citizenship. At the same time, it is an arrangement that enables people who have substantial ties to more than one political community because of their residence, family ties, or place of origin to protect their vital human interests in each. Thus the unitary model fails both descriptively and prescriptively to take the issue of dual citizenship into account.

There is another kind of dual citizenship that is even more important than the simultaneous holding of two state citizenships, namely, membership in two political communities within the same state. In a federal system like Canada's, everyone belongs to at least two political communities, each of whose jurisdiction and sovereignty is limited by and intertwined with the other's. The rhetoric of state sovereignty simply obscures this legal and political reality. Sovereignty, like property, is best conceived as a bundle of rights that can be parcelled out in many different ways. The rights and duties of political membership for people who live in Canada (and in many other federal systems) are not exhausted by the rights and duties created by the federal government, nor is the federal government necessarily supreme in confrontations with the provinces.

It is a fundamental conceptual, empirical, and normative mistake not to be open to the possibility that the units in a federal system are significant political communities and that membership in such communities is an important form of citizenship. Whether that is true or not will vary from case to case and over time. In the late eighteenth and early nineteenth centuries, American states were political communities that rivalled or surpassed the federal government in their powers and their significance for the identities of many of their citizens. That is no longer true today in the United States, but it is true of the political units of other federal systems like Switzerland, Belgium, Canada, and Spain, although the significance of the units as political communities and *loci* of citizenship may vary even within the same state, something I discuss in the next section.

The development of the European Union (EU) has lead to the creation of legal rights and duties for individuals distinct from the ones they possess as citizens of any given European state. In this case, of course, no one doubts the importance of citizenship in the component units (the states); rather the question is whether citizenship in the overarching unit (the EU) has any normative or empirical significance. While it is true that the individual's claim to membership in the EU is mediated through citizenship in a member state and that the depth and meaning of European citizenship are in dispute, we should not overlook the fact that individuals who are members of the EU can advance legal claims before European courts apart from and even in opposition to the legislation and court rulings of the state in which they are citizens. This fact alone fits badly with the unitary model's picture of the organization of legal rights, and it is entirely possible that these sorts of legal arrangements will become stronger and be extended in various ways. Whether that is desirable or not is an open question, but it certainly cannot be ruled out as empirically or conceptually impossible or normatively undesirable on the basis of the one person, one citizenship presupposition of the unitary model.

Finally, there is the question of what the unitary model presupposes about the distribution of rights among citizens. In the modern world—and in some earlier contexts as well—legal citizenship is closely linked to a norm of equality. To be a citizen is to be an equal citizen, at least in principle. Everyone must be equal before the law. There can be no second-class citizens.

But what does equality really mean in this context? The revolutionary French state abolished aristocracy and proclaimed the principle of equal citizenship but distinguished between active and passive citizens, partly on the basis of property ownership. The US Supreme Court declared in 1896 that the equal citizenship of African–Americans was not violated by state policies of enforced racial segregation. Of course, no one would defend such distinctions today, but the question of what equal citizenship requires and permits has obviously not disappeared.

Should all citizens have exactly the same rights and duties? If that were taken to mean a prohibition on any legislation that distinguished one group of citizens from another, it would prohibit all legislation, including legislation regarding taxation, property, traffic, and so on. The real debate is about what legal arrangements reflect and enhance our commitment to equal citizenship and what arrangements violate or obstruct it. This is not a question that can be answered in purely formal terms. What it requires is that we consider whether particular ways of treating people differently can be defended as compatible with a conception of justice as evenhandedness. This requires immersion in concrete contexts and cases.

As we have seen previously in this book, it can be argued that a commitment to equal citizenship requires distinct legal rights for cultural minorities. In this debate and in related ones regarding gender, sexual orientation, race, physical or mental condition, and so on, both sides in the debate appeal to an ideal of equal citizenship. All this shows that even the legal dimension of citizenship is more complex and multiple than the unitary model suggests.

The Psychological Dimension

Another way to belong to a political community is to feel that one belongs, to be connected to it through one's sense of emotional attachment, identification, and loyalty. I call this the psychological dimension of membership.

On the conventional understanding of citizenship, there is a tight fit between the legal and psychological dimensions of citizenship. It is expected, both empirically and normatively, that people will feel a strong sense of emotional identification with, and only with, one political community, namely, the state in which they possess legal citizenship. (Again, the assumption is that people have only one legal state citizenship and that only states really matter as forms of political community). The conventional view does not deny that people may have other important forms of collective identity besides citizenship, and that these other identities may influence the political ideas and activities of citizens. Nevertheless, people are assumed to draw their primary *political* identity from membership in the state. Citizens are supposed to be patriotic, to love their country. One of the objections to dual citizenship is that people who hold more than one citizenship are likely to have dual or multiple loyalties, identities, and attachments. Where will their primary commitment be in cases of conflict? What happens to the unity and the integrity of the political community if there are competing national attachments?

I do not think this conventional view is entirely wrong, but just as it neglects multiplicity in the legal dimension it misses the reality of multiplicity in the psychological dimension, and the complexity of the relationship between the legal and psychological dimensions of citizenship. The conventional view is right to distinguish psychological citizenship—one's sense of oneself as a member of a political community—from other forms of collective identity. Ethnicity, gender, sexual orientation, and disability are all examples of factors that may be relevant to one's personal identity and may be linked to a sense of group identity that is morally and politically relevant. Such group identities can be vitally important to people. They can serve as a focus for political mobilization, leading people to challenge public policies and the prevailing public culture. The groups may be described and experienced as communities. But these sorts of communities are not usually described or experienced as *political* communities, that is, as groups that possess (or aspire to) extensive self-government. People do not normally think of themselves as citizens of these sorts of groups. By contrast, not only states but also the units of a federal system are frequently described and experienced as political communities and use the language of citizenship. And groups that think of themselves as nations or national minorities frequently have self-government rights or seek them.[2] In the rest of this section therefore, I will focus only on contexts where this sense of membership in a political community is in play.

Consider first some of the ways in which people's attachments, loyalties, and identities may not correspond to their legal status. In Canada, a law called the Indian Act provided that Indian women lost their formal legal status as Indians if they married men without such status. This rule followed the widespread practice among Western states of making the citizenship status of women follow that of their husbands. Presumably, many of the women who lost their legal standing as members of their political community in this way nevertheless retained a much more powerful sense of identification with and loyalty to their communities of origin than to the ones they had been required to join. Immigrants and their descendants often feel a sense of loyalty and attachment to the country of origin, regardless of whether they retain legal standing as citizens there. Jews often feel a powerful sense of loyalty and attachment to Israel, even if they have no formal legal connection to it.

If people who lack the legal status of citizenship sometimes feel that they belong to a political community, people who have legal status as citizens sometimes feel very little attachment to or emotional identification with the political community in which they have this status. More generally, the degree of identification or attachment that legal citizens feel probably varies

---

[2] As I observed in Chapter 3, Kymlicka is entirely right to draw our attention to the fact that immigrant groups typically do not demand self-government rights and to argue that the differences between the aspirations of immigrants and national minorities are morally and politically relevant. I would not draw the line between such groups as sharply as Kymlicka does, for reasons spelled out in previous chapters, but I do think the differences in demands matter and cannot be entirely attributed to false consciousness or adaptive preference formation.

widely among individuals and groups and may vary a good deal over time within any given individual or group. To be slightly more precise, we might distinguish further between identity and attachment, noting especially that it is possible to have a strong sense of one's political identity as a member of a given political community without a corresponding sense of attachment to it. Identity may depend significantly on one's personal geographical history and on the availability of alternative political identities, while attachment may depend more on the congruence between one's own commitments and those of the community, including the extent to which people experience a sense of welcome in the political community for other aspects of their identities (e.g. race, religion, culture, sexual orientation, and so on). For example, one may think of oneself as a citizen of the United States or Canada or Fiji without feeling any strong sense of patriotism or attachment to the political community.

How might this variability in the sense of belonging, the psychological dimension of citizenship, be relevant to the legal dimension of citizenship? One answer is that it should not be relevant at all. Citizenship should be treated as a threshold concept. Once over the threshold, all are to be treated alike. We do not and should not hand out more legal rights (or legal duties) to some—say, the more patriotic—and fewer to others—say, the less patriotic.

That seems to me a largely valid principle, whose importance is brought home by the failure of so many states to respect it in ways that are profoundly objectionable. For example, in Chapter 9, I will argue that the lesser attachment of Fijian Indians to Fiji is morally irrelevant to the question of their legal status as citizens. Still, the principle does require a few qualifications.

First, what counts as equal treatment is always contestable and frequently contested. One clue about possible objectionable inequalities in citizenship rights—though it does not constitute proof of them—might be found by considering those citizens who do not feel a strong sense of identity or attachment, especially those who feel alienated from and hostile towards the political community. In some cases, disaffection may be created by particular constructions of 'equality' or particular configurations of 'equal rights'. Think, for example, of policies requiring separate but equal accommodations for different races or requiring all to close their shops on the same day, a day that corresponds to the religious practices of some and not others or requiring all to bare their heads as a sign of respect, a practice that reflects respect in some cultures and not in others. All these policies can be presented as ways of instantiating equal rights but experienced by some as forms of inequality and exclusion. In such cases, the disaffection might be alleviated, at least in part, by alternative constructions of equal rights that paid less attention to formal equality and more attention to the requirements of even-handed justice in particular contexts. This may invite the objection that I am now proposing to give more rights to the less patriotic, but I'll take that chance.

The second qualification is even more important for the purposes of this chapter. Consider cases—as in federal states or in the European Union—where people are members of two or more political communities at the same time and where these communities divide up the powers and jurisdictions between them. There are many different reasons for dividing powers and jurisdictions in one way or another, but the question I want to focus on is whether the psychological dimension of citizenship is one of them. How should such institutional arrangements be related, if at all, to patterns of political identity and attachment?

The conventional understanding of the state and citizenship is not much help here because it does not have much space for any version of federalism that goes beyond issues of administrative convenience. It insists, in ways that I think are often problematic, on the sovereignty of the state and thus the subordination of other forms of political community, whether internal to the state (e.g. provinces) or external (e.g. the EU). With respect to citizenship, the conventional view is that state citizenship should take priority as a locus of political identity, that other forms of citizenship ought to be subordinate, both legally and psychologically.

As an empirical matter, it can certainly be the case that people feel a stronger identification with and attachment to one of the constituent political units of a federal system than they do to the federal government. For example, public opinion surveys have shown that francophones living in Quebec tend to identify more strongly as Québécois than as Canadians and to express a strong attachment to this identity (Kalin 1995; Kymlicka 1995: 191). Francophone Québécois tend to think of themselves as citizens of Quebec first and most strongly and most affectionately, as citizens of Canada second and more weakly and less affectionately (though, of course, one should keep in mind what I said earlier about variability within groups and within a given individual, especially across time).

If this is the psychological reality, how should the rest of Canada respond to it? In particular, what should we make of this psychological reality from a normative perspective? One possibility is to criticize francophones for having such attitudes, to demand that they identify more strongly with Canada. One hears this sort of view expressed, implicitly and explicitly, often enough, but I confess I am unable to see the point of it. Justice neither requires nor prohibits the efforts to construct political structures, institutions, and policies that will strengthen or weaken the collective identities that are in play here. Justice does set some limits to the ways in which collective political identities may be constructed, prohibiting certain kinds of exclusions from citizenship and the political community. In my view, for reasons spelled out in Chapter 5, the Quebec nationalist project generally falls well within the limits of what justice permits in these matters.[3] I do not see why francophone Québécois have any obligation, moral or otherwise, to identify more strongly as Canadians. I think that it would be better for Canada as a political community if they felt a stronger sense of identification with Canada, but I do not see why this makes it morally incumbent upon them to do so.

There are various other possibilities. I will mention five (some of which could be combined in various ways:

1. Adjust the institutional arrangements of federalism (and hence, directly or indirectly, the legal rights and duties of citizens) so that they reflect the psychological realities of differentiated political identities. In other words, on this view, the federal government should play a stronger role in the lives of the citizens of other provinces than it would in the lives of the citizens of Quebec. This kind of arrangement goes under the label asymmetrical federalism and a partial (if formally unacknowledged) version of this has been the actual practice in Canada for some time.

Some people oppose asymmetrical federalism on principle, arguing that any such arrangement is incompatible with a commitment to equal citizenship, but it seems to me that this argument depends on an entirely formal view of equal citizenship. The alternative, as I have argued before, is to see that a substantive commitment to equality sometimes requires the legal recognition of differences. Asymmetrical federalism provides one mechanism for achieving that. It is a form of evenhanded justice that takes reasonable account of the differences between Quebec and the other provinces. Still, questions of degree are important here. At some point asymmetry slides into something else. Moreover, I would not claim that this political arrangement is morally required, only that it is morally permissible and has certain advantages in Canada's current situation.

2. Decentralize radically to all the provinces, in the name of equality (whether provincial equality or equal citizenship or both). This is a course recommended by some on the right in Canada who favour decentralized government generally and less government overall. The solution would presumably strengthen provincial identities and weaken Canadian identity everywhere, at least if political identities are significantly shaped by the institutional allocation of power. In that respect, it does not correspond to the existing (asymmetrical) patterns of political identification in Canada. As I just noted, I do not find the view that equal citizenship always requires identical legal arrangements persuasive, and I would add here that I do not see why the idea of provincial equality should be regarded as morally compelling. On the

---

[3] One important qualification to this claim would involve Quebec's stance towards aboriginal peoples which is deeply problematic in ways similar to Canada's. I explore these issues in relation to Canada in Chapter 8. Apart from the treatment of aboriginal people, I think the Canadian nationalist project also falls within these parameters of justice for the most part, but this is not usually questioned in the way that Quebec's project is.

other hand, while I find this course of action politically unattractive because it would reduce the capacity of the federal government to address national problems and to engage in redistributive programmes, I would not say that there is anything intrinsically unjust about it. It, too, could plausibly be defended as compatible with evenhanded justice.

3. Try to find a positive, rather than a critical, basis for strengthening the identification of Québécois with Canada. I think that there is a lot to be said for this approach if one can find a way to do it effectively. Alan Cairns has argued (plausibly) that this was the political strategy behind Pierre Trudeau's advocacy of the creation of the Charter of Rights and Freedoms in 1982 (Cairns 1992). Trudeau wanted the Charter to become a symbol to which all Canadians would feel attached because all would share the fundamental liberal values it expressed. He hoped that the existence of this common set of formal legal rights would help to create a sense of common citizenship and a shared political identity among Canadians. In fact, the Charter itself recognizes all kinds of legally relevant differences among Canadians, including a variety of collective rights, but that did not necessarily detract from and may even have enhanced its usefulness as a symbol of shared political identity in Canada.

This alternative provides a useful reminder that it is not only minorities who may seek to shape and reinforce collective identities through political institutions and policies. Indeed, much political contestation involves competing collective identities because what people regard as their interests often depends on how they think of themselves and on how they think about the identity of their community. Again, there are ways of constructing collective identities that are morally objectionable, but if we think that we ought to recognize significant space for democratic self-determination, then we have to leave considerable room for the construction and competition of collective identities.

In many ways, Trudeau succeeded in his project. The Charter is extremely popular, even in Quebec, and is the thing most often cited when people are asked what it means to be Canadian. Yet Trudeau did not manage to transform the primary political identification of most Québécois with Quebec, and in important ways his strategy may have backfired by politicizing the Constitution and leading the Québécois to feel that only major constitutional changes (or formal sovereignty) could provide adequate recognition for their identity (Ajzenstat 1995).

4. Do nothing. This may be the least bad alternative under the circumstances, in the sense that it does not make things worse. Still, it leaves an important problem unaddressed. It seems to me that it would be deeply unfortunate for Canada as a political community if the Québécois stay within Canada only out of a sense of regrettable necessity, that is, out of a fear of the potentially high and very uncertain economic costs of separation, rather than

out of a positive identification with Canada as a political community. Maintaining political unity on the basis of regrettable necessity might be a prudent decision. It might be better for the rest of Canada as well as for Quebec than separation, but it would be unfortunate. A community held together only by regrettable necessity will presumably find it more difficult to act collectively and to induce its members to make sacrifices for a common good and a shared future when the sense of common identification is so weak. It will find it harder to pursue evenhanded justice in many areas.

5. Find some way to embrace 'deep diversity' (to use Charles Taylor's term) as a positive basis for unity and a common identity. Taylor puts it this way:

For Quebeckers and for most French Canadians, the way of being a Canadian (for those who still want to be) is by belonging to a constituent element of Canada, *la nation québécoise*, or *canadienne-française*. Something analogous holds for aboriginal communities in this country; their way of being Canadian is not accommodated by first-level diversity. . . .

To build a country for everyone, Canada would have to allow for second-level or 'deep' diversity, in which a plurality of ways of belonging would also be acknowledged and accepted. Someone of, say, Italian extraction in Toronto or Ukrainian extraction in Edmonton might indeed feel Canadian as a bearer of individual rights in a multicultural mosaic. His or her belonging would not 'pass through' some other community, although the ethnic identity might be important to him or her in various ways. But this person might nevertheless accept that a Québécois or a Cree or a Déné might belong in a very different way, that these persons were Canadian through being members of their national communities. Reciprocally, the Québécois, Cree, or Déné would accept the perfect legitimacy of the 'mosaic' identity (Taylor, 1993: 182–183).

This approach goes further than asymmetrical federalism in the sense that it affirms, and does not merely yield to, the multiplicity and variety of political identities in Canada. Taylor focuses not on the institutions but on the underlying political culture in which those institutions are embedded and through which they are interpreted. To put it another way, it would only be possible to establish asymmetrical federalism as something more than a covert concession to necessity if Canadians were to adopt the sort of attitude Taylor describes here.

As Taylor suggests, most of the points made about the psychological identification of the Québécois as citizens could be made even more strongly about aboriginal people in Canada. If their current institutional capacities are much less fully developed (after over a century of systematic destruction of these capacities), their political identities are clearly much more sharply distinct from Canadian citizenship than those of any other people who live in Canada, including the Québécois. (Of course, like all identities, the identities of aboriginal people vary across individuals and even within the same individual over time.) Many aboriginal people, especially though not exclusively those who live in a territory where aboriginal people constitute a majority, think of themselves as members of this or that people or this or that community and aspire politically for the people to which they belong to govern itself as much as possible. Some aboriginal people do not regard themselves as Canadian citizens even in legal terms (seeing Canadian citizenship as an identification forced upon them against their wills), and many others see it as a very weak identity. Even more than the Québécois, aboriginal people seem linked to Canada primarily by a sense of regrettable necessity, necessity defined here as the need for ongoing transfers of resources (even if conceived as justified entitlements) and/or as the non-viability of small, economically and organizationally limited political units in the modern world.

What might change that sense of regrettable necessity into something more positive? What might create a sense of common citizenship between aboriginal people and other Canadians? Again, I think that Taylor's conception of deep diversity points in the proper direction. In Chapter 8 I explore more fully what it might mean if Canadians were to take that conception seriously in their dealings with aboriginal people.

The Political Dimension

Let me turn finally to the political dimension of citizenship which is concerned with the way people may share in collective agency. I will focus on the issue of representational legitimacy. Who may act authoritatively on behalf of and in the name of the political community and why?

The conventional view is closely tied to the understanding of citizenship as primarily a legal status establishing certain rights and duties. On this view, representational legitimacy depends upon being selected by voters in fair and free elections. One has only to look at South Africa or the former Soviet Union to see how powerful this view is and why it must be the first and most fundamental element in any democratic theory of representational legitimacy.

But is it sufficient? I think not. I pass by here a number of problems with respect to elected officials: the enduring question in democratic theory of the relation between representatives and those who voted against them; the issue of alienated or apathetic voters; the deep scepticism about all elected officials. There are other problems of legitimacy when key decisions are made by people not subject to elections and formal democratic control, whether in the public or private sphere (central bankers, the World Bank, the International Monetary Fund, European Community bureaucrats, capitalist investors) (Pauly 1997).

The question I am concerned with is how we should think about representational legitimacy in a particular context of conflicting claims: when the representational legitimacy of people elected through conventional democratic mechanisms is challenged either by another set of elected representatives (provincial officials claiming that they, rather than federal politicians, speak for the Québécois) or by spokespeople not directly elected by those for whom they claim to speak (leaders of aboriginal organizations claiming that they, rather than elected politicians, speak for aboriginal people).

I want to suggest that representational legitimacy must depend partly upon issues of identity as well as upon legal electoral procedures free of fraud and violence. Where the issues at stake are closely tied to powerful, politically relevant identities, the representational legitimacy of elected officials will appropriately depend on the extent to which they can be seen as having been chosen by people with the politically relevant identities in contexts where the issues connected to those identities were clear.

When feminists criticized the judiciary committee considering charges of sexual harassment against Clarence Thomas because it was composed entirely of men who 'just didn't get it', the criticism had a powerful resonance and appropriately so, despite the fact that roughly half of the voters who had elected these senators were women. Even most men could understand that most men's experiences and interests have been very different from women's experiences and interests in this area, so that it was much more problematic for men to claim to represent women on this issue than it would be, say, on free trade or general health legislation, even though there might be important differences between men and women in such areas as well.[4]

The same dynamics are at play in Canadian politics as a result of the fact that people have multiple and overlapping national identities. Alan Cairns, a distinguished commentator on Canadian politics, objects to the way minority leaders have deployed their identity claims in recent political debates to challenge the representational legitimacy of federal politicians:

Both Québécois and aboriginal nationalists act as if their people did not have dual identities and loyalties, one of which is legitimately represented by the federal government. Instead, they implicitly deny, or at least downgrade, the 'other' identity of Québécois and aboriginal peoples as Canadians. They treat the Canadian identity as that of the other, of the external party that sits on the other side of the table and therefore speaks as an outsider, through Quebec and aboriginal leaders, to Québécois and aboriginal peoples (Cairns 1993: 193).

---

[4] For an insightful discussion of the problem of representation with special attention to the position of women and African–Americans in the United States, see Williams (1998). For other important discussions of these issues, see Young (1990), Phillips (1993, 1995), and Kymlicka (1995). My comments here do not even attempt to address most of the questions about representation raised in these rich works. My goal is simply to highlight some of the ways in which multiple and overlapping citizenships raise questions about the legitimacy of conventional forms of representation.

Cairns goes on to note that federally elected members of Parliament no longer seem able to speak for the Québécois or aboriginal people they were elected to represent, and he concludes that the 'theory and practice of representation are in disarray' (Cairns 1993: 193). Sometimes Cairns seems to admire the political skill of the nationalists in delegitimating duly elected representatives; sometimes he seems frustrated as though they should not be able to get away with it.

For my part, I find this development both understandable and defensible. The nationalists are skilful, of course, but I think they win these legitimacy struggles for other reasons, namely, that our conventional electoral mechanisms presuppose a degree of shared identity between voters and the people elected to represent them that it has not been plausible to assume in the cases Cairns cites.

Cairns wrote his article before the appearance of the *Bloc Québécois*, a political party that emerged in the 1993 federal election to compete for seats in Parliament. It exists only in Quebec and its central political goal is Quebec sovereignty. It was very successful, winning enough seats to become the official opposition party in Parliament. In the subsequent election, it lost a few seats and its status as the official opposition, but it still elected by far the largest contingent of Quebec MPs. It is formally distinct from, though it has close ties to, the *Parti-Québécois* which is a party that contests only provincial elections in Quebec and also has sovereignty as its central goal. The *Bloc* sees its role as transitional and temporary, whereas the *Parti-Québécois* aims to become the governing party in a newly independent Quebec.

The struggle over representational legitimacy has shifted in a significant way with the appearance of the *Bloc Québécois*. Previously, the question of who could speak for Quebec voters with regard to issues of Quebec's distinct identity and interests was clouded by the fact that federal elections tended to focus on other issues, while such questions had been central in Quebec's provincial elections since the emergence of the *Parti-Québécois* in the early 1970s. This gave provincial officials a representational legitimacy on these issues that was hard for federal officials to match. Now the *Bloc Québécois* enjoys the same sort of representational legitimacy, but if the *Bloc* were to lose most of the seats it now holds, the representational legitimacy of the federal officials elected in their place would be greatly enhanced on issues relating to Quebec's distinct identity. In the last federal election, however, the *Bloc* held onto most of its seats and hence to its representational legitimacy.

The issue is even clearer with respect to aboriginal people. Over the past several years, when considering changes in the Constitution that would take account of the claims of the Québécois and of aboriginal peoples, federal officials have engaged in formal negotiations with aboriginal leaders. Cairns suggests that this practice is anomalous: from the perspective of the conventional theory, national representatives should be selected through parliamentary elections.

Instead, these arrangements gave extraordinary representational authority to the leaders of organized groups who were not subject to direct election by the people they were to represent.

Now it would be perfectly possible to challenge the representational legitimacy of these aboriginal leaders. For example, an organization of Indian women argued that these predominantly male aboriginal leaders did not adequately represent the perspectives and interests of aboriginal women. But the aboriginal women offered an alternative form of representation of aboriginal people by aboriginal people. I doubt that Cairns means to suggest that members of parliament who were neither aboriginal people themselves nor elected in constituencies composed primarily of aboriginal people could claim to speak effectively on behalf of aboriginal people. I do not see how any non-aboriginal person could claim to speak politically on behalf of aboriginal people, unless directly authorized to do so by an aboriginal constituency, because the political salience of aboriginal identity is so apparent.

Thus, the political dimension of citizenship points to the need for judgements about the fit between electoral mechanisms and political identities in assessing representational legitimacy, even when people share a common legal citizenship. My goal here is not to settle the question of what sort of representation is legitimate, but rather to open the question up. In some cases, special forms of representation may be appropriate, and in others not. In some cases distinct institutional arrangements may be desirable, and in others not.

To summarize, a contextual approach to political theory encourages us to begin thinking about citizenship by reflecting upon existing practices. In this chapter, I have tried to show that the practices of Canada (and of some other states as well) differ sharply from the unitary conception of citizenship that emerges from a conventional view of the nation-state. What we find is not singularity and exclusivity, but multiplicity and overlap along legal, psychological, and political dimensions. I have argued that these practices are at least morally permissible and, in some respects, morally required ways of recognizing claims of collective identity. We ought at least to be open to these sorts of practices as ways of addressing the problem of citizenship in multinational states. So, the conventional conception of citizenship is an intellectual and moral prison from which we should escape. What is needed is a more complex conception, one that is open to multiplicity and that grows out of practices we judge to be just and beneficial.

8

Citizenship and the Challenge of Aboriginal Self-Government: Is Deep Diversity Desirable?

In Canada, as in many other countries with aboriginal inhabitants, the government exercises much more direct control over the lives of aboriginal people than it does over most of the population. For a long time, and with increasing emphasis in recent years, representatives of aboriginal people in Canada have been demanding that the government give up this control. For the most part, however, they are not advocating that aboriginal people should simply be treated like other citizens. Instead, what they want—and what they argue is required as a matter of fundamental right—is a distinct set of institutions and arrangements through which aboriginal people can govern themselves within Canada.

One important obstacle to the project of aboriginal self-government has been the hegemony of the unitary model of citizenship, the widespread view that any form of differentiated citizenship would be incompatible with the inclusion of aboriginal people in a Canadian political community in which they were full citizens and all citizens were treated equally. In the previous chapter, I argued that the unitary model was inadequate and that our conceptions of citizenship should become more open to multiplicity. In this chapter, I will pursue that theme in more detail through a discussion of the relationship between Canadian citizenship and aboriginal self-government. I want to explore further the vision of differentiated citizenship that Charles Taylor has labelled 'deep diversity', an arrangement in which many aboriginal people would have a self-governing aboriginal community as their primary locus of political identity and participation while still being Canadian citizens. I will not attempt to spell out what this sort of deep diversity might entail in specific detail. That would be far too ambitious for this chapter.[1] My goal instead is to anticipate and meet two key objections to the project of deep

---

[1] The best discussion of these issues can be found in the *Report* of the Royal Commission on Aboriginal Peoples (1995).

diversity: the first, that common citizenship requires, at a minimum, that fellow citizens be subject to the same legal regime at least with regard to the protection of basic rights and liberties; the second, that the sort of differentiated citizenship that aboriginal self-government would create would be incompatible with the need for civic integration or what Will Kymlicka has called 'the requirements of social unity'.

I do want to enter a preliminary caution. The unitary model of citizenship does provide an ideal of *equality*, and, in the name of equal citizenship, provides grounds for criticizing policies and practices that exclude or marginalize distinct groups of citizens. Many of the injustices that aboriginal people have suffered in Canadian society have come precisely from the fact that they have not been treated as equal citizens, however equal citizenship is defined. The widespread denial of basic rights—to say nothing of equal opportunity—for aboriginal people in education, in health care, in the economy, in the criminal justice system, and in many other spheres has been too well documented to repeat here.

If the requirements of equal citizenship were met, even on the terms of the unitary conception, the conditions under which aboriginal people live in Canada would be vastly better than they are. It may well be the case, as many advocates of aboriginal self-government suspect, that the Canadian government will never meet even its own standards for equal citizenship, but that is no reason to abandon entirely the critical perspective those standards bring to bear.

Whatever form a non-unitary conception of citizenship might take, it will not legitimate the fundamental violations of equal citizenship that aboriginal people now suffer so frequently. In short, the unitary conception of equal citizenship provides a critical standard that should not be entirely abandoned in the search for an alternative conception of citizenship that respects aboriginal difference more fully. I hope to show below that it is possible to preserve elements of this unitary ideal of equal citizenship while transcending it in some respects.

In pursuing this inquiry, I adopt three presuppositions. First, I assume the moral legitimacy and desirability in principle of aboriginal self-government. While there are many ways in which aboriginal rights to self-government can be articulated, evaluated, and defended, I will not pursue that discussion here.[2]

---

[2] For an illuminating account of the justifications for aboriginal self-government, see Macklem (1995). Of course, not everyone accepts these justifications. The demand for aboriginal self-government has met with a mixed reaction from the non-aboriginal population in Canada. Some people, both officials and ordinary citizens, support the basic project while others oppose it. The support and the opposition depend in part on how aboriginal self-government is conceived and how people imagine it will develop. For example, some government officials see aboriginal self-government as a useful vehicle for downloading costs and responsibilities without transferring resources and powers. Needless to say, this is not the vision of aboriginal self-government that aboriginal leaders have in mind. They aim at something much more substantive than administrative decentralization and cost containment. At the same time, some oppose aboriginal self-government precisely because they imagine it will be vastly more expensive than current arrangements. In this chapter, however, I want to put questions about financial issues to one side and focus instead on a more fundamental theoretical concern, namely, the question of how a substantive vision of aboriginal self-government fits with the idea of citizenship.

Rather I will assume a commitment to aboriginal self-government in principle in order to consider how such a commitment might affect our thinking about citizenship.

Aboriginal self-government can take many different forms, and, given the variety of circumstances in which aboriginal people find themselves, many different ways of institutionalizing aboriginal self-government will be required to meet the needs of aboriginal people. To take one important example, the vast majority of aboriginal people live outside reserves or other territories likely to fall under the administrative control of aboriginal governments. Many of them live in urban areas. Their relationships to the federal and provincial governments in Canada may be very different from those of aboriginal people living on aboriginal land. Nevertheless, I will focus primarily on the latter.

I want to focus on the strongest possible model of aboriginal self-government because that is the context that poses the strongest possible challenge to conventional understandings of citizenship. If, as I think, it is possible to reconcile the strongest form of aboriginal self-government with an attractive conception of Canadian citizenship, then *a fortiori* it should be possible to reconcile other forms of aboriginal self-government with Canadian citizenship. Thus the conception of differentiated citizenship that I will defend here should be regarded as an ideal type, describing one end on a continuum of possible relationships between aboriginal people and Canada. There might be many hybrid forms of citizenship, and many, perhaps most, aboriginal people will find themselves somewhere along the continuum rather than at the end that I describe. But for theoretical purposes, it is especially important to analyse this end-point.

My second presupposition is that most aboriginal people living within the geographical territory identified as Canada will continue to be legal citizens of Canada, whatever forms of aboriginal self-government emerge from current and future negotiations. One important way in which the situation of aboriginal people in Canada differs from that of the Québécois is that independent statehood is not a realistic option for most aboriginal peoples. Since aboriginal self-government will be exercised *within Canada*, it is important to reflect upon what being within Canada means both to aboriginal people and to non-aboriginal people and to consider what Canadian citizens share in common and what they do not. This sort of reflection is important even if one accepts (as I do) the claim of aboriginal people that their right to self-government is a fundamental moral right (or an 'inherent' right in the term often used in Canadian discussions) rather than a discretionary delegation of political authority from the Canadian government.

Thirdly, I assume the usefulness of an inquiry informed almost entirely by Western political theory. Any non-aboriginal person like me who writes about the topic of aboriginal self-government is bound to think about the problem

of perspective. The concept of citizenship has a long history in Western political thought and is intimately associated with other concepts such as justice,
democracy, and political community. Given the differences between the
cultures of aboriginal peoples and the cultures of non-aboriginal peoples, is it
appropriate to offer a normative analysis that draws exclusively on non-
aboriginal traditions of thought?

Certainly not, in my view, if it is put forward as the one right way to think
about these issues. But on the other hand, non-aboriginal Canadians cannot
and should not avoid thinking about what aboriginal self-government
implies for the nature of the Canadian political community as a whole. In
thinking about alternative ways of living together, there are characteristic
puzzles, problems, and concerns that arise for people who share the Western
tradition of political thought (though, of course, there are many differences
and disagreements within that tradition). Those who share the (various) traditions of aboriginal thought may identify a different set of puzzles, problems,
and concerns. The goal of my reflections therefore is not to use the concept
of citizenship to provide definitive answers to questions about how aboriginal people and non-aboriginal people should live together in Canada, but to
contribute to a conversation in which aboriginal authors also participate from
their own perspectives.[3] More precisely, my goal is to identify particular
concerns about aboriginal self-government that arise from within the
Western tradition and to show how these can be addressed from within that
tradition's own resources.

As always, our reflections can be helped by paying attention to context. I
want to draw attention to two contextual features in the next two sections:
first, the multiplicity of aboriginal identities in Canada; second, the meaning
that Canadian citizenship has acquired for aboriginal people over the past
two centuries.

Aboriginal Multiplicities

So far I have been using the terms aboriginal people and aboriginal peoples.
These are useful terms for purposes of drawing a contrast between aboriginals
and non-aboriginals, but the generic term aboriginal conceals significant
differences of identity, culture, and collective life among those who count as
aboriginal, differences that become highly salient when one turns to the
question of how they think of their own political identities. The Canadian
government officially recognizes three distinct kinds of aboriginal people.

---

[3] Again, the Royal Commission on Aboriginal Peoples (1995) and many of the supporting
documents provide an especially valuable source of aboriginal contributions.

The first and most familiar category is composed of people conventionally called 'Indians' in Canada as in the United States, though in Canada they generally refer to themselves as First Nations for reasons that will become apparent. This category includes various groups of people long settled in North America who were displaced, often violently, by European settlers and their descendants. These people have been subject for over a century to explicit, highly formalized mechanisms of regulation and control, often involving the setting aside of specific areas of land ('reserves') for particular groups. (These lands were sometimes different from and always much smaller than the territories the groups had occupied prior to the arrival of the settlers). Despite the existence of these reserves (or because of the terrible social conditions characteristic of most of them), most First Nations people do not live on the reserves. As we shall see in the next section, 'Indians' were both excluded from and coercively included within Canadian citizenship in ways that have important implications for contemporary discussions of citizenship.

The decision of 'Indians' to call themselves 'First Nations' reflects their appreciation for the politics of language. The term 'nation' is, of course, a European concept with no precise correlate in aboriginal culture, but 'Indians' noticed that in Western discourse there was considerable sympathy for the view that 'nations' deserved self-determination and they noticed that the Québécois had used the rhetoric of nationhood to good effect in Canadian political debates. Since they had traditionally lived in distinct, self-governing communities with ties to particular territories and distinct languages and ways of life, they rightly judged that they had as good a claim (if not a better one) to the term than either Canadians or the Québécois and that appropriating it as a self-designation would be rhetorically useful in communications with non-aboriginal people about their desires to govern themselves (as it has been).

The use of the adjective 'First' in First Nations also serves an important political function. One important trope in Canadian political discourse has been to say that the French and the English were the 'founding nations' of Canada. This phrase serves to legitimate the priority given to French as an official language throughout Canada as compared with the treatment of the languages of immigrant groups which are sometimes more widely spoken than French in a given area but enjoy no official status. Even more importantly, the concept of two founding nations has often been used by the Québécois to justify demands that Quebec not be treated merely as one province among ten but rather as an entity co-equal with the rest of Canada (on the grounds that Quebec should be regarded as the contemporary embodiment of the French founding nation). The use of the term 'First' by First Nations people draws attention to the chronological priority of aboriginal people in settling Canada and thus implicitly challenges the myth of the two founding nations. In effect, the phrase says, 'If being in on the beginning of Canada entitles a group to equal treatment regardless of its current relative size, then *each* of the First Nations ought to be regarded as an equal to the French and the English'. The effect of this rhetorical move is that even people in English Canada who are sympathetic to Quebec are now far more reluctant to employ the phrase 'two founding nations'. This is a source of great irritation to Québécois who are more inclined to brush aside aboriginal objections, and it is one of many factors that has heightened tensions between aboriginal people and Quebec nationalists despite the fact that Quebec's record in dealing with its aboriginal inhabitants is no worse, and in some respects better than, the record of the other provinces or the federal government (although this is not a high standard). The phrase 'First Nations' would not have the same significance in a different context such as that of the United States where the trope of founding nations has no significant political role today.

The second category is 'Inuit', formerly referred to as Eskimo. These are the people of the far north. Apart from occasional intrusions by non-aboriginal Canadians into particular areas in pursuit of minerals and other natural resources, most of the people in this category did not have much contact with people outside their immediate communities until relatively recently, and many still do not. Because the territory where they live is vast, remote, and inhospitable, the Inuit as a whole have been subject to much less displacement than Indians, and indeed the Canadian government paid little attention to them until well into the twentieth century, and then often only in connection with assertions of territorial sovereignty.

The third category is the Métis. This term refers to the descendants of European (mainly French) trappers and aboriginal women. These people established distinct communities, cultures, and ways of life in the west of Canada during the eighteenth and nineteenth centuries. They were also subjected to a variety of forms of formal and informal domination, including armed repression, the execution of political leaders, and various forms of social and economic exclusion and discrimination. The Métis were formally recognized as aboriginal people only in 1982 with the adoption of the Charter of Rights and Freedoms as part of the Canadian Constitution. They generally now live lives more integrated with those of non-aboriginal Canadians than do the Inuit or the First Nations people. Collectively, they have been much less inclined to make land claims or to advance demands for self-government than other aboriginal people. The number of those identifying themselves as Métis has varied considerably, rising substantially in recent years as this heritage has come to be seen as a source of pride rather than shame and as this identity has carried fewer social costs (though it still offers few, if any, material advantages).

These three broad categories do not begin to exhaust the multiplicity of politically relevant aboriginal identities. Many, perhaps most, aboriginal people experience their primary communal identification at the level of the band or at least some collectivity smaller than these three categories. This is particularly true for First Nations people. The term itself draws attention to this multiplicity. The use of the plural deliberately highlights the fact that there are many different groups of aboriginal people, each of which has a distinct history, language, and culture and each of which thinks of itself as a self-governing community (e.g. Cree, Ojibway, Haida). Any satisfactory political arrangement will have to recognize and respect not only the differences between First Nations people and non-aboriginal Canadians, but also the differences among the various First Nations.

The primary identification of First Nations people with particular local historical communities is true even of aboriginal people who live in urban areas, although the character and strength of the communal identification of aboriginal people living outside aboriginal territory probably varies much more widely than it does among those who live on aboriginal land. For example, based on the testimony of aboriginal people to the Royal Commission on Aboriginal Peoples, it would seem that some aboriginal people in urban areas think of themselves as band members who just happen to be living elsewhere at the moment and who want to maintain strong ties to their bands, while others have a powerful sense of identification as aboriginal people, perhaps more specifically as Indian or Métis, perhaps even more specifically as Ojibway or Iroquois, but do not feel as powerful ties to a specific band or to specific aboriginal land (Royal Commission on Aboriginal Peoples 1992, 1993a, 1993b, 1993c).

The institutionalization of aboriginal self-government may intensify the split already present between aboriginal people living in diasporas and those living in homelands.[4] It seems reasonable to assume that the most effective and far-reaching forms of aboriginal self-government will emerge in contexts in which aboriginal peoples possess a territorial land base and constitute the overwhelming majority of people living in that territory. If these new aboriginal governments become the focal points of identity and action for those whose daily lives are affected by them, as will be the case if they work well, the gulf between those who live inside such territorial units and those who live outside may well widen. If the governments are successful in revitalizing aboriginal culture within these local political communities, those who live inside and those who live outside may come to feel that they no longer share the same way of life or the same fate. In short, the common bonds and common identity may weaken.

---

[4] One might draw an analogy here with the way in which the decision by francophones in Quebec to focus their nationalist project on gaining control over and strengthening the political capacities of the Quebec government led to a weakening of the bonds between francophones inside Quebec and francophones in the rest of Canada. See Chapter 5 for a discussion of these dynamics.

At the same time, there will be forms of collective aboriginal organization that transcend these primary communities of identification (however those are constructed legally). Some of these may well reflect existing or past ways in which aboriginal peoples have organized themselves collectively on a larger scale. There is a rich diversity of cultural approaches to draw upon here, as, for example, in the Confederacy and Grand Council systems that characterized groups like the Iroquois and Ojibway. On the other hand, economies of scale and the requirements of dealing with the federal and the provincial governments both administratively and politically will make it necessary for aboriginal peoples to rely upon existing and new regional and pan-Canadian organizations that are not rooted in the same way in cultural traditions. In such cases, questions about representational legitimacy are apt to arise with respect to these larger organizations. Will aboriginal people have a direct voice in the selection of leaders for such organizations and in the discussion of their policies or will all connections with these organizations be mediated through the primary communities? If the former, then a stronger sense of community and membership may emerge with respect to the wider aboriginal community or some parts of it.

Thus the institutionalization of aboriginal governments may contribute to the evolution of aboriginal identities in another way, namely, by increasing the salience of the category 'aboriginal' and its subcategories 'Indian', 'Inuit', and 'Métis'. While aboriginal cultures have traditionally been local cultures, to a considerable extent, and identities likewise primarily local (though the picture is more complex for a number of groups like the Iroquois, Ojibway, and Haida), over the years both bureaucratic categorization and oppositional political action have created some basis for a common aboriginal identity, and especially for a common First Nations identity despite the tremendous diversity among the various peoples. While aboriginal self-government will strengthen local identities in some respects, the economic, administrative, and political requirements of self-government will all generate the need for much more cooperation among different aboriginal communities than in the past. It is at least possible then that many people will develop a stronger sense of identification with the aboriginal community as a whole and even a sense of aboriginal citizenship (in the sense of membership in a genuine overarching aboriginal community or in some significant subset). Of course, this sort of development is even more likely among that vast segment of the aboriginal population that lives in cities or in other areas where aboriginal people do not constitute a majority of the inhabitants.

Partly as a result of such developments, the aboriginal community as a whole may face complex institutional questions about representation and political legitimacy. For example, will each aboriginal government be represented in larger bodies on an individual basis or will factors like population count? How will the huge population of aboriginal people living in urban areas be represented? Will the relations of aboriginal people to overarching political entities be entirely mediated through local governments and organizations or will there be some sense of more direct connection between aboriginal leaders and aboriginal people? Of course, aboriginal organizations already face these questions and we need not assume that the institutional answers must reflect one principle. Nevertheless, the current situation has a certain fluidity and ambiguity with respect to organizational representation which it may be more difficult and less desirable to maintain in the future, and new patterns of identification among aboriginal people could make the organizational issues more salient and more difficult to resolve.

This points to the possibility of overlapping forms of aboriginal membership and to the possibility that psychological membership may be fluid and shifting. The legal dimension of membership cannot be as shifting and fluid as the psychological one, but the appropriateness of establishing legal rights and obligations with respect to a particular community may depend in part on the rights and obligations established with respect to others, and the appropriateness of the overall set of arrangements will presumably have some relationship to the kinds of identification and loyalty that people feel with respect to different communities. In that sense, some of the puzzles about what membership in the Canadian political community means may be reproduced (in somewhat different fashion) within the aboriginal community.

In sum, in thinking about citizenship and aboriginal self-government, one has to consider multiple possible *loci* of authority and identification. While the chapter will focus primarily on the question of how the existence of aboriginal governments linked to primary communities of identification should affect our thinking about the nature of Canadian citizenship, I will try to keep these other aspects in view as well.

Meaning in Context: Canadian Citizenship as a Tool of Coercive Assimilation

A contextual approach to political theory requires one to pay attention to the way concepts have been used historically because this is bound to shape the way a new discussion of those concepts is heard. With respect to the concept of citizenship, it is not only the conventional conception of citizenship but also the particular history of Indian policy in Canada that is bound to make those aboriginals classified as Indians especially wary of what it might mean to be included as Canadian citizens and dubious about the possibility of reconciling Canadian citizenship and aboriginal self-government.[5] (In this

---

[5] This section draws on Miller (1991: 110, 114, 190, and 206), and on Cairns (1995).

section, I use the term Indian rather than First Nations because it is the term used by the Canadian government in the official policies I am trying to describe, and it would be confusing to switch back and forth between the terms Indian and First Nations in this context.) For Indians, inclusion as citizens has been intimately associated with policies of forced assimilation.

For most of the nineteenth and twentieth centuries, Indians were treated more as subjects than citizens. Enfranchisement and full citizenship status were initially provided as a reward for becoming 'civilized', that is, for adopting Euro-Canadian values and practices and repudiating Indian culture and identity. Hence Canada's legislature passed an Act for the Gradual Civilization of the Indian Tribes in the Canadas in 1857 which laid out the terms under which Indians could become full citizens and drop their Indian status. Between 1857 and 1876, however, only one Indian was enfranchised under these provisions. So, more coercive techniques were employed, most notably the introduction of a system of compulsory residential schools in which Indian culture was severely repressed. Despite this, few Indians, even among those educated by Euro-Canadians, were willing to trade their Indian status and give up their links to their Indian communities for the sake of full Canadian citizenship. Only 250 Indians sought enfranchisement between 1857 and 1920.

Frustrated by this resistance, the government in 1920 made it possible to enfranchise Indians and thus strip them of their Indian status without their consent. The goal of this policy was consistent with what had preceded it: 'Our object is to continue until there is not a single Indian in Canada that has not been absorbed into the body politic' (D. C. Scott, Deputy Minister of the Department of Indian Affairs, 1920, as quoted in Miller 1991: 207). Thus, for a long period of Canadian history, full Canadian citizenship was treated as incompatible with a distinct Indian identity.

In 1960, the Diefenbaker government extended the franchise and full Canadian citizenship to Indians without abolishing special Indian status. This policy reflected a somewhat more ambivalent stance towards Indian culture and community than previous policies. On the one hand, the denial of the franchise to Indians had explicitly been premised upon the inferiority of Indian culture and the subordinate status of Indian communities, so that removing this stigmatizing difference without requiring the abandonment of Indian culture and community could be interpreted as a move in the direction of an egalitarian version of differentiated citizenship, that would grant equal respect to Indians without denying their distinctive position in relation to the rest of Canadian society.

On the other hand, Indians did not seek this extension of the franchise nor were they consulted about it. Moreover, it has not been entirely benign in its effects. The fact that Indians now have the right to vote like other citizens has the effect of legitimating, at least in the eyes of some, the authority of elected officials to make policies that affect Indians, while the relatively small and dispersed character of the Indian electorate ensures that they will have little actual effect on electoral outcomes.[6] Furthermore, as Boldt points out, the extension of the franchise 'lends symbolic legitimacy to the fiction that Indians have given democratic consent to Canadian sovereignty and citizenship, and that their primary commitment is to the Canadian regime. Thus it undermines Indian claims to 'peoples' rights' under the U. N. charter' (Boldt 1993: 83). This is not just a hypothetical point. Canada has explicitly challenged attempts by Indians to use UN forums for indigenous peoples on the grounds that Indians are Canadian citizens (Boldt 1993: 48).

This is an important issue for aboriginal people.[7] Aboriginal peoples in Canada want to have standing in international fora dealing with the rights of peoples, especially indigenous peoples. They want access to these fora to gain recognition and respect on the world stage as distinct cultural communities and political actors. In addition, these fora would provide additional ways of challenging the hegemonic policies of the Canadian government. Given the history and present circumstances of aboriginal people within Canada, the desire of aboriginal people to achieve international recognition as distinct peoples seems to me entirely justifiable and the Canadian government's posture entirely indefensible. Thus, whatever its original motivations, the extension of the franchise and full Canadian citizenship to Indians has been used strategically by the Canadian government to protect itself against challenges from Indians.

Subsequent official discussions of Indian policy during the 1960s reflected the same ambiguous messages about the implications of Canadian citizenship for Indians. The Hawthorn–Tremblay Report in 1966 argued for a positive reconciliation of Canadian citizenship and Indian status, coining the phrase 'citizen plus' to communicate the conviction that Indians should have all the normal entitlements of Canadian citizenship and some distinctive additional ones as well directly related to Indian status (and using the phrase 'citizen minus' to characterize the situation of Indians under previous policies). Clearly, the goal here was to achieve some sort of evenhanded justice, granting distinctive entitlements out of a sense that this was a fair way to respond to the history and circumstances of Indians in Canada.

---

[6] See Cairns (1993, 1995) for expressions of concern about the fact that the duly elected representatives of the Canadian state are not perceived to be legitimate spokespeople for aboriginal people and the previous chapter for a critical discussion of this view.

[7] It is also an important issue for the Québécois. Quebec has persistently sought distinct recognition on the world stage, so that Quebec's language and culture can receive acknowledgement and respect outside of Canada and so that Quebec's identity is not completely submerged under Canada's outside Canada's borders (Taylor 1993: 52–3). While full recognition would require independent statehood, Quebec has in fact managed to assert a distinct presence outside Canada, in part through its role in *La francophonie* and more importantly through its establishment of immigration offices in many countries. While the latter arrangement irritates partisans of a unitary theory of sovereignty, it is now well established and it has worked fairly smoothly in practice. The Canadian state has not crumbled as a result of Quebec's ability to act abroad and in its own name.

By contrast, the Trudeau White Paper of 1969 proposed to abolish all legal distinctions between Indians and other Canadians on the grounds that such distinctions were incompatible with liberal egalitarian and democratic values. This approach was motivated by a conception of justice as neutrality, which required an abstraction from differences of history and circumstances in the allocation of citizenship rights. Thus the White Paper once again linked Canadian citizenship with assimilation. This aptly named White Paper generated such fierce opposition among Indians that the government was ultimately forced to abandon it.

In sum, much of Canadian Indian policy has had as its fundamental goal the transformation of Indians into Canadian citizens like any others. With this background, it would not be surprising to find Indians committed to self-government to be wary and sceptical about the positive insights to be gained from reflection on the concept of citizenship.

The situation is a bit different for other aboriginal people. For Inuit and Métis, the concept of citizenship may carry less historical baggage simply because they did not have the kind of distinct *legal* status that Indians possessed in the Canadian polity, so that the concept of citizenship is not so intimately associated for them with attempts to eliminate their distinctive identity as peoples. This historical difference helps to explain why Inuit and Métis are less hostile than some Indians to the Charter of Rights and Freedoms, one of the primary symbols of contemporary Canadian citizenship, as I will discuss below.

Legal Equality and Cultural Difference: Should the Charter Apply to Aboriginal People?

Let me turn now to the objections that can be posed to the project of aboriginal self-government. Why would anyone suppose that aboriginal self-government might be incompatible with Canadian citizenship? One answer is that some advocates of aboriginal self-government have insisted that the Charter of Rights and Freedoms (Canada's constitutional bill of rights) should not apply to aboriginal governments. The view that the fundamental rights and freedoms of individuals must be protected against governmental abuse lies at the heart of the liberal conception of citizenship. So, many people think that if Canadians are to enjoy any kind of common citizenship, the Charter of Rights and Freedoms must apply to all Canadian citizens, including aboriginal people, in all jurisdictions in Canada.

Why would (some) aboriginal people object to this? Let me answer this question first in more general terms with regard to culture, government, and justice, and then more concretely with respect to the Charter.

Political and legal institutions are simultaneously cultural institutions in ways that are sometimes invisible to those who share the culture. The distinctiveness of aboriginal cultures brings the cultural thickness of Canadian institutions more sharply into view. Many aboriginal people see themselves as belonging to peoples with highly developed, richly differentiated languages, histories, customs, practices, understandings, and ways of life. They believe aboriginal governments will be able to reflect and express the distinctive cultures of the peoples they govern, and partly for that reason they believe a system of aboriginal self-government will be more legitimate and more satisfactory to aboriginal people than the existing political arrangements.[8] If that is correct, living under an aboriginal government might indeed feel like a very different experience from living elsewhere in Canada (Turpel: 1991).

Here a contrast between the aspirations of aboriginal people and those of the Québécois may be illuminating. As a province within Canada, Quebec enjoys full legislative jurisdiction in some areas and shares others with the federal government. Quebec has consistently sought to expand the scope of its legislative powers in relation to the federal government, and, of course, some Québécois want Quebec to become an independent state. In some respects and on some issues, this desire for political autonomy may reflect a sense that Quebec has a different cultural tradition and that it is important for the Québécois that the laws reflect that difference. Thus, for example, Quebec's legal system reflects the traditions of the French Code Civil rather than the English common law. For the most part, however, and leaving aside the crucial issue of language which I discussed in Chapter 5, the cultural differences do not run so very deep. Whatever the particular differences of detail in the content of the laws, the general patterns of the ways in which Quebec's legal system regulates family, business, and social relations would seem familiar to a resident of Ontario or, for that matter, to a resident of the United States or France. Public opinion surveys have repeatedly shown that the Québécois share the same basic liberal value orientations as people in other parts of Canada. Indeed, most modern industrial Western liberal democratic capitalist states have similar legal arrangements and underlying value systems in this broad sense. Thus the impetus for Quebec to control its own legislation comes more from a commitment to collective autonomy ('We want to choose for ourselves how to do things' 'We want to be masters in our own home') than from a sense of collective difference ('Our way is different from your way'). This characterization is not intended as a denigration of collective autonomy which is an important dimension of the ideal of self-determination.

For aboriginal peoples, the cultural differences run much deeper than

---

[8] Some scholars fear that aboriginal governments will not be able to meet these cultural expectations and that precisely for that reason too much attention is paid to aboriginal self-government at the expense of other ways of preserving aboriginal cultures (Boldt 1993).

language and variations on a liberal theme. Do aboriginal peoples share the same principles of justice as the rest of the population of Canada? That is a hard question to answer. All principles require mediation, instantiation, embeddedness in some concrete social context. Different forms of mediation have different advantages and disadvantages, different features and quirks, and may fit together more or less well with other forms of mediation. But, sometimes the particularity of the mediation overwhelms the abstract principle it allegedly instantiates. Or, to put it another way, people are supposed to experience the realization of principles of justice through various concrete institutions, but they may actually experience a lot of the institution and very little of the principle. That can be true, of course, even in the context of a shared background culture, but the problem becomes more acute where the background culture is not shared by people subject to the institutions.

In the face of deep cultural differences within a state, it may be appropriate and even necessary to try to construct alternative forms of mediation, forms more congruent with non-dominant cultures. But if the forms of mediation are sufficiently different, it may be hard to tell whether they really do instantiate the same principles.

How do these general propositions inform aboriginal objections to the Charter? Let me say first that not all aboriginal people oppose the Charter. The Métis, who first gained constitutional recognition with the Charter, want to keep it but supplement it with a Métis Charter. One major organisation of First Nations women favours the Charter as a bulwark against what they see as a male-dominated leadership insensitive to the rights and interests of women. But those aboriginal people who do oppose the Charter generally do so in the name of cultural difference.

Why are some aboriginal people opposed to the Charter?[9] Well, not, they would say, because they want to be able to prevent other aboriginal people

---

[9] Some Québécois are also opposed to the Charter (though it is relatively popular even there). The explanation for the opposition varies. Some think Quebec's commitment to liberalism since the Quiet Revolution is a thin veneer spread over the traditional Catholic anti-liberal culture that characterized Quebec for much of its history, and that the opposition to the Charter springs from these deep anti-liberal roots. Others argue that Quebec is committed to a liberalism of a different kind from that of English Canada, one that is less individualistic and more in keeping with continental traditions. (Taylor 1993). There may be something to this second account, but, in my view, the opposition comes primarily not from the sorts of cultural differences that the first two accounts posit, but from political differences rooted in a desire for collective autonomy. I am most persuaded by an account that traces Quebec hostility to the Charter to the fact that the Charter is not just a neutral instantiation of liberal ideals but a political document, explicitly designed by Pierre Trudeau to link Canadians as individual citizens to the Canadian state and thus to serve as a unifying symbol of Canadian citizenship, with the goal of undercutting Quebec nationalism (Cairns 1992). In fact, the Charter has now become a powerful symbol of Canada, and especially of the common commitments implied by Canadian citizenship, for many Canadians, especially in English Canada. This third account takes Quebec's liberalism seriously and points to the fact that Quebec has its own Charter of Rights and Freedoms, adopted before the Canadian Charter and embodying many of the same sorts of liberal protections, and to the fact that the nationalists who oppose the Canadian Charter celebrate Quebec's. The issue on this account is less the content of the Charter than its origins and identity.

from practising their religion, or to restrict their freedom of expression, or to deny them equal treatment. They know firsthand that these are bad things to do because these are the sorts of things that have been done to them since the Europeans arrived and that continue to be done.

Then perhaps they do share the same basic principles of justice and what they want is that the principles should actually be respected in practice, in which case the Charter might be a good first step? Well, not exactly. Aboriginal cultures vary from one aboriginal people to another, and there are many aboriginal peoples in Canada, but most, if not all, of them are very wary about articulating basic principles of justice in the language used by liberal democratic theorists. There is a richly elaborated, highly refined tradition of discourse associated with words like 'rights', 'justice', 'democracy', and, I might add, 'citizenship', You might say that even abstract principles and concepts turn out to be thickly mediated forms of expression, and it is that thick mediation that is particularly worrisome. Some aboriginal writers suggest that their traditions emphasize responsibilities more than rights and the well-being of the community rather than the claims of the individual, but they also see even these formulations as alien and distorting in important respects (Turpel: 1991).

These general concerns about cross-cultural communication pale in comparison to the concern about what the Charter would mean in practice. After all, the Charter is not a philosophical formulation of moral principles, but a set of legal concepts and categories that will be interpreted and applied by particular people (not, need it be said, aboriginal people), people selected and trained in certain ways (and not others), people attuned to certain considerations (and not others), people taught to regard certain forms of communication (and not others) as intellectually respectable and relevant. Who will have actual, effective power to make Charter claims and for what ends will they make them?

As this line of argument suggests, opposition to the Charter in the name of the cultural distinctiveness of aboriginal peoples cannot be reduced to simple formulas about the relative weight attached to different values (e.g. gender equality versus collective self-government by aboriginal people).The issue is also how the Charter is likely to work in practice.

Some aboriginal feminists oppose having the Charter apply to aboriginal governments not because they think the male aboriginal leadership is fine or that the situation of aboriginal women is unobjectionable, but rather because they think that using the Charter to supervise and restrict the operations of aboriginal governments will do a lot to limit the viability of aboriginal self-government without doing much to enhance the equality of women within aboriginal communities (Turpel 1991). In other words, the formal guarantees of gender equality provided by the Charter may not actually translate into meaningful social equality between men and women, but having the Charter apply to aboriginal self-government could greatly limit the capacity of aboriginal people to develop their own distinctive political arrangements for self-governance.[10]

The Charter is not something that directly translates abstract individual rights into social realities. It is not applied liberalism, pure and simple, but liberalism applied in and through a set of legal institutions with their own distinctive norms, practices, interpretations, and modes of reasoning. These are often alien enough to the non-lawyer who shares the basic cultural commitments in which the legal system is embedded; they are bound to be all the more alien to aboriginal peoples who have seen the ways in which such legal institutions have been used over many years to justify and legitimate the dispossession and domination of aboriginal peoples. Thus, it seems reasonable for aboriginal people (even if they are male leaders) to respond with scepticism to the view that the only thing the Charter will be used to do is to protect the equality rights of aboriginal women or other basic human rights, not to limit or prevent aboriginal people from running their affairs in other ways that seem good to them (perhaps even most of them, women and men alike) but bad to non-aboriginal Canadians.

My intention here is not simply to endorse the view that the Charter should not apply to aboriginal governments but rather to show why that view, which is the one most in tension with the conventional understanding of citizenship, is nevertheless a defensible and plausible one. Some aboriginal peoples want to address the issues of cultural difference by drawing up their own aboriginal Charters and by having these subject only to aboriginal courts, not Canadian courts. Others (including the Inuit Tapirisat) argue that it would be acceptable for the Canadian Charter to apply to aboriginal governments so long as those governments have the same override powers as the federal and provincial governments.

This latter position seems especially difficult for non-aboriginals to challenge. As I argued in Chapter 2, the override itself is an arrangement that reminds us that there may be many different ways of protecting fundamental rights and freedoms, and what will work best in a particular political context depends partly on the character of the culture of the people whose rights and freedoms are being protected. In any event, given that the federal and provincial governments have override powers, not to grant the override to aboriginal governments would be to say, in effect, 'We don't trust you not to abuse this power, even though we do trust these other governments not to do so'. Do aboriginal women, for example, have more reason to trust the wisdom and commitment to equality of the non-aboriginal (mainly male) justices

---

[10] The Charter's guarantees regarding gender equality currently apply to aboriginal women, but they have done little to address the many serious problems that aboriginal women face. Would the situation have been even worse in the absence of these guarantees? Perhaps, but it seems more plausible to suppose that the Charter is simply not an effective tool to address these problems.

who interpret and apply the Charter than the wisdom and commitment to equality of aboriginal governments? Again, my point is not to insist on a particular answer to this question, but rather to suggest that an insistence that aboriginal governments should have override powers seems entirely reasonable. Of course, as I noted in Chapter 2, some Canadians think the override clause is a bad idea altogether, but in a context in which all the other governments in Canada have it, to deny it to aboriginal governments would be to send a powerful message about relative power and trust.

In summary, the Charter is embedded in a complex, costly, and alien legal system. Aboriginal opponents of the Charter have no confidence that such a densely mediated form of justice will, in fact, do justice to aboriginal people. On the contrary, they can point to a long history of the aboriginal experience of the rule of law in Canada's liberal democratic regime. It is not, to put it mildly, a happy experience. So now, just when the political struggles of aboriginal people in Canada seem to have opened some prospect for aboriginal peoples to reclaim some significant degree of control over their own communities after a long and destructive period of subordination, the insistence by some non-aboriginal people that the Charter must apply to aboriginal governments in an unchecked fashion is quite understandably experienced by some aboriginal people not as a way of protecting individual aboriginals but as a reassertion of collective hegemonic control (Turpel 1991).

Beyond Regrettable Necessity

A second fundamental line of objection to the kind of differentiated citizenship that aboriginal self-government would create is that it cannot perform one of the key functions of citizenship: civic integration. On this view, members of a political community should be able and willing to work together, to understand one another, to seek agreement on issues, to compromise where necessary to reach agreement, to respect each other's legitimate claims, to trust one another, and even to make sacrifices for one another.[11] From this perspective, the danger of aboriginal self-government and of the related concept of differentiated citizenship is that the emphasis they place on the recognition and institutionalization of difference could undermine the conditions that make a sense of common identification and thus mutuality possible.

We see again here the importance of the psychological dimension of citizenship. If aboriginal people and non-aboriginal people do not feel themselves to be members of the same community in some significant sense, they

---

[11] See Miller (1995) for a persuasive articulation of the importance of these concerns.

may not be willing to make the compromises and sacrifices required for people to live together well. They may adopt more instrumental attitudes in their dealings with one another.

I think that this line of argument presents an important challenge to the idea of differentiated citizenship. It would be highly desirable for Canada (or perhaps any political community) to have a mutuality of understanding, trust, and concern among the citizenry. But I want to argue that this kind of civic integration is more likely to result from differentiated citizenship, properly understood, than from any alternative conception of citizenship. Paradoxically, greater respect for difference is more likely to generate more genuine unity than any attempt to manufacture that unity directly. Nevertheless, differentiated citizenship does carry certain risks of increasing the divisions between aboriginal and non-aboriginal people in Canada. To assess those risks, both normatively and politically, we must place them in the proper perspective.

First, it may be helpful to ask what actual alternatives critics of differentiated citizenship might have in mind. There is a tendency in some discussions of this issue to slide, often implicitly and perhaps unconsciously, from the legitimate claim that a good political community will be built upon mutual understanding, trust, and concern among its members to the much more problematic one that these orientations are now characteristic of the relationship between aboriginals and non-aboriginals in Canada and that differentiated citizenship would somehow undermine them.

As I have shown above, the whole history of efforts to promote unitary citizenship in Canada with respect to aboriginal people is a history of forced assimilation. The most recent attempt to move strongly in the direction of unitary citizenship, the White Paper of 1969, was decisively repudiated by aboriginal people. It is surely impossible to generate dispositions of mutual understanding, trust, and concern by means of the compulsory imposition upon aboriginal people of a unitary citizenship they do not want. In that respect, when the theory of unitary citizenship is assessed in the actual context of Canadian history and Canadian political realities, it appears far more idealistic, even naïve, than the theory of differentiated citizenship that I have been presenting.

It is important also to remember that I have characterized the kind of differentiated citizenship that would flow from aboriginal self-government as an ideal type, describing one end on a continuum of possible relationships between aboriginal people and Canada. Aboriginal people do not fit a single mould, and however they are categorized and subdivided, the members of these groups do not fit a single mould.

As I noted above, most aboriginal people live outside reserves or other aboriginal territory, and most of those live in cities. Among this population, some aboriginal individuals may well want to reject any form of differentiated citizenship and insist on their possessing the same rights and responsibilities as non-aboriginal Canadians (though these are not as uniform as we sometimes unthinkingly assume). That is an option that should certainly be left open to them. And of the group that rejects differentiated citizenship, some may reject their aboriginal identity, others may hide it, and still others may assert it proudly.

Further along the continuum, aboriginal people would possess varying degrees of differentiated citizenship. If all goes well, they will have more opportunities than today to live their lives in and through aboriginal institutions, but so long as they live outside aboriginal-controlled territories, they are bound to have many connections and interactions with federal and provincial governments. For them (as for the group that rejects differentiated citizenship), the issue is not whether they will have any direct links to the various non-aboriginal governments in Canada, but what the quality of those links will be and how that will affect their feelings about Canada as a political community. No genuine civic integration can be achieved so long as aboriginal people continue to be subject to deep and pervasive racism.

Finally, consider those aboriginal people who will be living in aboriginal communities where self-government is most extensive. If civic integration is about creating dispositions towards mutual understanding, trust, and concern, then it is not clear why these dispositions have to be the product of a direct relationship to the federal government rather than the product of relationships to the federal government and other Canadians mediated primarily through aboriginal political communities. If aboriginal people feel that the communities with which they most deeply identify have space for self-determination within Canada and that the representatives whom they regard as legitimate are treated with respect and have an effective voice in their (inevitably frequent) interactions with federal and provincial governments and with the non-aboriginal Canadian public, including a voice in shaping their legal connections with Canada, then aboriginal people may well develop a sense of identification with and attachment to this larger community of which their community is a respected and integral part. Even if aboriginal people continue to view the federal government as representing 'them' not 'us'—a tendency that may be unavoidable given the relative sizes of the aboriginal and non-aboriginal populations and the salience of aboriginal identity—they may nevertheless come to think of Canada as a political community to which they belong.

Canada as a political community need not be regarded as identical with or reducible to the federal government. As Taylor points out, we do not all have to belong to Canada in the same way. For some, including many aboriginal people, Canada might be seen as the interactive product of its constituent communities, including the federal government, and people may feel they belong because they identify strongly as members of one or more of these constituent communities.

To put some of these points another way, given the history and present circumstances of aboriginal people in Canada, it would be unreasonable to expect most of them to have a strong positive identification with and attachment to Canada as a political community. As I noted in the previous chapter, that is why so many aboriginal people feel tied to Canada by a sense of regrettable necessity. But that sense of regrettable necessity need not be taken as permanent and unchangeable. A more positive psychological attachment to Canada is not likely to emerge, however, at least not primarily, from an improvement in the legal and institutional connections between individual aboriginals and Canadian governments (although such improvements are both desirable and necessary). For aboriginal people, the psychological dimension of citizenship—the sense of identification with and attachment to Canada, the sense of belonging—is most likely to emerge as a long-term outgrowth of the exercise of legal and participatory citizenship in ways that actually promote the fundamental cultural interests of aboriginal peoples.

Let me take the argument one step further. I would hypothesize that the success (or failure) of the most far-reaching experiments in aboriginal self-government might have a significant effect on the psychological citizenship even of those aboriginal people who do not participate directly in the experiments themselves, by marking out an important set of boundaries regarding the possibilities for aboriginal people in Canada.[12] What might transform the sense of regrettable necessity on the part of aboriginal people into a positive identification with and attachment to Canada would be for the Canadian government and non-aboriginal Canadians to embrace a conception of differentiated citizenship like the one Taylor sketches and I pursue here. This would enable non-aboriginal Canadians to perceive aboriginal self-government as something that could contribute to the strength and depth of Canada as a political community and would enable aboriginal people to experience their relationship with Canada as something that could support rather than undermine their aspirations to live as aboriginal people. To pursue this course would require us non-aboriginal Canadians to make an effort to acknowledge the thickly mediated character of our own practices and ideas and to try to understand more about the thickly mediated character of aboriginal practices and ideas. A shared identity that precedes genuine inclusion in common deliberation is hegemonic.

If my argument is correct, then the only effective way to promote the civic integration of aboriginal people is through the kind of differentiated citizenship described in this and other chapters. It is only that form of citizenship that will give rise to the psychological attachment to Canada which is in turn the necessary precondition for the dispositions to mutual understanding, trust, and concern that characterize civic integration.

---

[12] This hypothesis stands in some tension with, but I think is not ultimately incompatible with, my hypothesis above about diaspora effects.

There is a second, more direct way in which differentiated citizenship contributes to civic integration: its emphasis on dialogue about difference. To some the phrase 'differentiated citizenship' suggests nothing but an emphasis on what separates us. To put the objection in its harshest form, some hear the aboriginal demand for self-government as a way of saying, 'Give us the money and then shut up and leave us alone'. No doubt this does reflect what some aboriginal people feel, and it may reflect what most of them feel at one time or another. That is an understandable reaction to a relationship in which, for a long time, the non-aboriginal side has had most of the power and has done a lot of talking and very little (serious) listening. But it is clearly not an attitude that can sustain a long-term relationship. And the concept of differentiated citizenship articulated here shows why it is not the right way to think about the meaning of aboriginal self-government.

If we start instead from the assumption that aboriginal and non-aboriginal Canadians both care about justice but think about it differently, and if we try to explain ourselves to each other, we might arrive at arrangements that feel like more than a satisfactory bargain, arrangements that combine mutual compromise and mutual understanding in ways that create genuine common bonds. And that is the sort of basis on which a shared identity could be built, and eventually perhaps even a genuinely shared citizenship.

My ideal of differentiated citizenship thus entails a dialogue between aboriginal people and non-aboriginal people over the meaning of justice. A dialogue over justice is not an instrumental relationship. Rather it is the kind of relationship that, when it works, gives rise to mutual understanding, mutual trust, and mutual concern. Such a dialogue would strengthen ties between aboriginal people and non-aboriginal people in Canada, not weaken them, and deepen not diminish the attachment of aboriginal people to Canada. It offers a way of transforming what is currently a highly instrumental and unequal relationship into one based on reciprocity and mutual commitment.

Of course, there is no guarantee that a dialogue about justice will work. Perhaps we will not be able to find mutual understandings and mutually acceptable compromises. But it is an illusion to suppose that an emphasis on current common bonds offers any more hope. The current relationship between aboriginal people and the Canadian government is a disaster. The bonds we share now are the bonds of our history and current connections. But these bonds cannot serve as the basis for civic integration for most aboriginal people; they are the ties of regrettable necessity. Regrettable necessity explains why we are connected enough to make the effort to enter into the dialogue, but the dialogue itself offers the best hope for transforming the bonds into something more positive.

So far I have been focusing on the problem of civic integration with respect to aboriginal people, that is, on the question of what effects differentiated citizenship would have on the attitudes of aboriginal people towards Canada and towards non-aboriginal Canadians. I have argued that differentiated citizenship would be more likely than any alternative to promote civic integration among aboriginal people while conceding that there could be no guarantee of success.

But this is only part of the story. Civic integration also involves non-aboriginal people. Some critics of differentiated citizenship for aboriginal people are concerned primarily with its effects upon the attitudes of non-aboriginal people. There are worries that differentiated citizenship for aboriginal people will undermine non-aboriginal Canadians' feeling that aboriginal people are members of the Canadian political community and hence entitled to equal treatment and concern. One consequence over time might be an erosion of the willingness of non-aboriginal Canadians to provide financial transfers to support aboriginal self-government.

I think that this is a realistic concern, but that it is important to evaluate this possible development critically as well as realistically, from the perspective of principle as well as from the perspective of prudence. In other words, we should be concerned not only with the likelihood but also with the legitimacy of this sort of reaction.

Sometimes this anticipated decline in mutuality on the part of non-aboriginal Canadians is presented as a reasonable and perhaps inevitable response to a decline in mutuality on the part of aboriginal people as reflected in their pursuit of self-government and differentiated citizenship. But this account is clearly wrong, if the analysis of differentiated citizenship that I offered above is accepted. It is the current relationship that lacks genuine mutuality and differentiated citizenship that offers the best hope of creating it. So, if non-aboriginal Canadians are truly committed now to mutual understanding, trust, and concern in their relationships with aboriginal people in Canada, they should embrace differentiated citizenship and aboriginal self-government. Yet non-aboriginal Canadians may not see this, in part because the myth of unitary citizenship is so powerful and widespread.

We are faced then with a paradox and a dilemma. The paradox is that the very concepts and institutions (aboriginal self-government, differentiated citizenship) that seem the most promising in terms of leading aboriginal people to feel as though they really belong to Canada as a political community are ones that may lead non-aboriginal Canadians to feel as though aboriginal people no longer belong. This would not happen if non-aboriginal Canadians understood the concepts and institutions correctly, but a misunderstanding seems likely (though perhaps not inevitable).

The dilemma is how to respond to this paradox. We have seen in this chapter why differentiated citizenship for aboriginal people is the best way to meet the demands of justice and equality and even the most promising way to promote the civic integration of aboriginal people. Yet the fact that something is right does not guarantee that it will triumph in history. Aboriginal people need hardly be reminded of that. But if aboriginal people were to abandon or significantly modify their project of self-government out of fear that non-aboriginal Canadians might react negatively and detach themselves further from aboriginals, how could their legitimate demands ever be met and what could possibly promote their civic integration with non-aboriginal Canadians? Such a course would seem to me to reflect a resigned acceptance of the view that their relationship with non-aboriginal Canadians is and can only be an instrumental one, defined fundamentally and unalterably by the disparities of wealth and power. That would be a sad development not only for aboriginal people but for all those who aspire for Canada to become a political community in which all of its members are integrated on the basis of a genuine mutuality.

9

Democracy and Respect for Difference: The Case of Fiji

In the introductory chapter of this book, I suggested that we gain as political theorists by reflecting upon unfamiliar cases. I turn now to a case that will certainly fit in that category for most of my readers: the case of Fiji.

Fiji is a small island state in the South Pacific whose population is composed primarily of two groups: 'Fijians' (the descendants of the people who originally settled the island thousands of years ago) and 'Indo-Fijians' (the descendants of people who were brought to Fiji from India as indentured labourers under the British colonial regime in the late nineteenth and early twentieth centuries).[1] The tensions and conflicts between these two groups raise a number of important theoretical questions about the moral relevance of culture, identity, and history. On the one hand, efforts to protect Fijian culture against the pressures of modern liberal institutions and values have been central to Fiji's history for over a century, and, today, in large part due to those efforts, Fijians are much better off than many comparable indigenous groups in other countries. On the other hand, for many decades Indo-Fijians have pressed for equal treatment with other groups in Fiji, first in relation to the European colonists and more recently in relation to Fijians, advancing their demands in the name of liberal democratic principles and arguing for political and economic arrangements in which group identities would play no formal role.

What makes the case of Fiji particularly rich and rewarding for purposes of theoretical reflection is its moral complexities and ambiguities. The two

---

[1] The terminology used to identify the two groups deserves some comment. Many scholars who write about Fiji, including ones who are themselves of Indo-Fijian descent or who are clearly sympathetic to Indo-Fijians, distinguish simply between Indians and Fijians without any suggestion that this sort of terminology might be sensitive. However, Mayer (1963) noted that the term 'Indo-Fijian' had been adopted by a 1961 Commission and seemed preferable to 'Fiji Indian'. A number of recent scholars have adopted this term, and I am following their usage. (On the other hand, a graduate student at the University of Toronto who grew up in Fiji and emigrated with his family to Canada told me that in the circles he knew, people thought of themselves as Indians and would be insulted to be called Fijian Indians, and even more so Indo-Fijians.) The use of the term 'Fijian' to identify the indigenous ethnic group is universal in the literature, and so I follow it although it might seem to prejudice certain questions about membership that I want to explore.

groups in conflict here both arouse our moral sympathies—at least they do mine. On the one hand, the Indo-Fijians are the descendants of victims of an exploitative colonial labour system and a system of colonial rule that unjustly privileged Europeans over them. I admire their struggles and achievements. And because the appeals of the Indo-Fijians to liberal democratic principles are rooted in a history of challenges to European domination, I do not see how one could treat them as ideological rationales for the perpetuation of privilege. Instead, their liberal democratic principles appear as critical and constructive ideals—connected to their own interests, to be sure, but moral principles that have to be taken seriously.

On the other hand, Fijians appear in some respects to be an even more vulnerable and threatened group. When North Americans think of indigenous peoples, we tend to think of people conquered by the violence or ensnared by the deceit of European settlers and their descendants, people decimated by disease and driven from their lands, now impoverished and powerless minorities in countries overwhelmingly populated by the descendants of immigrants from many different lands. That has been the fate of indigenous peoples in North America and in many other places as well, including Australia and New Zealand.[2] If one cares about human well-being, one has to worry about what makes people end up so badly off and to ask what might prevent such a fate.

The situation of Fijians invites reflection on one possible avenue of escape, namely, a systematic effort to protect a traditional way of life and to enable it to evolve over time. By comparison with other indigenous peoples, Fijians appear to be in an enviable position. Their numbers, after an initial period of decline in the colonial era, stabilized and grew and they now constitute over half of the population of Fiji. While not affluent, they have enjoyed a relatively secure material and social life. They certainly have not suffered from the extreme social disintegration—high rates of unemployment, crime, alcoholism, and suicide—that has befallen many other indigenous groups. I will argue below that it is reasonable to attribute much of the present situation of Fijians, and hence their relative well-being, to the fact that Fijians have been able to maintain a relatively stable and coherent collective way of life over the last century or so. That fact in turn seems due in significant measure to the policies of cultural preservation pursued in Fiji. And, as I will argue below, it seems plausible to suppose that policies more in keeping with liberal individualism—for example, an insistence on individual, alienable title to land as opposed to the collective, inalienable form of ownership adopted in Fiji—would have had

---

[2] Australia and New Zealand were colonies that the European settlers in Fiji took as models, hoping that the colonial government in Fiji would adopt policies encouraging European settlement and leading to the development of Fiji along similar lines. Had this course been followed, it seems highly doubtful that Fijians would have fared as well as they did under the policies actually adopted (Reynolds 1982).

disastrous consequences for Fijians as such policies did elsewhere. But if one accepts these claims, it would seem hard to conclude that efforts at cultural preservation, even when this goes against the grain of liberal institutions, are always a bad idea, from a moral point of view.

Thus the attempt to preserve a distinctive Fijian way of life opens a fruitful avenue for examination of the liberal commitment to pluralism. One of the concerns of this book has been to explore what sorts of cultural differences we ought to respect as a way of affirming a commitment to equality, what sorts we should tolerate or accommodate, and what sorts we should reject. The case of Fiji presents an important opportunity to deepen our reflections on these issues. If liberals are ever going to be open to, even supportive of, non-liberal cultures and ways of life, where better than in a case where a traditional, non-liberal culture seems to be or to have been both viable and good for most of those who shared it and where it would be very costly in terms of human well-being if the culture were to disintegrate either from lack of support or from a deliberate (but unsuccessful) attempt at transformation? Yet the steps that have been taken to preserve Fijian culture do conflict in important ways with conventional liberal views and arrangements. So, exploration of this case may reveal a lot about liberalism and cultural difference.

The methods used to protect and recognize group identity in Fiji vary widely, from collective ownership of land and special veto powers for Fijian chiefs to ethnically based political arrangements to a military coup justified in the name of the protection of the Fijian way of life. One could simply reject (or, less plausibly, affirm) all of these, but I think it is preferable to think more deeply about the case to see whether there are ways to reconcile our sympathies for both Fijians and Indo-Fijians. Can one criticize the coup but endorse institutions and practices that contributed to the sense of ethnic identity that lay behind the coup? Can one endorse an ideal of equal citizenship and insist that Indo-Fijians are morally entitled to be treated as equal citizens yet still defend the constitutional entrenchment of certain rights and privileges for Fijians? I will argue for an affirmative answer, with qualifications, to these questions and try to show how they cast new light on familiar debates about cultural difference.

The chapter begins with a brief history of Fiji, designed to present the essential background information needed to understand my discussion of the case. I then defend the claims of the Indo-Fijians to equal citizenship, considering and rejecting various arguments against this based on history and culture. The bulk of the chapter, however, is devoted to a defence of two policies deliberately aimed at preserving Fijian culture: the creation of a system of inalienable collective ownership of the land and the institutional reinforcement of deference to chiefly authority through various means. I consider and reject arguments that these measures were inauthentic, unfair, and undemocratic.

A Short History of Fiji

There is an extensive scholarly literature on Fiji, and thus inevitably much scholarly debate about how to interpret Fiji's past and present.[3] This section is intended to provide a descriptive background so that the reader can think intelligently about the particular theoretical questions that I subsequently address. I have tried as much as possible to present a summary overview which does not prejudice the normative discussion to follow. In other words, I hope that the account I am providing in this section would be accepted as accurate both by those whose primary sympathies lie with the efforts to preserve a distinctive Fijian way of life and by those whose primary sympathies lie with the Indo-Fijians or with attempts to transform Fijian society in directions required by liberalism, capitalism, and/or democracy. At the same time, I recognize that in this book 'the case of Fiji' is inevitably the story that I tell about Fiji. Any such narrative is an interpretation. It is bound to contain controversial and contestable elements and to reflect, in ways of which I am only partly conscious, my own particular angle of vision. Someone else would tell the story differently. But that does not mean that there is no point in my trying to tell it.

Fijians and the Colonial Regime

Fiji is a collection of islands in the South Pacific originally settled thousands of years ago by people of Melanesian origin.[4] The current population is around 790,000. In the nineteenth century, Europeans began to arrive in the islands, first as traders, then as missionaries, later as commercial farmers. They

---

[3] The principal sources for this section are the following: Ali (1980, 1986); Alley (1986, 1997); Bayliss-Smith *et al.* (1988); Belshaw (1964); Burns (1963); Fisk (1970); France (1969); Gillion (1962, 1977); Howard (1991); Jayawardena (1980); Lal (1983, 1986, 1988, 1990, 1997); Lasaqa (1984); Lawson (1991); Legge (1958); Macnaught (1982); Mamak (1978); Mayer (1963, 1973); Nation (1978); Nayacakalou (1975); Newton (1970); Norton (1977, 1986); Premdas (1995); Roth (1973); Scarr (1980, 1984, 1988).

[4] Even discussion of the ancient history of Fiji is fraught with contemporary political overtones. Some scholars argue that the original settlers of Fiji came from Melanesia with a relatively egalitarian culture and social structure and that the strongly hierarchical orientation of contemporary Fijian culture can be traced to later arrivals from Polynesia, who arrived both as peaceful migrants and as armed invaders a thousand years ago. By drawing attention to the cultural diversity within the Fijian tradition and by linking the contemporary chiefly establishment to people who were not the original inhabitants and who used violence to establish their presence, these critics hope to undercut the claims of the chiefs to a central and legitimate place in Fijian culture and tradition. (Howard 1991: 16–18). By contrast, other scholars present a picture of Fiji's ancient history in which the original settlers developed Polynesian culture in Fiji and neighbouring Tonga, while later migrations brought different cultural elements from other parts of Melanesia. On this account, concern for status and the other elements of a chiefly cultural were present from the beginning (Scarr 1984: 1–3). While I make no attempt to settle this particular issue, I discuss below the moral relevance of historical claims about continuity and change with regard to the chiefly class in Fiji.

formed alliances with some of the Fijian chiefs, facilitating attempts to centralize power. In 1874, as a strategy for dealing with internal political conflicts and external political and economic pressures, the high chiefs of Fiji ceded dominion of the islands to the British Crown. The formal Cession was unqualified, but the chiefs received verbal assurance that the new government would keep the interests of the Fijians paramount. Arthur Gordon, the first governor of the colony, apparently took this promise very seriously (to the dismay of the European settlers) and developed a number of policies to protect traditional Fijian society as he understood it. In particular, he instituted an administrative system for governing the Fijians through their traditional rulers and in accord with their own customs; he prohibited the sale of Fijian land; and he drastically restricted the employment of Fijians as agricultural workers on European plantations.

The colonial system that Gordon instituted to preserve traditional Fijian society also transformed it profoundly. As one scholar puts it:

The regional varieties of kinship and social organization in old Fiji, the underlay of colonial reconstruction, defy summary analysis and description: suffice to emphasize here that the colonial order devised and imposed new, very much simplified principles of authority and territorial organization which may or may not have meshed with pre-existing sociopolitical realities. (Macnaught 1982: 3)

Gordon's system of administration created provinces and districts and established formal lines of authority from the village to the district to the province. He assigned chiefs to fill these positions largely (though not exclusively) in accordance with his perception of their hereditary status and rank. This scheme drew more upon the strongly hierarchical arrangements of eastern Fiji than of other regions (though it altered them as well), thus strengthening the role of chiefs in Fijian society. Gordon also established the Great Council of Chiefs, a periodic assembly of the provincial leaders and other lesser officials, to advise the governor on Fijian affairs. Although it had not existed previously, this group came to be seen by most Fijians and non-Fijians as the final authority on the interpretation of Fijian custom and tradition.

To secure the inalienability of Fijian land, Gordon and later administrators somewhat arbitrarily chose the *mataqali*, a kinship or household group, as the 'authentic' land-owning unit. Moreover, they defined the *mataqali* in law in a way that corresponded to practice in only one part of Fiji. The previous system of land tenure had been much more complex, informal, and fluid. Gordon also gave legal sanction to customary obligations such as the obligation to provide one's chief with certain goods and services (*lala*) or to work under his direction on communal projects which included such tasks as building and maintaining houses, improving the water supply, clearing land, and providing visitors with food. More broadly, Fijians were legally required to obey their chiefs 'in all things lawful according to their customs'

(Macnaught 1982: 43). To reinforce the prohibition on Fijians indenturing themselves on the plantations, he made it an offence for Fijians to leave their villages for more than sixty days without the permission of local authorities and arranged for taxes to be paid in kind and on the basis of collective assessments, rather than in cash by individuals.

Under this regime, Fijians were participants in a distinctive culture and way of life that had significant continuities as well as discontinuities with what had preceded colonization. Most of them lived in rural villages rather than in towns or on independent homesteads. The villages were the centre of their social and economic life. The local authorities were chiefs (rather than Europeans). Ordinary people spent their time in the tasks connected with subsistence agriculture and their communal labour obligations. They had little contact with the cash economy. Various aspects of the culture and of the institutional arrangements emphasized cooperation and sharing within a hierarchical framework and discouraged individual acquisitiveness or the production of surpluses. Some villages were involved in trading networks, but again these were embedded in social relationships that sharply limited the possibilities for profit. Fijians placed great emphasis on courtesy and customary modes of respect, as well as on public ceremonies and festivals (which the chiefs were expected to sustain).

Over time, the colonial authorities eliminated the most restrictive features of this system (e.g. the limitations on mobility and access to the labour market, the legal obligations to obey the chiefs and provide them with labour). They eventually introduced electoral mechanisms to make local governmental authorities more accountable to ordinary Fijians. The policies of colonial officials oscillated over the years between reinforcing the communal system of village life and encouraging an individualistic, profit-seeking orientation to economic activity. There were few notable successes in these entrepreneurial activities, however, and many failures. Much of the best agricultural land was leased to non-Fijians for commercial farming, and many Fijians worked at least part of the time as wage labourers. At the same time, even those most in favour of the communal system recognized the need for some significant transformation of Fijian life. As Fiji moved towards independence in the post-World War II era, colonial officials acknowledged an obligation to prepare Fijians to participate in modern economic and political institutions, including the market economy and, eventually, democratic politics. Subsistence would no longer suffice. Greater educational opportunity, economic development, and an improvement in the material conditions of life of ordinary Fijians were essential.

Indo-Fijians

When Fiji became a British colony, maintaining the Fijian way of life was not the only concern of the colonial government. The European farmers wanted labour for their plantations. Since the government had precluded the use of Fijians (to the intense displeasure of the planters), some alternative source had to be found. To satisfy these demands, Gordon arranged for the importation of indentured workers from India, a system that was finally stopped in 1916 as a result of criticisms from India. Most of the workers stayed on after their labour contracts had expired, taking up agriculture on their own. There was also a small but steady stream of free immigrants from India who came to set up small businesses or to engage in commercial farming. By 1921, there were about 61,000 Indo-Fijians in Fiji—39 per cent of the population. By the mid-1940s, Indo-Fijians outnumbered Fijians, largely because of higher birth rates and lower mortality rates, trends that continued until about the mid-1960s when Indo-Fijians constituted about 51 per cent of the population and Fijians about 46 per cent. During the 1970s and 1980s, the difference between the two groups narrowed, largely because of the greater emigration of Indo-Fijians, although Indo-Fijians still constituted a slightly larger proportion of the population (48.6 per cent) than Fijians (46.2 per cent) at the time of the 1986 census. A surge in emigration of Indo-Fijians following the 1987 coup has now made Fijians a clear majority of the population.[5]

The experience of the Indian immigrants was, of course, very different from the experience of the Fijians. The indenture system was hard and degrading. It was impossible to maintain traditional Indian cultural patterns and values, especially the religiously sanctioned caste system which required the careful separation of castes from one another in occupations, marriages, living arrangements, and many other aspects of social life. On the ships and plantations, these traditional distinctions largely disappeared. New patterns of social differentiation eventually emerged, but on different bases. Religion was far less central to social life in Fiji than it had been in India. The Indo-Fijians emphasized more secular goals like material prosperity, social mobility, and individual achievement. They tended to focus on economic activity. This is not to say that they abandoned Indian culture altogether. In language, religion, dress, and social practices, the Indo-Fijians maintained and preserved a distinct identity that clearly marked them as culturally different from both Fijians and Europeans.

Upon being released from indenture, many of the Indo-Fijians set up independent households on land leased from Fijians. The Indo-Fijians engaged in commercial, rather than subsistence, agriculture, especially in growing sugar cane. Often they hired Fijians as day labourers. (Sometimes these workers were the ones from whom the Indo-Fijians were leasing the land). Occasionally, Fijians refused to renew leases with the intent of engaging in commercial farming themselves. But these attempts were rarely successful,

---

[5] Alley (1997) estimates that 70,000 Indo-Fijians emigrated after the coup and cites Fijian government estimates of the resident population in 1995 as 50.7% Fijian and 43.5% Indo-Fijian, with others at 5.8%.

and the Indo-Fijian tenant farmers complained bitterly about the unfairness and insecurity created by refusals to renew leases. More politically effective complaints came from the Australian company holding a monopoly on sugar refining in Fiji which feared a disruption in the orderly supply of sugar cane.

In 1940, in response to these complaints, the government, with the agreement of the Great Council of Chiefs, set up the Native Land Trust Board to control 'all native land not required for immediate use and to administer such land in the best interests of Fijians' (Gillion 1977: 191). In practice, this meant that most of the land stayed in the hands of the Indo-Fijian tenant farmers because they could pay the rent. Despite ongoing insecurities about long-term leases (which remain a crucial political issue today), Indo-Fijians came to dominate commercial farming (replacing the Europeans) and small retail trade. They eventually took over significant parts of the transport and construction industries. Because Indo-Fijians also placed great emphasis on the acquisition of higher education (partly for cultural reasons, partly as compensation for their insecurities about land tenure), they came to dominate the professions and many white-collar jobs. Overall then, Indo-Fijians (as a group) became much more successful economically than Fijians (as a group), though there is considerable variation within each group and Fiji is a relatively poor country.

Group Relations

At the beginning of the colonial period, there was almost no contact between Fijians and the Indo-Fijians who were brought in as labourers. Over time, contact increased a little as the Indo-Fijians left the plantations and set up independent homesteads, leasing land from the Fijians, or established small businesses which supplied goods to the Fijians. Still, the dominant pattern was (and is) one of separateness, a pattern that was deliberately reinforced by colonial policies.

The gulf between the two groups is enormous. Fijians and Indo-Fijians speak different languages. The Fijians speak Fijian, the Indo-Fijians mainly Hindi, although most members of both groups also speak English. They have different religions. The Fijians are mostly Christians (having been converted in the nineteenth century). The Indo-Fijians are predominantly Hindu, although a significant minority (15 per cent) is Muslim. Cultural practices with regard to diet, marriage, and family relationships also differ. Occupations tend to be dominated by one group or the other. In towns they live in different neighbourhoods. There is almost no intermarriage between the groups, and there are few social friendships, except occasionally at the elite level. Formally, the educational facilities and teachers are now shared in common, but *de facto* segregation is widespread. Most unions and private associations are formally open but dominated by one ethnic group or the other. There are two teachers' unions, one for each. The army is composed overwhelmingly of Fijians, and the civil service predominantly so, while the professions are primarily occupied by Indo-Fijians.

These social differences are accompanied by mutual suspicion and contempt. Ethnic stereotypes are pervasive. Fijians regard Indo-Fijians as greedy, selfish, and cunning. Indo-Fijians see Fijians as lazy, uncivilized, and dupes of traditional authorities. Despite these mutually hostile attitudes, there was relatively little overt ethnic conflict prior to the coup, and still not much today compared with many societies. Most interactions occur in commercial settings and are marked by common courtesies. The extreme separation between the two groups has limited the arenas of competition and thus reduced the likelihood of conflict. Again, this is changing as more Fijians seek advanced education and economic opportunities.

Colonial Politics

In politics as elsewhere, the differences between Fijians and Indo-Fijians have been profound. From the early 1920s, Indo-Fijians agitated for equal citizen-ship among all the inhabitants of Fiji and a common franchise. In these early stages, the focus of their demands was on the Europeans who had political rights and political power, not the Fijians who were excluded from the fran-chise like the Indo-Fijians. The Indo-Fijians appealed both to an historic promise of equal treatment made at the beginning of the indenture system and to general principles.[6] During World War II, Indo-Fijian leaders urged their followers not to serve in the army unless they were given the same pay and treatment as European soldiers (which was out of the question from the British perspective). During the postwar period, Indo-Fijian leaders urged that Fiji become independent from Britain and adopt a system of self-government consistent with democratic principles.

The Fijian political experience was quite different. From early on, Fijian leaders expressed fear of Indo-Fijian political power, indeed domination, even before Indo-Fijians outnumbered Fijians. As the population trends became clearer, Fijian fears increased. Unlike the Indo-Fijians, the Fijian leaders gener-ally did not resent European political superiority. They had come to trust that the colonial government would indeed put Fijian interests first and would interpret that as requiring the maintenance of traditional chiefly authority. To be sure, there had been conflicts between Fijians and the European settlers who had pressed during the early years of the colony for policies and institu-tions more favourable to European interests. But by the 1930s, the Europeans too began to feel threatened by the Indo-Fijians and saw the strategic advant-ages of alliance with the Fijians.

---

[6] A document known as the 'Salisbury Despatch' was the basis of the Indo-Fijian claim that a promise had been made (Lawson 1991: 129–30).

Fijian leaders were content with Fiji's status as a colony; in fact, the British pushed them towards independence. Fijian leaders feared democracy as corrosive of traditional patterns of rule. They themselves had insisted on the maintenance of a separate Fijian administration. They did not press for the franchise but resisted it until it became inevitable (in the early 1960s).

During World War II, Fijian leaders, in contrast to the Indo-Fijian leaders, encouraged young men to join the British army without demanding equal pay or equal treatment with the Europeans. A substantial number volunteered, fought bravely, and returned to form the core of the Fijian armed forces. This historical experience was a major factor contributing to the continued predominance of Fijians in the Fijian armed services.

The 1970 Constitution and its Aftermath

During the 1960s, as Fiji began to move towards independence, the British introduced more participatory political arrangements. Both the Indo-Fijians and Fijians organized political parties that drew support primarily from their own ethnic group, although the Fijians had a strong alliance with the relatively small number of people who did not belong to either of the main groups.[7] In 1970, Fiji became independent and adopted a new constitution endorsed by both major parties. The new constitution was built upon the principle of ethnic representation. It established a bicameral system based upon the Westminster model, but with a special role for the Upper House or Senate. The Senate had twenty-two members: seven nominated by the Prime Minister, six by the Leader of the Opposition, and one by the Council of Rotuma. The remaining eight were nominated by the Great Council of Chiefs, and they had effective veto power over an important range of legislation. No substantive changes could be made with regard to citizenship, the composition of parliament or the judiciary, or key legislation affecting Fijians without the support of three-quarters of both Houses. In addition, legislation affecting 'Fijian land, custom, and customary rights' required the support of at least six of the eight Council of Chiefs nominees. Thus the Senate institutionalized protections for chiefly authority and established Fijian rights and interests in key areas.[8]

The House of Representatives had fifty-two seats. For twenty-seven of these seats (the communal seats), both the candidate and the voters were designated by ethnic identification. Thus there were twelve seats for which the candidate had to be Fijian and only Fijians could vote, twelve seats for which for which the candidate had to be Indo-Fijian and only Indo-Fijians could vote, and three seats reserved for candidates and voters who were neither

---

[7] This 'other' category included the Rotumans (who have a distinct identity and formal representation in the Fijian political system), other Pacific Islanders, people entirely or partially of European or Chinese descent, and a few others. They constituted about 5% of the total population.
[8] For a discussion of the 1970 Constitution, see Lal (1990: 76–81) and Lawson (1991: 184–94).

Fijian nor Indo-Fijian. For the other twenty-five seats (the national seats), the candidates were to be selected on the basis of ethnicity, but elected by all voters in the constituency. Of these, ten seats were reserved for Fijian candidates, ten for Indo-Fijian candidates, and five for the 'General Electorate'.

Under this arrangement, the Alliance Party, which drew most of its strength from Fijians, won the election of 1972. In 1977, however, a new party—the Fijian Nationalist Party—emerged and appealed for the votes of Fijians. This party advocated Fijian supremacy and even the deportation of the Indo-Fijian population. This split the ranks of the Fijians, and the National Federation Party, which drew most of its strength from Indo-Fijians, actually won two more seats than the Alliance Party in 1977 but was unable to form a government because of infighting and political ineptitude. When new elections were called in 1977, most Fijians returned to the Alliance Party which won handily and won again with a diminished majority in 1982. In 1985, a new party emerged—the Fijian Labour Party—which advocated a multi-ethnic, democratic socialist platform and sought to build links between the disadvantaged in both major groups. The Labour Party became the senior partner in an alliance with the National Federation Party during the 1987 election, and the coalition managed to win twenty-eight seats to the Alliance's twenty-four.[9] It formed a government with Timoci Bavadra, a Fijian commoner, as Prime Minister and the cabinet almost equally divided between Fijians and Indo-Fijians.

The election results led to some public protests, even rioting, by Fijians, but things seemed to be settling down when, a month after the election, the Fijian army staged a (bloodless) coup whose goal was, or quickly became, the firm establishment of Fijian political hegemony. Fiji severed its links with the British Commonwealth, established a Republic, and adopted a new constitution that guaranteed Fijians a significant majority of the seats in Parliament, eliminated cross-voting, and strengthened the power of the chiefly establishment in the Senate.[10] After some years under this arrangement, however, internal divisions among Fijians and international political and economic pressures led to the adoption of a new constitution in 1997 which closely resembles the 1970 Constitution in many respects, though it contains important new strategies for encouraging political coalitions across ethnic lines and more firmly establishes protections for individual rights.

Citizenship, Justice, and History: Who Belongs?

With this historical background in view, we can consider some of the questions raised by the case of Fiji. I begin with a defence of the Indo-Fijians' claim

---

[9] The Labour Party and its allies actually won fewer total votes than the alliance, but they won four key 'swing' seats by narrow margins, and so gained a clear legislative majority.

[10] See Lawson (1991: 289–90) on the new constitution and (255–9) on the coup. For a more detailed discussion of the coup, see Howard (1991: 243–340).

to equal citizenship. My position on this is likely to be less controversial than some of the ones I defend later, but it provides an opportunity to explore some important questions about the moral relevance of history and cultural differences.

The slogan of the Fijian Nationalist Party, 'Fiji for the Fijians', expresses the view of many Fijians, including those who supported the coup and the subsequent political reforms entrenching Fijian hegemony. In this view, the Indo-Fijians should be regarded as second-class citizens, at best, perhaps even as temporary visitors to be returned to India or sent elsewhere as soon as possible. For many Fijians, the fact that they are descended from the original inhabitants of the islands has been central to their self-understanding, their identity, their sense of themselves. The centrality of land in Fijian culture suggests an attachment which goes far beyond its instrumental use and which is tied up with this sense of self. They care about Fiji and feel that it is rightly theirs. They are the Fijians. The others who live there are outsiders, immigrants even if they were born and raised there. They place great weight on the Deed of Cession, the agreement which established Fiji as a colony, which, according to their interpretation, included an historic promise by the British government that their interests would always be kept paramount and thus implicitly acknowledged that those who came to Fiji from other places and their descendants would not have the same sort of claim to membership.[11]

The Indo-Fijians in Fiji have a far more ambivalent attitude to the land where they live. Virtually all of them were born and raised there, and in many cases their parents and grandparents were as well.[12] Certainly they do not belong anywhere else. They would not fit in traditional Indian village society and few have any desire to live in India. On the other hand, they generally see Fiji as a land where their ancestors lived in harsh bondage, where their own contributions have never been acknowledged fully, and where they are still regarded as outsiders. Though they know of no other home, many do not feel Fiji to be home (Ali 1980). For many, India, or an idealized conception of India is far more central to their identity than Fiji. Their relation to Fiji is far more instrumental than that of the Fijians.[13] Although some Indo-Fijians call themselves Fijians in some contexts, they normally use the term exclusively for Fijians. Even prior to the coup, more Indo-Fijians than Fijians emigrated,

---

[11] The Deed of Cession itself was actually unconditional and contained no explicit references to the paramountcy of Fijian interests. Nevertheless, Gordon the first governor claimed that verbal assurances to this effect had been given to the Fijians and he and later officials interpreted it in this way, so that it has become a formal convention, recognized in legislative acts and in the preamble to the 1970 Constitution, to read the Deed as providing some recognition of, and guarantee for, the special position of indigenous Fijians (Lawson 1991: 58–60).

[12] By the early 1960s, over 90% of the Indo-Fijians had been born in Fiji (Mayer 1963: viii.)

[13] One might ask to what degree the Indo-Fijians' form of attachment is the product of their being made to feel as though they do not really belong and are not welcome. If Indo-Fijian citizens feel less committed and have a more instrumental attitude to Fiji than their Fijian counterparts, perhaps that is more a reaction to their treatment than a reason for treating them differently.

and the number of émigrés has grown enormously since 1987. More would probably go, if they could get into Australia or Canada or the United States, where there would be greater economic opportunities than in Fiji.

Do these differences between Indo-Fijians and Fijians matter for the question of who ought to be a full citizen, entitled to equal rights and equal treatment within the political community of Fiji? The Indo-Fijians say no. Like the Fijians, they appeal in part to an historic promise by a British colonial official, in their case to the Salisbury Despatch of 1875 which pledged that if the government of India would support the recruitment of Indian indentured labour for other British colonies, then Indian settlers, after completing their term of indenture, would enjoy 'privileges no whit inferior to those of any other class of Her Majesty's subjects resident in the colony'.[14] But they appeal also to liberal democratic principles. They are morally entitled, they say, to be treated as full members and equal citizens, in no way inferior to the Fijians.[15]

I agree completely with the claim of the Indo-Fijians. They ought to be treated as equal citizens. But my response is, in the first instance, an intuitive one. I will try to defend my view, but I should say at the outset that I have more confidence in the judgement than in the theory that I provide to justify it. To put it another way, whatever the limits of the positive argument I am about to offer, I suspect that most people will share my intuitive judgement and I doubt that anyone will be able to offer a good argument *against* equal citizenship for the Indo-Fijians.

Justice and Citizenship

One way to think about the issue is to ask what justice requires, if anything, with regard to the citizenship status of Fijians and Indo-Fijians. Of course, a great deal of contemporary political theory, especially theories about justice, start with the assumption that the issue of membership in the political community is settled and the only question is what citizens owe one another (Rawls 1971). But the case of Fiji shows why the question of who belongs is also vital. So, how should we think about that question?

The question has two parts: (1) who is entitled to citizenship? (2) what sorts of citizenship are people entitled to? With regard to the first, I submit that, at a minimum, anyone born and brought up within the borders of a modern state is morally entitled to citizenship in that state. I recognize, of

---

[14] Unfortunately for this argument, the government of India did not agree to cooperate in the proposed schemes, so the status of the promise was clouded. Some have argued that it was a contingent promise, and so, no longer binding when the government of India rejected the offer. Others have argued that the promise of equal status was a background presupposition of all arrangements for indentured labour, and they cite subsequent administrative reports to support this claim (Lawson 1991: 128–31).

[15] The arguments by Indo-Fijians go back to their long struggle for a common roll (Gillion 1977: 130–56).

course, that this principle is not part of international law and is not compatible with the citizenship laws of many countries, but I propose to defend it anyway. Even for one not born and raised in a state, the longer one's residence, the stronger one's moral claim to belong and hence one's moral claim to citizenship. By these criteria, virtually all of the Indo-Fijians have very strong claims to citizenship. With regard to the second question, I submit that citizenship in the modern state must be treated as a threshold concept. Once over the threshold, one is entitled to be treated as an equal. No modern state can legitimately have different ranks of citizenship. There should be no second-class citizens. To be a citizen ought to mean that one is an equal citizen. Hence, Indo-Fijians must be treated as full members and equal citizens of Fiji. In support of both these claims, I will appeal both to abstract principles and to concrete intuitive judgements that I think are widely shared.

The first claim is the harder one to defend because it is less central to political theory and practice. But think of cases where a state has excluded people born and raised in the community from citizenship. Nazi Germany did it under the Nuremberg Laws. South Africa did it under apartheid. These were not the worst evils of either regime by any means, but surely their policies of exclusion from citizenship on the basis of race, religion, and ethnicity were centrally connected to what we find most morally abhorrent about those regimes. Of course, many contemporary states have citizenship laws that do not grant citizenship to everyone born and raised within its borders, and these policies do not arouse the same intuitive moral outrage as the policies of Nazi Germany and South Africa under apartheid. But that is largely because the implications of the formal citizenship policies are largely muted by other policies and practices that acknowledge *de facto* many of the moral claims of those born and raised within the state, especially their right to stay and to be treated with respect and dignity.[16] Moreover, the numbers of people in such a position have typically been quite small, until recently, and so not very visible.

Consider again the case of the long-term foreign residents in Germany which I first discussed in Chapter 2. As a way of exploring your own intuitive sense of what justice requires, ask yourself what your reaction would be if Germany were to expel the hundreds of thousands of people born and raised in Germany by Turkish or Yugoslav or other immigrant parents. My own reaction is that any such expulsion would be morally reprehensible. But why? After all, the people in question are not citizens. Yet the Germans have not

---

[16] For example, 'guestworkers' and their descendants in Germany enjoy most of the same social and economic rights that German citizens have, a fact that certainly makes their lives better than they would be if these benefits were tied more tightly to citizenship. The same separation between social, economic, and legal rights (except for political participation) and citizenship can be found in almost all Western industrialized countries, although some recent developments, such as the recent US. legislation denying certain social benefits even to lawful permanent residents, threaten to erode this status (Brubaker 1989: 156, 160–2).

expelled them, even selectively on the basis of unemployment, despite some strong economic incentives and internal political pressure to do so. It is clear that many Germans think it would be morally wrong to expel these people. Again the question is why?

One clue to the answer lies in language. These people have often been described by German commentators as 'second-generation immigrants', though they have never lived anywhere other than Germany and sometimes speak no other language than German. Their children are described as 'third-generation immigrants'.[17] But an immigrant is someone who comes from somewhere else to live in a new country, not someone born and raised there. The parents or grandparents of these people were immigrants. They are not. This oxymoronic language reveals the moral contradictions at the heart of the German policy. These people have a moral right to stay in Germany because they have a vital human interest in being able to continue to live in the community in which they were born and raised. The Germans know this, which is why they cannot bring themselves to kick the people out. But, until recently, most Germans could not quite bring themselves to acknowledge that these people really belonged, which is why they continued to call them 'immigrants'.

Any moral theory that claims to respect the moral equality of persons will set severe limits to the moral right of the state to expel inhabitants. The same moral considerations that set limits on the moral right of a state to deny citizenship to the children of its current citizens or to strip people of citizenship and expel them also set limits on the expulsion of people who have lived in a country all their lives, whatever their citizenship status. Adults who have spent most of their lives in a community have the same sort of moral right to stay, because they have the same sort of interest at stake.[18] Moreover, if 'second and third-generation immigrants' have a moral right to stay in Germany, as even most Germans concede, they also have a moral right to become German citizens if they choose, in part so that their moral position as members of the community can receive formal legal acknowledgement and protection and in part so that they may participate in political life, on the familiar liberal democratic principle that people should not be governed without their consent.[19] The new German government has recognized this and has committed itself to passing a law which will give most people born and raised in Germany the right to become citizens rather easily if they wish to do so.

The Indo-Fijians are legal citizens of Fiji. But even if they were not, they

[17] See, e.g. Hailbronner (1989: 77) for this way of characterizing foreign permanent residents in Germany.

[18] The interest of the state here is normally related to length of residence. There are important questions of degree here, and difficult questions about where it is or is not reasonable to draw a line. I am emphasizing clear cases, however, because length of residence is not a serious issue for the Indo-Fijians.

[19] For a fuller argument on this point, see Carens (1989) and Barbieri (1998).

would have a moral right to stay and to become citizens. It would be wrong to expel them.

If the first part of the argument is granted—the right of the Indo-Fijians to stay in Fiji and to keep the Fijian citizenship they possess—the second part—the argument for equal citizenship—should be easier to establish. Again, states like Nazi Germany and South Africa that have openly rejected the principle of equal citizenship stand as the archetypes of moral wrong. No one has to debate the merits of their policies today. Of course, most Western states also denied formal equality of citizenship on the basis of race, class, religion, ethnicity, and gender in the not too distant past, but almost no one defends these practices today or suggests that we should return to them. On these issues there is a moral consensus or as close to a consensus as one gets.

The crucial abstract principle underlying this consensus is the assumption of human moral equality whether that is expressed in terms of the moral equality of persons or in terms of equal consideration of the interests of all individuals or in some other form. This assumption is central to the modern liberal tradition. It is commonplace to argue that a commitment to the moral equality of persons entails a commitment to equal political citizenship.

Of course, acceptance of the principle of equal citizenship does not settle every question, as we have seen throughout this book. I have argued at a number of points already that the principle of equal citizenship may permit or even require certain differences and distinctions among citizens, and I will argue below that it permits some of the differences created by the 1970 Fijian Constitution. But a commitment to equal citizenship does not permit a distinction among citizens on the basis of a difference in degrees of attachment to the community (whether putative or real), much less one that would purport to deduce that difference in attachment from ethnic identification. Those who cry 'Fiji for the Fijians' are not advocating a form of differentiated citizenship that they claim reflects a commitment to equal citizenship. They do not regard the Indo-Fijians as equal citizens. Their goal is domination, not respect for difference or evenhanded justice.

Justice and History

One possible objection to the line of argument I have developed so far is that it ignores history. Fijians certainly place great weight on the historical promise they say the British made in the Deed of Cession that their interests would be paramount. In my view, a commitment to equal citizenship does not require us to ignore history. On the contrary, it requires us to pay attention to history in trying to judge what evenhanded justice requires in particular circumstances. In this section, I will show first why appeals to the Deed of Cession carry no moral weight, and secondly, how history is morally relevant to the claims of Indo-Fijians to membership in Fiji. In later parts of the chapter, I will argue that historical circumstances contribute to the moral justification of certain kinds of special arrangements for Fijians.

The appeal of the Fijians to the Deed of Cession's supposed guarantee that their interests would be kept paramount cannot plausibly be used as a justification for the subordination or expulsion of the Indo-Fijians, because if the guarantee meant what some Fijians have claimed it meant, the British had no right to make such a promise. If A promises B to keep C and C's descendants in perpetual servitude in return for a promise by B to obey A, this promise provides no compelling moral reason for perpetuating the servitude of C and her descendants, if that servitude is itself unjust. In other words, a promise to do wrong deserves no moral respect and justifies nothing. So, to rely on the Deed of Cession's guarantee as a moral justification for the treatment of Indo-Fijians, one would have to show that the British were morally justified in not treating the Indo-Fijians equally.

In fact, there is no reason to believe that those like Gordon and the others who promulgated the idea that the Deed of Cession guaranteed the paramountcy of Fijian interests intended the sort of dominance by Fijians that some later interpreters have claimed the Deed warrants. The real issue at the time was whether the interests of the European settlers would override any real concern for the indigenous Fijians. Understood properly as a commitment to protect the Fijians against domination and exploitation by European settlers, the doctrine of the paramountcy of Fijian interests was morally defensible and indeed desirable. But such a commitment would not warrant any action towards the Indo-Fijians who were themselves clearly subjected to domination and exploitation by the European settlers in Fiji. Even if one argued that the British importation of Indian labourers violated the promise to protect the Fijians' interests (an argument that is deeply problematic given their crucial role in preventing the exploitation of Fijian labour on the plantations and in contributing to the economic development of the island), it would not follow that the Fijians would be justified in treating the Indo-Fijians as less than equal citizens, much less in expelling them.[20]

[20] One of the familiar moral conundrums of the real world is the fact that those in power are often able to arrange circumstances so that oppressed groups are pitted against one another. For example, landless peasants in Brazil are now encouraged by the powerful, including some governmental officials, to clear and settle land in the Amazon basin, displacing the indigenous people who have traditionally lived in that area. Is it wrong for the peasants to take over these lands? Speaking broadly, I think the answer is yes, but it is easy to see why the peasants act as they do and hard to criticize them because they too are so clearly victims. Assume, for the sake of this argument, the following (which I take to be largely true but won't try to prove): the peasants are landless because most of the arable land is in the hands of a tiny, powerful elite. This is a highly unjust distribution, but land reform is not feasible because of the power of the rich landowners. The peasants are hungry, needy, and desperate, but any attempt to wrest land from the wealthy, though morally justifiable, would be doomed to failure. Taking the land of the Indians, which no doubt seems underutilized from the peasants' perspective as well as from that of the central government, is the only realistic option for them to improve their very bad situation. It is not justifiable, but it is perhaps morally excusable in a way that the behaviour of the landowners is not, though their behaviour, too, is perfectly understandable from the perspective of self-interest.

My rejection of the Fijian claim about the moral force of the Deed of Cession is not an argument for regarding history as morally irrelevant. After all, the Indo-Fijians' claim to equal citizenship is itself rooted in history. It is the particular history of the Indo-Fijians that establishes their moral claims in Fiji.

To explore the importance of this, it may be helpful to draw attention briefly to other cases involving immigrants where my own moral sense of who belongs and what justice requires would be somewhat different from the case of Fiji. Take the case of recent French immigrants to New Caledonia. The number of Europeans in New Caledonia has greatly increased in the last few decades with the result that Europeans now outnumber natives. This development was, at least in part, the outcome of a deliberate policy by the French government encouraging immigration as a way of forestalling any demand by the natives for independence. In other words, it was a deliberate manipulation of the principles of equal citizenship and majority rule to maintain French hegemony over the island.[21]

Suppose that a combination of native insurgency, international pressures, and changing world conditions led to independence for New Caledonia in the next few years. Would the recent French immigrants be entitled to claim equal citizenship? Do they belong? If it was wrong for the French government to have encouraged and facilitated their arrival in the first place—and from the story I have told that seems clearly to be the case—does the fact of their having arrived give them legitimacy? I ask these as genuine, not rhetorical questions. On the one hand, there would be something perverse about rewarding the French policy with moral recognition for the new settlers. On the other hand, they are not soldiers obeying orders but individuals with lives and claims of their own. Are they to be held responsible for the policy? Should they have known better? What about earlier arrivals who have been there for many years? How about those of European descent who have been born and brought up there? The latter, at least, belong and are entitled to equal citizenship on the basis of my earlier analysis. But if the French can delay long enough, a European majority will have grown up in New Caledonia with just this sort of claim.

This illustrates one of the deep puzzles about the relation between history and morality. On the one hand, if we simply accept the claim that the passage of time reduces the moral importance of the origins of a situation, we seem to create an (additional) incentive for those who do not care about morality to ignore it, namely, that over time those who care about morality will feel less inclined, indeed less entitled to try to do anything about the injustice that has been perpetrated. On the other hand, it seems problematic to penal-

---

[21] This policy is alluded to in a letter from Pierre Messmer, Prime Minister, to his secretary of state at the French Overseas Department—Overseas Territories, 1972 (Coulon 1985: 231).

ize present generations for what their ancestors have done.[22] These questions arise with respect to large minorities or even majorities introduced by other imperial powers into lands with existing populations with a long-standing cultural identity and tradition: Chinese in Tibet, Russians in the Baltics, to cite only a few.[23] I don't feel as though I have a clear answer to such cases. Whether one accepts or rejects the claims of the settlers to full membership, something of moral importance is lost. But however one answers these difficult questions, they do not apply to the Indo-Fijians, almost all of whom were born and brought up in Fiji and have known no other home. In this case, at least the passage of time is great enough to establish their right to belong beyond all reasonable doubt.

Ironically, the tension between morality and history is more apparent with regard to the legitimacy of the Fijians' share of political power than it is with regard to the membership of the Indo-Fijians. One of the greatest concerns of Fijian leaders was the fact that, since the mid-1940s, Indo-Fijians had outnumbered Fijians. Fijian leaders feared that numerical superiority would lead to Indo-Fijian political dominance in an electorate polarized along ethnic lines. Much of the Fijian resistance to independence and to democratic institutions, especially a common electoral roll, stemmed from fear of this demographic reality. But as a result of the coup, and subsequent discriminatory policies, many thousands of Indo-Fijians emigrated, changing the demographic balance significantly. Now Fijians constitute the majority of the population and have a significant numerical advantage over the Indo-Fijians (50.7 per cent to 43.5 per cent). So, the morally illegitimate coup and its aftermath have created a situation in which Fijians can maintain political control

---

[22] David Hume made an even stronger claim about the ways in which the passage of time affects morality: 'Time and custom give authority to all forms of government . . . and that power, which at first was founded only on injustice and violence, becomes in time legal and obligatory' (Hume 1888: 566). Indeed, he argued that time alters even our moral evaluation of a given event so that 'a king, who during his life-time might justly be deem'd an usurper, will be regarded by posterity as a lawful prince' if his family keeps the throne (Hume 1888: 566).

Israelis sometimes speak of 'building facts on the ground' with their settlements on the West Bank. This refers, I think, not just to sociological facts but to moral facts. Over time, even people who opposed the settlements initially, may come to feel that it is not right to uproot those who have settled. This is not necessarily, or not simply, a cynical manipulation of morality, because many Israelis feel the settlements are entirely justified morally but for reasons which are not persuasive to others who will, however, feel their moral views of what justice requires shift the longer the settlements stay. In the same vein, some people would say that it was not right to displace the Palestinians to create Israel, but now that Israel exists and has existed for so long, it would be wrong not to accept its existence as legitimate. Those who see the founding of Israel as fully justified from a moral point of view might not be entirely happy with this qualified form of acceptance, but they would none the less welcome the support it provides when others advance challenges to Israel's basic existence. Of course, those now being displaced are also well aware of the ways in which time will weaken their moral claims (in the eyes of others, not their own) and so of the importance of resisting as vigorously as possible now, especially since they can expect that the moral sympathy they now receive from outsiders may fade over time. This is not a recipe for tranquillity.

[23] Small minorities do not pose quite the same kind of moral problem because acknowledging their claims will not affect the fundamental identity of the political community in the same way as acknowledging the claims of a new group with close to a numerical majority.

through democratic institutions (if they stay united). Yet there is no morally legitimate way to undo this shift in political power.[24]

Whose Justice?

One way to characterize my argument in the last several pages is to say that the requirements of justice set moral limits to the claims that may be advanced in the name of identity and culture. One obvious challenge to this line of argument is to ask the question 'Whose justice?' (MacIntyre 1988). This takes us back to the concerns I initially addressed in chapter two. If different cultures embody different moral views, at least to some extent, isn't it a form of cultural imperialism to use the standards of one culture to judge another? Who are we to say what is just or unjust in Fiji? Indeed, in resisting international criticism of the coup, the most powerful line of argument that the Fijians have been able to advance has been the claim that any Western criticism of the coup and of the treatment of the Indo-Fijians is a form of neo-colonial imperialism (Lawson 1991: 262).

This line of defence, supported by other island states in the region, led the governments of Australia and New Zealand to retreat from what had initially been quite critical responses to the coup. In my view, they retreated too far, but I do not want to develop that argument here. In this chapter, I am interested primarily in the question of how we judge such issues from a moral perspective as outside and unofficial observers. It may well be proper for public officials to feel more constrained in their criticism of other countries than private citizens, at least in some circumstances. There is, of course, a certain irony in the Fijian invocation of the charge of colonialism, given the resistance of the Fijians to decolonization, but this does not prove the charge untrue.

I do not think that this challenge can be dismissed out of hand. There is a real danger that in making moral judgements about other societies, we will be led astray by misunderstandings or misinterpretations of practices and institutions different from our own. On the other hand, every repressive security apparatus is quick to say 'If you understood our situation—which is very different from yours—you would understand why we have to do these things'. It would be a moral mistake to take such claims about difference at face value.

---

[24] People sometimes describe the coup and the subsequent policies favouring Fijians as a form of 'ethnic cleansing' because it has resulted in the departure of so many Indo-Fijians. I think this is inappropriate. The term 'ethnic cleansing' came into common usage several years ago in connection with the (mainly) Serbian practices in Bosnia and Serbia of killing large numbers of people and driving others out at the point of a gun because they were members of the wrong ethnic group. No such violence has occurred in Fiji. It is not a defence of the coup or the subsequent policies to observe that this is a difference that matters morally.

So, we cannot and should not abandon the task of judging.[25] We cannot because such judging is implicit in as ordinary a daily practice as reading the newspaper. Part of what makes a story newsworthy is the assumption that it contains information that engages our moral sensibilities. Think of reports about ethnic massacres in Rwanda, the resistance of people in East Timor to Indonesian authority, the repression of dissidents in China. These stories are newsworthy in no small part because of the moral concerns they evoke. We should not abandon the task of judging because no defensible moral view can really refuse all judgements about other societies. Consider again archetypal cases like slavery in the United States, the Holocaust under the Nazis, apartheid in South Africa. Would a moral approach that refused to pronounce on such cases be worthy of serious consideration? When unarmed, peaceful marchers are shot down simply for objecting to the current regime or its policy (as they have been in any number of places), do we really need to inquire into the intricacies of local culture before expressing moral condemnation?

No one can defend murder on the grounds of cultural difference and indeed no one tries to. Repressive regimes deny that they commit murder. They say that the protestors had guns or threatened the security forces in some way or that the massacre never really took place. And, of course, if any of these claims were true they would change our moral judgement. This means that there is a limit to any plausible claim of moral or cultural relativism. What that limit is, and where the appeal to cultural difference begins to have some moral bite, is precisely the issue that I am trying to explore here, first by specifying the limits to appeals to cultural difference in moral arguments about Fiji and then by arguing below that cultural difference does matter morally within those limits. In that way, I am trying to put into practice here the precepts I put forward in Chapter 2.

One answer to the challenge that we are imposing our own moral views on others is to note that the view that we should not do this is also one of *our* moral views. It is a characteristically liberal view really, one not shared by a number of other cultural perspectives. In one sense it is a truism that we start from our own moral perspective. Where else could we start from? The point is that our moral perspective contains both moral principles about justice that we think apply to the actions of people outside our own society and moral principles about respecting the autonomy of others that we think limit our right to judge how others live their lives, individually and collectively. We normally suppose there to be some tension between these different principles but not an actual contradiction. So, the question is how to apply these different principles to the case of Fiji.

To answer this question, we must unpack it a bit. First, someone might

---

25 For an instructive discussion of the problem of judging as an outsider, see Beiner (1991).

argue that in raising the issue of equal citizenship and the liberal democratic principles that underlie it, I am introducing principles and ideals that are foreign to the traditions and cultural values of Fiji, that have no roots in the Fijian community. But this begs a crucial question about what the community is and who belongs. For the challenges I have raised from a liberal democratic perspective are the very ones that Indo-Fijians have been raising for decades in their demand for formal political equality among all citizens and a common franchise that does not recognize ethnic distinctions (Gillion 1977: 130–56). To claim that these liberal democratic principles are morally irrelevant to Fiji because they are not rooted in the culture of the Fijian community would be to accept (as having normative force) a definition of the Fijian community that excludes or at least marginalizes the Indo-Fijians who live in Fiji, to suggest that they do not really belong.

Secondly, let's consider the culture of the Fijians. Does it really entail a significantly different set of moral commitments from the ones I have drawn upon in defending the claims of the Indo-Fijians? The key principle in my argument was the principle of moral equality, a principle central to the Christian tradition. Christianity has been an essential ingredient in Fijian culture for over a century, and most Fijians who argue for the paramountcy of Fijian interests do not attempt to defend their position by appeal to pre-Christian values. Of course, some Fijian Christians deny that their religious commitments entail an obligation to respect the equal rights of the Indo-Fijians.[26] There were many official Christian apologists for segregation in the United States and apartheid in South Africa, too. But those who argued that segregation and apartheid were incompatible with Christian principles had the better of the argument. The critics of Fijian domination have the better of the argument, also, and for the same sorts of reasons. For the most part, though, the Fijians have not attempted to mount a reasoned defence of the coup and the subsequent policy of subordinating the Indo-Fijians, apart from the sorts of claims I have already criticized above.

It is tempting to describe the coup as simply a power grab, but I do not think that such a description would accurately reflect the support for the coup and especially for the post-coup reforms among the Fijian community. Many Fijians did feel that the coup was justified. In that sense, there is a deep difference between their views and those of an outside observer like me (although the most recent constitutional reform seems to reflect a shift in the views of at least some Fijians). In any event, I do not think that this difference reflects a deep cultural difference about the nature of justice. To a large extent, what the Fijians put forward are simply claims of identity and entitlement: 'We are the Fijians; we were here first'. The same sort of sense of identity and

---

[26] Indeed, fundamentalist ministers are some of the key leaders in the nativist movement. (Howard 1991: 318–19). For an instructive discussion of the role played by religious leaders and institutions and leaders in Fiji's recent politics, see Premdas (1995).

entitlement is common enough in other parts of the world, including Western Europe and North America and has often led to much worse forms of repression of those defined as 'other' than the Indo-Fijians have suffered. So, we have no need or warrant to appeal to special features of Fijian culture to account for these views, and, by the same token, they are just as subject to the moral criticisms (however ineffective these may be in changing behaviour) that have been applied to those seeking ethnic domination in other countries.

Justice, Culture, and History: How Difference Matters

Thus far, I have been arguing that cultural difference doesn't make much difference, at least to our judgements about Fiji. But now I want to turn to the aspects of the case where I think culture and history do matter in the sense of legitimating institutions and practices that might seem morally problematic to many at first glance, and that still seem morally problematic to some after long reflection. In much of this book, I have been considering the virtues and defects of various ways of recognizing distinctions of identity and culture. In Fiji, the project has been not merely to recognize Fijian culture but to preserve and protect it against the corrosive effects of liberal values and institutions.

This is the sort of enterprise that seems very troubling to many of those who write about culture and politics. As Jeremy Waldron puts it in a well-known article, 'To *preserve* a culture is often to take a 'favored' snapshot version of it, and insist that this version must persist at all costs, in its defined purity, irrespective of the surrounding social, economic, and political circumstances' (Waldron 1992: 788, emphasis in original). Using the political authority of the state to preserve a group's culture raises a number of difficult questions from a liberal perspective. Isn't a culture that is deliberately preserved through public action necessarily an inauthentic culture? Doesn't the attempt to preserve a collective cultural identity inevitably falsify that identity by freezing it in some respects and transforming it in others, in neither case responding only to the internal imperatives of the culture itself. Who speaks for the collective? Doesn't external support for a cultural leadership show that there is something problematic about its claim to internal legitimacy? Shouldn't individuals be free to choose whether to accept, modify, or reject their inherited cultural identity, and isn't that freedom restricted when steps are taken to preserve a culture?

I think the case of Fiji offers an opportunity to show that the challenges posed by these difficult questions can be met under some circumstances. I will focus on two policies deliberately aimed at preserving Fijian culture: the creation of a system of inalienable collective ownership of the land and the institutional reinforcement of deference to chiefly authority through the establishment of a separate Fijian administration, creation of the Great Council of Chiefs, and other means. I will consider and reject the charges that these measures were inauthentic, unfair, and undemocratic, charges that are implicit in the questions above and explicit in some of the best discussions of Fiji. I will argue instead that these measures of cultural preservation were compatible with evenhanded justice.

In elaborating the objections to these measures of cultural preservation, I will rely heavily on what I regard as the best scholarly work on the politics of Fiji: Stephanie Lawson's *The Failure of Democratic Politics in Fiji* (Lawson 1991). Lawson's work is particularly valuable from my perspective because she is so clearly critical of most of the efforts to preserve Fijian culture that no one could reasonably accuse her of distorting her interpretation to favour preservation. Yet, because she is so scrupulously fair-minded in her presentation, much of the evidence she provides supports the case for cultural preservation in ways that she herself does not acknowledge or perhaps even recognize.

As the analysis proceeds, it will be helpful to keep in mind the distinction between what is morally permissible and what is morally required. Up till now, I have been focusing largely on the latter sort of argument, claiming that it was morally required to treat the Indo-Fijians as equal citizens. But I do not want to make so strong a moral claim about the efforts to preserve Fijian culture. Rather I want to argue that these measures taken were morally permissible—that is, one possible set of steps it was legitimate to take, even though other, quite different ones might not have been wrong.

Continuity and Change in History, Culture, and Morality: Justice and the Ownership of Land

Consider first the question of whether the arrangements regarding the ownership of land are justifiable. There is no question that the fact that the Fijians collectively own 83 per cent of the land has been a source of great power for them in relation to other groups, especially the Indo-Fijians, and that the latter's inability to buy land and their insecurity about the length and renewals of leases has been a source of great unhappiness in their community. Nevertheless, I think the practices of prohibiting the sale of Fijian land and exercising central control over its administration have been and are still justified.

There are three key points to the defence of the policy on land ownership. First, prior to this prohibition, Fijians were selling land, mainly to Europeans, and there is every reason to believe on the basis of the experience of other colonies that without this arrangement Fijians would have given up ownership of their land without receiving any substantial long-term benefits in return and without foreseeing the consequences for their collective way of life. So, this arrangement did protect a vital Fijian interest. Secondly, Fijian dominance in this area is balanced by the dominance Indo-Fijians have achieved in other areas of economic life. If the Fijians owned most of the businesses and occupied most of the key professional and white-collar positions as well, then it would be easier to make the case that this form of 'cultural preservation' was merely a means of perpetuating unjust privilege. Thirdly, despite the erosion of the traditional culture, it appears that the land is still central to the Fijian self-understanding. The attachment to the land is not merely instrumental; it is constitutive of the Fijian identity. Like the previous condition, this one could change. If both conditions changed, the justification of this arrangement would be greatly reduced. None of this is meant to suggest that the administration of the land and the conditions imposed on tenants could not be improved.

There are various objections that may be raised against this land policy. For purposes of exposition, I will divide the objections into two categories: ones that focus on the original adoption of the policy under the colonial regime and ones that focus on the continuation of the policy under current circumstances. Of course, the two categories of objections are often interrelated.

Context and Contingency in the Evaluation of the Past: Objections to Colonial Land Policy

Let me begin with the objections that Lawson raises to colonial land policy. Lawson observes that Gordon, the first colonial governor, set up a uniform system of inalienable land ownership with the rights held in a particular communal unit. This was, she says, very much at odds with traditional practice. First, land had not been inalienable prior to the colonial regime. More importantly, this communal unit had not been a landholding unit for most Fijians and had played a relatively minor role in most Fijian communities prior to this colonial practice. Now it has come to be seen by most Fijians as the traditional landholding unit, but the rigidities imposed by this arrangement have led to significant inequalities in ownership between different units because of variation in fertility and mortality among units. Those inequalities could have been addressed under the more fluid, pre-colonial arrangements but there is no easy solution today (Lawson 1991: 73–8).

Suppose that everything Lawson says about the transformation of traditional practices is true or largely so. What should we conclude? Was it a good policy or at least a morally permissible one? One important question is what the alternatives were and how good or bad they would have been.

The most likely alternative would have been a land policy designed to grant individual title to Fijians, and, more generally, to open up the land more fully for commercial exploitation. Would that have been desirable? Something like it was in fact tried. Lawson tells us that a later governor, Everard im Thurn, worried about the subordination of ordinary Fijians to their chiefs. He wanted to promote individualism among the Fijians, including a sense of economic ambition. To this end and as a way of reducing the chiefs' control, he wanted to have English taught in the village schools, not just to the children of the chiefs.[27] But his most dramatic innovation was a policy designed to reverse the previous assumption that 'all non-alienated lands, occupied or otherwise, had Fijian "owners" ' (Lawson 1991: 89). With the enthusiastic support of the European settlers, he tried to open up 'underutilized' land for commercial purposes. Between 1905 and 1908, 105,000 acres were sold and 170,000 put under-long term lease, a significant portion of the best agricultural land in Fiji. Gordon, the first governor, was then in the House of Lords, and when he learned of this policy he used his influence to put an end to it, and it was not subsequently renewed.

Was Gordon's intervention and the failure of this new land policy to be regretted? Here is Lawson's own assessment: 'It was, of course, fortunate at that time that the European population was prevented from encroaching too far upon the land—whether the land was occupied or not. In other ways, however, the consequences have not been so fortunate . . .' (Lawson 1991: 90). This seems a striking statement given Lawson's general position on preservation. What lies behind her ambivalence? In what ways was it fortunate and in what ways unfortunate?

With regard to the Fijians, Lawson seems to think the prohibition on the sale of land was unfortunate because it reduced incentives for individual economic activity and because it was an integral part of Gordon's overall strategy of cultural preservation which she sees as a conservative orthodoxy. But listen to what she acknowledges to be the advantage of the policy for the Fijians:

[It] discouraged an influx of white immigration which might have been expected had the land been thrown open for settlement. Unlike the neighbouring colonies of Australia and New Zealand, the indigenous population could not be pushed further and further off their lands to make way for white expansion (Lawson 1991: 77).

If these are the advantages and disadvantages, the preferable course for Fijians seems clear. Australia and New Zealand were the models that the settlers wanted to emulate and that Gordon wanted to avoid. Whatever the economic and social costs to Fijians of Gordon's plan, they pale beside the costs of the alternative suffered by the indigenous peoples in Australia and New Zealand.

---

[27] Lawson is not entirely clear about what became of this proposal but it seems to have been dropped because of resistance from the chiefs. The governor's persistence with his land policy may suggest where his true priorities lay (Lawson 1991: 86–7).

Lawson has nicely articulated precisely the sort of considerations that I think ought to be taken into account in our moral judgements: plausible historical possibilities and factors that the actors facing a situation could reasonably be expected to consider. We cannot just compare the path Fiji actually took with some hypothetically benign course in which the Fijians harmoniously developed ethnicly integrated economic and political institutions, effectively transforming their cultural traditions in ways that enabled them to compete successfully as individuals with other groups, if that imagined course was not in any sense a real historical possibility. Various efforts were made under the colonial regime to make Fijians more individualistic and to orient them more towards the market. Many of these were spectacular failures. None was particularly successful. Of the two paths which were clearly open, Gordon's and the more liberal individualistic one pushed by his successor, I see no grounds even on Lawson's own account for preferring the latter, if one is concerned about the welfare of the Fijians in the short or long run. If there was some third and superior alternative, we need some specification of what it might have been and how it might have worked.

I must acknowledge that there is a danger in the emphasis I am placing on the importance of historical context, namely, that one can accept too readily constraints which, however real, should themselves be subject to criticism. It is a deep problem for political theory as to how one is to incorporate the constraints of history without losing one's critical and theoretical perspective.[28]

This dilemma is brought home all the more forcefully when we turn our attention to the group which has thus far remained off-stage in this part of the discussion: the Indo-Fijians. As Lawson notes, one major consequence of the policy on the inalienability of Fijian land is that the Indian population and their descendants were doomed by it to become and remain 'a landless majority in their adopted country' (Lawson 1991: 77). If land is crucial to the well-being of the Fijians, it is also crucial to the well-being of the Indo-Fijians. Their insecurities about land are one of their central long-standing complaints. Did and does the rule against alienation adequately respect their moral claims?

Certainly the costs of this policy for the Indo-Fijians should count against it. Are the costs great enough to judge it on balance to have been or to be morally wrong? Again, thinking about this in historical context is perplexing. Should we ask whether the policy should have been adopted in the actual historical context, assuming that the system of indentured labour and white domination were to be in place? That seems odd. Surely both of those features of the colonial system were much more deeply problematic from a moral perspective than the inalienability of land. Why would we focus exclusively on the latter?

---

[28] For an attempt to wrestle with this sort of problem, see Carens (1996).

We could instead ask whether such a policy would have been justified if the rest of the colonial policy had been just, assuming that is not an oxymoron. But then we drift so far from reality that we begin to lose the bearings that we need to make an intelligent judgement about the question. Do we assume away white domination and the indenture system? How about the colonial government? How about the incursions of the European settlers that made becoming a colony seem like an attractive option to some of the Fijian leaders? Remember that the most powerful argument in favour of the policy is the role it played in preserving the Fijians from the fate suffered by indigenous peoples in Australia and New Zealand. Do we want to say that that fate was unfortunate but just? I doubt it. If not, when we remove injustice hypothetically from the situation, we remove much of the rationale for the policy. It was, after all, a defensive policy. The Fijians did not practice strict inalienability before the arrival of the Europeans, but alienability within the internal, non-capitalist Fijian context was not such a threat to the well-being of most Fijians.

Perhaps we should focus exclusively on the issue of land policy because altering it was a realistic possibility, as is evidenced by the actual, if temporary, change in the early 1900s, while the other morally problematic arrangements—such as, white domination, indenture—were inevitable under the circumstances. But inevitable in what sense? What this really means is that the Europeans were so firmly in power and had such ability to defend their vital interests, that no fundamental challenge to them could succeed. (Indeed, it is remarkable what Gordon was able to do to limit their claims). But here we confront again the question of what should be taken as a given for purposes of moral theory and what should be subjected to critical analysis.

Cultural Change, Paternalism, and Moral Legitimacy: Objections to Contemporary Land Policy

It is tempting to try to avoid these conundrums by refusing to judge the past (in the name of avoiding anachronism) and skipping to the present. John F. Kennedy and Pierre Trudeau were fond of saying that we can only be just in our own time. So, we can ask whether it is just now for the Fijians to hold their land inalienably in collective units. I will try to address that question, though I'm afraid the issues raised above about appropriate realistic constraints won't go away, and not only because the present will soon be the past.

The basic picture seems to be this. A somewhat fluid set of arrangements with regard to land in pre-colonial Fiji became much more rigid and fixed with the assignment of inalienable rights to collective units. This helped to protect the Fijians from the disasters suffered by indigenous groups in neighbouring colonies, but it also had the effect of changing Fijian culture, making land and these collective units more central than before. Now the threat of a European takeover of the land is greatly reduced, but the Fijians feel threatened by the Indo-Fijians' desire for land. Ordinary Fijians seem to feel a powerful attachment to the land and to have a lot at stake in their sense that they own the land, even when they do not live on it or work it themselves. Lawson herself indirectly attests to the power of this attachment when she notes critically that Fijian politicians have exaggerated the threat to Fijian ownership of the land that an Indo-Fijian-dominated government would pose as a way of stirring up support for themselves and opposition to Indo-Fijians (Lawson, 1991: 2–5). Her criticism of the tactic is entirely appropriate, but it is essential to see that the tactic can work only if Fijians care about the land at least, or perhaps especially, as a symbolic (i.e. cultural) issue. In other words, the Fijians themselves seem to regard continued Fijian ownership of the land as a vital interest.

We do not have to accept that perception at face value. One could argue, as Lawson does, that some of the features of Fijian culture are the product of a manipulative system of socialization. But I want to defer examination of that criticism to the discussion of chiefly authority. Instead, I want to focus here on the question of whether cultural change undermines the moral legitimacy of claims made in the name of culture.

I have noted how Fijian attitudes towards land were altered by the colonial policies designed to protect them. Is that a reason for discounting the present attachment? I don't see why. The Fijian attachment to the land clearly has deep pre-colonial roots even if it was more fluid then. Similarly, the communal units that own the land are not simply the creation of the colonial regime even if they did not generally have ownership rights over the land prior to Gordon's policy.

Even if both the attachment to the land and the land-owning unit had been entirely created by the colonial regime, to take an extreme hypothesis, it is not clear why that would discredit them if people were deeply attached to them over 100 years later. Remember, I am setting to one side here the issue of manipulation of the culture for the sake of internal domination. By hypothesis, we are dealing with a case where the cultural commitments in question are neutral or benign in their effect on those who hold them, but where they derive, at least in part, from some source exogenous to the culture.

As I see it, all cultures are subject to exogenous influences. That does not prove that there are no legitimate cultural commitments or attachments. What makes something a legitimate part of people's culture, regardless of its origins, is the fact that they have internalized it, made it their own, integrated it with other aspects of their culture. Of course, one can argue about whether that has actually occurred in a given case, but as I have tried to suggest, the depth of the Fijian attachment to the land today does not seem to be in dispute. What people regard as important is, in some respects at least, contingent and variable. But if they see something as important, we should take it seriously if we wish to take them seriously. That does not settle the question of what is to be done in cases of conflicting claims. It does mean, however, that external observers cannot simply employ the external origins of a cultural institution as a basis for declaring it inauthentic and then use its putative inauthenticity as a reason for rejecting the moral legitimacy of efforts to proect and preserve it.[29]

So, Fijians today are entitled to treat their land as a vital interest because of the role it plays in their culture. But what about Indo-Fijians? They have vital interests at stake here too. For the Indo-Fijians, as far as I can tell, the concern with regard to the land is an economic interest rather than a cultural one. I do not mean to suggest that this economic interest is less vital. It may be more vital in some contexts. But it does suggest that some compromise might be possible that would respect the security interests of Indo-Fijian farmers without challenging the cultural claims of Fijians to ownership. Indeed, the Indo-Fijians themselves seem to recognize this and did not object to the constitutional entrenchment of Fijian ownership of the land either in the 1970 Constitution or in the 1997 Constitution, although they were prepared to argue about many other matters. It is a familiar legal point that ownership is a bundle of rights, and that these rights can be organized differently for different purposes. Under these circumstances, it should be possible to find some arrangement that meets the concerns of both Indo-Fijians and Fijians. Under other circumstances, that might not be the case.[30] What justice requires then is evenhandedness, a willingness to take the interests of different groups into account in a fair way, combined with a recognition that the interests of different groups may not be the same.

A second line of criticism focuses not on the effect of inalienable collective ownership on groups but on its effects on the freedom of individual Fijians. After all, if individual Fijians or Fijian communal units do not want to sell their land, they do not have to do so. No one will force them to sell. If they do want to do so and the chiefs want the land to be inalienable in order to prevent it, the chiefs are acting paternalistically.[31] To put it another way, shouldn't we regard collective, inalienable land rights as an internal restriction designed to keep Fijians from changing their own culture and isn't that precisely the sort of arrangement that Kymlicka argued was morally objectionable from a liberal perspective?

---

[29] I emphasize external observers because claims about origins can sometimes play a role in internal debates within cultures about questions of authenticity, and there is no reason for outsiders to object to such debates.

[30] It is not unknown for two different groups to have powerful cultural attachments to the same land. In such cases, a just solution is harder to achieve, perhaps even impossible, but we do not advance the cause of justice by denying that cultural concerns matter. That they do matter is sometimes the only thing the conflicting groups can agree upon and must be the starting-point for reflection.

[31] At one point Lawson gives a lengthy and approving discussion of another author who develops precisely this argument (Lawson 1991: 191).

Now the first point to note in response is that even Lawson does not seem to think this sort of argument would have been an adequate reason for permitting Fijians to sell land at the beginning of the colonial period. The implication of the passages I cited earlier seems to be that the widespread alienation of Fijian land then, however voluntary, would have been a disaster for the Fijian people as it was for indigenous peoples elsewhere. One could perhaps argue that Fijians today do not need as much protection against potential Indo-Fijian domination as their ancestors needed against European domination. I think that there is something to that claim, but we cannot overlook the greater economic success of the Indo-Fijians and therefore the possibility that the ownership of land would become concentrated in their hands if Fijian land were not inalienable. That outcome is a problem only if one accepts the argument advanced earlier that ownership of the land is central to Fijian culture and that a significant erosion of that culture would be bad for Fijians. But that just throws the paternalism argument back one step further. If particular Fijians want to act in ways that undermine their own culture, why shouldn't they be free to do so? Isn't the attempt to preserve a culture through a practice like making land inalienable an unjustified form of paternalism?

Kymlicka himself cites collective inalienable land as an example of an external protection that has an internal restriction as its unavoidable by-product. He notes that land is often central to indigenous cultures but says that the land base:

is vulnerable to the greater economic and political power of the larger society. History has shown that the most effective way to protect indigenous communities from this external power is to establish reserves where the land is held in common and/or in trust, and cannot be alienated without the consent of the community as a whole (Kymlicka 1995: 43).

He observes that this arrangement prevents individual members of an indigenous community from using land as collateral for purposes of borrowing and says that does restrict their liberty but that this is 'a natural by-product of the external protection' (Kymlicka 1995: 44).

Kynlicka's account is not likely to satisfy a conventional liberal. From that perspective, the most direct restriction is not on the ability of an individual to use the land as collateral but on the ability to sell it, perhaps as a way of raising money to leave the community and start a business. So, Kymlicka does not directly address the issue of paternalism. But what the charge of paternalism implicitly presupposes is a particular cultural and institutional background in which private property is the norm, and even Kymlicka falls into this trap by treating the inability to use reserved land as collateral as a regrettable restriction on liberty. Capitalist private property was not the cultural and institutional context from which Fijian collective and inalienable ownership emerged (even though, as we have seen, the colonial scheme changed the traditional landholding arrangements). It is not the natural order of things. Even in a conventional capitalist setting, not all land is individually held and alienable. The inability of individual Americans to sell 'their' piece of the Grand Canyon or to use it as collateral is not normally construed as a restriction of individual liberty despite the potentially high value of a house lot on the rim. Of course, some people would like to commodify and market-ize all publicly owned lands and do see every form of collective ownership as a restriction of individual freedom, but most people can see that there are various collective goods that require or are enhanced by collective ownership of land.

From one perspective, the Fijian land arrangements are not properly construed as an example of paternalism but rather as an unfamiliar use of a familiar technique for dealing with collective action problems and external-ities, both of which are present in this case. As Russell Hardin has argued, making certain rights inalienable or restricting the range of actions of the members of a group to which one belongs is a perfectly intelligible way of protecting one's interests in a context in which collective action problems or externalities create incentives for individuals to act in ways contrary to their more important interests (Hardin 1988: 92–6). This is not necessarily a form of paternalism if by paternalism is meant requiring people to conform to pol-icies or rules in ways that go against their own best judgements of their inter-ests but which others believe will be in their interest. When constraints are self-imposed as a way of avoiding collective action problems, it is misleading to call them paternalistic.

From this perspective, the policy on inalienable collective ownership of land in Fiji is far less paternalistic today than it was when it was introduced. Then it was primarily the result of a judgement by the colonial government about what would be good for the Fijians, not something they had chosen for themselves. Today, by contrast, the policy has the strong and explicit support of a substantial majority of Fijians.[32] Keeping land inalienable is not a form of paternalism but rather a way of respecting the demands of most Fijians. Of course, this still leaves open the question of whether it is legitimate to require the minority of Fijians who do not share this view to conform to it, but that is a familiar problem in any situation where democratic decisions must be made about the provision (or non-provision) of collective goods in the absence of a consensus. It is not an infringement of freedom in any signific-ant sense to refuse to sell off the Grand Canyon in response to the demands of a small minority.

In sum, the constitutional entrenchment of inalienable land rights is morally permissible because it offers one way to protect interests that most

---

[32] This conclusion seems to me the obvious implication of Lawson's discussion of the way the issue plays politically, although she herself does not draw this inference.

Fijians regard as vital and that would be vulnerable in the absence of this institutional arrangement because of collective action problems. It is one component of an evenhanded solution, the other part of which would require much greater security for Indo-Fijian tenants. Are collective and inalienable land rights for Fijians morally required? It seems to me that they were morally required at the beginning of the colonial period because no other feasible arrangement would have protected Fijians from losing most of their land and culture. But I would not go so far as to insist that they are morally required in today's world because Fijians are gradually integrating themselves into the market economy. As they do so, the moral urgency of maintaining the distinctive Fijian culture diminishes. While the constitutional entrenchment of inalienable land rights is a morally permissible arrangement today, there may well come a time when the maintenance of inalienable land rights would no longer be primarily a way of protecting a vital aspect of Fijian culture, but rather just a way of achieving economic advantage in relation to the Indo-Fijians. If that should occur, the policy would no longer be morally defensible. When such a point is reached is, of course, subject to interpretation and debate like every other substantive moral judgement one can make about this case or any other.

Authenticity, Interests, and Democracy: Three Challenges to the Moral Legitimacy of Chiefly Authority

Let me turn now to the issue of the institutional reinforcement of deference to chiefly authority through the establishment of a separate Fijian administration, creation of the Great Council of Chiefs, and other means. I begin with an overview of the case for and against these measures and then pursue the main objections in more detail.

The chiefs and their supporters have claimed that respect for chiefs and deference to chiefly authority have long been a central part of traditional Fijian culture. This was, at least ostensibly, an important part of the original justification for constructing a separate administration and giving the chiefs a key role in running it, in other words, that this way of organizing colonial political and legal institutions was the most congruent with indigenous Fijian culture.

Whenever one encounters a formal system of separate treatment on the basis of race or ethnicity, one is bound to ask whether such an arrangement is unjust in the way that apartheid in South Africa or segregation in the Old South was unjust. But as I argued in Chapter 4, it is essential to distinguish between separate arrangements as a form of respect for difference and separate arrangements as a form of domination. Fiji's separate institutions were not like apartheid or segregation because they did not grow out of and perpetuate ethnic or racial domination. On the contrary, most of these institutions were designed to protect Fijians *against* domination especially by the European settlers. In a more positive sense, they were intended to preserve traditional values and the Fijian way of life. But this was not dependent upon the subordination of any other group. Having a separate Fijian administration, for example, did not stigmatize the Indo-Fijians and Europeans who were excluded from its jurisdiction or deprive them of any powers they ought to have possessed. By contrast, the refusal to grant Indo-Fijians the franchise at a time when the Europeans had it clearly was a symbol of and a contributor to the subordinate position of the Indo-Fijians *vis-à-vis* the Europeans.

The separate Fijian institutions were different. Indeed, it seems clear that these institutions contributed to the Fijians' lower rate of economic success. On the other hand, in traditional Fijian culture, as we have seen, economic success was not very important, and as we saw in Chapter 4, it is appropriate to respect differences in aspirations that grow out of cultural commitments so long as these are not the product of adaptive preference formation or internalized subordination. In this case, it seems reasonable to say that the Fijians wanted the insulation the institutions offered and that the reduced economic opportunities may well have been a price worth paying for the possibility of prolonging the traditional way of life.

Today, that way of life seems no longer to be viable because of population growth and the desire for economic growth. There are too many people and not enough land for a way of life based upon subsistence agriculture. But an agriculture that aims at producing a substantial surplus is not as congruent with the values and practices of the traditional Fijian way of life. Moreover, many Fijians are no longer willing to live in the traditional ways. Even the Fijian leadership, in the past the group that has most emphasized the importance of maintaining the traditional way of life, now expresses great concern about the relative position of Fijians in the general economic competition. As Fijians come to want the same things that other members of society do, the case for separate institutions declines. This development reminds us that cultures are never stagnant and can evolve substantially even in the context of measures designed to preserve them.

The separate administration is not the only way in which Fijian chiefs exercise special power as part of the effort to preserve Fijian culture. Consider the entrenchment in the 1970 Constitution of Fijian rights and their protection through the veto power given the Great Council of Chiefs in the Senate. (A similar arrangement exists in the new 1997 Constitution.) The justification for this sort of special arrangement must be that the interests being protected are vital and yet vulnerable without these special protections. I have already argued above that the interests were vital. As to their vulnerability, I suspect that the fates of indigenous peoples elsewhere, and even nearby, provided sufficient reason for Fijians to be concerned. As with the separate institutions discussed above, the goal of these arrangements seems to have been protection of the Fijians rather than domination by the Fijians of the Indo-Fijians. The Senate did not initiate legislation, and the veto power only affected the areas most relevant to the protection of Fijian culture. In short, here was an institutional arrangement specifically designed for the preservation of culture (potentially, depending on demographic developments, a minority culture) that was morally justifiable.

Against this, Lawson draws our attention to what she calls the myth of Fijian cultural homogeneity. Much of what is called traditional Fijian culture, Lawson argues, is really a product of the colonial regime. It created the Great Council of Chiefs and the separate Fijian administration and, in doing so, greatly strengthened the power of some hierarchical elements in Fijian society at the expense of other, less hierarchical elements. Diversity and dissent among Fijians were repressed. To the extent that Fijians today think of themselves as sharing a common culture which entails respect for chiefly authority, this is the result of years of hegemony by chiefs and their representatives who have introduced a powerful system of socialization to convey a limited and inaccurate picture of Fijian culture.

According to Lawson, the costs of perpetuating this myth have been high. The separate institutions and formal ethnic divisions in colonial and independent Fiji that were defended in the name of the myth exacerbated ethnic divisions in Fiji and led to the emergence of a party system based on ethnicity. This in turn undermined the legitimacy of democratic politics, especially the idea of a democratic opposition that might legitimately succeed to power through elections, and so ultimately led to the coup.

In sum, Lawson argues that the institutionalization of deference to chiefly authority distorted Fijian culture, that it served the interests of the Fijian chiefs at the expense of the Fijian people, and that it undermined desirable democratic institutions and practices in Fiji as a whole (Lawson 1991: 93–117). I will explore each of these objections in turn.

Authenticity and Cultural Change

First, consider the issue of authenticity. I have already touched on aspects of this issue in my discussion of the place of land in Fijian culture, and now I will explore it further. Let me recall the general concern about authenticity that I raised earlier. Some people object to any effort at cultural preservation on the grounds that every culture is indeterminate and contested and that the idea of preserving a culture inevitably privileges one particular understanding of the culture over others and rigidifies the culture in an artificial way (Waldron 1992: 761–5). That objection can be raised even when the efforts at preservation are being carried out by institutions like museums and, even if (as is often not the case) the museum officials are members of the community whose culture the museum is trying to preserve (Welsh 1992: 841–6). The objection takes on added force when political authority is used to maintain an ongoing way of life. Is it morally legitimate for those with political power to promote their interpretation of a 'shared' culture and to determine what measures shall be taken to preserve it? What, besides force, makes their view of the culture authoritative?[33]

However problematic political efforts at cultural preservation may seem in a liberal democratic society with its institutional mechanisms for deliberation, choice, and dissent by the citizenry, they are likely to seem even more problematic in societies where authority is said to rest on tradition rather than choice. How do we know that what is put forward as a 'shared culture' is not merely a self-serving ideology designed to preserve existing patterns of privilege and power? How do we know whether those without power really accept and share this culture? If they are silent, is it because they agree or because they have no means of voice? If the traditional culture is to be preserved in the name of the people who share it, don't we have to know what they think, how they see their own culture, whom they regard as legitimate spokespersons?[34] And even if ordinary people do accept the legitimacy of 'traditional' authorities, how do we know that their acceptance is not just the product of a manipulative system of socialization?[35]

---

[33] This problem is further complicated when it is a question of a minority culture so that those from the minority culture who have political power within their own group are nevertheless subject, at least potentially, to political constraints from the majority outside the group. What if a minority within the minority appeals to this overall majority in the name of the minority's own culture which the dissidents may say those in power are not respecting? For example, native women in Canada have argued that the Canadian government should not permit them to be excluded from membership in their bands and expelled from their reservations for marrying non-natives when the same rules do not apply to native men who marry non-native women. When those sympathetic to native self-government argue that the native women should not use Western concepts of equality between the sexes to challenge traditional native practices, the women sometimes reply that the male chiefs are not following traditional native culture which varied considerably from one tribe to another and often permitted women who married non-natives to remain with their tribe. They point out that the exclusionary rule, at least in its universal form, was imposed by an earlier Canadian government in the name of Western patriarchal values that many native groups did not share but which some male chiefs have come to accept because it suits their interests to do so (Jamieson 1978: 79–88). So far as I can tell, however, this particular sort of complication about who speaks in the authentic voice of the tradition has not yet arisen among the Fijians themselves, though variants of it are perhaps implicit in some of the challenges to the chiefs.

[34] Perhaps someone will object that such a question entails the (moral) imposition of our own liberal democratic values on other cultures. But then the objector must explain why we ought to respect other cultures at all. As I argued above, it is not possible in practice to sustain a radically relativistic view of the morality of other cultures, i.e., a view that sets no limits on what count as morally legitimate social arrangements and cultural values.

[35] Now that Marxism is in such disrepute, terms like 'false consciousness' are shunned. There are indeed good reasons to be wary of any claim that someone else's self-understanding is false. One risks riding roughshod over any view of the world that does not comport with one's own. On the other hand, it would require a wilful blindness to deny that manipulative socialization has played an important role in maintaining patterns of unjust domination with regard to race, class, and gender, both in our own society and in others. The challenge therefore is to find a critical perspective which is at the same time open to the possibility of genuine differences among people's values and commitments.

Lawson's critique shows why all of these concerns are directly relevant to the issue of chiefly authority in Fiji. She points out that before Fiji became a colony there was considerable regional variation in patterns of authority and social organization. While chiefs played some significant social role in all parts of pre-colonial Fiji, it was only in the eastern region of the main island that a strongly hierarchical pattern of chiefly rule predominated. The colonial regime, with the cooperation of the eastern Fijian chiefs, defined this strongly hierarchical pattern as *the* traditional system of Fijian rule, using it as the key structural element for purposes of colonial administration. Different patterns were forcibly suppressed and all of Fiji was required to conform to this model. Hierarchical relationships were formalized to meet the requirements of administration, and in some cases entirely new hierarchical institutions, most notably the Great Council of Chiefs, were created by the colonial regime. According to Lawson, this arrangement might be attributed as much or more to the familiar colonial strategy of indirect rule as to any real desire to respect traditional patterns of Fijian authority. At the very least, the hierarchical dimensions of Fijian culture were dramatically reinforced by the institutions of colonial administration. So, according to Lawson, chiefly authority in its current form is not a deeply rooted, long-standing element of a common Fijian culture, as its defenders would have it, but rather, in important respects, a relatively recent addition created in no small part to serve the needs of the colonial regime.

If chiefly rule is as tainted by its colonial connections as Lawson argues, why do the Fijian people put such store by their chiefs today? Lawson's answer to this question seems ambiguous. At times, she suggests that it is only the chiefs themselves, not the Fijian people, who are attached to chiefly hierarchy (Lawson 1991: 99, 107). At other points, she seems to be saying that ordinary Fijians do accept chiefly hierarchy as central to the Fijian way of life, but only because the chiefs have established and maintained their position through fear, superstition, and propaganda. She says, for example, that 'a century of propaganda' accounts for why ordinary Fijians accept the current patterns of socio-political organization, including landholding, as long-standing and traditional for all Fijians, despite the evidence of historians to the contrary (Lawson 1991: 96). Among other techniques, Lawson says, the chiefs have insisted that they alone are authoritative interpreters of Fijian tradition and then have used that interpretive authority both to bolster their claims to exercise legitimate social authority and to influence the understanding of particular social and political issues.

Overall then, Lawson argues that the chiefly hierarchy rests its claim to legitimacy on appeals to a traditional Fijian culture which it misrepresents. Because existing patterns of chiefly rule have deeper roots in colonialism than in pre-colonial Fijian culture, chiefly hierarchy in its present form is not an authentic expression of indigenous Fijian culture.[36] She explicitly considers and rejects an argument to the effect that what matters is the attachment of past and contemporary Fijians to their forms of social organization, including chiefly authority, rather than questions of historical origins. Lawson objects that such a position implies that 'the legitimacy of the "tradition" embodied in the uniform structure [of contemporary Fijian social organization] is not derived from any consideration of its origins, but from the purpose it has come to serve' (Lawson 1991: 99).[37]

Lawson's objection is well worth considering. An appeal to tradition is a claim about continuity. If there is no continuity, doesn't the appeal fail? To put it another way, attachment and interest are not the same as authenticity. The fact that people are attached to some institution or benefit from some practice tells us nothing about their relation to past institutions and practices. But isn't the relation to the past what matters if the institution or practice is defended on the grounds of 'tradition'?

Suppose we answer the last question affirmatively. What sort of relation with the past, how much continuity, is necessary for something to count as 'traditional'? To put it another way, under what circumstances does it make sense to talk of 'preserving' some aspect of a culture? It makes no sense to insist that any element of change in an institution or practice renders it non-traditional. All cultures evolve and change. It is the sense of continuity within change that the idea of tradition evokes. Consider, as an analogy, the idea of being faithful to a constitution. As the debates over constitutional interpretation show, there are no simple answers to the question of what counts as continuity in constitutional law (Levinson 1988).[38]

Let us move from the abstract to the concrete. Was there enough continuity between pre-colonial Fijian culture and the institutions and practices created by the colonial regime to justify a claim that the new order was traditional in some meaningful sense, that it was a way of preserving Fijian culture? Lawson herself seems to concede as much, saying 'The system did much to preserve the indigenous culture and way of life, even though some aspects of these were of dubious value' (Lawson 1991: 3). The quotation illustrates Lawson's scepticism about the merits of the traditional Fijian way of life, and that is another important issue to which I will turn shortly. But just as authenticity is distinct from the question of current attachment, so it is also distinct from the question of whether what is authentic is good on other grounds.

[36] Lawson never uses the word 'authenticity' but this concern is implicit in the logic of her critique.

[37] Lawson's argument comes in the context of a critique of Macnaught (1982). In my view, that is in part an unfair criticism. However, pursuing this issue would take me too far from my main concerns.

[38] Of course, one solution is to deny the possibility of continuity altogether, but like all forms of radical scepticism this is a difficult position to maintain. A more defensible position is to insist that any particular claim to continuity is contestable.

Perhaps what is most important in determining whether there is enough continuity to regard the post-colonial Fijian culture as authentic is that the Fijians themselves treated the continuity as significant. If the question of authenticity is essentially a question about how to appraise a relationship with the past that includes elements of both continuity and discontinuity, it would seem reasonable to let the people whose culture and history are in question be the judges of whether contemporary institutions and practices should be regarded as authentically traditional. This is not the same as saying whatever institutions and practices they accept are authentic. Rather it is to say that whatever institutions and practices they accept as traditional are authentic. For example, most Fijians seem to accept legislatures and elections as legitimate social institutions in the sense that no significant segment of the Fijian population suggests that it would be appropriate today to choose political rulers purely on the basis of heredity, to rule by fiat, and so on. But no one claims that these institutions are traditional. Of course, people in a given culture may disagree among themselves about what is authentic. But in the case of the Fijian people, there seems to be surprisingly little disagreement on such key issues as whether a deep attachment to the land and respect for chiefly authority are authentic elements of Fijian culture and whether the contemporary institutional incarnations of these values are legitimate.[39]

One scholar who explicitly acknowledges the ways in which the arrangements of the colonial regime drastically modified traditional Fijian practices asserts none the less that these arrangements were something that 'Fijians rapidly made their own and defended tenaciously for a century as the bulwark of their neo-traditional identity, of everything that was still distinctively Fijian' (Macnaught 1982: 4). In other words, this is what the Fijians themselves thought they could maintain of the old ways under new conditions, what they could preserve even if in changed form. If that description is correct, then chiefly authority as institutionalized by these arrangements ought to be considered an authentic part of Fijian culture. In other words, the issue of authenticity should not be used by people outside a culture to call into question institutions and practices that those within the culture regard as legitimate reflections of their heritage.

Suppose that the apparently widespread acceptance of such institutions and practices as authentic elements of the tradition is the product of lies and coercion. Suppose those in power mislead ordinary people about their actual history and traditions, presenting relatively recent innovations as things that date back to time immemorial, and repressing those who would challenge

---

[39] Lawson devotes several pages of one chapter to a discussion of various manifestations of dissent or discontent by commoner Fijians with regard to chiefly rule in the Fijian administration under the colonial regime (Lawson 1991: 117–23). What struck me in reading these pages was the relative paucity of examples she could cite. To my eyes, these pages confirmed rather than challenged the conventional view that these arrangements were widely accepted.

their hegemonic view of the culture. Lawson suggests that the Fijian chiefs have done exactly that with regard to the arrangements regarding the land and chiefly rule (Lawson 1991: 104–11). Can an authentic tradition and legitimate authority be built on lies and coercion? Presumably not. But one might also ask whether any actual system of political socialization is likely to be entirely free of myths and whether any actual form of political rule reproduces itself without the use of power. While truth and unfettered consent provide powerful critical ideals, we should not use those ideals to declare an actual political system such as Fiji's inauthentic and illegitimate unless we are prepared to judge other actual systems by the same standards. But if all actual systems fail to meet the standards, as I think would clearly be the case, then the most important task may be to calculate degrees of inauthenticity and illegitimacy, in short, to distinguish bad from worse.

If lies and coercion are really the key to a political system, then one would expect the legitimacy of the system to collapse when the lies are exposed and the coercion removed. The collapse of communism in Eastern Europe provides an obvious illustration. Decades of systematic socialization and indoctrination turned out to be extremely ineffective when criticism and choice were widely permitted.

In Fiji, whatever coercion might have sustained the system of chiefly rule in earlier times—for example, the early colonial regulation legally requiring Fijians to obey their chiefs in all things lawful according to custom—has long since been removed.[40] With the introduction of democratic elections, a clear route was open for dissatisfied Fijians to challenge the hegemony of the chiefly establishment and some have taken that route. For example, the chiefly establishment is dominated by chiefs from eastern Fiji, and Fijians from the western part of Fiji have sometimes tried to build a political movement on the basis of regional dissatisfactions with the status quo. Even the Fijian Nationalist Party was, in certain respects, a reaction against the chiefly establishment and has occasionally employed populist rhetoric against the chiefs. Much of the political rhetoric of the Fijian Labour Party provided an implicit challenge to chiefly authority and offered Fijians an alternative political identity based on social and economic interests rather than ethnicity and culture. But none of these political challenges was able to draw more than a relatively small number of Fijians away from the Alliance Party (which represented the chiefly establishment) and then only for a brief period. Perhaps the Fijian Labour Party would have done so if it had been permitted to govern and had carried out the sort of cross-ethnic programme to which it was committed, but it appears to have won only about 9 per cent of the Fijian vote in the 1987 election. As I see it, these political patterns confirm what most

---

[40] The coup was a form of coercion, of course, and one that I think rendered the political system established by it illegitimate, as I will argue further below. But it is not this that Lawson has in mind in alleging the importance of coercion to chiefly rule.

observers of Fiji report, that support for the chiefly leadership is not unanimous but is nevertheless very strong even in the face of challenges to that
leadership from within the Fijian community. Of course, the chiefs enjoy
political advantages because of their positions, but those in power always
enjoy advantages even in democratic politics. The point is that it is not plausible to attribute the ongoing acceptance of chiefly authority to raw coercion.

But what about manipulation and deception? Again the question of degree
is important. Lawson and others object that the chiefly establishment misrepresents history and tradition, presenting a uniform picture of what was in fact
a diverse tradition and concealing the colonial origins of the institutions of
chiefly authority. No doubt the defenders of chiefly authority do present a
sanitized and mythical picture of the Fijian past, but again some such mytho-
logizing is a feature of the political culture and childhood socialization system
of every society. It matters that it is not a lie (even if it is a drastic oversim-
plification) to say that chiefly rule was the traditional form of authority in Fiji
prior to colonial rule. After all, oral traditions remain strong in Fijian society.
For the Fijian chiefs to pass on this mythical picture of the Fijian past, they
had to have the initial cooperation of people who had lived through the
actual past. If most of these people had found the discrepancies between the
official picture and their own experience too jarring, they might have passed
on an alternative understanding to their children. Nor is it clear why they
would cooperate in a massive deception in the absence of effective coercion
to require them to do so. It is easy, on the other hand, to understand why they
would cooperate in a process of mythologization that they found congenial to their own sensibilities.

There is a second important point here about the limits to any claim that
Fijian tradition, and especially chiefly authority, is based on deception. There
was no significant censorship in Fiji prior to the coup. Any number of scholarly books have been written debunking these myths about the Fijian past.
For example, Peter France launched a famous attack on the myths about
Fijian tradition with respect to land (France 1969). Such works are readily
available in Fiji. One may object that these works are accessible only to an
educated and sophisticated audience, but the contrast with societies that
make a systematic effort to restrict and control information is significant.
Again, political opponents of the chiefs were free to try to make use of these
findings. In short, the fact that Fijian chiefs are not impartial purveyors of the
truth about Fijian traditional culture does not prove that chiefly authority is
inauthentic, that it is not really a significant element in Fijian traditional
culture.

Lawson also seeks to undermine the authenticity of the chief's position in
Fijian society when she asserts that 'pre-Christian superstitions, together with
some later Christian accretions, must be seen as having played at least as
important a role in maintaining chiefly status and authority as any other

factor' (Lawson 1991: 102). Again, suppose that her description is accurate. It is not clear why this would call into question the *authenticity* of chiefly authority so long as these 'pre-Christian superstitions' and the 'later Christian accretions' are seen as authentic parts of Fijian culture. Indeed, the introduction of Christianity into Fiji provides an interesting illustration of an outside cultural influence that is acknowledged by all, yet not rejected as alien even by the most ardent Fijian nationalists. On the contrary, Christianity has become part of the Fijian way of life and is one of the features of that way of life that differentiates Fijians from most Indo-Fijians (Howard 1991: 371).

In sum, I think the challenge from inauthenticity fails. The legitimacy of the special role given Fijian chiefs in protecting Fijian culture is not undermined by the fact that they have not had this role from time immemorial.

To avoid misunderstanding, let me emphaize that I am *not* claiming that cultural practices and institutions deserve political recognition and support simply because they are regarded as authentic by those who participate in them.[41] Rather I am trying to criticize the idea that cultural practices and institutions can be shown to be inauthentic (and hence unworthy of support) if they can be shown to be contingent, constructed artefacts that have changed over time and that serve the interests of some more than others.

Is Chiefly Authority Good for Fijians?

A second important element in Lawson's critique is the claim that efforts to preserve Fijian culture through the separate administration, the Great Council of Chiefs, and so on served the interests of the chiefly class, not ordinary Fijians. This part of the challenge focuses on the substantive consequences of these arrangements. Was and is chiefly authority a good thing for the Fijians, even assuming that it was and is an authentic part of their culture?

This question takes us back to the issue I discussed earlier in this chapter about judging cultures other than our own and permits us to explore it further in a context where the arguments for respecting difference appear stronger to me. The position I will defend is one that gives some weight both to universal norms and to particularity. Let me say at the outset though that I am uncertain about the views I am putting forward and I feel the attraction of both more universalistic and more relativistic positions.

How should a North American like me try to answer a question like the one I have posed about the merits of chiefly authority in Fiji? I will leave aside, though only for the moment, the question of how the role of chiefly authority among Fijians affects the interests of others, especially Indo-Fijians.

---

[41] This is the position attributed to me by James Johnson in a critique of the earlier version of this argument presented in Carens 1992 (Johnson 1999). Whatever the ambiguities of that earlier text, this is not a position I wish to defend.

Obviously, one important objection to chiefly authority is the claim that it subverts democratic culture and institutions within Fiji as a whole. I will return to this issue shortly. For the moment, I want only to concentrate on the question of whether it is good for Fijians.

I do not intend to exclude by inadvertence the possibility that we should not try to answer such questions at all. I have tried to indicate above why a principled refusal to judge other cultures at all seems to me both morally wrong and practically impossible. This does not mean, however, that we should not refrain from some sorts of judgements about other cultures, and I will explore below the possibility that this issue fits in that category.

I will lay out two basic alternatives: criticizing Fijian culture, including chiefly authority, in the name of liberal ideals and standards or defending it in the name of respect for cultural difference. There are different ways of defending Fijian culture, however, and I will explore three of them. Then I will set out my own position which draws on all of these arguments but basically defends Fijian culture (and chiefly authority as part of it) with qualifications.

One possible answer to the question of whether chiefly authority is good for the Fijians is to say that what is good for the Fijians is the same kind of social order as the one we have, namely, liberal democracy and capitalism with its accompanying culture of individualism and economic acquisitiveness. From this perspective, chiefly authority is bad because it is deeply contrary to these values and this sort of social order.

From the beginning of the colonial period, and even earlier, many European observers of Fiji advanced this sort of argument. They regarded the chiefly hierarchy as exploitative and despotic. Of course, the nineteenth-century critics were not trying to bring economic equality and democracy to the Fijians but rather liberal economic freedoms, especially with regard to land and labour. They saw chiefly authority as an obstacle to that because they saw it as a crucial element in Fijian communalism, a way of life that subordinated the interests of individuals to the interests of the community and especially, they argued, to the interests of the head of the community.

Here is what they found objectionable about traditional Fijian life as they understood it.[42] The members of a Fijian village were expected not only to show personal deference to the local chief but also to contribute to his material subsistence, farming for him, supplying him with mats and cloth, and so on. (The chief's entitlement was called his *lala*.) At the same time, they were expected to participate in a variety of tasks that one could not easily do for oneself, such as building houses and canoes, and to assist in the duties of communal maintenance. It was the chief's right and responsibility to call

---

[42] The following descriptions of Fijian practices and the Europeans' reactions to them is based on Macnaught (1982).

upon people to provide labour for such activities and to direct it. Also, people had extensive obligations to friends and relatives, most notably in the practice of *kerekere* under which one's friends and relatives could 'request' one's personal property, a request that it would be shameful to refuse. The conflict between these communal practices and any individual opportunities or incentives for industry and accumulation seemed both obvious and objectionable to the early Europeans (Macnaught 1982: 20–1). It was no wonder that the Fijians did not seek to go beyond subsistence agriculture in their economic activity.

What the European settlers wanted was to make it possible for individual Fijians to sell their land and their labour for cash, the latter primarily taking the form of indentured contracts to European planters. To facilitate this, they wanted the colonial government to impose poll taxes on Fijians, a policy that had been adopted elsewhere with the desired effect of forcing people to supplement their employment in subsistence agriculture with some sort of activity that generated a money income. Of course, the colonial government did indeed have to raise taxes from the Fijians, but to the dismay of the colonists, Gordon and his associates devised a system of indirect taxation, building on the *lala* rights of the chiefs so that ordinary Fijians effectively paid taxes in kind by working in communal fields whose produce, often a cash crop, eventually went to support the colonial government. In addition, as I noted above, Gordon prohibited Fijians from engaging in indentured labour on the plantations on the grounds that the departure of men for the plantations would destroy the communal system of labour that made Fijian village life possible. Further, he prohibited ordinary Fijians from leaving their villages without the permission of their local chief and gave the chiefs the legal authority to enforce this and all traditional communal obligations. And, of course, he prohibited the sale of Fijian land and established a legal regime based on communal holdings.

Gordon's contemporary critics did not argue that his efforts were objectionable on the grounds that they were transforming traditional Fijian culture, although, as we have seen, that claim is true in important respects. Rather they objected on the grounds that Fijian culture was not worth preserving or that there was a positive moral obligation to transform it to fit with the norms of British liberalism. These sorts of arguments have been a staple of a certain kind of criticism ever since. Thus two major reports published around 1960 as part of the process of preparing Fiji for independence blamed the economic backwardness of Fijians (compared with other inhabitants of Fiji, especially the Indo-Fijians who obviously had not begun from a position of privilege) on the Fijian communal culture. And, like the earlier critics, they saw chiefly leadership as a key element in maintaining that communalism and thus retarding the economic progress of Fijians (summarized in Lawson 1991: 57–8, 109–10).

More recent critics like Lawson have repeated these critiques of the negative economic effects of Fijian culture and added an emphasis on the conflicts between democratic values and the values on which chiefly authority rests. Since chiefly authority is acquired as a hereditary status and requires deference from commoners towards chiefs, it stands in deep and ineradicable tension with the democratic idea that the legitimacy of public authority should rest on the choices of the governed and with the ethos of equal citizenship required to sustain democratic institutions.[43]

What should we make of these criticisms? To those who have some sympathy for traditional Fijian culture and the attempts to preserve it, the criticisms, especially those of the economic liberals, may appear smug and supercilious, an example of what Macnaught calls a 'clichéd liberalism' that simply assumed the moral superiority of Western and especially British culture and too often ignored the actual devastating effects of social reforms based on such liberal premises in Fiji and elsewhere (Macnaught 1982: 103). So, let us turn now to that alternative.

One approach to defending Fijian culture, including chiefly authority, celebrates its differences from the liberalism that purports to criticize it. Many of the very features of Fijian society that liberal critics have found so objectionable are the ones that have seemed most admirable to some of the colonial administrators and to many of the Western scholars who have written about Fiji. In particular, they have found admirable a communal culture that embodies principles of mutual caring and reciprocity, that places concern for the common good above individual advantage, that discourages acquisitiveness and encourages respect for others (Macnaught 1982: 160–3). So, even at the level of moral ideals, Fijian communalism seems to many (including me) to offer an attractive alternative to the possessive individualism of liberal capitalism.

At the level of practice, too, the contrast between Fijian communalism and liberal capitalism often favours Fijian communalism if one cares about the well-being of the ordinary person, and especially about those at the bottom. Macnaught, for example, draws attention to the almost complete absence of violent crime or destitution and to the high quality of housing in Fijian village society during the first decades of colonial rule (Macnaught 1982: 70). As liberal reforms took root, these conditions began to deteriorate. Another author stresses the protection that this way of life still provides against the

---

[43] Lawson's principal argument is that the perpetuation of the neo-traditional Fijian order, and especially its emphasis on chiefly authority, prevented the development of a sufficiently strong democratic culture to sustain the transfer of legitimate power from a party representing the chiefly establishment to a party representing Indo-Fijians and, to a lesser (but potentially greater) extent, Fijian commoners. In this section, however, I want to focus on arguments about the merits of chiefly authority for Fijians themselves, leaving for later a discussion of effects on Indo-Fijians. And part of Lawson's argument is that this undemocratic culture of chiefly authority was bad for the Fijians themselves.

risks of capitalist life (Fisk 1970: 45). A Fijian commercial farmer or entrepreneur who fails is not bereft of all support. One can always return to the less affluent but secure existence of village life. Fijian communalism has not produced a high level of surplus or material affluence, but it has produced enough for the basic material wants of all, while maintaining a rich ceremonial and social life. Given the experiences of other societies, there is good reason to suppose that a more rapid or radical transformation of Fijian culture in a liberal direction would not have improved the lives of most Fijians.

Let me add one qualification to all this. Most of these observers do not celebrate chiefly authority as such. They are apt to see chiefs as more responsive and responsible to the people, less exploitative and domineering than the critics. But in the main, they see chiefly authority as an integral element of Fijian communal life and therefore something to be respected if one respects that way of life.

So far, I have described a defence of Fijian culture that celebrates the ways in which it differs from much Western liberal individualism. There are two alternative forms of defence that also deserve mention. First, one might argue that Western liberalism is morally superior to Fijian culture but that it was not, or is not, readily applicable to Fiji. On this view, which has been embraced (if only for political reasons) by some Fijian traditionalists and which fits as well with certain forms of British imperialist thought, any attempt to transform Fijian culture and institutions rapidly and radically in a Western liberal direction would cause more harm than good, because the history of Fiji has not prepared Fijians to adapt well to such an alternative.[44] From this perspective, chiefly authority is seen not as a good in itself or as an essential element in a

---

[44] One prominent advocate of this view was Ratu Sir Lala Sukuna, the leading Fijian official in the 1940s and a remarkable figure who is acknowledged by his critics as well as his admirers to have been a person of extraordinary ability and vision. Sukuna was a member of a leading chiefly family and a profound student of Fijian custom and tradition (which is not to suggest that he was an impartial interpreter). At the same time, he had been a brilliant student at Oxford where he was drawn to the aristocratic conservatism of Sir Henry Maine. Thus he moved easily between two worlds but was sceptical about the possibility of bringing those worlds together, at least in the near future. A 1944 speech in support of the return to indirect rule illustrates his characteristic approach to the problem of political and social change in Fiji. He offered a politic acceptance of the principles of equality and democracy as ideals but denied their immediate applicability to Fijian society on historical grounds. (In fact, in other contexts, it seems clear that Sukuna was hostile to democratic equality in principle, for the sorts of reasons that critics since Plato have always advanced: democracy is directed at the satisfaction of the unregulated desires of the masses rather than at rule for the common good by the wise few. But such a view would have been difficult to defend publicly in the midst of World War II). Sukuna advocated a gradual, evolutionary transformation of Fijian society in a democratic and egalitarian direction, but stressed the importance of preserving the strengths of the traditional Fijian way of life in the process of transformation. In practice, his reforms and policies placed far more emphasis on preserving chiefly authority, village society, and other aspects of the Fijian way of life (as he interpreted it) than on introducing cultural and institutional changes that might make it possible for Fijians to adapt successfully to the liberal democratic, capitalist environment that was being imposed on Fiji by historical forces that it could not have resisted successfully even if it had had the collective will to do so. For an excerpt from the speech see . Lawson (1991: 113). For a sympathetic biography of Sukuna, see Scarr (1980).

culture that has significant intrinsic merits as compared with liberalism. Rather the argument is simply that liberalism is not a viable alternative for historical reasons, so that it is necessary to settle for the inferior but viable alternative of traditional Fijian culture. The great danger is that efforts at reform could destroy the traditional culture without successfully replacing it with anything superior. The result would be anomie and disorder, a far worse condition for Fijians then their situation under the traditional culture.

The other alternative is to defend Fijian culture on grounds that link cultural difference more closely to moral relativism. On this view, it is inappropriate, perhaps even wrong, for us as outsiders to try to pass judgement on the merits of Fijian culture, including chiefly authority, provided that it meets certain minimal moral standards such as not sanctioning the murder of the innocent. Just as we ought to respect the rights of individuals to make their own decisions about the good life and how to achieve it, we must recognize that different individuals will define the good differently. Therefore, we ought to respect the rights of cultural collectives to develop and transmit their own understandings of value and goodness, recognizing that different cultural collectives will have different understandings and practices. For both individuals and collectives, some minimal standards must be respected, and how these are to be specified is bound to be contested. Moreover, it is always possible to define minimal standards that are so extensive and demanding that they really amount to a comprehensive universal morality that governs all significant aspects of individual and collective life. But if this subterfuge is not adopted, then the principle of not judging others—call it the 'mind your own business principle'—tells us that we should refuse on principle to answer the question I posed at the beginning of this section about whether or not chiefly authority is a good thing for the Fijians. This question is one that the Fijians themselves must decide on the basis of their own understanding of the good. This line of argument has obvious affinities with the position of Michael Walzer, discussed in Chapter 2, and it might seem to suggest that Fiji could be used to answer the question I posed there as to whether there are contemporary states that are just even though undemocratic.

The three different defences of Fijian culture that I have identified stand in some tension with one another, perhaps even to the point of outright conflict. I am drawn most strongly to the first defence, the one celebrating the goodness of the Fijian way of life, yet I think that there is something to be said for each of the defences and even for the opposing critique of Fijian culture in the name of Western institutions and values. There are two crucial issues here: the first is the question of how far minimal moral standards extend; the second is the question of whether we ought to make moral judgements about institutions and practices that meet minimal moral standards (whatever those may be) or whether instead we should simply acknowledge the rights of others to conduct their lives as they see fit within the sphere of the morally permissible.

I have already argued for the applicability of minimal moral standards to Fiji in my discussion of the rights of Indo-Fijians to equal citizenship. Let me try to explore that issue further by taking up some hypothetical questions about the course of Fijian cultural evolution. According to the reports of early nineteenth-century visitors to Fiji, Fijian culture included at that time such practices as the ritual killing of slaves in connection with the building of chiefly houses and canoes and the killing of the widows of chiefs upon the deaths of their husbands (Calvert and Williams 1859; Scarr 1984). Suppose that these practices were still part of Fijian culture today. Would we be obliged not to pass judgement so as to respect their autonomy or their cultural difference from us? One could argue, of course, that we ought not to intervene to try to change the culture because indigenous cultures like Fiji's tend to change with greater exposure to other cultures and deliberate intervention to change a culture often does more harm than good. But could anyone argue that we should, as a matter of principle, show respect for such practices as killing slaves or widows because these practices constitute part of the cultural life of others? I cannot imagine how one would try to defend that view.

Suppose someone did not try to defend a strong form of moral relativism directly, but rather tried to challenge the moral relevance of my example. It would be fair for the critic to point out that these sorts of reports tend to be characterized by bias, exaggeration, and misinformation; that the legal regimes of some Western states during the same period sanctioned both chattel slavery and the violent subordination of wives to their husbands; and that the question is purely hypothetical because Fijian culture has not included such practices for over a century.

Consider what each of these objections implies. The first merely suggests that we have the facts wrong or that there is some way to tell the story of these practices that will make them seem unobjectionable (without committing us to the principle that we shouldn't judge other cultures).

The second objection makes a valid historical point but its implications for our moral reasoning are unclear. As I argued in Chapter 2, there is a problem of anachronism in making moral judgements about the past, but that does not mean that we can simply refuse to make such judgements. What would it be like to tell the story of slavery and its abolition in America without incorporating any moral judgements into the story? I do not mean to imply that the moral judgements are easy or uncontested. On the contrary, think of the question of whether we should admire or despise (or both admire and despise) Abraham Lincoln, Robert E. Lee, and John Brown. These judgments are still debated today.[45] But what would it be like to feel obliged not to make any moral judgements about this history?

---

[45] For one thoughtful exploration of this period that is clearly informed by a passionate moral commitment, see Cover (1975).

Thinking about the past from a moral perspective is a lot like thinking about other cultures from a moral perspective. In both cases, it is easy and dangerous to adopt a smug and superficial assumption about the moral superiority of our own time and place, an assumption that enables us to avoid self-examination and self-criticism. In both cases, it can reasonably be argued, we have to pay attention to context and circumstance before passing judgement. But can we avoid judgement altogether? What would it mean to live in a moral world in which we made no moral judgements about past practices and actions? How would we know what to praise or blame, what to preserve or reform? A moral world unguided by the past seems, almost literally, unimaginable to me.[46] But a moral world guided by the past is one in which we make moral judgements about the past. Similarly, a moral world informed by our knowledge of other cultures is one in which we make judgements about other cultures, judgements about what to condemn, what to admire, and what to accept as different.

The third objection, focusing on the hypothetical character of my question, I find more difficult to answer. On the one hand, I think actual cases are usually a more fruitful focus for reflection than hypothetical ones. Hypothetical cases tend to serve the interests of the argument for which they are constructed. Actual cases encourage reflection because of the complexity and ambiguity they contain. They are more apt to take us in unanticipated directions and to broaden our sense of what matters. That is why I chose to focus on the actual case of Fiji, rather than some imaginary island state whose history could be tidied up to serve the interests of the points I wanted to make. On the other hand, this is a contingent judgement. Hypothetical cases can be illuminating and challenging, and I see no reason why they should be excluded in principle. Part of what I am trying to explore in this section is how much my moral judgements about the legitimacy of preserving Fijian culture are shaped by the fact that Fijian culture is not radically (but only somewhat) at odds with liberal values and institutions. To explore that issue, it seems helpful to imagine greater divergence than we find at present, and the most plausible sort of divergence is the kind that can actually be found in Fiji's past.

Suppose that no one wants to defend the killing of slaves or widows. We are still a long way from the institutions and practices of liberal democracies. Fiji's most violent practices had disappeared by the time of Cession or soon after, but the colonial regime clearly included a number of illiberal policies. Take, for example, the restrictions on personal mobility, requiring people to get the permission of the chief to leave the village for any extended period, and the absence of formal democratic procedures for selecting rulers. Leave

---

[46] By 'moral world' I do not mean simply a philosophical system but a way of thinking that guides and informs actual moral judgements. In fact, there are few, if any, philosophical systems of morality that do not incorporate, implicitly or explicitly, judgements about the past.

aside here the question of how we should judge such policies in their original context. Suppose they were reintroduced today as part of the movement to preserve traditional culture. How should we respond?

In terms of Kymlicka's distinction between external protections and internal restrictions, such policies would constitute a prime example of what he calls internal restrictions, and it seems to me that we would be justified in criticizing such policies as a violation of individual freedom. Again, this doesn't mean that we should try to intervene in any way. I'm not even interested here in the question of whether we should try to communicate this criticism to the Fijians. The question is whether this sort of judgement is a morally inappropriate form of cultural imperialism. I think not. These freedoms—the freedom to leave the village and to vote for officials—seem to me to be part of the minimal moral standards that any regime should be expected to meet. I do not mean to suggest that there could never be circumstances in which it would be justifiable not to meet these standards, but rather that they should be taken as norms that apply to all societies, so that departures from them could not be justified simply by saying 'That's not the way we do things around here'. To justify violating these standards, one would have to show how the violation is necessary to meet some urgent public interest that could not be met in another way that respected the standards, and how it would eventually be overcome.

There is another reason why these freedoms set moral limits to Fijian institutions and practices: they are essential today to support the claim that Fijian culture deserves to be protected and preserved. One major argument for why we should respect Fijian culture and attempts to preserve it is that this is what the Fijians themselves want. That argument itself is built on democratic principles: people are entitled to get the kind of public policies and institutions they want (within limits). One major reason for believing that Fijians want to preserve their culture, including some forms of chiefly authority, is that they continue to live in the villages and they keep voting for political parties that make these concerns a central element of their appeals to the electorate. In other words, this claim about what Fijians want has received considerable validation from the right of individual mobility and from liberal democratic processes of free and contested elections.

Of course, we all know the weaknesses of such processes as methods of validating what people want. Freedom of movement can seem hollow if there is no reasonably attractive place to which one can go. People may not be satisfied with their choices in elections. Nevertheless, whatever the weaknesses of liberal democratic procedures, they are far more reliable as indicators of what people want, in most cases, than the alternatives. Would we want to defend the preservation of Fijian culture and chiefly authority against the wishes of the Fijian people?

That last question is not purely rhetorical. One could argue that the traditional culture (including chiefly authority) has been good for Fijians, whether they know it or not, and that it should be preserved whether ordinary Fijians would vote for it or not. That is certainly the sort of position that some Fijian leaders took in the past.[47] I would not want to say that such an argument could never be valid, though I think that the chances of its being valid in the contemporary world grow increasingly remote. But I do not think that such an argument is plausible in Fiji today. Much of the recent history and recent experience of chiefly leadership does not inspire confidence in their ability to lead effectively or in their selfless dedication to the common good.

In sum, minimal moral standards set significant constraints on morally permissible cultural variation. If the institutions and policies of independent Fiji before the coup seem morally permissible, as I have generally argued that they do, that is because they generally respected basic individual freedoms and political rights. Within the limits set by minimal moral standards, there can still be an important range of cultural variation. Here, it seems to me that the arguments in defence of Fijian culture are potentially complementary. One can think that Fijian culture ought to be respected and preserved both because it is the Fijians' and they want to preserve it, and because one has formed an independent judgement that it is an admirable culture that provides meaning and structure to the lives of the people who participate in it. The former is a prerequisite. As I argued above, it would be hard to defend cultural preservation if the Fijians themselves did not want it. But the latter judgement adds considerable weight as we saw in Chapter 4. It is easier to defend limited departures from liberal democratic norms for the sake of preserving a culture when the culture is one that evokes admiration, not just toleration.

Finally, if a moral defence is to be offered of the earlier policies and practices that constrained freedom and limited democracy, it should be one that emphasizes context and the limited range of feasible alternatives at the time, rather than one that seeks to deny the relevance of liberal democratic standards to Fiji in the name of cultural difference. On the other hand, not every aspect of the liberal tradition deserves equal weight. In particular, the possessive individualism that seems to animate so many critics of traditional Fijian culture reflects a vision of the human good that has itself been subject to considerable moral criticism on the basis of deeper liberal commitments. Whatever side one takes in this debate, the arguments should open up a space within democratic politics within which people are morally free to choose among competing visions of how society ought to be organized.

Democracy and the Preservation of Fijian Culture

The third challenge to the legitimacy of the efforts to preserve Fijian culture focuses on the way such efforts contributed to the failure of democratic politics

---

[47] See the discussion of Ratu Sukuna in note 44.

in Fiji. In this view, the efforts to preserve Fijian culture were not morally justified, even if those efforts themselves violated no moral principles and led to the
preservation of an authentic Fijian culture that was good for Fijians, because of
the negative impact those efforts had on democracy in Fiji and thus on the
other citizens, especially Indo-Fijians.

Lawson argues that the vision of Fijian culture that emerged from the colonial regime, with its emphasis on the homogeneity of the Fijian tradition and
the centrality of chiefly authority, greatly contributed to the salience of
ethnic identity in Fiji and thus led inexorably to the definition of political
differences along ethnic lines. The separate administration and other institutions designed to preserve Fijian culture led to the view that separate forms of
political representation were desirable, a view that was institutionalized in the
electoral system adopted in the 1970 Constitution which made the ethnic
identity of the voters and of the representatives a central feature of the
system. When this was combined with the principle (deeply embedded in
Fijian culture) that Fijian interests should be paramount, it led to the sense
among Fijians that representatives of the 'other' group, Indo-Fijians, could
not legitimately hold political power over Fijians, even as a result of free elections. So, democratic principles were respected only so long as they put representatives of Fijians in power. When a party that drew most of its support
from Indo-Fijians won in 1987, the Fijians felt justified in overthrowing it by
force.

There is a lot to be said for Lawson's argument, but I think she overstates
the historical constraints in some respects and understates them in others.
When this imbalance is redressed, it is still possible to justify the efforts to
preserve Fijian culture, including chiefly authority, as a morally permissible
course of action.

Consider the coup first. The first point to make is that it is possible to
defend the efforts to to preserve Fijian culture and still condemn the coup.
That is certainly my position. Fijian defenders of the coup have argued that
the coup was necessary to preserve traditional Fijian culture, especially the
collective Fijian ownership of land which was alleged to be threatened by the
new government (Dean and Ritova 1988). So far as I can tell, there is no
reasonable foundation for these allegations.

Some members of the new government, among them the Fijian Prime
Minister who was himself a commoner, had criticized certain aspects of
chiefly rule, including the high incomes some chiefs received from their share
of land revenues. Greater security for tenant farmers was a long-standing and
deep concern within the Indo-Fijian community and one that the new
government might have tried to address. And, reading between the lines, one
might infer that some of those associated with the new government regarded
the system of collective Fijian ownership of the land as outmoded and unjust.
But there is no evidence that the new government had any intention of trying

to alter the existing arrangements with regard to land or that they would have had the capacity to do so even if they had wanted to. As I noted above, Fijian land rights and the other central elements of the traditional way of life were constitutionally entrenched and the Great Council of Chiefs had an effective veto power over any changes in these areas, both substantively and procedurally through its veto over legislation affecting the judiciary.

To be sure, one can easily overstate the security provided by constitutional guarantees. If those with political power are unwilling to respect a constitution, its formal guarantees can easily prove worthless. But again, there is no evidence at all that the new government had any inclination not to respect the Constitution or any effective capacity not to do so. On the contrary, it was the coup makers who violated the Constitution in overthrowing a democratically elected government that had operated scrupulously within the letter and spirit of the law. In sum, ungrounded fears about threats to the Fijian way of life did not and could not justify the coup.

Some may find my wording altogether too cautious. They might say, 'Suppose the government had wanted to transform the traditional Fijian way of life, including its provisions regarding land ownership. That would still not justify a coup, at least so long as the government stayed within the law. That is what democracy is all about—the right of the majority to make changes.' That is the sort of challenge I imagine. But that response glides over some deep difficulties in constitutionalism and in democratic theory.

With regard to constitutionalism, who decides whether the government is staying within the law? One cannot assume American answers—which are themselves contested—to these questions. Recall that Fiji was a former British colony with a parliamentary system.

With regard to democratic theory, there is the familiar question of the limits to what the majority may do to the minority and what the minority is entitled to do if the majority transgresses those limits. Suppose, for example, that a democratically elected government, representing a majority of voters, is embarking on a programme of religious or ethnic discrimination, even persecution, and that the minority—as is rarely the case—is in a position to prevent this through a coup. Is it evident that a coup would never be justifiable under those circumstances? I do not think so, although I would not say either that these circumstances necessarily legitimate a coup. These are complex questions, but I do not propose to pursue them here because the problems they raise simply do not apply to the case of Fiji or to the behaviour of its government.

Even if one can distinguish between the efforts to preserve Fijian culture and the coup, supporting the former and condemning the latter, does that distinction really matter if Lawson is right that the previous efforts to preserve Fijian culture led to the coup? The problem is that Lawson makes the sequence seem at times almost inevitable. It is always tempting to suppose that what did happen, had to happen. Yet she herself concedes that the coup was not inevitable. Rambuka, the coup leader, had two superiors who were loyal to the Constitution. Had they received word about the plot, they might well have been able to forestall it (Lawson 1991: 286). Bavadra's government probably would have stayed in power, and the story of Fiji would have had a different line of development.

It is a striking fact that ten years after the coup, a new constitution was adopted which is even more firmly rooted in liberal democratic norms than the 1970 Constitution.[48] For example, the new constitution explicitly contemplates the possibility of a non-Fijian Prime Minister, prohibits discrimination on the basis of race or ethnicity, and guarantees individual rights in a variety of ways. (At the same time it maintains the sorts of protections for Fijian land ownership and a separate Fijian administration that were provided in the 1970 Constitution). This sort of development is not always what happens after a military coup conducted with the goal of ensuring the domination of one ethnic group over another. It suggests that the democratic culture of Fiji may be considerably more robust than Lawson supposed and the anti-democratic effects of the efforts to preserve Fijian culture far less severe. Of course, with the first elections under the new constitution scheduled for 1999, it remains to be seen how well it works in practice.

What about Lawson's complaint that the efforts to preserve Fijian culture and the subsequent political arrangements based on ethnicity led to polarized ethnic identities? There is something to her concern, but as was the case with her critique of collective land ownership, it is not evident what historically possible alternatives would have been superior. If Gordon had not created the separate administration in the first place, perhaps no one from India would have come to Fiji and the problem (in its present form) would not exist. But then perhaps the Fijians would have suffered the fate of indigenous groups in Australia and New Zealand.

If we take the late nineteenth and early twentieth-century developments as a given and focus on more recent policies, the differences of ethnic identity are a reality that have to be taken into account even if one seeks to transcend them. Consider, for example, the complex system of ethnic representation established in the 1970 Constitution (which I described in my short history above).This system was apparently designed with two goals in mind. First, the communal seats were intended to guarantee that each of the major ethnic groups would have some representatives looking out for its

---

[48] The new constitution embodies most of the elements proposed by a three-person Fiji Constitution Review Commission which was established in 1995. The main difference is that the Commission recommended that roughly two-thirds of the seats in the new parliament be open (i.e. neither voters nor candidates restricted on the basis of ethnicity) and one-third reserved for ethnic groups in proportion to their share of the population. The constitution that was adopted reverses the proportion of open and ethnic seats. For discussions of the Commission's proposals, see Alley (1997) and Lal (1997).

interests (as defined by the voters within the group itself). Secondly, the national seats were intended to encourage political parties to form alliances across ethnic lines. Thus, for example, the National Federation Party (NFP) which appealed primarily to Indo-Fijians had to find Fijians willing to run under its banner in order even to contest the Fijian national seats in constituencies where Indo-Fijians constituted a majority of the voters. It followed that each major party was likely to have members in its caucus who did not belong to the dominant ethnic group in the party.

On the whole, the system appears to have achieved the first goal but not the second, at least not in a substantive sense. It is true that both parties nominated and elected candidates from the other ethnic group, but these candidates had only a marginal impact on the policies, rhetoric, and voter support of the parties. A Fijian elected almost entirely with Indo-Fijian votes was simply not a credible representative of the Fijian community; so too for Indo-Fijians elected with Fijian votes. To use the language of Chapter 7, they enjoyed no representational legitimacy. The major exception to this was where the candidate represented some disaffected sub-group. For example, Indian Muslims sometimes supported the Alliance Party rather than the Hindu-dominated NFP.

Was this electoral system with its emphasis on ethnicity morally justifiable? Here my judgement coincides with that of the Street Commission which was established in 1975 to review these arrangements (which were regarded as temporary) and make recommendations for a more permanent system. Given the depth of ethnic divisions in Fiji, it was essential to provide some guarantee of representation to all three ethnic communities. To adopt a system that pretended to be blind to ethnicity in the Fijian context would have been to ignore the underlying social realities in a way that would not have improved them. Perhaps of equal importance, in the context of Fijian political history such an apparently neutral reform would inevitably have been perceived as a partisan triumph for the Indo-Fijians who had long demanded a Westminster-type of system with a common electoral role and majority rule. So, what the commission aimed at was an arrangement that satisfied the requirements of evenhanded justice in the particular context of Fiji's history.

But the Street Commission also thought that Fiji needed to take steps to transcend these deep ethnic divisions. It recommended electoral reforms which would have eliminated any ethnic restrictions on voters and candidates for some of the seats in parliament and would have used techniques of proportional representation to prevent domination by one group. (These proposed reforms were blocked by the ruling Alliance Party which drew its support primarily from Fijians). Again I agree with the Commission. As I have argued above, the extreme separation of the two communities is no longer viable. If Fiji is to have any sort of decent future, it must construct a politics that is not entirely based on ethnicity. The new 1997 Constitution takes this as its fundamental goal and includes a number of mechanisms designed to encourage power-sharing and political cooperation across ethnic divides, in addition to reforms of the electoral system that go beyond what the Street Commission proposed. Thus the liberal democratic norm of a common franchise among all citizens does constitute one important goal towards which these latest reforms should and do point.

Two final comments on the relationship between democracy and chiefly authority. My own sympathies lie, like Lawson's, with the members of the Fijian Labour Party. I admire the goals they were pursuing—building a multi-ethnic, democratic, and egalitarian society in Fiji—and I admire the skill and dedication with which they pursued these goals. By contrast, the Fijian chiefs appear, at least in the literature that I have read, to be a privileged elite primarily concerned with protecting their own interests. But it is a fundamental democratic principle that people have a right to choose their leaders, even bad leaders. Prior to the 1987 election, the vast majority (normally over 90 per cent) of Fijians voted quite consistently for their chiefs or for a party built around chiefly leadership. Even in the 1987 election, which they lost, the chiefly leadership retained the support of an overwhelming number of Fijians. Again, let me emphasize that I am not defending the coup or calling into question the legitimacy of the Labour Party government. The point is that if one were to ask which politicians spoke most for Fijians, the answer would be obvious—just as in previous elections, if one had asked which party spoke for most Indo-Fijians, the answer would have been obvious. If one accepts the arguments of the previous section that this electoral support cannot be attributed to coercion, manipulative socialization, or mendacity (beyond what is characteristic of most democratic politics), then there is an important sense in which a concern for democracy provides a reason for respecting the place of chiefs in Fijian society as well as for criticizing it.[49]

Finally, it is important to recognize that the absence of measures to preserve Fijian culture would have provided no guarantee of post-colonial ethnic harmony. One has only to glance around the world to see that failures greatly outnumber successes when it comes to ethnic harmony and democratic government in post-colonial regimes. Before the coup, Fiji was widely cited as one of the most promising stories, a multi-ethnic democracy with no ethnic violence (Scarr 1988: 6.) The mere fact that the coup occurred does not mean that the belief that it was one of the most promising societies was incorrect.

---

[49] In the two elections that took place after the coup (1992 and 1994), the Fijian vote was divided, suggesting that support for chiefly authority may finally be waning. Indeed, because of divisions among Fijians, Rambuka the coup leader, who now heads the party most closely associated with the chiefs, had to govern after the 1992 election with the help of the Labour Party (the party whose government he had overthrown) and after 1994 with the help of the General Electors (the ones who were neither Fijian nor Indo-Fijian).

And if that prior judgement was correct, then that suggests that the efforts to preserve Fijian culture were not necessarily bad, even from the perspective of their impact on the long-term prospects for building a democratic society in Fiji.

Conclusion

I want to conclude this discussion of Fiji by drawing explicit attention to the many ways in which the case revisits the concerns of previous chapters, shedding new light on them because of the distinctive way in which they emerge in the context of this case.

The questions about the cultural variability of justice raised in Chapter 2 seem particularly salient when we think about Fiji. Is it appropriate to use liberal principles to assess the justice of institutions and practices on an island whose history and cultural traditions are very different from the ones in which liberal understandings developed? Whether you agree with my views or not, your answer to this question is one good indicator of where you stand on the broader issue. Thus, seeing how people respond to a case like Fiji is one way of making the abstract challenge of moral and cultural relativism concrete.

As we have seen, from the late nineteenth century up until the present, those with political power in Fiji have taken steps to preserve and protect the traditional culture of Fijians. This provides a link to Chapter 3's concern with the moral status of group-differentiated rights for cultural minorities, though the case of Fiji recasts the problem in a number of ways. In many ways, the phrase 'distinct societal culture' seems to fit the Fijians better than it would many minority groups, because the social differences between Indo-Fijians and Fijians are so great and because there has been a separate Fijian administration. Yet there are no distinct geographical boundaries that could be drawn between most Fijians and most Indo-Fijians, the Fijians' cultural attachment to the land extends over the entire territory of Fiji, and Fijians are not really a minority because they have constituted about half the population for most of the period in question. In all these ways, the Fijians do not fit well with Kymlicka's picture of a national minority whose cultural interests can be protected through territorial self-government. On the other hand, the measures used to protect Fijian culture that I have argued were justifiable (inalienable land rights, veto powers for Fijian chiefs) are precisely the sorts of things Kymlicka recommends. This suggests again, I think, the extent to which Kymlicka's analysis remains valuable even if one rejects the concept of societal culture.

In Chapter 4 I argued that the fact that the Amish do less well as a group than other Americans with regard to conventionally valued social and economic achievements is a justifiable inequality because it is the product of an internal Amish culture that does not value these achievements. In Fiji, the traditional culture also discouraged economic and educational achievements, and the efforts at cultural preservation kept most native Fijians out of the market economy and tied to their local villages. By contrast, the Indo-Fijians, partly because of their own cultural heritage and partly because of their circumstances in Fiji, were more inclined to pursue commercial, professional, and educational opportunities. The result was the development of substantial inequalities between the groups, with the Indo-Fijians much higher on average in terms of conventional indicators of social and economic success, though Fijians, unlike the Amish, were both active and efficacious in the political arena. I have argued that this pattern of group inequality, like that between the Amish and other Americans, was justifiable. In recent years, however, the cultural norms have changed and Fijians have begun to seek greater access to educational and economic opportunities. This illustrates the general point (less visible in the Amish case) that culture is dynamic, and it raises questions that I have not had the space to pursue about the consequences of these changes for the justification of current inequalities. Should special efforts be made to assist the current generation of Fijians seeking economic and educational advancement or should a lower success rate for them be viewed as the legitimate consequence of the earlier cultural commitments? The latest Fijian Constitution has provisions for affirmative action for Fijians but also for any others who are socially or economically disadvantaged. Are those provisions justifiable? But these are questions for another day.

In a comparison of Quebec and Fiji, it is the contrast that is particularly illuminating. In Chapter 5, I discussed Quebec's policies with regard to the integration of immigrants, noting that Quebec emphasized the importance of linguistic adaptation for immigrants and at the same time observing how Quebec's identity was being transformed as a result of the immigrants' inclusion. I also argued that no liberal political community could reasonably expect more of immigrants by way of cultural adaptation than Quebec was expecting. In Fiji, the Indo-Fijians are no longer immigrants, of course, but it is significant that language has never been a serious issue in the conflicts between the groups. So far as I can tell, no serious effort has ever been made, even by Fijian nationalists who speak of Indo-Fijians as immigrants, to get Indo-Fijians to speak Fijian or to make Fijian communal culture the dominant culture of the political community, perhaps because the Fijians realize that such moves would inevitably open the Fijian cultural community to substantial numbers of non-Fijians, and, as in Quebec, might ultimately change the identity of the community itself. For Fijians, unlike Québécois, the cultural community remains thick, particularistic, and relatively exclusive but not co-extensive with or identified with the political community. It is morally permissible for the cultural community to retain these characteristics and for the political community to adopt measures aimed at preserving the Fijian cultural community, in part because there is no effort to extend the sway of Fijian culture. This does not challenge my claims about the limits to the kinds of cultural adaptations a political community can demand, but it serves as a useful reminder that sometimes these issues take very different forms in different contexts.

There are Muslims in Fiji—a minority of the Fijian Indian population—but this is not central to the case as I read it. Rather the link between Chapters 6 and 9 comes through questions about the moral status of cultures thought to be illiberal. In both cases, I have argued for more flexible and open-minded readings of cultural practices and more appreciation for the ways in which liberal commitments themselves should open space for pluralism.

In Chapter 7 I drew attention to the possibility that people could have multiple political memberships, sometimes in overlapping political communities, and discussed some of the ways in which representational legitimacy might depend on identities. In the Fijian case, the separate administration for Fijians provides a partial analogue to the overlapping political communities discussed in Chapter 7, and identities have been seen as crucial to representational legitimacy both in the design and in the working of electoral systems in Fiji. I have argued, however, that the ethnic designation of seats and voting rolls in Fiji should be regarded as a regrettable and temporary necessity, something that is contrary to the liberal democratic norm of a common franchise and something that should ultimately be overcome as the latest Fijian constitutional reforms intend. By contrast, the multiplicities of membership and identities and the related overlapping political communities in Canada (and in some other federal systems as well) may reflect an appropriate long-term way of responding to interdependence amidst deep diversity, if these projects can be sustained.

The key connection between Chapters 8 and 9 is the fact that both are concerned with attempts by indigenous peoples to preserve their cultural traditions in the modern world. Indeed, the sharp contrast between the plight of aboriginal peoples in Canada—whose fate is sadly typical of that of indigenous peoples in lands settled by European colonizers—and the much better condition of native Fijians is one of the most powerful arguments on behalf of the efforts at cultural preservation that were undertaken in Fiji in the late nineteenth century and suggests that it is appropriate to be cautious about dismantling the remnants of that system today, especially the arrangements for collective, inalienable land ownership.

I conclude with a comment about the moral relevance of history, an issue that runs through a number of the chapters but is particularly salient to my discussion of the case of Fiji. It is a commonplace to say *that* history matters for moral judgements but less common, especially for theorists, to say explicitly *how* it does. In this chapter I have tried to do so.

I have argued that the Fijian account of history, with its emphasis on the British promise to keep their interests paramount, would not justify the exclusion of Indo-Fijians from citizenship, even if it were true, because the Indo-Fijians have been established in Fiji for so long (which is itself a moral claim built on history). By contrast, I claimed that the colonial governor in the late nineteenth century made the morally right choice in seeking to protect the Fijians' culture and way of life, even though the policies he adopted—establishing a more rigid form of collective and inalienable native Fijian land ownership, setting up a separate Fijian administration, enhancing the power of the Fijian chiefs—transformed the Fijians' culture and way of life. It was the right choice because the only historically viable alternative was one that would have led to the acquisition of most of the land by European colonists and to the destruction of the Fijian culture and way of life with predictable horrible consequences for the well-being of native Fijians. I have argued further that the cultural transformations resulting from colonial policies did not render the subsequent Fijian culture as it has developed up to the present inauthentic because the Fijians themselves have generally seen that subsequent culture as an authentic extension of their traditional way of life, and their judgements are the ones that count on this question. Moreover, I have rejected an interpretation of history that places the blame for the failures of democratic policies in Fiji on the efforts to preserve traditional Fijian culture. Finally, I have contended that the deep social separation between native Fijians and Indo-Fijians—itself largely a product of these earlier efforts to preserve Fijian culture—made it reasonable in the mid-twentieth century to create separate voting lists and to reserve seats based on ethnicity, even though these arrangements should be regarded as regrettable and temporary.

If my arguments are accepted, and perhaps even if they are only conceded to be relevant, it has implications for our assessment of institutions and practices elsewhere, including much more familiar contexts like the United States and Canada. For what the arguments show is that claims about what justice requires in a particular case can never be settled at the level of abstract principle but always requires an interpretation of history and context. In contexts that are familiar to us, this interpretation is often presupposed implicitly and perhaps unconsciously. Yet if the interpretation were made explicit, its contingent and contestable character would become more apparent. The case of Fiji, whose history is both so different and so obviously relevant, makes this general point easier to grasp. In sum, by thinking carefully about the case of Fiji, a small and distant island, we acquire new and illuminating perspectives on a range of concerns about culture, citizenship, and community that animate contemporary theoretical debates.

10

Conclusion

What have we learned from this contextual exploration of culture, citizenship, and community? One clear lesson is that claims about culture and identity appear in many different forms in politics. There is no master principle that enables us to determine when we should respect claims advanced in the name of culture and identity and when we should deny them, although the idea of evenhandedness often points us in the right direction.

The discussion of immigrants to Quebec in Chapter 5 and of Muslim immigrants in Chapter 6 shows that the liberal principle that people should be as free as possible to pursue their own conceptions of the good and to revise those conceptions if they wish remains important. It sets significant limits to the way political communities may promote particular cultural commitments, even commitments to fundamental liberal norms like gender equality. Nevertheless, this book shows that this principle alone cannot provide an adequate guide. It does not capture the variety of ways in which liberal political communities already do take culture and identity into account in their institutions and policies or the ways in which they should. Let me elaborate.

First, if we think concretely about how political communities try to institutionalize liberal principles (like the principle that people should be free to pursue their own conceptions of the good), we can immediately see that there is no such thing as applied liberalism, pure and simple. Every institution is thickly embedded in some particular cultural context with its own language, traditions of discourse, norms of behaviour, patterns of recruitment, and so on. A commitment to cultural neutrality cannot itself be realized in the world in a way that is culturally (and politically) neutral. I have used discussions of the Canadian Charter in Chapters 3, 5, 7, and 8 to illustrate this point. The fundamental purpose of the Charter is to protect basic liberal democratic rights and freedoms (hence making it possible for people to pursue their own conceptions of the good), yet, as I have shown, the ways in which it does this can seem problematic to aboriginal people, to the Québécois, to other Canadians, and to people outside Canada. The reasons for objecting to the Charter vary, and, to some degree, conflict, but, in each case the objection is tied to the ways in which the Charter emerges from and reflects a specific cultural and political context. In a related vein, Chapter 2's discussion of the symbolic significance of the focus on genital mutilation in contemporary discussion of immigration, Chapter 8's discussion of the use of Canadian citizenship as a tool in an assimilationist Indian policy, and Chapter 9's discussion of the way a common electoral roll in Fiji was seen as a partisan political proposal favouring the interests of Indo-Fijians illustrate in different ways how the meaning of liberal concepts and arguments can be affected by the cultural and political contexts in which they are situated.

Secondly, the idea that people should be free to pursue their own conceptions of the good stands in some tension with the ideal of equal opportunity. We cannot try to equalize every opportunity, and in choosing which opportunities to make equal (however equality is defined), we cannot avoid employing some determinate conception of the good. The usual theoretical strategy here is to try to adopt a minimalist conception (like Rawls's primary goods) that will fit with or be useful to as many different views as possible, but no such conception is really culturally neutral or comprehensive. This becomes very clear when one confronts the claims of cultural communities whose view of the good conflicts in important ways with the widely shared, minimalist conception in a context where the liberal conception is dominant. I discuss the cases of the Amish in Chapter 4, aboriginal peoples in Canada in Chapter 8, and Fijians in Chapter 9, using Kymlicka's phrase about culture as a context of choice in a more open-ended, pluralist way to illustrate the general point. Making sure that people have (equal) access to some options may have negative effects on the availability of others, perhaps the ones that they (or their parents) regard as most important in life. The situation is particularly complex when children are involved, because what is at issue is precisely how their cultural contexts of choice will be constructed. Again, the thickly mediated character of liberal social institutions is a relevant consideration. We should not imagine that social institutions like public education systems and markets are culturally neutral, critical-thinking, option-generating machines. They are mechanisms of socialization and preference formation with regard to lifestyles, values, and behaviour. The appropriate response in such situations is to acknowledge that the value of conventional liberal rights and institutions cannot be separated from their effects on people's lives. (The same is true, of course, of alternatives to these liberal rights and institutions). So, in deciding what arrangements to adopt, we should take into account not only our commitment to provide certain standard kinds of opportunities but also what people actually want and, especially, in the case of children, what we think is good for them. And in thinking about what is good, we should take an open-minded stance, trying to think in broad terms about the conditions of human flourishing and the likely effects of imposed liberal institutions in particular contexts, not simply assuming the superiority of liberal arrangements in every context. Where different, morally relevant considerations conflict, we should try to treat them evenhandedly, balancing them in an appropriate manner instead of insisting that a single perspective must triumph. As the cases I have cited show, liberal practices at least sometimes reflect this sort of stance.

Thirdly, quite apart from situations of conflict between equal opportunity and the other options people want to pursue, people have a range of legitimate interests related to culture and identity that cannot be met merely by the commitment to let each person pursue his or her own conception of the good (or by any other single principle). Usually these interests have some of the features of collective goods, although they may be met through many different means, ranging from collective provision (direct or indirect, full or partial) to individual entitlements. Sometimes these interests are so important that they give rise to fundamental moral rights. At other times, they fall within the range of interests that it is permissible but not necessary to satisfy, in other words, the stuff of ordinary politics. It would require a radical reform to eliminate these sorts of cultural concerns from the politics and policies of contemporary liberal democracies. Majority cultural groups are able to use their power in the normal democratic process to satisfy their interests, though often they do not even have to do so consciously because their culture already shapes most social institutions and practices. Nevertheless, minority cultural groups are often able to get support or recognition or accommodation for their cultural concerns, through a combination of political activity and appeals to an implicit or explicit conception of justice as evenhandedness. I use the discussion of language issues in Chapters 3 and 5 to illustrate these sorts of interests. The provision of collective, inalienable land rights to Fijians provides another example.

Fourthly, the principle that people should be free to pursue their own conception of the good says nothing about the political location of that pursuit. The conventional assumption is that people belong to a single political community and the identity of that community is not in doubt. As Chapters 3, 5, 7 and 8 show, that assumption is deeply problematic. The Québécois and aboriginal people in Canada (and many people elsewhere in the world) belong legally and psychologically to more than one political community, and at the same time the communities may overlap and intertwine. People's multiple political identities are variable and shifting and linked to their cultural concerns in complex ways. Actual political arrangements already often take these variables into account to some extent. There is no single arrangement required by justice, though there may be many circumstances (as in the case of aboriginal peoples) when ignoring these multiplicities would be profoundly unjust. Under these circumstances, the only morally appropriate way to think about appropriate political arrangements or suitable conceptions of citizenship is to take these differences of culture and identity explicitly into account, trying as much as possible to aim at evenhandedness.

In sum, many questions about what justice requires or permits with regard to culture and identity cannot be addressed adequately so long as we imagine that justice requires only that political communities take a hands off approach to such issues. Too many relevant considerations are screened from view. That is why one major lesson that emerges from this contextual exploration of culture, citizenship, and community is the importance of what I have called the concept of justice or fairness as evenhandedness. The term 'evenhandedness' evokes democratic norms of balance, proportionality, and compromise. It enables us to consider rather than ignore the cultural claims being advanced by various people in various contexts: minority language groups with different sizes, concentrations, and histories putting forward a wide array of demands with regard to language rights; groups like the Amish seeking to keep their way of life separate from the wider society; immigrants trying to secure space for their own practices and traditions within the wider society, even though some of their practices and traditions conflict with prevailing ones; groups like the Québécois and aboriginal peoples in Canada, many of whose members think of themselves as belonging to multiple political communities and who want that multiplicity to be recognized and accepted; groups like the Fijians and the Indo-Fijians who share a common political community but are sharply divided by differences of culture and identity. Readers may disagree with the particular judgements that I have made about the cultural claims that emerge from these cases, but I hope they will agree that this concept points in the right direction and draws our attention to relevant considerations.

At the same time, all these efforts to take differences of culture and identity into account remain morally constrained by fundamental principles of human freedom and equality, which entail, among other things, commitments to gender equality and democracy. This may seem to stand in tension with some of the claims I have just made: the commitment to gender equality is inevitably constrained to some extent by the commitment to allowing people to pursue their own conceptions of the good; there is a danger of mistaking particular, culturally specific interpretations of liberal principles for the principles themselves; and we ought to be open to the recognition of human flourishing even if it appears in ways of life that are at odds with conventional liberal practices. Nevertheless, I have tried to show in Chapters 2, 4, 5, 6 and 9, that the moral constraints of democracy, freedom, and equality do matter, that they set significant limits to the range of morally acceptable ways of responding to differences of culture and identity.

Finally, I hope that the book has provided a glimpse of how much political theory can profit from paying more careful attention to what goes on in the world, and that others are encouraged to pursue what I have called a contextual approach to political theory. Let me note just two of the benefits which would follow.

First, Chapters 2 and 3 are intended to reveal, among other things, how a contextual approach can help in the critical reading of texts. It is a common enough move in discussing a theory to pose some counter-example (real or hypothetical) that seems intuitively not to fit with the line of argument being advanced, but I have tried to show what can be gained by pursuing real cases much more seriously. Thus thinking through the examples used by Walzer and Kymlicka reveals some fundamental flaws and contradictions in their theoretical accounts. The critical light shed by careful examination of cases will be even more illuminating when applied to other theorists, most of whom say far less than Walzer and Kymlicka about the concrete implications of their arguments.

Secondly, one of my goals has been to broaden the range of examples that people have in mind when they construct and assess theoretical arguments. When someone like Jeremy Waldron criticizes the idea of cultural preservation, has he thought about a case like Fiji and would he be prepared to reject all the measures taken to preserve Fijian culture? (Waldron 1992) When Rawls presents his theory of political liberalism, has he thought about the questions raised by linguistic and national minorities like the Québécois and aboriginal peoples in Canada (Rawls 1993)?[1] I am painfully aware, however, of (at least some of) the limitations of this book, especially with regard to what is left out. Think how our reflections might be enriched if we had normative discussions of what justice requires in responding to differences of culture and identity in a much wider range of cases. These are urgent issues everywhere in the world. I know of work already in progress that juxtaposes the theoretical accounts of Rawls, Kymlicka, Taylor, and Young with the historical and social realities of India, Nigeria, Northern Ireland, and Sri Lanka.[2] As more of this sort of work is done, we will have a much richer set of reference points for our inquiries, and those of us writing in what is sometimes called the Anglo-American tradition will be able to become much more self-conscious about the presuppositions and limitations of our arguments.

[1] Rawls does discuss the cases like the Amish (although he does not mention them by name) where a cultural or religious group opposes what he calls 'the culture of the modern world' and seeks to limit their children's exposure to it in the educational system, but not groups that aim at internal collective political autonomy while remaining linked to the wider political community (Rawls 1993: 199–200). Donald Moon, a political liberal who does discuss the Quebec case, fails to take into account the significance of the multiplicity and overlap of political identities in Canada and thus treats Quebec's failure to provide a publicly funded education in English to the children of non-English speaking parents as an example of 'pluralist encapsulation' (Moon 1993: 182). As a whole, however, I would applaud Moon's concreteness, his openness to cultural differences, and his sensitivity to the exclusionary tendencies of liberalism.
[2] At the University of Toronto, Boye Ejobowah has completed a political theory dissertation dealing with the accommodation of ethnic differences in Nigeria, Ashok Acharya is writing about India, and Damian O'Leary is studying Northern Ireland. At MIT, Ram Manikkalingam has completed a thesis that looks in part at the conflict in Sri Lanka.

REFERENCES

Ahmed, Leila. 1992. *Women and Gender in Islam: Historical Roots of a Modern Debate*. New Haven: Yale University Press.

Ajzenstat, Janet. 1995. 'Decline of Procedural Liberalism: The Slippery Slope to Secession'. In *Is Quebec Nationalism Just? Perspectives from Anglophone Canada*, ed. Joseph H. Carens. Montreal: McGill-Queen's University Press: 120–36.

Aldeeb Abu-Salieh, Sami. 1994. 'To Mutilate in the Name of Jehovah or Allah: Legitimization of Male and Female Circumcision'. Unpublished paper. Available from the author at Ochettaz 17, 1025 St Sulpice, Switzerland.

—— 1996. 'The Islamic Conception of Migration'. *International Migration Review*. 30 (1): 37–57.

Ali, Ahmed. 1980. *Plantation to Politics: Studies on Fiji Indians*. Suva: University of the South Pacific and Fiji Times and Herald, Ltd.

—— 1986. 'Fiji: Political Change, 1874–1960'. In *Politics in Fiji*, ed. Brij V. Lal. Winchester, Mass.: Allen & Unwin: 1–27.

Alley, Roderick. 1986. 'The Emergence of Party Politics'. In *Politics in Fiji*, ed. Brij V. Lal. Winchester, MCatherine. ass.: Allen & Unwin: 28–51.

—— 1997. 'Fiji at the Crossroads? After the Constitutional Review Commission'. *The Round Table*. 342: 245–56.

al-Quaradawi, Yusef. 1993. *The Lawful and the Prohibited in Islam*. Trans. M. Mo Syed Shukry. Kuwait: International Islamic Federationist Student Organization.

Arneson, Richard, and Shapiro, Ian. 1996. 'Democratic Autonomy and Religious Freedom: A Critique of *Wisconsin vs. Yoder*'. In *Political Order: NOMOS XXXVIII*, ed. Ian Shapiro and Russell Hardin. New York: New York University Press.

Aulagnon, Michéle. 1994. 'Enlever le voil, c'est être libre'. *Le Monde*. 2 Oct.: 10.

Bader, Veit. 1997. 'The Cultural Conditions of Transnational Citizenship: On the Interdependence of Political and Ethnic Cultures'. *Political Theory*. 25 (6): 771–813.

Badinter, Elisabeth, Debray, Régis, Finkielkraut, Alain, de Fontenay, Elisabeth, and Kintzler, Catherine. 1989. 'Profs, ne capitulons pas'. *Le Nouvel Observateur*. 2 (8): 58–9.

Barbieri Jr. William A. 1998. *Ethics of Citizenship: Immigration and Group Rights in Germany*. Durham, N.C.: Duke University Press.

Bardach, Ann Louise. 1994. 'Women are Being Abused, Even Mutilated . . . All in the Name of Islam'. *Reader's Digest*. January: 78–82.

Bauböck, Rainer. 1994. *Transnational Citizenship: Membership and Rights in International Migration*. Aldershot: Edward Elgar.

Bayliss-Smith, Tim, *et al.* 1988. *Islands, Islanders, and the World: The Colonial and Post-Colonial Experience of Eastern Fiji*. Cambridge: Cambridge University Press.

Beiner, Ronald. 1991. 'In Nationalist Wonderland'. *Jerusalem Reporter*. 6 June.

—— 1992. *What's the Matter with Liberalism?* Berkeley: University of California Press.

Belshaw, Cyril S. 1964. *Underneath the Ivi Tree: Social and Economic Growth in Rural Fiji*. Berkeley: University of California Press.

Benhabib, Seyla. 1987. 'The Generalized and the Concrete Other: The Kohlberg–Gilligan Controversy in Feminist Theory'. In *Feminism as Critique: On the Politics of Gender*, ed. Seyla Benhabib and Drucilla Cornell. Minneapolis: University of Minnesota Press.

Boddy, Janice. 1989. *Wombs and Alien Spirits: Women, Men and the Zar Cult in Northern Sudan*. Madison: University of Wisconsin Press.

—— 1998. 'Violence Embodied? Circumcision, Gender Politics, and Cultural Aesthetics'. In *Rethinking Violence against Women*, ed. R. Emerson Dobash and Russell P. Dobash. Thousand Oaks, Calif.: Sage: 77–110.

Boldt, Menno. 1993. *Surviving as Indians: The Challenge of Self-Government*. Toronto: University of Toronto Press.

Bouchard, G., Rocher, F,. and Rocher. G., 1991. *Les Francophones québécois*. Montreal: Conseil scolaire de l'île de Montréal.

Brubaker, William Rogers. 1989. 'Introduction'. In *Immigration and the Politics of Citizenship in Europe and North America*, ed. William Rogers Brubaker. Lanham, Md.: German Marshall Fund and University Press of America: 1–27.

—— 1992. *Citizenship and Nationhood in France and Germany*. Cambridge, Mass.: Harvard University Press.

Buchanan, Allan. 1990. 'Justice as Reciprocity versus Subject-Centered Justice'. *Philosophy and Public Affairs*. 19 (3): 227–52.

Buenker, John, and Nicholas, Burckel. 1977. *Immigration and Ethnicity: A Guide to Information Sources*. Detroit: Gale Research Company.

Burns, Alan. 1963. *Fiji*. London: HMSO.

Burtt, Shelly. 1994. 'Religious Parents, Secular Schools: A Liberal Defense of Illiberal Education'. *The Review of Politics*. 56 (winter): 51–70.

Cairns, Alan. 1992. 'Reflections on the Political Purposes of the Charter: The First Decade'. In *The Charter: Ten Years Later*, ed. Gerald A. Beaudoin. Cowansville, Que.: Les editions Yvon Blais Inc.: 163–91.

—— 1993. 'The Fragmentation of Canadian Citizenship'. In *Belonging: The Meaning and Future of Canadian Citizenship*, ed. William Kaplan. Montreal: McGill–Queens University Press: 181–220.

—— 1995. 'Aboriginal Canadians, Citizenship and the Constitution'. In *Reconfigurations: Canadian Citizenship and Constitutional Change*, ed. Douglas E. Williams. Toronto: Maclelland & Stewart: 238–60.

Calvert, James, and Williams, Thomas. 1859. *Fiji and the Fijians*. New York: Appleton & Co.

Carens, Joseph H. 1985. 'Compensatory Justice and Social Institutions'. *Economics and Philosophy*. 1: 39–67.

—— 1987. 'Aliens and Citizens: The Case for Open Borders'. *Review of Politics*. 49 (2): 251–73.

—— 1989. 'Membership and Morality: Admission to Citizenship in Liberal Democratic States'. In *Immigration and the Politics of Citizenship in Europe and North America*, ed. William Rogers Brubaker. Lanham, Md.: German Marshall Fund and University Press of America: 31–49.

—— 1990. 'Difference and Domination: Reflections on the Relation between Pluralism and Equality'. In *Majorities and Minorities: NOMOS XXXII*, ed. John W. Chapman and Alan Wertheimer. New York: New York University Press: 226–50.

—— 1992. 'Democracy and Respect for Difference: The Case of Fiji'. *University of Michigan Journal of Law Reform*. 25 (3–4): 547–631.

—— 1994. 'Cultural Adaptation and Integration: Is Quebec a Model for Europe?' In
  From Aliens to Citizens: Redefining the Legal Status of Immigrants, Ranier Bauböck.
  Aldershot: Averbury Press: 149–86.
—— ed. 1995*a*. *Is Quebec Nationalism Just? Perspectives from Anglophone Canada*.
  Montreal: McGill-Queen's University Press.
—— 1995*b*. 'Complex Justice, Cultural Difference, and Political Community'. In
  Pluralism, Justice, and Equality, ed. David Miller and Michael Walzer. Oxford: Oxford
  University Press: 45–66.
—— 1996. 'Realistic and Idealistic Approaches to the Ethics of Migration'. *International
  Migration Review*. 30 (1): 156–71.
—— 1997*a*. 'Liberalism and Culture'. *Constellations*. 4 (1): 35–47.
—— 1997*b*. 'Dimensions of Citizenship and National Identity in Canada'. *The
  Philosophical Forum*. 28 (1–2): 111–24.
—— 1997*c*. *Citizenship and Aboriginal Self-Government*. Ottawa: Royal Commission on
  Aboriginal Peoples.
—— and Williams, Melissa S. 1996. 'Muslim Minorities in Liberal Democracies: The
  Politics of Misrecognition'. In *The Challenge of Diversity: Integration and Pluralism in
  Societies of Immigration*, ed. Rainer Bauböck, Agnes Heller, and Aristiole R. Zolberg.
  Aldershot: Avebury Press: 157–86.
Coleman, Doriane Lambelet. 1996. 'Individualizing Justice through Multiculturalism:
  The Liberals' Dilemma'. *Columbia Law Review*. 96: 1093.
—— 1998. 'The Seattle Compromise: Multicultural Sensitivity and Americanization'.
  Duke Law Journal. 47 (4): 717–83.
Constitution Act 1982. 1983. Ottawa: Minister of Supply and Services Canada.
Coulon, Marc. 1985. *L'irruption kanak: de Calédonie à Kanaky*. Paris: Messidor.
Cover, Robert. 1975. *Justice Accused*. New Haven: Yale University Press.
Dagger, Richard. 1997. *Civic Virtues: Rights, Citizenship, and Republican Liberalism*. New
  York: Oxford University Press.
Dean, Eddie, and Ritova, Stan. 1988. *Rabuka: No Other Way*. New York: Doubleday.
Dinnerstein, Dorothy. 1976. *The Mermaid and the Minotaur: Sexual Arrangements and
  Human Malaise*. New York: Harper and Row.
Divine, Robert. 1957. *American Immigration Policy*. New Haven: Yale University Press.
Dorkenoo, Efua, and Elworthy, Scilla. 1992. *Female Genital Mutilation: Proposals for
  Change*. 3rd edn. London: Minority Rights Group.
Eisenberg, Avigail. 1994. 'The Politics of Indiviudal and Group Difference in Canadian
  Jurisprudence'. *Canadian Journal of Political Science*. 27 (1) (March): 3–21.
Elster, Jon. 1983. *Sour Grapes*. Cambridge: Cambridge University Press.
Engineer, Asghar Ali. ed. 1987. *The Shah Bano Controversy*. Bombay: Orient Longman.
Esposito, John L. 1991. *Islam: The Straight Path*. Expanded edn. New York: Oxford
  University Press.
—— 1992. *The Islamic Threat: Myth or Reality?* New York: Oxford University Press.
Feldblum, Miriam. 1993. 'Paradoxes of Ethnic Politics: The Case of Franco-Maghrebis in
  France'. *Ethnic and Racial Studies*. 16 (1): 52–74.
Fishkin, James S. 1983. *Justice, Equal Opportunity, and the Family*. New Haven: Yale
  University Press.
Fisk, Ernest K. 1970. *The Political Economy of Independent Fiji*. Wellington: A. H. & A. W.
  Reed.

France, Peter. 1969. *The Charter of the Land: Custom and Colonization in Fiji*. Melbourne: Oxford University Press.

Fraser, Nancy. 1997. *Justice Interruptus: Critical Reflections on the Post-socialist Condition*. New York: Routledge.

—— 1998. 'From Redistribution to Recognition?: Dilemmas of Justice in a Post-socialist Age'. In *Theorizing Multiculturalism*, ed. Cynthia Willett. Malden, Mass.: Blackwell.

Gainer, Bernard. 1972. *The Alien Invasion: The Origins of the Aliens Act of 1905*. London: Heinemann Educational Books.

Galeotti, Anna Elisabetta. 1993. 'Citizenship and Equality: The Place for Toleration'. *Political Theory*. 21 (4): 585–605.

Galston, William. 1982. 'Defending Liberalism'. *American Political Science Review*. 76 (Sept.): 621–29.

—— 1991. Liberal Purposes: Goods, Virtues, and Diversity in the Liberal State. Cambridge: Cambridge University Press.

Garrard, John. 1967. 'Parallels of Protest: English Reactions to Jewish and Commonwealth Immigration'. *Race*. 9 (1).

Gaspard, Françoise, and Khosrokhavar, Farhad. 1995. *Le Foulard et la République*. Paris: Éditions La Découverte.

Gellner, Ernest. 1983. *Nations and Nationalism*. Oxford: Blackwell.

Gilligan, Carol. 1982. *In a Different Voice: Psychological Theory and Women's Development*. Cambridge, Mass.: Harvard University Press.

Gillion, Kenneth L. 1962. *Fiji's Indian Migrants: A History to the End of Indenture in 1920*. Melbourne: Oxford University Press.

—— 1977. *The Fiji Indians: Challenge to European Dominance 1920–1946*. Canberra: Australian National University Press.

Gitlin, Todd. 1995. *The Twilight of Common Dreams*. New York: Metropolitan Books.

Glazer, Nathan. 1975. *Affirmative Discrimination: Ethnic Inequality and Public Policy*. New York: Basic Books.

—— 1983. *Ethnic Dilemmas*. Cambridge, Mass.: Harvard University Press.

—— 1997. *We Are All Multiculturalists Now*. Cambridge, Mass.: Harvard University Press.

Government of Quebec. 1990. *Vision: A Policy Statement on Immigration and Integration*. Montreal: Ministère Communautés culturelles et de l'immigration.

Green, Leslie. 1994. 'Internal Minorities and their Rights'. In *Group Rights*, ed. Judith Baker. Toronto: University of Toronto Press: 100–17.

Gutmann, Amy. 1993. 'The Challenge of Multiculturalism in Political Ethics'. *Philosophy & Public Affairs*. 22 (3): 171–206.

—— and Thompson, Dennis. 1996. *Democracy and Disagreement*. Cambridge, Mass.: Harvard University Press.

Hailbronner, Kay. 1989. 'Citizenship and Nationhood in Germany'. In *Immigration and the Politics of Citizenship in Europe and North America*, ed. William Rogers Brubaker. Lanham, Md.: German Marshall Fund and University Press of America.

Haley, Alex. 1966. *The Autobiography of Malcolm X*. New York: Grove Park.

Hammar, Tomas. 1989. 'State, Nation, and Dual Citizenship'. In *Immigration and the Politics of Citizenship in Europe and North America*, ed. William Rogers Brubaker. Lanham, Md.: German Marshall Fund and University Press of America: 81–95.

Hardin, Russell. 1988. *Morality within the Limits of Reason*. Chicago: University of Chicago Press.

Hegel, Georg Wilhelm Friedrich. 1962. *Philosophy of Right*. Trans. T. M. Knox. Oxford: Clarendon Press; 1st pub. 1821.

Higham, John. 1963. *Strangers in the Land: Patterns of American Nativism*. New York: Atheneum.

—— 1975. *Send These to Me: Jews and Other Immigrants in Urban America*. New York: Atheneum.

Horowitz, Donald L. 1985. *Ethnic Groups in Conflict*. Berkeley: University of California Press.

Hosken, Fran. 1983. *The Hosken Report: Genital and Sexual Mutilation of Females*. 3rd edn. Lexington, Mass.: Women's International Network News.

Hostetler, John. 1980. *Amish Society*. 3rd edn. Baltimore: Johns Hopkins University Press.

Howard, Michael C. 1991. *Fiji: Race and Politics in an Island State*. Vancouver: UBC Press.

Hume, David. 1888. *A Treatise of Human Nature*, ed. L. A. Selby-Bigge. London: Clarendon Press; 1739.

Huntington, Samuel. 1993. 'The Clash of Civilizations?' *Foreign Affairs*. 72 (3): 22–49.

Jamieson, Kathleen. 1978. *Indian Women and the Law in Canada: Citizens Minus*. Ottawa: Minister of Supply and Services.

Jayawardena, Chandra. 1980. 'Culture and Ethnicity in Guyana and Fiji'. *Man*. 15: 430.

Johnson, James. 1999. 'The Politics of Cultural Authenticity'. Unpublished paper.

Kalin, Rudolph. 1995. 'Ethnicity and Citizenship Attitudes in Canada: Analyses of a 1991 National Survey'. *Nationalism and Ethnic Politics*. 1(3): 26–44.

Kiss, Elizabeth. 1996. 'Group Rights in Principle and Practice: A Cautionary Tale from Central Europe'. Unpublished paper.

Koso-Thomas, Olayinka. 1987. *The Circumcision of Women: A Strategy for Eradication*. London: Zed Press.

Kraybill, Donald. 1989. *The Riddle of Amish Culture*. Baltimore: Johns Hopkins University Press.

Kukathas, Chandran. 1996. 'Liberalism, Communitarianism, and Political Community'. *Social Philosophy and Policy*. 13 (1): 80–104.

—— 1997. 'Cultural Toleration'. In *Ethnicity and Group Rights: NOMOS XXXIX*, ed. Ian Shapiro and Will Kymlicka. New York: New York University Press.

Kutler, Stanley. 1984. *The Supreme Court and the Constitution*. 3rd ed. New York: Norton.

Kymlicka, Will. 1989*a*. *Liberalism, Community and Culture*. Oxford: Oxford University Press.

—— 1989*b*. 'Liberal Individualism and Liberal Neutrality'. *Ethics*. 99 (4): 883–905.

—— 1995. *Multicultural Citizenship: A Liberal Theory of Minority Rights*. Oxford: Oxford University Press.

—— 1997*a*. *States, Nations and Cultures: Spinoza Lectures*. Amsterdam: Van Gorcum.

—— 1997*b*. 'Do We Need a Liberal Theory of Minority Rights? A Reply to Carens, Young, Parekh and Forst'. *Constellations* 4 (1): 72–87.

Lacoste-Dujardin, Camille. 1990. 'Les Fichus islamistes: approche ethnologique d'une stratègie d'anti-intégration'. *Hérodote*. 56: 14–44.

Lal, Brij V. 1983. *Girmitiyas: The Origins of Fiji Indians*. Canberra: Journal of Pacific History.

—— 1986. 'Politics Since Independence: Continuity and Change, 1970–1982'. In *Politics in Fiji*, ed. Brij. V. Lal. Winchester, Mass.: Allen & Unwin: 74–106.

Lal, Brij V. 1988. *Power and Prejudice: The Making of the Fiji Crisis*. Wellington: New Zealand Institute of International Affairs.

—— 1990. *Fiji: Coups in Paradise: Race, Politics, and Military Intervention*. London: Zed Press.

—— 1997. 'Towards a United Future: Report of the Fiji Constitution Review Commission'. *The Journal of Pacific History*. 32 (1) June: 71–84.

Lasaqa, Isireli. 1984. *The Fijian People: Before and After Independence (1959–1977)*. Canberra: Australian National University Press.

Lawson, Stephanie. 1991. *The Failure of Democratic Politics in Fiji*. Oxford: Clarendon Press.

Legge, J. D. 1958. *Britain in Fiji, 1858–1880*. London: Macmillan.

Leveau, Remy. 1992. 'Maghrebi Immigration to Europe: Double Insertion or Double Exclusion?' *Annals of the American Academy of Political and Social Science*. 524: 170–91.

Levinson, Sanford. 1988. *Constitutional Faith*. Princeton: Princeton University Press.

—— 1990. 'The Confrontation of Religious Faith and Civil Religion: Catholics Becoming Justices'. *DePaul Law Review*. 39 (summer): 1047–81.

—— 1992. 'Religious Language and the Public Square'. *Harvard Law Review*. 105 (June): 2061–79.

Levy, Jacob T. 1997. 'Classifying Cultural Rights'. In *Ethnicity and Group Rights: NOMOS XXXIX*, ed. Will Kymlicka and Ian Shapiro. New York: New York University Press.

—— 1995. 'Liberal Civic Education and Religious Fundamentalism: The Case of God v. John Rawls'. *Ethics*. 105 (Apr.): 468–96.

MacIntyre, Alasdair. 1988. *Whose Justice? Whose Rationality?* Notre Dame, Ind.: University of Notre Dame Press.

Macklem, Patrick. 1995. 'Normative Dimensions of the Right of Aboriginal Self-Government'. *Queens Law Journal*. 21: 173–219.

Macnaught, Timothy J. 1982. *The Fijian Colonial Experience*. Canberra: Australian National University Press.

McRoberts, Kenneth. 1991. *English Canada and Quebec: Avoiding the Issue*. North York, Ont: Robarts Centre for Canadian Studies.

Macedo, Stephen. 1990. *Liberal Virtues: Citizenship, Virtue, and Community in Liberal Constitutionalism*. Oxford: Clarendon Press.

Mamak, Alexander. 1978. *Colour, Culture and Conflict: A Study of Pluralism in Fiji*. Rushcutters Bay, Australia: Pergamon Press.

Mayer, Adrian C. 1963. *Indians in Fiji*. London: Oxford University Press.

—— 1973. *Peasants in the Pacific: A Study of Fiji Indian Rural Society*. 2nd edn. Berkeley: University of California Press.

Memon, Kamran. 1993. 'Family: Wife Abuse in the Muslim Community'. *Islamic Horizons*. 23 (Mar./Apr.): 12–19.

Mernissi, Fatima. 1987. *Beyond the Veil: Male–Female Dynamics in Modern Muslim Society*. Bloomington, Ind.: Indiana University Press.

—— 1991. *The Veil and the Male Elite: A Feminist Interpretation of Women's Rights in Islam*. Trans. Mary Jo Lakeland. Reading, Mass.: Addison-Wesley Publishing Co.

Miller, David. 1995. *On Nationality*. Oxford: Oxford University Press.

—— and Walzer, Michael. eds. 1995. *Pluralism, Justice, and Equality*. Oxford: Oxford University Press.

Miller, J. R. 1991. *Skyscrapers Hide the Heavens: A History of Indian–White Relations in Canada*. Rev. edn. Toronto: University of Toronto Press.

Modood, Tariq. 1998. 'Anti-Essentialism, Multiculturalism and the "Recognition" of Religious Groups'. *The Journal of Political Philosophy*. 6 (4): 378–99.

Monnet, Jean-François. 1990. 'A Creil, l'origine de l'affaire des foulards'. *Hérodote*. 56 (Jan.): 45–54.

Moon, J. Donald. 1993. *Constructing Community: Moral Pluralism and Tragic Conflicts*. Princeton: Princeton University Press.

Morgan, Kathryn Pauly. 1991. 'Women and the Knife: Cosmetic Surgery and the Colonialization of Women's Bodies'. *Hypatia*. 6 (3): 25–53.

Moruzzi, Norma Claire. 1994. 'A Problem with Head Scarves: Contemporary Complexities of Political and Social Identity'. *Political Theory*. 22 (4): 653–72.

Myers, Robert A. *et.al.* 1985. 'Circumcision: Its Nature and Practice among some Ethnic Groups in Southern Nigeria'. *Social Science and Medicine*. 21 (5): 581–8.

Narayan, Uma. 1997. *Dislocating Cultures: Identities, Traditions, and Third-World Feminism*. New York: Routledge.

Nation, John. 1978. *Customs of Respect: The Traditional Basis of Fijian Communal Politics*. Canberra: Australian National University Press.

Nayacakalou, R. R. 1975. *Leadership in Fiji*. Melbourne: Oxford University Press.

Nedelsky, Jennifer. 1997. 'Embodied Diversity and the Challenges to Law'. *McGill Law Journal*. 42: 91–117.

Newton, W. F. 1970. 'Fijians, Indians, and Independence'. *Australian Quarterly*. 42 (1): 33–40.

Norton, Robert E. 1977. *Race and Politics in Fiji*. St Lucia, Australia: University of Queensland Press.

—— 1986. 'Colonial Fiji: Ethnic Divisions and Elite Conciliations'. In *Politics in Fiji*, ed. Brij V. Lal. Winchester, Mass.: Allen & Unwin: 52–73.

Parekh, Bhikhu. 1990. 'The Rushdie Affair: Research Agenda for Political Philosophy'. *Political Studies*. 38 (4): 695–709.

—— 1991. 'British Citizenship and Cultural Difference'. In *Citizenship*, ed. Geoff Andrews. London: Lawrence & Wishart.

—— 1994a. 'Equality, Fairness, and the Limits of Diversity'. *Innovation*. 7 (3): 289–308.

—— 1994b. 'Cultural Diversity and Liberal Democracy'. In *Defining and Measuring Democracy*, ed. David Beetham. London: Sage: 199–221.

—— 1994c. 'Superior People: The Narrowness of Liberalism from Mill to Rawls'. *Times Literary Supplement*. 25 Feb.: 11–13.

—— 1997. 'Equality in a Multicultural Society'. In *Equality*, ed. Jane Franklin. London: Institute for Public Policy Research.

Pauly, Louis W. 1997. *Who Elected the Bankers?* Ithaca, NY: Cornell University Press.

Perry, Michael J. 1982. *The Constitution, the Courts, and Human Rights*. New Haven: Yale University Press.

Phillips, Anne. 1991. *Engendering Democracy*. University Park, Pa.: Pennsylvania State University Press.

—— 1993. *Democracy and Difference*. University Park, Pa.: Pennsylvania State University Press.

—— 1995. *The Politics of Presence*. Oxford: Clarendon Press.

Plato. 1991. *The Republic of Plato*. Trans. Allan Bloom. New York: Basic Books.

Premdas, Ralph. 1995. *Ethnic Conflict and Development: The Case of Fiji*. Aldershot: Avebury Press.

Rawls, John. 1971. *A Theory of Justice*. Cambridge, Mass.: Harvard University Press.

—— 1993. *Political Liberalism*. New York: Columbia University Press.

Raz, Joseph. 1994. 'Multiculturalism: A Liberal Perspective'. In Joseph Raz, *Ethics in the Public Domain*. Oxford: Clarendon Press: 155–76.

—— and Margalit, Avashai. 1994. 'National Self-Determination'. In Joseph Raz, *Ethics in the Public Domain*. Oxford: Clarendon Press: 110–30.

Reaume, Denise, and Green, Leslie. 1989. 'Education and Linguistic Security in the Charter'. *McGill Law Journal*. 34 (4): 777–816.

Reynolds, Henry. 1982. *The Other Side of the Frontier*. Victoria: Penguin Books.

Roth, G. K. 1973. *Fijian Way of Life*. 2nd edn. Melbourne: Oxford University Press.

Rousseau, Jean-Jacques. 1978. *On the Social Contract, with Geneva Manuscript and Political Economy*, ed. Roger D. Masters ; trans. Judith R. Masters. New York: St Martin's Press; 1st pub. 1762.

Royal Commission on Aboriginal Peoples. 1992. *Public Hearings: Overview of the First Round*. Ottawa: Minister of Supply and Services.

—— 1993a. *Public Hearings: Focusing on the Dialogue: Discussion Paper 2*. Ottawa: Ministry of Supply and Services.

—— 1993b. *Public Hearings: Overview of the Second Round*. Ottawa: Ministry of Supply and Services.

—— 1993c. *Public Hearings: Exploring the options: Overview of the Third Round*. Ottawa: Ministry of Supply and Services.

—— 1995. *Report*. Ottawa: Ministry of Supply and Services.

Russell, Peter. 1991. 'Standing Up for Notwithstanding'. *Alberta Law Review*. 29: 293–309.

Sa'dawi, Nawal. 1980. *The Hidden Face of Eve: Women in the Arab World*. Trans. Sherif Hetata. London: Zed Press.

Sandel, Michael. 1982. *Liberalism and the Limits of Justice*. Cambridge: Cambridge University Press.

Scarr, Deryck. 1980. *Ratu Sukuna*. Canberra: Australian National University Press.

—— 1984. *Fiji: A Short History*. Sydney: Allen & Unwin.

—— 1988. *Fiji: Politics of Illusion*. Kensington: Australian National University Press.

Schuck, Peter. 1998. *Citizens, Strangers, and In-Betweens*. Boulder, Colo.: Westview Press.

Shklar, Judith. 1991. *American Citizenship: The Quest for Inclusion*. Cambridge, Mass.: Harvard University Press.

Silverman, Maxim. 1992. *Deconstructing the Nation: Immigration, Racism and Citizenship in Modern France*. London: Routledge.

Simon, Robert, L. 1990. 'Pluralism and Equality: The Status of Minority Values in a Democracy'. In *Majorities and Minorities: NOMOS XXXII*, ed. John W. Chapman and Alan Wertheimer. New York: New York University Press: 207–25.

Spinner, Jeff. 1994. *The Boundaries of Citizenship: Race, Ethnicity, and Nationality in the Liberal State*. Baltimore: Johns Hopkins University Press.

Spiro, Peter. 1997. 'Dual Nationality and the Meaning of Citizenship'. *Emory Law Journal*. 46: 1411–85.

Tamir, Yael. 1996. 'Hands Off Cliterodectomy'. *Boston Review*. 21 (3):

Taylor, Charles. 1993. *Reconciling the Solitudes: Essays on Canadian Federalism and*

Nationalism, ed. Guy Laforest. Kingston and Montreal: McGill–Queen's University Press.

—— 1994. 'The Politics of Recognition'. In *Multiculturalism: Examining the Politics of Recognition,* ed. Amy Gutmann. Princeton: Princeton University Press.

Toubia, Nahid. 1995. *Female Genital Mutilation: A Call for Global Action.* 2nd edn. New York: Rainbow/Women Ink.

Tully, James. 1995. *Strange Multiplicity: Constitutionalism in an Age of Diversity.* Cambridge: Cambridge University Press.

Turpel, Mary Ellen. 1991. 'Aboriginal Peoples and the Canadian Charter: Interpretive Monopolies, Cultural Differences'. In *Canadian Perspectives on Legal Theory,* ed. Richard Devlin. Toronto: Edmond Montgomery Publications, Ltd.: 505–38.

United Nations Commission on Human Rights (UNCHR). 1986. *Report of the Working Group on Traditional Practices Affecting the Health of Women and Children.* New York.

Wadud-Muhsin, Amina. 1992. *Qur'an and Woman.* Kuala Lampur: Penerbit Fajar Bakti Sdn. Bld.

Waldron, Jeremy. 1992. 'Minority Cultures and the Cosmopolitan Alternative'. *University of Michigan Journal of Law Reform.* 25 (3–4): 751–93.

Walker, Brian. 1997. 'Plural Cultures, Contested Territories'. *Canadian Journal of Political Science.* 30 (2): 211–34.

Walzer, Michael. 1977. *Just and Unjust Wars.* New York: Basic Books.

—— 1983. *Spheres of Justice: A Defense of Pluralism and Equality.* New York: Basic Books.

—— 1994. *Thick and Thin: Moral Argument at Home and Abroad.* Notre Dame, Ind.: University of Notre Dame Press.

—— 1995. 'Response'. In *Pluralism, Justice, and Equality,* ed. David Miller and Michael Walzer. Oxford: Oxford University Press: 281–97.

—— 1997. *On Toleration.* New Haven: Yale University Press.

Weitzman, Lenore. 1985. *The Divorce Revolution.* New York: The Free Press.

Welsh, Peter H. 1992. 'Repatriation and Cultural Preservation: Potent Objects, Potent Pasts'. *University of Michigan Journal of Law Reform.* 25 (3–4): 837–65.

Whyte, John. 1990. 'On Not Standing for Notwithstanding'. *Alberta Law Review.* 28: 347.

Wilkins, William Henry. 1892. *The Alien Invasion.* London, Methuen.

William, Jean-Claude. 1991. 'Le Conseil d'État et la laïcité'. *Revue Française de Science Politique.* 41 (1): 28–58.

Williams, Melissa. 1998. *Voice, Trust and Memory: Marginalized Groups and the Failings of Liberal Representation.* Princeton: Princeton University Press.

Winter, Bronwyn. 1994. 'Women, the Law, and Sexual Relativism in France: the Case of Excision'. *Signs.* 19 (4): 939–74.

World Health Organization (WHO). 1986. 'A Traditional Practice that Threatens Health—Female Circumcision'. *WHO Chronicle.* 40 (1): 250–74.

Young, Iris Marion. 1989. 'Polity and Group Difference: A Critique of the Ideal of Universal Citizenship'. *Ethics.* 99: 250–74.

—— 1990. *Justice and the Politics of Difference.* Princeton: Princeton University Press.

—— 1997. 'Deferring Group Representation'. In *Ethnicity and Group Rights: NOMOS XXXIX,* ed. Will Kymlicka and Ian Shapiro. New York: New York University Press.

Zwang, Gérard. 1978. *La fonction érotique.* 3rd edn. Paris: Robert Laffort.

INDEX